BATTLE OVER BAVARIA

The B-26 Marauder versus the German Jets - April 1945

ROBERT FORSYTH
with Jerry Scutts

BATTLE OVER BAVARIA
The B-26 Marauder versus the German Jets - April 1945

Colour Artwork by Eddie J. Creek and Jerry Scutts
Technical Drawings by Arthur L Bentley

CLASSIC
PUBLICATIONS

Preface
by
Jerry Scutts

Should the contemporary reader of *Luftwaffe* history attempt to compare the triumvirate of Hitler, Göring and Galland with leaders on the American side, the task would indeed be a difficult one. While Franklin Roosevelt was virtually a household name, fewer members of the public could have named Henry 'Hap' Arnold or most division, wing or group commanders although one would shrink from making any comparisons between the US President and Army Air Forces chief with the *Reichsmarschall* or his *Führer*!

The 'third man' on the American side would be even more difficult to name but Jimmy Doolittle might be a contender as a Galland contemporary. He and a few other high ranking AAF officers were known to certain sectors of the American public at large. But in general and despite a positive approach to publicity, what her military men were doing 'over there' during the war was little known outside a select circle of colleagues, relatives and close friends.

For the men at the front it is not overstating the point that under certain circumstances, in some god-forsaken corner of Europe (and there were plenty of those) anonymity had its place; much of the war, from a squadron or group commander's viewpoint was routine and generally unspectacular. To such individuals combat flying, mercifully free of politics, was a job they had been well trained to do as professional airmen.

That said, the AAF publicity machine was active and it thrived throughout the war. Achievement was recognised both nationally and by home town exposure in the press, on radio and in newsreels – but there were no Adolf Gallands wearing American uniform.

Rarely, if ever, was a US officer given the awesome responsibility handed to Galland – neither was there a need for anything comparable to his elite force on the Allied side although one could cite dozens of units that were obliged to prove new weapons and tactics. Somebody always had to be first. And regarding the operational deployment of the world's first practical jet fighter, in Galland's case, to paraphrase the apt title of his autobiography – he was not only among the first but also the last.

ROBERT FORSYTH has studied the history of the 1939-1945 European air war for many years. His particular interest lies in the internal politics of command and operations of the German air force during that conflict and his first book, *JV 44 - The Galland Circus,* has been acclaimed as a " ... staggering work of reference on one of the most controversial units in Germany's wartime *Luftwaffe*". The inspiration for *Battle over Bavaria* came from his research into the operations of JV 44 and the men who both flew with and against that unit, many of whom he has either interviewed or corresponded with.

A former shipping industry executive, he now works as a founding partner in Classic Publications. He lives in Kent, England.

JERRY SCUTTS was trained at art college and worked as a professional journalist until 1987. He is now a full time historian/writer specialising in military aviation and naval operations. After working as a press officer for the UK Civil Aviation Authority he left to become editor and publisher of the popular 1980s magazine *Combat Report*. He has written more than forty books and articles ranging from the various air forces of World War Two through to USAF operations in Vietnam and his most recent works include *Messerschmitt Bf 109 – The Operational Record, Bf 109 Aces over North Africa and the Mediterranean* and *B-26 Marauder Units of the Eighth and Ninth Air Forces*. He lives in London.

First published in Great Britain in 1999 by Classic Publications, Friars Gate Farm, Mardens Hill, Crowborough, East Sussex TN6 1XH England.

© 1998 Colour Illustrations – Eddie J. Creek
© 1998 Colour Illustrations – Jerry Scutts
© 1998 Line Drawings – Arthur Bentley

ISBN 0 9526867 4 0

Book and Cover design by Colin Woodman Graphic Design
Origination by Colourwise Limited, Burgess Hill, West Sussex, England
Printed in Italy by Officine Grafiche D^eAgostini

CONTENTS

Author's Introduction

This book has evolved from the writing of another. May 1996 saw the publication of my book *JV 44 - The Galland Circus* in which I attempted to recount the history and operations of what is perceived to be one of the most famous yet most controversial of *Luftwaffe* units. *Jagdverband* (JV) 44 comprised a curious assortment of some of Germany's most talented and experienced *Experten* – fighter aces – as well as a large number of young, barely trained and untested pilots. The unit's origins lay essentially, as the reader will discover, in the unrest, competitiveness and downright incompetence which dogged the senior ranks of the *Luftwaffe's* fighter force during the closing stages of the Second World War. The unit existed only for some nine or so weeks before the Third Reich surrendered. Remarkably, it was equipped with the world's first operational jet fighter, the Messerschmitt Me 262, an extremely potent machine, which perhaps more than any other, symbolised the coming revolution in post-war aircraft design.

Fueling the controversy surrounding JV 44 has been the post-war claim that, despite the populist legend of "German design and last minute defiance against all odds" the unit, in truth, accomplished – in tactical terms – very little; that many of its so called "aces" were burnt out – suffering from nervous exhaustion and an inability to accept or even handle the advanced technological concept of a jet aircraft; that many of its less accomplished personnel simply did not or could not fly operations and that consequently, the "legend" is transparent. Put in more fundamental terms – JV 44 was unsuccessful at shooting down American bombers – the task for which it was formed – and was apparently a waste of badly needed human and mechanical resources.

Strangely however, research for *JV 44 - The Galland Circus* led me to believe otherwise. Through considerable correspondence and dialogue with various parties in the United States and by studying original USAAF documents, not only did the truth begin to emerge, but also the story of a little told aspect of the European air war, namely the short but bitter battle waged over southern Germany in April 1945 between the bomber crews of the American B-26 Marauder and the pilots of Adolf Galland's "Squadron of *Experten*". This was almost a "private" war, since it was fought in a series of brief but violent encounters between four units; JV 44 and the 17th, 323rd and 344th Bombardment Groups. There were, of course, other American units which encountered Galland's jets at this time, but it was predominantly these three groups which bore the brunt of their attacks. JV 44 was in Bavaria to defend the German jet aircraft production facilities and the Marauders were there to bomb them. There were many former survivors of that battle who were able to testify that the German jets *did* take their toll in a fearsome and deadly manner and also that time and time again, despite a severe blood-letting from the guns and rockets of the jets, the Marauder came back. But what was most surprising, was how many US survivors, in their letters, related to me how their respective intelligence organisations offered no warning or information on the jets. They had no idea who or *what* had hit them – and when they *were* hit it was – to paraphrase two former B-26 air crew – "like a bat out of Hell".

I was able to include a part of this story in my earlier book, but more, much more came to light as a result of the willingness and generosity of many former "Marauder Men".

This is their story.

Robert Forsyth
Kent, England

Acknowledgements

I wish to record my thanks to a number of individuals who contributed time, advice, material and recollections without which this book could not have been written. In particular, I am grateful to James H.Kitchens, III for "pointing the way" and to Major General (Ret) John O. Moench for his energy and support for this project in its early days; to Ronnie Macklin, a special thank you for so willingly and generously sending regular parcels of photographs; to Robert Harwell and Bill Baird for their patience and support and to Jerry Scutts for writing various parts of the text and for his help in areas where I must confess to having little or no knowledge! Thanks must also go to Jack Havener for contributing his superb photographs. Thanks too to Eddie J. Creek for his assistance and generosity with German photographs.

The following aircrew took part in The Battle over Bavaria and I thank them for their contributions (post-war ranks given where known):

William Allan (17th BG)
William D. Baird M.D (17th BG)
Ed Brandt (17th BG)
Bernard J. Byrne (17th BG)
Orrin Cloud (17th BG)
Oliven T. Cowen (365th FG)
Randle J. Dedeaux (17th BG)
Henry Dietz (17th BG)
Donald P. Edelen (17th BG)
Norman G. Farley (344th BG)
James J. Finnegan (50th FG)
Robert L. Harwell (344th BG)
Jack Havener (344th BG)
Wayne J. Hutchinson (17th BG)
Ronnie Macklin (17th BG)
Maj.Gen. USAF (Ret) John O. Moench
    (323rd BG)

William P. Morton (344th BG)
Donald Mushrush (17th BG)
William H. Myers (365th FG)
Henry "Hank" Pryse (344th BG)
Johnny Quong (344th BG)
Robert M. Radlein (323rd BG)
Carl S. Schreiner (17th BG)
Don Sinclair (344th BG)
Capt. USAF Res (Ret)
William N. Snead (17th BG)
Lt.Col. USAF (Ret) John W. Sorrelle Jr.
    (323rd BG)
James L. Stalter (344th BG)
Capt. USAF (Ret) James L. Vining
    (323rd BG)
Don Wilson (17th BG)
Warren E. Young (17th BG)

I was also fortunate enough to be able to consult (though I think the word is "pester") former members of JV 44, some sadly no longer alive today, who kindly agreed to offer their various recollections, photographs and documents either in person or by correspondence. They are Adolf Galland, Walter Krupinski, Hans-Ekkehard Bob, Eduard Schallmoser, Klaus Neumann, Herbert Kaiser, Erich Hohagen, Franz Stigler, Werner Gutowski, Werner Roell, Leo Schuhmacher and Rudolf Nielinger. I would also like to mention the kind assistance of Wolfgang Späte and Horst Amberg of the *Gemeinschaft der Jagdflieger*.

My thanks also to Nevill Basnett, Arthur Bentley, Walter J. Boyne, J. Richard Smith, Dipl.Ing. Jochen Haberecht-Kaiser, Nick Beale, Jürgen Rosenstock, Peter Petrick, James V. Crow, Eric Mombeek, David Wadman, Rudolf Schallmoser, Roger Freeman, Peter J. Hatcher, Dr. Stanley W. Akers of the Bierce Library at The University of Akron, Heidi Galland, Lillian J. Couture, Carlos A. Herrera Jr., Lorenz Rasse, Henry Sakaida, Mary K. Wagner, Jean-Yves Lorant, Philip Jarrett, Philip Savides and Rick Chapman.

Thanks also to my wife, Sally-Kate, for going through it all over again.

R.F.

Foreword
by
Generalleutnant a.D. ADOLF GALLAND

Jagdverband 44 must have been one of the most unusual and short-lived flying units of the *Luftwaffe,* formed, as it was, towards the end of that force's brief existence. It was an end full of turbulent events, the extent, importance and consequence of which today can only be imagined with great difficulty.

The Commander-in-Chief of the *Luftwaffe,* Hermann Göring, as a result of his inertia and lack of success, had completely lost Hitler's confidence and respect. This was a well known and widely discussed subject within the *Wehrmacht* (the German Armed Forces), the Party organisation and particularly within the Waffen SS. The fact that military command of the *Wehrmacht*, and especially that of the army, was vested in Hitler alone, had catastrophic consequences. The complete collapse of the armed forces quickly followed.

The war in the air had turned into a disaster for Germany. Hitler, who lacked virtually all understanding of air war strategy, categorically refused a last minute switch to a policy of determined air defence following the Hamburg catastrophe. The weak Hermann Göring, who had only recently advocated an exactly opposing point of view, did not attempt to object. In this desperate situation, the new jet aircraft, particularly the Me 262, provided the only, if not small, hope. But jet aircraft development had been delayed on the highest orders, and consequently it was not possible to introduce them into operational service at such short notice.

I never envisaged that, on the highest orders, the Me 262 – our fighter pilots greatest hope – would be built and employed operationally only as a *"Blitzbomber"*. Nobody in the *Jagdwaffe* understood this insane directive. Rather than execute this order however, it would have made much more sense to have granted all the bomber wings earmarked for re-equipping onto the Me 262 with leave until the end of the war. But the order was executed! As a result of the enemy's total air supremacy by both day and night, the ultra-fast Me 262 was requested for – and diverted to – numerous other tasks.

This then, was the situation existing within the *Luftwaffe,* when Hitler intervened in my personal affairs by ordering me to set up a small unit, namely *Jagdverband* 44, with which I was to prove that the Me 262 was indeed a superior fighter aircraft. The fact that this had already been demonstrated beyond any doubt by *Kommando Nowotny* and JG 7 was not taken into consideration.

One has to understand these developments and the resulting situation – only roughly sketched by me here – in order to appreciate the evolution of *Jagdverband* 44 and its short history.

Through interviews and research into every available source, Robert Forsyth, the author of this book, has achieved this brilliantly. *Jagdverband* 44 was established on 24 February 1945, and – in theory – dissolved again on 3 May 1945, at which time it was redesignated "IV./JG 7". In practice however, this was never carried out. It had only archival significance and I learned of it only long after the war. In retrospect, an operational life-span of just eleven weeks is an absurdly short period, particularly if one considers the turbulent times just before the military collapse.

Hardly any statements or reports were submitted by the unit and virtually no photographs were taken. The war correspondents had long since gone home or had been made prisoners of war. The destruction of nearly all known records finished it all. There are now hardly any living witnesses. Under such circumstances, it is astonishing what information the author has been able to collect during the course of his most thorough research. All earlier attempts to tell the story of *Jagdverband* 44 have either failed or been abandoned.

There is no need for me to comment or add to the chapters of this volume which deal with the operations of *Jagdverband* 44 and I only wish to say that the author has done nothing less than the ultimate. Contributing chiefly to my opinion is the fact that he has succeeded in correctly presenting, in such great detail, the catastrophic circumstances of the period, the mood and the spirit of the participants.

Commander, *Jagdverband* 44

(This edited foreword was written originally for JV 44 - The Galland Circus by Robert Forsyth, Classic Publications, 1996)

Foreword

by
ROBERT L. HARWELL

President of the B-26 Marauder Historical Society
Formerly 344th Bombardment Group

I found Robert Forsyth's *Battle over Bavaria* without equal. Although elements of the history of the USAAF and other units facing the new Me 262 in World War Two are known to a few, both these persons as well as those not directly involved should find this book informative.

A comparison of the German hierarchy and the American command would be difficult to make but it would appear that mistakes were made on both sides – and opportunities lost.

By March 1945, I had completed 67 B-26 Marauder combat missions with the 344th Bombardment Group (M) – both as co-pilot and pilot. While I and other air crews had been warned about the Me 262, we had no real understanding of its potential. Much as many others, I had not encountered the Me 262 in combat and, in hindsight, I can say that I was blessed for those who did a face-to-face with the Me 262 often suffered heavily.

If the German hierarchy had been able fully to develop and refine this new aircraft (and produce and man it in quantity), I doubt if the USAAF, and especially the B-26 Marauders, would have fared as well as they did. Through the Me 262, Germany had a great opportunity that, fortunately, was not exploited.

As all medium bomber crews will remember, we never gained the recognition we deserved for the extensive role we played in achieving air superiority, in destroying the enemy's capability on the ground, in severing the enemy transportation lines, in attacking the enemy missile sites and, most of all, in assisting the ground forces when they joined the attack in Europe. Perhaps through this book some new light will be shed on these achievements of the medium bomber forces.

One thing that this book makes clearer to me is the revelation that here was a neophyte military force in day-to-day combat with a trained and seasoned professional air force of warriors who were gaining aircraft credits when most of our Air Force was still in high school.

A second thing that Forsyth brings home is the impact of power struggles that can and do emerge within the system. Such struggles can lose sight of the real issues at hand and

1st Lt. Robert Harwell, 344th BG, (back row, centre) with his crew lined up in front of B-26B 7I-F (S/N 42-95903) HARD TO GET at Stansted Mountfichet, England, July 1944. Harwell, who was commisioned in December 1943 and served with the 344th until March 1945, flew this aircraft on several occasions, though it was also the personal machine of Col. Delwin D. Bentley, commander of the 497th Squadron and later deputy commander of the 322nd BG. HARD TO GET was indeed "hard to get" and survived the war without damage from either flak or fighters. Seen here with Harwell are – (back row l-r) J. Kenyon (Pilot); Harwell (Pilot); L. Fenster (Bombardier/Navigator); (front row) K. Boucher (Armourer-Gunner); A. Gorgowicz (Radio-Gunner); F. Gebert (Engineer-Gunner).

weaken the structure. This ongoing battle probably contributed greatly to the demise of the German war machine – but all governments and military forces are subject to such influences. Let us hope that we can avoid them as we face the future.

When we weigh the facts it becomes very clear that in World War Two, we held a great advantage in quantity of men, machines and logistics and that advantage made a difference. To a lesser degree, we held an advantage in quality. We need both attributes as we move forward to address new challenges and let us never forget that.

Robert L Harwell

Foreword

by

Major General JOHN O. MOENCH, USAF (ret)

Formerly 323rd Bombardment Group
Historian, B-26 Marauder Historical Society

The history of the Martin B-26 Marauder, an aircraft that served in World War II not only in the forces of the United States but also with the Royal Air Force, South African Air Force and Free French Air Force, is one of great men and women accomplishing great deeds often in the most difficult of circumstances.

Remarkably, much of the history surrounding this aircraft comes from the pens of writers from Britain and the Commonwealth. Robert Forsyth is, without doubt, one of those outstanding writers.

The unique feature of *Battle over Bavaria* is that it approaches the story from both the American and German sides of the encounter.

The survivors of this battle are now of rapidly diminishing numbers. Robert Forsyth has painstakingly sought information from these persons and other historical sources of record and has presented his findings in a most comprehensive format.

As a person who spent the war in the cockpit of a B-26 Marauder and who was a participant in the engagements with the *Luftwaffe's* Me 262, I found *Battle over Bavaria* not only to be most interesting but also to hold to the facts.

10

Foreword
by
WILLIAM D. BAIRD, M.D.

Formerly T/Sgt. and Gunner, 34th Squadron, 17th Bombardment Group
Secretary of 17th Bomb Group/Wing Reunion Association

April 1945. The war was – or should have been – over. What was left was "mop-up". We at last had come to the end of it and all of us were aware that celebrations would soon be in order.

We had seen an earlier hint of things to come. A small aircraft had once come over our formation, high up. It dove at us, missing the formation by over 100 feet and disappeared below. Then it came up and again missed the formation.

We were told that it was a "jet aircraft". It went away and did not reappear.

Until 24 April...

On the 24th, the 34th Squadron lost two aircraft to jets. On the 25th, we were again approached but they were kept at bay by our fighters. Then, on the 26th, we were hit again and lost an additional plane.

Of the aircraft lost, three men survived. Our gunners accounted for two of the jets.

We flew three more missions, "gravy runs" on an undefended target. Then the war was over.

Many men were lost in that war, but the losses that week in April were the most senseless.

PART ONE INSTRUMENTS OF WAR

Professor Willy Messerschmitt confers with his test pilot Fritz Wendel in front of a latest batch of production Messerschmitt Bf 109 G fighters. Wendel made the first test flight in the Me 262 V1 prototype fitted with the combination of a Junkers Jumo 210 piston engine as well as two BMW 003 turbojets on 25 March 1942. During this flight both turbojets failed.

The Messerschmitt Me 262A-1a jet fighter: Willy Messerschmitt's revolutionary masterpiece. The example shown here is a standard production variant and illustrates the 18.5 degree swept back wing with the automatic leading edge slats in the open position.

ONE

MESSERSCHMITT Me 262

Perhaps more than any other aircraft designed, manufactured and operated by Germany during the Second World War, none was dogged more by politics, controversy and argument than the revolutionary Messerschmitt Me 262, the world's first operational jet fighter.

For reasons largely attributable to misguided beliefs, personal ambition, hidden truths and limited industrial incapacity, the troubled development of the Me 262 represented one of the greatest examples of technical and tactical mismanagement in the history of the Third Reich.

One man, possibly more than any other, who was forced to contend with and suffer from this mismanagement was *Generalleutnant* Adolf Galland. Credited by at least one Nazi armaments industry official as the "real father" of the Me 262, Galland was the raven-haired, cigar smoking son of an estate manager from Westerholt in Westphalia who, at the age of 29, had been appointed *General der Jagdflieger* – Commanding General of the *Luftwaffe* Fighter Arm – upon the unwelcome death of the previous incumbent, the legendary fighter ace Werner Mölders.

Generalleutnant Adolf Galland.

At the time of his appointment and as one of only seven living holders of the coveted *Ritterkreuz* with Oakleaves, Swords and Diamonds, Adolf Galland had been plucked from his command as *Kommodore* of the famous JG 26 on the Channel Front, a unit to which he had belonged since May 1940 and with which he had flown successfully over England during the difficult summer months of the Battle of Britain. He had accumulated more than 70 confirmed victories over the English Channel and, like Mölders, had developed a reputation as a proficient tactician. As a member of the *Legion Condor* during the Spanish Civil War, he had been one of the early advocates of ground-attack operations in support of land forces and the stream of reports that he presented to his superiors was well received.

Oberst. Johannes Janke, former *Gruppen-kommandeur* of IV./JG 51 and later commander of 7. *Jagddivision* was a fellow cadet with Galland at the Army *Kriegsschule* in Dresden in 1934. He remembers Galland as "...a very good pilot and an excellent shot, but ambitious and he wanted to get noticed. A parvenu. He was crazy about hunting anything, from a sparrow to a man."

Reichsmarschall Göring (second from left) visits JG 26 on the Channel Front. Galland, the Geschwaderkommodore (fourth from left) regularly proposed innovative tactics to Göring.

Thus it was hardly surprising that the exploits and accomplishments of this dashing, extrovert young officer attracted the eyes of both Hitler and Hermann Göring. Galland quickly became one of the *Reichsmarschall's* favourite "sons", perhaps because he embodied the image of the modern fighter pilot. A popular officer and commander blessed with natural leadership qualities who both worked and played hard, Galland had never been afraid to express his fears and misgivings. During the Battle of Britain, he took great pains to spell out to Göring the folly of trying to take on the British Spitfire in turning dog-fights where he knew the RAF fighter enjoyed superior performance. Instead, Galland pushed for hit-and-run, nuisance tactics which advantaged the fast Bf 109. Like Mölders, he was also an innovator, experimenting with schemes as diversified as fitting telescopic sights into his cockpit to masterminding a complex air-cover operation on 12 February 1942 over the English Channel. Better known to the British as 'The Channel Dash', this was also the first time the Fw 190 was used in a major action. The operation was the escape of three of the German Navy's capital ships, *Scharnhorst* and *Gneisneau* and the cruiser *Prinz Eugen,* from their enforced confinement in the French port of Brest to the sanctuary of the

Adolf Galland made frequent visits to the front-line fighter units. Here, he is seen at Achmer airfield during late 1943 whilst on an inspection to Erprobungskommando 25, the anti-bomber weapons testing and evaluation unit. One of E.kdo 25's Me 410 "destroyers" fitted with a 50mm cannon and telescopic sight can be seen in the background.

German ports of Kiel and Wilhelmshafen via the Straits of Dover in broad daylight. He succeeded.

At the time of being awarded the Diamonds to the *Ritterkreuz* in January 1942, Galland had amassed 94 aerial victories. In November of that year, at the age of thirty, he was promoted to *Generalmajor*, the youngest General in the German armed forces.

Though initially reluctant to relinquish his command of JG 26 for the complex power politics of senior command in Berlin, Galland approached the inherent demands of his new position as *General der Jagdflieger* with considerable verve, tenacity and creativity. These attributes, however, frequently led to violent personality clashes with the megalomaniacal Göring who often viewed Galland's radical proposals for strengthening and reforming the *Jagdwaffe* as indirect criticism of his own shortcomings.

Cracks and strains in the relationship between the *Reichsmarschall* and his fighter general began to appear as early as the spring of 1943 when Göring demanded that his fighters stay airborne longer to deal with the increasing threat of American daylight bombers over the *Reich*. When Galland endeavoured to point out the loss of manoeuvrability incurred by both the standard *Luftwaffe* fighter types – the rugged, radial-engined Fw 190 and the regularly re-worked Messerschmitt Bf 109 – based in France and the Low Countries by carrying twin drop-tanks in order to increase flying time, Göring, could not grasp it. Looking to save face with Hitler and preserve his popularity with the German people, he promptly directed Galland to issue orders that no pilot was to jettison his tanks unless actually hit by enemy fire.

Later that year, as the Allied daylight raids intensified, Galland reasoned that it would be prudent to limit the number of machines and operations flown by the home defence *Geschwadern* against individual enemy raids to allow sufficient repair and re-grouping of aircraft that had landed on emergency fields. Only by carefully conserving strength and by efficient management of its most precious resources, namely its *pilots*,

There were also endless meetings and conferences: here Galland attends one of those meetings with the aircraft designer, Kurt Tank (second from right), designer of the Fw 190.

could the *Jagdwaffe* hope to cause any damage to the bombers. Unimpressed, Göring demanded instead that all available units be thrown against every raid wherever and whenever possible, regardless of the American escort fighters now accompanying the bombers into *Reich* airspace. According to *Generalfeldmarschall* Erhard Milch, the *Luftwaffe's* chief of armament procurement: "Göring just could not grasp it."

Consequently, as the *Jagdwaffe* began to suffer unacceptably high levels of attrition during late 1943, Göring could only assume that the lack of any decisive victory over the Americans, a nation which, in any case, he considered capable only of manufacturing "fancy cars and refrigerators", was due to nothing but cowardice on the part of his fighter pilots. Had he not heard Galland talk of *Jägerschreck* – Fighter Fear?

As Galland wrote in his post-war memoirs: "Göring began to lay increasing blame on the *Jagdwaffe* and as I felt I had earned the right to answer him back, we were soon at loggerheads... he proceeded to comment on the *Jagdwaffe's* lack of spirit... he got into such a state that he hurled reproaches and accusations at us to the effect that we had been loaded with honours and decorations but had proved ourselves unworthy of them, that the *Jagdwaffe* had been a failure as early as the Battle of Britain and that many pilots with the highest decorations had faked their reports to get Knight's Crosses over England." In a moment of fury whilst in one meeting with Göring, Galland ripped his *Ritterkreuz* from his throat and slammed it down on the table. "For six months after that I did not wear my decorations."

Throughout late 1943, the air war over the *Reich* continued to escalate. The pressure was on. Galland took harsh, deliberate steps to radically improve his fighter pilot selection and training programmes. He wanted the best of what was available and that meant tough, stringent psychological testing of all potential aircrew. Some found his standards too hard to bear and as one *Luftwaffe* fighter-control NCO based in Sicily revealed following the *General der Jadgflieger's* brief assignment to the island in 1943: "During the two months he spent with us, we came to know him as a man who was both proud and vain. He was dreaded by pilots under his command; whenever they came back from a sortie, his first question was *"Where have you been?"*... Galland was particularly hard on pilots who had taken part in many operations but who had won no victories. Although he was always scrupulously careful about his personal appearance, Galland was temperamentally very moody and excitable and was easily upset by trivialities. We suffered particularly from his

irascibility, which affected all of us and made us unsure and nervous of ourselves."

Galland forged ahead, proposing the opening of new schools with sufficiently qualified instructors and facilities for blind and bad weather flying, skills which were now needed in order to equal the capability of the Allied opposition. He was even prepared to take the surplus pilots of other branches of the *Luftwaffe* as a means of reducing overall training hours and fuel usage. But perhaps his greatest hope lay in a new aircraft that been quietly undergoing trials at Leipheim and Lechfeld in the south of Germany – the Messerschmitt Me 262.

On 17 April 1943, the accomplished fighter ace and commander of the Me 163 equipped experimental rocker fighter testing unit, *Erprobungskommando 16*, *Hptm.* Wolfgang Späte, test flew the Me 262 V2, a prototype aircraft which had been fitted with Jumo 004 A-0 turbojet engines in October of the previous year. As the first service officer to fly the new jet fighter, his reactions were viewed as encouraging. In his subsequent report to Galland, Späte wrote:

"Flight characteristics are such that an experienced fighter pilot would be able to handle this aircraft. In particular, the increase in air speed when compared to the fastest conventional fighter deserves attention. Maximum speed at ground level measured so far is 780 km/h (485 mph). This is not expected to decrease markedly when armament and radio equipment have been fitted... The superior horizontal and climbing speeds will enable the aircraft to operate successfully against numerically superior enemy fighters. The extremely heavy armament (six 30 mm guns) permits attacks on bombers at high approach speeds with destructive results despite the short time the aircraft is in the firing position. As a fighter-bomber, and carrying bombs, the aircraft

Hptm Wolfgang Späte was the first Luftwaffe officer to fly the Me 262; his reactions were encouraging.
Below: The Me 262 V3 takes off from Leipheim airfield on 18 July 1942. This was the third prototype; by October 1943 it was achieving a test speed of 950 km/h (590 mph).

would still be faster than any enemy fighter... The aircraft deserves the highest attention; its development should receive the greatest possible support..."

A month later, fired by Späte's favourable recommendations, Galland test flew the Me 262 V4 during a visit to Lechfeld and made his now famous comment that in flying the machine "...it felt as if angels were pushing." As far as performance was concerned, even in its prototype variants, the Me 262 was, indeed, a formidable and ground breaking aircraft. As early as October 1943 an Me 262 prototype, the Me 262 V3, was achieving test speeds of 950 km/h whilst eight months later, the Me 262 S2 reached 1,004 km/h in a dive. In terms of offensive load, it was planned to install one 30 mm MK103 cannon and two 20mm MG151/20 cannon. Galland, captivated by the speed and the tactical opportunities that the new aircraft now offered as a fighter, immediately set wheels in motion by sending an urgent teletype message to Milch in which he said:

"The aircraft represents a great step forward and could be our greatest chance; it could guarantee us an unimaginable lead over

Ground crew attend to an Me 262 of Erprobungskommando 262, the first jet fighter trials unit. One mechanic assists the pilot with his harness straps and controls, while the other fits a wire "basket" to the turbojet intake to prevent damage from objects being sucked in.

the enemy if he adheres to the piston engine. The flying qualities of the airframe make a very good impression. The engines are extremely convincing, except during take-off and landing. The aircraft opens completely new tactical possibilities."*

Galland also advocated the immediate cancellation of the Me 209, the intended replacement for the Bf 109, so as to allow production of at least 100 Me 262s by the end of 1943. The enthusiasm in this message may have been a little premature; shortly afterwards, the director of testing at Messerschmitt, *Dipl.Ing.* Gerhard Caroli, offered his own, more realistic appraisal of the Me 262 in which he warned, amongst other things, of problematical ailerons, high forces on the elevators and rudders, inadequate directional stability, poor stall behaviour and insufficient fuel injection. But despite *Prof.* Willy Messerschmitt's misgivings over the cancellation of the Me 209, Galland got

Milch's support and immediate priority was given to an initial Me 262 building programme. It was to be plagued from the start; firstly, production of the Me 209 *was* re-instated as a result of Messerschmitt complaining directly to Hitler and thus emphasis diverted from the Me 262 project – secondly, an American air-raid on the Regensburg assembly plant in August successfully destroyed a number of crucial fuselage jigs and acceptance gauges and forced the company to relocate its project office from Augsburg to Oberammergau in the Bavarian Alps, and, thirdly, the promise of 1,800 skilled workers needed to tool-up two production lines proved fickle and they arrived late resulting in the loss of almost three million man hours in nine months.

On 2 November 1943, Göring, accompanied by Milch, visited the bomb damaged Regensburg works and met *Prof.* Messerschmitt. It was at this meeting that a new, previously unforeseen dimension crept into the troubled production saga of the Me 262 – the hand of the *Führer.* "When the enemy attempts a landing in the West," announced Göring, "And the first signs of confusion appear on the beach as tanks, guns and troops are unloaded and a terrific traffic jam ensues, these fast machines, even if only a few of them, should be able to race through the heavy fighter screen, which the *Führer* expects in the event of such an attack and drop bombs into this confusion."

Göring demanded of Messerschmitt whether the Me 262 could carry bombs externally. *"Herr Reichsmarschall,"* Messerschmitt replied, "It was intended from the beginning that the machine could be fitted with two bomb racks so that it could drop bombs, either one 500 kg or two 250kg. But it can also carry one 1,000 kg or two 500 kg bombs..."

Göring beamed. "That answers the *Führer's* question..."

Three days later, however, Göring and Milch were at Dessau where they met Dr Anselm Franz of the Junkers engine company. Bombs or no bombs, an aircraft cannot fly without engines. The design of the Me 262 incorporated a pair of Jumo 004 turbojet engines mounted beneath the wings, each unit comprising an eight stage axial flow compressor, six separate combustion chambers and a single stage turbine. The first production engines were delivered in May 1943 having been improved by modifications to the compressor and the turbine entry nozzles which increased static thrust from 840 kg to 900 kg. Two months later however, in July, it was noticed that there were still "inconsistencies" in engine performance, with the engines on the prototypes V3 and V4 suffering from burning after shutdown. The summer was dogged by flame-outs and leaking and igniting fuel and when Franz welcomed the *Reichsmarschall* and the *Generalluftzeugmeister* to Dessau he warned them of difficulties still being experienced with individual components including the turbine wheel which suffered from vibration and the control system where there was difficulty in opening and closing the throttles. "It cannot be guaranteed with certainty," Franz admitted, "That we will have the problem at upper altitudes rectified by the time series production begins so that the pilot will be able to open and close the throttles without worrying about a flame-out."

Göring seems to have been unworried by this, for on 26 November, he invited Hitler to Insterburg in East Prussia which was located conveniently near to the *Wolfschanze* HQ, in order that he could view a display of some of the *Luftwaffe's* latest jet aircraft and guided missiles. After a bungled commentary on the proceedings by Göring, the Me 262 V6 streaked past flown by *Flugkapitän* Gerd Lindner. Hitler was impressed. He asked whether the aircraft was able to carry bombs. Messerschmitt, also in attendance, eagerly stepped forward and again reiterated that the jet could carry a bomb-load of 1,000 kg. A tense silence followed with no protests and shortly afterwards, Göring ordered the necessary trials to commence.

That Hitler asked if the Me 262 was able to carry bombs may have been a misguided question from a man who had little appreciation or knowledge of air strategy and aircraft design, but, at the same time, it was perfectly understandable since every other front-line *Luftwaffe* combat aircraft had already proved itself adequately capable of carrying bombs or performing in the fighter-bomber role. What was different about the Me 262? It must also be remembered that, ultimately, this was a totalitarian state ruled by a dictator whose authority and power was absolute and it is therefore hardly surprising that efforts were made to convert the Me 262 into a fast bomber in order to satisfy Hitler's whim. Furthermore Späte's report to Galland back in April had also indirectly supported the notion of deploying the Me 262 as a fighter-bomber.

It is also not surprising then, that the ambitious and dynamic *Generalmajor* Dietrich Peltz, as *General der Kampfflieger* – Commanding General of the Bomber Arm – flew the Me 262 V6 on 20 December 1943 without, as far as is known, any adverse reaction, despite the fact that the Jumo 004s were still subject to such teething problems as diffuser failures and starter engine and fuel pump jamming. Peltz was nevertheless impressed by the aircraft and, like Galland, viewed it as a priority design.

Dietrich Peltz was born in 1914 in Thüringia and his rise through the ranks of the *Luftwaffe's* officer corps had been extraordinarily rapid. A successful *Stuka* and bomber pilot and able

All wheels down, "White 5", an Me 262 of Erprobungskommando 262, makes its landing approach at Lechfeld.

The few service officers who flew Me 262 prototypes viewed the aircraft as a priority design. Generalmajor Dietrich Peltz (right), the commander of the Luftwaffe bomber arm, test flew the V6, seen here (below) at Lechfeld in November 1943 following a demonstration flight for Willy Messerschmitt and Göring.

tactician with experience gained over Russia and the Mediterranean, he had been appointed *General der Kampfflieger* at the age of twenty eight. By mid 1943, as a protégé of Göring's, his future at the very highest echelons of *Luftwaffe* command seemed secure, despite the fact, in a later capacity, he was to earn himself notoriety.

Under pressure from Hitler who was hungry for retaliation against England, Göring decided to place Operation *Steinbock* – the bombing of key "strategic" targets in the British Isles, particularly London – on a priority footing. To this end in November 1943, he appointed the newly promoted *Generalmajor* Peltz to the position of *Angriffsführer England* – Attack Leader England – giving him command of IX. *Fliegerkorps*. In reality, IX. *Fliegerkorps* was a hotchpotch of 550 hastily scraped together, fuel-starved bomber aircraft hauled into France from Russia and the Mediterranean – a

Above: Hitler's option: an Me 262 A2-a bomber of 1./KG 51 at dispersal at Rheine in late 1944.

Right: The superbly elegant, almost timeless design qualities of the Me 262 are seen here to full effect on this Me 262A-2a of Kommando Schenk.

Below: Two SC 250s are slung below this Me 262 A2-a. Although this photo shows the four standard gun ports in the nose, in the bomber variant generally two MK 108 30 mm cannon were fitted.

collection of literally *anything* that could carry a bomb. The "offensive" opened in January 1944 and limped on for four months, plagued from the start by technical and navigational difficulties, lack of accurate bombing and heavy losses over southern England. Eventually, *Steinbock* was called off and the battered remnants of IX. *Fliegerkorps* began to pull back into Germany, its crews uncertain of what the future might hold for them.

Typically however, Peltz was undaunted by the failure of the campaign he had been assigned to lead. In his mind, there was no time to sit and lick wounds and though IX. *Fliegerkorps* could hardly be described as an "asset" in terms of aircraft, its component *Gruppen* still boasted several hundred fully trained, but redundant bomber pilots. With the urgent demand for experienced air crew to fly in the home defence, Peltz, approached Göring with the radical but quite understandable suggestion of retraining and converting IX. *Fliegerkorps'* bomber pilots into jet fighter-bomber pilots. Peltz's reasoning was logical; his bomber pilots could probably make a better job of home defence than the apparently overworked and exhausted

Jagdwaffe and, given the new Me 262 jet fighter and their training in blind and bad weather flying and handling multi-engined aircraft, they could *also* adapt to flying high-speed fighter-bomber missions on the western front in an aircraft which nothing the Allies had could touch.

Though Peltz's theory may have been music to Göring's ears, Galland's enthusiasm for the proposal was less than warm. "I recommended that the IX. *Fliegerkorps* and its component units be disbanded and the pilots – they had very good material and the average pilot was well experienced – should attend fighter conversion courses and should then be incorporated into existing fighter units. In opposition to this, Peltz demanded that his *Fliegerkorps* should remain intact at all costs and should be completely retrained under *his* command and then sent into autonomous operations because he had far greater hopes of the "spirit" within his own *Korps*. He had made rash promises and had said that he could form a *Korps* which could operate in bad weather and that the only way this *Korps* could ever be efficiently brought back into action was if it was kept together and re-enforcements were arranged accordingly. I countered this by saying that that was irrelevant and thereby aroused the anger of the "fat gentleman" and was given a terrible telling-off, point by point and told that my suggestion was completely out of the question and that I was to make no mention of it again."

With Galland's misgivings silenced, Peltz began to keenly monitor the operations of the *Luftwaffe's* first fully equipped and operational Me 262 fighter and bomber units.

Remarkably, Galland had already initiated the establishment of the first jet fighter trials unit, *Erprobungskommando 262*, selecting as its commanding officer a serving member of his own staff, *Hptm.* Werner Thierfelder, an accomplished former *Zerstörer* pilot and *Ritterkreuzträger* who had flown over England, the Balkans and Russia. In his capacity as adviser to Galland on heavy fighter policy, Thierfelder had already flown the Me 262 several times and it is likely that he both encouraged and influenced the *General der Jagdflieger's* eventual decision to employ *Zerstörer* pilots as the first to convert over to the jet fighter.

So it was, that five days before Peltz flew the V6, Thierfelder moved into his newly assigned quarters at Lechfeld anticipating the arrival of twenty pilots.

Hptm Werner Thierfelder

Slowly they trickled in, together with the embryonic unit's first aircraft, the V5, V7, V8 and S1. However, the first production machines, together with some pilots from ZG 26, did not arrive until May 1944. That same month, on the Obersalzberg, Hitler had discovered from Milch, that contrary to his orders that the Me 262 be produced as exclusively as a fighter-bomber, the aircraft was, in fact, being built as a fighter. Hitler was exasperated and flew into a rage. Milch tried to reason: *"Führer,* even the smallest child can see that this is a fighter and not a bomber..."

In retrospect this may not have been a diplomatic remark for Hitler simply strengthened his resolve and ordered Göring to hold a meeting with those involved in the production of the Me 262 to sort things out once and for all. This took place on 29 May at which were present *Generaloberst* Günther Korten, the *Luftwaffe* Chief-of-Staff, Galland, Messerschmitt, Thierfelder, *Oberst* Walter Marienfeld, the acting *General der Kampfflieger* and representatives of the various aircraft testing establishments. Göring was erring towards safety and abiding by the latest *Führerbefehl.* "The *Führer* is rightly quite upset and says that everything he has ordered has not been carried out... The *Führer* wants the aircraft as a high speed bomber and not as a fighter at first. Nevertheless, he does not want further development as a fighter to be completely halted... He only wants all production aircraft to be bombers until further advised and that all emphasis be placed on the bomber sector... The machine may be a splendid fighter and may be flown as such, all very well, but he has doubts as to how, tactically, it can be used in the fighter role..."

An astonishing contrast between jet technology and its ground support equipment; an Me 262A-1a of Erprobungs-kommando 262 at the edge of the runway at Lechfeld, August 1944. The carts carry an auxiliary 24 volt electrical supply.

Me 262 A-2a "Black F" of Kommando Schenk seen here fitted with a ETC 503 bomb rack.

Göring immediately ordered the transfer of the Me 262 to the bomber arm in order to avoid "...further errors." Galland tried to protest, stating that in the Me 262, the *Luftwaffe* had, at last, the one aircraft capable of dealing with the super-fast British Mosquito bomber. His protests fell on deaf ears: "When the day comes that I can tell the *Führer* that the first *Staffel* of high speed bombers is ready," Göring vowed, "and that production is in full swing, then the *Führer* will authorise the machine as a fighter. I must now be able to rely on you to carry out this order with zeal and not frustrate my aims."

The wait was not long. The following month, *Maj.* Wolfgang Schenk, holder of the *Ritterkreuz* with Oakleaves and an extremely competent ground-attack pilot with experience gained over virtually every front that the *Luftwaffe* had fought on and who, at the time, was serving as a Tactical Adviser to the RLM's Technical Department, was chosen to form an experimental jet fighter-bomber unit. On 20 July 1944, the day that Count von Stauffenburg's bomb exploded in the *Führer's* headquarters, *Kommando Schenk* left its start-up base at Lechfeld and transferred to Châteaudun in France with nine Me 262s, six weeks too late to exploit their potency against the Allied landings in Normandy.

Meanwhile, *Eprobungskommando 262* had begun to make its first trial interceptions against Allied high-altitude/high-speed photo-reconnaissance aircraft over Bavaria when tragedy struck. Bounced by Mustangs over Kaufering on 18 July, having attempted to attack an American bomber formation, Werner Thierfelder successfully managed to bale out of his stricken aircraft but his parachute failed to open. Other members of the unit, however, attributed his death to technical failure, blaming damaged stator rings on both engines, proof that the Me 262 was still not completely ready for operations. Command of the embryonic jet fighter unit changed hands twice and there followed a period of isolated successes against Mosquitoes and P-38 Lightnings. In overall terms though, the effect of the unit against Allied operations was so small as to be hardly felt.

In France, the state of affairs surrounding *Kommando Schenk* was even worse. Affected by the critical ground situation in Normandy, the unit had flown no operations and had been forced to embark on a series of steady withdrawals from Châteaudun to Étampes to Creil to Juvincourt. Reinforcements were sent from Lechfeld, but of nine Me 262s dispatched, only five arrived to take part in intensive bombing sorties mounted against targets along the Seine, to the north-west of Paris and in the Melun area. On August 28th, the unit was compelled to pull back yet again, this time to Chièvres in Belgium.

Far-sighted conventional fighter unit commanders were now aware of what the Me 262 could offer and began to make demands for its speedy integration into the *Jagdwaffe's* arsenal.

Major Gerhard Stamp, *Gruppenkommandeur* of I./JG 300 and a former 300 mission bomber pilot who had converted to fighters, reported to OKL and the RLM in the summer of 1944 that:

"...A change in the air situation over the Reich is not possible with the forces at present available. If, on the other hand, the *Luftwaffe* could operate in sufficient strength with these new types of aircraft, then we might effectively beat the enemy's fighters and thus bring about a change in the whole situation. The Me 262 is capable of fulfilling these expectations... The operational intention would be to intercept bomber formations and their escorting fighters at, or before, the German border and force them to jettison their auxiliary tanks. The *Luftwaffe* would thus regain not only technical but also moral superiority during combat. The fighters would be forced to give up their free-lance tactics in which they range over nearly the whole front and the bombers would have to keep closer together on account of their weaker escort. They would however make a much better target for our defences."

Major Walter Nowotny.

Fighting hard to prove its worth as a fighter, Galland had taken advantage of Hitler's compromise of 20 August to allow every twentieth Me 262 that rolled off the production line to go the *Jagdwaffe*. The questionable operations of *Erprobungskommando 262* were bolstered by the establishment of two short-lived associate *Einsatzkommandos* based respectively at Rechlin-Lärz and Erfurt-Bindersleben, the former validating itself by claiming two Mosquitos and two P-38 Lightnings, the latter failing to embark on any operations in its own right before its incorporation into *Kommando Nowotny* the following month.

Kommando Nowotny was the next stage of development along the hard road towards convincing the leadership of the benefit of mass Me 262 fighter deployment. Galland had picked *Major* Walter Nowotny, the highly decorated twenty three year old Austrian fighter ace who, following a career that saw 255 confirmed victories in Russia with JG 54 and the award of the Diamonds to the Knights Cross, had transferred to France to command a school *Geschwader*. He would now command the new, expanded jet fighter unit. Following the initial intention

Major Wolfgang Schenk

to establish the unit with 52 aircraft on 25 September 1944, it was found that the only pilots capable of flying the jet were the remaining 15 of the original *Erprobungskommando* 262. Nevertheless, a form of primitive and hurried conversion

training began to take shape, with Nowotny applying himself to the task with as much energy as he could muster. By 29 September, *Kommando Nowotny* had some 30 Me 262s divided into two *Jagdgruppen*.

October, its first full month of operations, saw the unit struggle to get to grips with its machines and during the period 4-13 October, ten valuable jet fighters were either destroyed or damaged due to take-off or landing accidents. Nowotny's pilots, most of them drawn from conventional single-engined fighter units, lacking sufficient training in instrument flying and with only two or three intended training flights, found the jet with its effortless speed, short endurance and rapid descent, difficult to handle. On top of this, the choice of Achmer and Hesepe as its operational bases meant that the *Kommando* was constantly in the line of flight of approaching American bomber formations and thus prey to their marauding escort fighters.

Flying ceased altogether due to bad weather until 28 October when another pilot was killed, this man having the ignoble honour of making five flights in the Me 262, four of which involved crashes. The Messerschmitt test pilot, *Flugkäpitan* Fritz Wendel was alarmed and reported:

"...The commander, Nowotny, is a successful Eastern Front pilot but is unfamiliar with the present situation in the west and at 23 is not the superior leader personality necessary to guarantee the success of this vital operation... There is a variety of opinions among the pilots and *Staffelkapitäne* as to the most suitable tactical employment of the Me 262, indeed, there are even contradictory views. Clear tactical objectives and corresponding instructions of the pilots are lacking. The majority of the pilots have received far too little instruction on the Me 262... Instruction on type is particularly bad at *Kommando Nowotny*. The *Gruppe* Technical Officer at Hesepe... is a complete layman, who has, himself, destroyed two aircraft as a result of carelessness or inadequate training."

In France, Schenk's jet fighter-bomber operations were, at least, beginning to achieve more favourable results. Throughout early October, *Kommando Schenk* had carried out several hit-and-run raids, often using single machines or formations of two aircraft carrying up to a maximum of 108 SD-2 anti-personnel bombs, against RAF airfields in Belgium and Holland. On 2 October, for example, five raids were made resulting in 35 British casualties. On 12 October another lone raider accounted for one Spitfire destroyed at Grave and another nine damaged with several more casualties. Owing to this initial success, the *Kommando* was rapidly incorporated back into its mother unit, KG 51, and I./KG 51 began to re-equip on the Me 262 ready for the bomber role.

For the fighters however, worse was to come. Galland, now worried by the increasing losses being sustained by his only jet-fighter unit, arrived at Achmer on 7 November for an inspection. After a tour of both Achmer and Hesepe, he retired to the unit's billet to discuss the problems of the past weeks and listen to the pilots' worries about the Me 262's technical shortcomings and lack of readiness. The next day an American bomber formation set out to raid the marshalling yards at Rheine and the Nordhorn Canal. Throughout the whole of this raid, *Kommando Nowotny* was only able to scramble four jets in total; two in the morning against the approaching bombers and two in the afternoon during the formation's return to England. In this latter action, *Major* Nowotny and *Leutnant* Schall took off. Schall succumbed to the dreaded Mustang escort and was forced to bale out. A little

later, Nowotny's voice was heard over the radio. "We stepped into the open." Galland later wrote. "Visibility was not good: six-tenths cloud. Seconds later an Me 262 appeared out of the cloud and dived vertically into the ground. There was black smoke and an explosion." Nowotny's last words, though garbled, had indicated that his aircraft was on fire and seconds later, in front of a horrified Galland, he crashed to his death.

Wendel was quick to point out:

"...withdrawal was ordered by General Galland who had been with the unit on November 7 and 8. I have already stressed the weakness and faults in the training of the *Kommando* in my last report. The pilots are only partly "fighter-trained"... Total victories during the period (October 1 to November 12, 1944) are 22 and 4 possibles. Losses to our own machines total 26 out of a delivery of 30."

To Adolf Galland, Nowotny's death did not just represent the loss of yet another valued and experienced fighter commander. The political and strategic implications were far graver. Dogged by the apparent and intolerable failure of the Me 262 as a fighter, he knew that he would soon be fighting for the *Jagdwaffe's* life.

Me 262 A-1a "Green 3" of Kommando Nowotny is towed past other aircraft belonging to the unit by a Kettenkrad motorcycle half-track.

TWO

BAT OUTA HELL II was the personal aircraft of Col. Carl Storrie, commander of the 387th BG. It is seen here upon arrival in the UK at Chipping Ongar, summer 1943.

MARTIN B-26 MARAUDER

Beautifully streamlined – arguably superior in this respect to any other World War II bomber – the Martin B-26 Marauder was a fast, strong and well armed aircraft. Powered by two 2,000 hp Pratt and Whitney R-2800-5 radial engines and usually carrying a six-man crew, it could deliver a bomb load of 2,000 lb (907 kg) over a 550 mile (885 km) radius. With an all-round performance comparable to that of its US contemporary the B-25 Mitchell and interestingly, its opposite number in the *Luftwaffe*, the revered Junkers Ju 88, the Marauder turned in an outstanding combat record. All three types flew thousands of war sorties, often carrying the same bomb load at similar speeds over similar distances. But unlike the B-25 and Ju 88, both of which were adapted to many different roles, the B-26 flew the majority of its wartime missions purely as a medium bomber, delivering its ordnance in straight and level flight, usually in close formation to offer crews the mutual protection of a defensive armament of up to twelve machine guns per aircraft (only seven guns were actually defensive on all B-26s, the four package guns and the fixed nose gun being more accurately offensive weapons for use by the pilot during strafing runs). Even on those many occasions when Marauders based in

the European Theatre of Operations (ETO) flew pathfinder, chaff dropping or flare ship missions, some of them at night, the effort was considered an integral part of the Army Air Force (AAF) medium bombing campaign which continued to be spearheaded by the B-26 groups.

The design of a Glenn L. Martin Company project engineer, Peyton M. Magruder, the B-26 first saw the light of day as Martin Model Number 179 in which form it won a design competition issued by the Material Division at Wright Field in March 1939. Recognising the clouds of war gathering over Europe, the US

Factory-fresh Omaha-built B-26C-5 s/n 41-34678. Note the central rudder trim tab hinge, a distinguishing feature between the C-5 model and earlier B-series Marauders.

Army Air Corps had embarked upon an expansion programme in which it required a "300 mile per hour bomber." A contract for 201 aircraft valued at nearly $16,000,000 was subsequently awarded to Martin in mid-September. Jigs were swiftly set up at Martin's Middle River Plant in Baltimore and mass production quickly followed with the first B-26 rolling off the assembly line to make its maiden flight on 25 November 1940 with the company's chief test pilot, William K. "Ken" Ebel, at the controls. Events proved satisfactory and within three months, the first four aircraft were delivered to the Army Air Corps.

An organised training infrastructure was first established by the air force with Transition Training Fields at MacDill Field, Tampa, Florida and Shreveport Field, Shreveport, Louisiana, with Laughlin Army Air Field at Del Rio, Texas· and Dodge City Army Air Field, Kansas following as Operational Training Unit bases. There were problems in these early days of acceptance with both instructors and pilots possessing no previous twin-engine experience endeavouring to master the quirks of the machine and ultimately leading to a somewhat unfair and exaggerated adverse reputation of the aircraft. The truth however, was that the number of accidents involving the B-26 Marauder during 1943-1944 fell below that associated with the B-25 Mitchell.

However, once committed to combat in the Pacific very early in its development the B-26 did well – almost too well. Opting to fly low altitude, surprise attacks against Japanese targets, a handful of B-26 crews achieved a creditable record against the crack interceptors of the Imperial Japanese Army and Navy. When the enemy threat in the Pacific was more or less contained, the B-26 was largely replaced by the more numerous and versatile B-25. Apart from the 22nd Bomb Group, which inherited nearly all the remaining Army Marauders in the theatre and flew them until late 1943, any B-26s in the Pacific at the end of the war were operated by the Navy and Marines on second line target towing and liaison duties

The AAF's southern European war theatre in the Mediterranean had an urgent need for medium bombers following the success of Operation Torch, the first major combat

Set apart by the distinctive yellow and black stripes of its tail band, this is a B-26 of the 558th Squadron of the 387th BG. The group was one of those that was heavily committed to operations during the Battle of the Bulge in December 1944. For its efforts, it was awarded a DUC in recognition of its attacks on heavily defended transportation and communications targets.

deployment of US troops against the Axis in November 1942. In response three Marauder groups, the 17th, 319th and 320th, were assigned to the Twelfth Air Force in North Africa. The 319th was the first to begin operations, in November, with the 17th following suit in December. The 320th's initiation to combat would come later, in April 1943.

Initially, B-26 war sorties in the Mediterranean Theatre of Operations (MTO) did not go well; by continuing to employ low altitude attacks, the 'short wing, short tail' Marauders suffered at the hands of the German defences when raiding such locations as airfields, supply dumps and seaports. The 319th found the going rugged and crews welcomed the expansion of the desert medium bomber force when the 17th began its operations a few weeks later. They too found operating conditions to be primitive; arriving at Telergma in Algeria, they found the weather cold and wet and ground crews slept in holes in the ground and ate their meals in the open whatever the conditions. The flight line of the 34th Squadron was "... nothing but a barren clay expanse" with the unit's aircraft parked amidst humble Arab dwellings. The 17th ran a series of operations against German occupied airfields, bridges, marshalling yards and armour parks in Tunisia and Sardinia. Still things did not go smoothly, for both groups were being handed far too many missions. Two groups represented a meagre effort, with little room for normal war attrition.

A secret 1943 report on the B-26's performance in the MTO was not encouraging vis-à-vis its future use and this coupled with a spate of training accidents in the US – which, as we have

"Hard-hitting medium bomber for daylight raids" was how the press described this aircraft. Photographed by official cameramen, B-26 s/n 41-31892 was among the earliest Marauders to arrive at Earls Colne, England in the late summer of 1943 as part of the 323rd BG assigned to the Eighth Air Force.

seen, were no worse than other American types and in some instances considerably better – had nevertheless marred its career in official USAAF circles. Committees were convened more than once to cancel the B-26 but fortunately this was never carried out.

In 1943 the 322nd Bomb Group (Medium) was assigned to the Eighth Air Force in England as the cadre of a new 3rd Bombardment Wing composed of medium bombers. Unfortunately, lacking any well defined tactical plan, the Eighth reinforced the 'low level' doctrine by laying on a mission to Imjuiden power station in Holland on 14 May involving twelve Marauders from the 322nd. The results were deemed acceptable in terms of aircraft losses – one B-26 was lost as a result of a crash

The graceful lines of the Marauder are shown off here on TOOTSIE (s/n 41-34787), a B-26 of the 456th Squadron, 323rd BG in England in January 1944. Just visible as a misty silhouette beneath Tootsie's fuselage is a B-17 Flying Fortress.

landing in England due to severe Flak damage; several other aircraft were damaged – and the new crews thought they had made a reasonable job of bombing, but subsequent reconnaissance revealed little apparent damage. Consequently, a repeat raid was laid on for 17 May – again at low level. This famous disaster when eleven out of twelve 322nd Group aircraft 'failed to return' having fallen prey to navigational error, collision, Flak and fighter attack, revealed the flaws in the doctrine.

Operating low flying bombers against an enemy possessing a well-honed early warning radar network linked into numerous anti-aircraft guns manned by highly experienced crews and supported by a deadly fighter force, was almost guaranteed to make tactical missions costly. Crew inexperience also played a very large part in this negative period – the B-26 could be very unforgiving if not treated with great respect. The aircraft itself was not completely free of technical faults, particularly in its weak nosewheel leg, which could give way in a hard landing and lead to a disastrous crash.

Fortunately however, the fact that the 3rd Bombardment Wing did not really need a tactical bomber force and had few operational plans as to how to deploy one, was not ultimately held to be any fault of Marauder crews or the aircraft itself. In mid-October 1943, the initial quartet of B-26 groups assigned to the Eighth – the 322nd, 323rd, 386th and 387th – moved base and became part of Air Support Command at a time when, in terms of tactical planning, there was very little to actually support – certainly not American armies in the field. The time was not however, wasted. Between the last raid of the first phase of B-26 operations over north-west Europe and the formation of the new

tactical Ninth Air Force on 16 October, the medium groups flew a steadily rising total of missions to the continent under heavy fighter escort, their crews gaining invaluable experience in adopting the most effective target approaches, flying in formation at altitudes which would increase bombing accuracy and minimise losses to flak and generally making their presence felt. The Ninth's Marauder groups soon became a force to be reckoned with.

Equipped with the famed Norden bombsight, the B-26s now attacked at heights between (on average) 12,000 ft (3,660 m) and 18,000 ft (5490 m). Tight, six-ship 'boxes' of bombers ensured that a good concentration of bombs was achieved. Release was by various methods – individual, box or pathfinder signal given by a lead bombardier, or 'toggler' as he was sometimes termed. Target approach altitudes varied; weather conditions could dictate that a lower level than normal be adopted in deference to the prevailing visibility, despite the increasing risk to the B-26s from Flak. Bombing on the leader's command was frequently necessary, and specialised pathfinder crews were often needed to navigate through to an obscured target and employ BTO – Bombing Through Overcast – techniques.

Total losses of individual Marauders – primarily to Flak – remained encouragingly low and in direct ratio to the number of sorties flown, they generally stayed that way. The greatest hazard to B-26 group operations became crew injury and incapacitation. Numerous crewmen were hospitalised when shrapnel penetrated the B-26's skin – near misses could sometimes be grimly effective in this respect.

Some European targets were so well defended by Flak artillery that after attacking them few aircraft returned to base without battle damage in varying degrees. But such was the plethora of tactical targets that Air Support Command began sending out double – morning and afternoon – strikes on given days and these increased as the date for the invasion of occupied France approached. The result was that individual Marauders – some so patched that their original finish needed regular attention, others seemingly leading charmed lives and coming

The loathed German "Flak" or anti-aircraft fire inflicted a terrible punishment on low-flying medium bombers throughout the war, but the Marauder proved very resilient. Here the effects of Flak can be seen on the port-side fuselage wall of a B-26 between the cockpit and the package gun blisters.

home time and again without a scratch – piled up impressive mission records (such as the 322nd Group's famed B-26B-25 *Mild and Bitter*, the first to survive 100 missions, and the same group's other old war-horse, *Flak Bait*, which notched up an outstanding 202 combat missions). These were facts that AAF senior command might have scoffed at only a few months previously. Combat was proving Martin's shapely medium was more than up to the task assigned it if it was deployed correctly.

Strong fighter cover, primarily by RAF Spitfire squadrons, but later by P-47s, P-38s and other types, unquestionably helped the admirable record achieved by Eighth ASC B-26 groups. Fortunately, German fighter opposition to medium bombers remained sporadic throughout the conflict, the *Jagdwaffe's* response being increasingly focused towards the greater perceived threat, that of the AAF's four-engined heavy bombers attacking strategic targets deeper into Germany. Furthermore, it no way detracts from the bravery of Marauder crews to state that however well they laid their bombs on various targets, some of these were surprisingly resilient and well able to absorb high explosive without succumbing.

Medium bombers, with their modest bomb sizes, could rarely hope to entirely eliminate some targets – but these could be neutralised by repeat raids. Airfields invariably required multiple visits and the process became one of a slow whittling down rather than a series of 'knock out' blows.

While the build-up towards Overlord proceeded in England, the Twelfth Air Force in North Africa was likewise strengthened, poised to support the Allied drive through North Africa and an eventual invasion of southern France. With more US groups in action in the desert and the *Luftwaffe* being gradually worn down, medium bombers could hone their technique and provide excellent support to the armies representing the 'Torch' force and Montgomery's Eighth Army. After the battle of El Alamein, the *Panzer Armee Afrika* was unable to prevent the link up of the two Allied armies and the loss of North Africa as a base of operations.

Allied commanders recognised that vital to the success of the forthcoming invasion of France was the gaining of local air superiority – but there was a fear that too much emphasis on targets in the Normandy area would clearly indicate to the Germans where Allied troops would go ashore. The tactical air forces were therefore given a long list of targets that encompassed virtually the entire coastline of north western

With their 2,000 hp Pratt and Whitney radial engines turning over, B-26 Marauders of the 322nd BG wait their turn for take-off on the taxiway at Andrew's Field, (Great Saling), England in September 1943. The 322nd carried the distinction of being the first B-26 group to embark on operations in the ETO but suffered catastrophic losses on a raid to Ijmuiden, Holland in May 1943.

Marauders cross the Italian coast.

France, Belgium and Holland and extended some 200 miles inland. This interdiction campaign had the ultimate advantage of not only preserving the area selected for the invasion but of creating great difficulties for the Germans in bringing fresh troops, supplies and equipment into the battle area over supply lines and dumps that had been hit in great depth, far behind the new front line.

Also, the B-26 groups were instrumental in preventing an offensive that could well have wrecked the entire invasion. Had the *Luftwaffe* been able to launch the V-1 flying bomb, the first of Hitler's *Vergeltungswaffen* (revenge) weapons, against the invaders in the numbers planned, the carnage could have been terrible. As it was, early Allied detection of the launching sites in France and reports from agents, led to a full operational plan, 'Operation Crossbow', for countering the threat from these new weapons. The majority of the first V-1 launching areas, nicknamed 'ski sites' because they included storage buildings with this distinctive shape, were located in the Pas de Calais area. These were heavily bombed under the operational codename 'Noball', a word that was to appear repeatedly in Ninth Air Force mission folders for months.

Being briefed to bomb innocuous-looking French fields gave B-26 crewmen newly arrived in England useful theatre orientation. A bonus was that V-1 sites generally lacked the heavy flak defences of other enemy targets, but these missions, which were not always 'milk runs', were vital. That the aerial campaign was successful was proven by the fact that not a single V1 could be launched against the forces of Operation Overlord on 6 June 1944.

By the eve of D-Day, the Ninth Air Force had its eight assigned groups, the four originals from the Eighth and a quartet of directly-assigned units. These were tasked with attacks on Noball sites and manufacturing plants, an interdiction campaign against the French road, rail and waterway transportation system in order to isolate the beachhead, and attacks on *Luftwaffe* aerodromes. Such missions were an extension of those that had been conducted in previous months, the latter an ongoing war of attrition against enemy air power.

So much had been accomplished by the tactical groups before the first Allied soldier put a foot on French soil on 6 June 1944 that relatively few dangers to Overlord came from bypassed targets along the Normandy coast. Even the efficient German radar network had enormous gaps in coverage, to the detriment of *Luftwaffe* formations which might have challenged the invasion.

Troops on the ground found however that bombing (and naval gunfire) can only achieve so much; German coastal defences at Normandy proved to be tough obstacles to overcome, particularly at Omaha beach. While aerial bombs had indeed hit the gun emplacements, these had been extremely strongly built and well sited. In some cases these positions were all but invulnerable to conventional aerial attack and could only be neutralised when stormed by troops. The crews of B-26s and other Allied bombers could only report that from their viewpoint tactical targets appeared to be smothered by explosions and at least damaged – but repeat missions had to be flown on numerous occasions.

One type of target that the Ninth's B-26 groups became adept at destroying was bridges. Small and thus difficult to sever from altitude, bridges in France and Germany were attacked by Marauders many times during the drive across Europe. In fact, "bridge busting" represented something of a campaign within a campaign as evident from the mission log of the 323rd Bomb Group which attacked bridge targets for nine consecutive days in May 1944. European bridge spans, often ancient and sturdily built of brick and stone, had to be heavily bombed in order to break them or at least to shake their supporting piers so badly that they became dangerously unsafe, especially for heavy

A B-26F-1 (s/n 42-96288) of the 598th Squadron, 397th BG releases its bomb load on a target somewhere over Europe in 1944. The aircraft wears little camouflage and is adorned with the group's yellow diagonal tail band. The 397th was the first Ninth Air Force bomb group to operate from the continent and later won a DUC for action against transportation targets in the Ardennes in December 1944.

vehicles or trains. Formations of B-26s carried a sufficient weight of explosives to achieve either of these twin goals and they were very widely deployed against all types of bridge target. By 6 June 1944 – D-Day – 4,400 tons of bombs had been successfully dropped on bridges in France by the Ninth Air Force and the command was proud to report that not a bridge remained intact along the Seine between Rouen to Mantes-Gassicourt.

BATTLE OVER BAVARIA

With Overlord a success, the Ninth Air Force continued to provide a fast and efficient air support service to the ground forces as they pushed their way out of the Normandy bridgehead. It was foreseen that response to rapidly-developing situations on the ground would be far faster when Allied tactical aircraft were operating from airfields in France and, following the planned movement of fighter-bombers to the continent, the first B-26 rapidly followed suit, with the 323rd, 387th, 394th and 397th BGs operational by the end of August.

Flak rather than fighter attack, continued to be the cause of the majority of B-26 losses although in contrast to the high number of sorties flown by Ninth Air Force groups, the percentage was well within broadly-defined limits established by AAF planners.

The Marauder's European combat debut had been made by the B-26B-4 with a redesigned, longer stroke nosewheel leg, four fuselage package guns for use by the pilot and provision for a pair of 'fifties in the rear hatches. The B-4 was supplanted in production by the much-improved B-26B-10 which boasted an increase of 6 ft (1.8 m) to its wingspan (56 sq ft (5.2 sq m) of additional wing area), and a larger vertical tail. Armament was again increased, to total a maximum of 12 machine guns. This included a fixed gun in the starboard side of the nose transparency which was, like the package guns, fired from the pilot's control column. The Marauder's nose area which already had a flexible centreline weapon of similar calibre for use by the bombardier, had thus become very crowded, so much so that the fixed gun was a short-lived addition.

An oxygen system change was made in the B-26B-15, which was also the last model to have the early 'stepped' tail gun position with two hand-held guns.

The next combat model, the B-26B-20, had a shorter-chord rudder, a streamlined Bell Type M-6 powered tail 'stinger' with

A combat box of Marauders of the 555th Squadron, 386th BG en-route to Normandy on one of at least three missions which the unit made on D-Day. The 386th earned itself a noble record as a result of bombing operations mounted against enemy airfields, transport and industrial targets, V-1 sites and ground support on D-Day, the subsequent campaign in Normandy and the Battle of the Bulge.

Above: Marauders of the 587th Squadron, 394th BG in formation south west of Paris, 12 June 1944.

Right: Six days after the invasion, a pair of B-26s belonging to the 587th Squadron, 394th BG are seen over Conflannes, France with their P-47 Thunderbolt escort close at hand. The nearest ship B-26B-55 (s/n 42-96210) was shot down the next day, 13th June, near Orleans. The group later won a DUC in August 1944 following exemplary bombing achievements against strongholds, ammunition dumps and bridge targets in Normandy.

two .50-in machine guns and incorporating armour protection for the gunner, and further oxygen system changes.

Centre of gravity problems had caused some concern to front line Marauder units and the B-26B-25 had its rear bomb-bay sealed to prevent overloading. Minor revisions on the B-26B-35 and -40 production blocks culminated in the B-26B-45, which deleted the single fixed nose gun, introduced a new combined bombing/gunnery sight for the pilot and had some revisions to the radio equipment. B-26B model production ended after the B-26B-50, which had a mechanism for emergency closure of the bomb doors and the B-26B-55, with an improved bomb sight.

Martin's plant at Omaha produced the B-26C starting in mid-1942 with the B-26C-5, which was, in fact, the first of the 'big wing' and revised tail Marauders. All subsequent B-26Cs were similar to their Baltimore-built equivalents (although some sub-types were unique to Omaha) and production terminated in the spring of 1944 with the B-26C-45. A small but important addition to the later model Marauders were 'stall strips'. Attached to the leading edge of the wing inboard of the engines, these strips broke the airflow sufficiently to ward off a low speed stall on landing.

The B-26F was the penultimate Marauder built at Baltimore. Otherwise similar to the B-26B-55, the F-1 had a 3.5 degree increase in wing incidence to provide improved lift on take off. Only B-26F-1s were delivered to the USAAF, the F-2 and F-6 sub types being built for the RAF.

The last production model was the B-26G, which incorporated the increased wing incidence and was built in eight principal blocks: B-26G-1, G-5, G-10, G-11, G-15, G-20, G-21 and G-25. Some early examples were fitted with the C-1 autopilot while all had a blast 'blanket' to protect the forward fuselage structure in the vicinity of the package guns, fuel line modifications, a full mechanical emergency landing system and revised fittings on all hydraulic lines.

There were further hydraulic line changes on the B-26G-5 and the G-10 introduced a spent cartridge case collector fairing below the tail turret to prevent ejected cases damaging aircraft following in formation. Otherwise externally similar, the B-26G-15 and G-20 respectively had the portable oxygen system removed and some further changes in radio equipment.

Late model B-26s were issued to combat units as required but most units operated a mix of Marauder sub-types until the end of hostilities. Many of the veterans bore witness to scores of sorties over enemy territory and for an aircraft that was on the point of cancellation more than once,

The 386th BG receives a visit from the "top brass" shortly before the D-Day landings: Air Chief Marshal Sir Trafford Leigh Mallory, commander of the Allied Expeditionary Air Force, chats with a member of the ground crew attending to THE YANKEE GUERILLA during an inspection tour of Allied airfields. Ultimately, the B-26 was protected by a total of twelve .50 calibre machine guns.

The B-26G was the last production model of the Marauder and incorporated increased wing incidence, a blast "blanket" to protect the forward fuselage, modifications to the fuel feed system and a mechanical emergency landing system.

the B-26 turned in an exceptional combat record. Many individual machines defied the doubters and flew 50, 75 and 100 missions or more and their crews were justifiably proud of their battle-scarred 'centenarians'.

Production breakdown for B-26 combat models was: B-26 and B-26A – 340; B-26B – 1,883; B-26C – 1,210; B-26F – 300 and B-26G – 893. When Baltimore completed the last B-26 in March 1945, a grand total of 5,266 Marauders had been built. To the front line bombers were added the ships that shouldered the vital but unsung duty of tuition for thousands of pilots and crewmen who would fly mediums 'in anger'. Thus Martin production extended to 640 AT-23s and TB-26s intended for training and target towing.

In total B-26s flew 129,943 sorties (in the ETO) to drop 169,382 tons of bombs. This effort claimed 911 aircraft destroyed to all causes which was less than 1 per cent of the sorties flown and the best for any US medium bomber. In the course of the European war, many Marauder crewmen were decorated for bravery and one pilot, Darryl Lindsay of the 387th BG, won a posthumous Medal of Honor. In addition, Marauder crews claimed 402 enemy aircraft destroyed.

The Marauder's overall performance in both war theatres was good and outstandingly so in Europe; by the time Germany surrendered, crews were placing their bombs very accurately indeed. Figures of 60 per cent falling within a 2,000 ft (609 m) radius of the target aiming point and 85 per cent hitting within 1,000 ft (305 m) were regularly achieved by units of the 9th Air Division in general and the 387th Group in particular.

Martin was contracted to complete B-26 production before the war ended (in March 1945), there being no plans by the air force to retain the type in its post-war inventory. Although this was seen as a rather unfortunate state of affairs at the time, the company was at least spared costly production overruns faced by many of its rivals which had difficulty turning off the production tap once the need for obsolescent aircraft had passed.

Declared obsolete when the European war ended, B-26s were scrapped, many of them in Germany. The surprisingly rapid demise of the Marauder continues to be a source of controversy among combat veterans, not least because precious few examples of the type exist today.

Above left: A typical scene found at many of the continental airfields serving the Marauder groups during 1944-45. Here THE OLD GOAT, a B-26G-1 (S/N 43-34213) of the 585th Squadron, 394th BG, sits on the perimeter track at Cambrai, France in February 1945 surrounded by the objects of war; bombs, fuel drum, access steps and servicing trolley.
Left: December 1944 and winter snows coat these B-26s of the 386th BG at their airfield at Clastres from where they flew sorties over the Ardennes during the Battle of the Bulge.

THREE

A P-47 caught by a German photographer whilst flying low over German positions in Italy, 1944

REPUBLIC P-47 THUNDERBOLT

A big, tough and highly effective combat aircraft, the P-47 Thunderbolt had been the 'stop-gap' escort fighter which was a literal life-saver to long-suffering Eighth AAF bomber crews battling their way through fighter infested skies over Germany in the summer of 1943. Later that year, the arrival in England of the P-51 Mustang to undertake long range bomber escort, indirectly pointed the way for the heavyweight P-47 to equip new groups trained to undertake tactical ground attack operations. Not that this was in any way a new role for the Thunderbolt, for P-47 fighter groups had regularly indulged in strafing ground targets en route back to England after escort missions for some time. Under the AAF policy of neutralising the German fighter force and gaining Allied air superiority prior to any invasion of the continent, Thunderbolt groups were to play a decisive part.

The most heavily armed single seat fighter in the AAF inventory, the P-47's weight of fire was approximately equal to that of the P-38 Lightning's single 20 mm cannon and four 0.50 in machine guns. The P-47D weighed in at 13,500 lb (6,123 kg) and was eventually cleared to carry up to 2,000 lb (907 kg) of external

ordnance. Without the benefit of special aiming devices or sights, pilots became adept at delivering high explosive 500 lb (227 kg) and/or 1000 lb (454 kg) GP bombs, combinations of 60 lb (27 kg) fragmentation bombs and 4.5 in (114 mm) air-to-ground rockets launched from triple M-10 'Bazooka' tubes. But the fire from eight .50 in (12 mm) Colt-Browning machine guns was often more than enough to heavily damage if not destroy, the majority of targets, from all kinds of structures on the ground, up through ships, locomotives, tanks, vehicles and aircraft. Anything supporting the German war effort was fair game to the American *Jabos'* which

BILLIE a P-47 sporting the "Fighting Cock" badge of the 66th Squadron, 57th FG, the longest-serving Thunderbolt fighter-bomber unit in the Mediterranean theatre. The group had taken delivery of its first P-47s in November 1943.

became a feared and hated thorn in the side of the *Wehrmacht* on the western front as well as to the German transport infrastructure. In this, the P-47 also proved a not insignificant psychological weapon.

When the Ninth Air Force was formed in late 1943, the fighter-bomber force had Thunderbolt groups assigned without delay, there being thirteen in the UK by the spring of 1944 out of an eventual total of eighteen.

An aircraft highly suited to the demands of ground attack work with its big Pratt and Whitney R-2800-21 radial engine

Below: The US press men who released this photo, described this P-47 Thunderbolt of the 57th FG, Twelfth Air Force – the "Black Scorpions" – as a "triple-threat work-horse". They were no doubt referring to the aircraft's awesome firepower consisting in this case of eight 0.50 in (12.7 mm) calibre machine guns, a pair of 500 lb bombs and a triple-tube 4.5 in (114 mm) M10 rocket launcher under each wing. So-equipped, this P-47 was one of those which took part in Operation Strangle, the massive air offensive designed to choke German supply lines in Italy. Based on the US Army infantry rocket, the M10, though possessing impressive destructive capability, was difficult to aim due to uncertain trajectory and the delay in reaching maximum velocity following release.

developing 2,300 hp and a top speed of 433 mph (697 km/h), the P-47D was far less vulnerable to ground fire than liquid-cooled powerplants, and a 'natural' in the role, one which its pilots took to with great flair. Attack techniques adopted by P-47 groups included shallow dive 'glide bombing' or steep angle dive bombing, both proving equally effective, depending on the type of target and the strength of the defences.

Pulling up sharply enough to create wingtip contrails, a P-47D with the unmistakable black/white checkerboard nose marking of the 78th Fighter Group at Duxford shows the shapely, purposeful lines of one of the most successful fighters of World War II. Like other Thunderbolt/Mustang units, the Duxford group tangled with the German jets and Lt Col Joe Myers of this squadron, the 82nd, scored the first US fighter victory over the Me 262. In terms of jet kills the 78th emerged as the third most successful in the Eighth Air Force with 14 destroyed.

It is no overstatement to say that the fighter-bomber was one of the true cornerstones of Allied victory in Europe, one without which the conflict might well have taken a different turn. Had troops not had such outstanding support, the European campaign would undoubtedly have been more costly and protracted. A positive attitude on the part of Army commanders in exploiting the assets of air support was another key factor in the overall success of the campaign in Europe. Commanders generally understood air power and had high praise for what the tactical groups could do to smooth their passage against a tenacious, skilled and at times, extremely strong defence.

As the air element of Overlord that would operate closest to American troops, the P-47 units faced a considerable responsibility. Fortunately, air-ground tactical co-ordination was brought to a very precise art during and after the invasion and fighter-bombers were able to make pin-point strikes on very small targets, at times mere yards from Allied positions. Directed by airmen riding in leading vehicles in mobile army columns and directing the strikes by map or photographic co-ordinates over radio links, this superb system placed the ordnance where it was needed, reduced the ratio of misses to hits and minimised casualties to friendly troops. Tactical aircraft were also greatly aided by the establishment of microwave radar units on the European mainland.

The skilful deployment of P-47 fighter-bombers often enabled the advance to proceed where it might otherwise have been delayed for days on end, with friendly troops being obliged to withstand a spiralling casualty rate, pinned down by enemy fire. German mobile units and fixed positions were overcome quickly by Allied troops with timely fighter-bomber intervention. And if the *Luftwaffe* chose to intervene, the P-47 was more than capable of warding off attack. With their predominant ground attack role the Ninth Air Force Thunderbolt groups flew numerous sorties without

Massed might of the Wolfpack includes a number of Thunderbolt models – and typical individualistic camouflage schemes sported by aircraft of almost the entire 56th Fighter Group. The 61st Fighter Squadron is represented here by razorback and bubbletop sub-types, all of which have the abbreviated black and white stripes which endured on the lower surfaces of Allied aircraft for some time after D-Day. The Wolfpack was credited with downing 6.5 German jets including 4.5 Me 262s.

even a sight of the *Luftwaffe* but there were times when the enemy appeared and air combat enabled a number of pilots flying with tactical groups to notch up enough aerial victories to become aces.

D-Day had been launched with the tactical fighters of the Ninth AAF based in the main on Advanced Landing Grounds in southern England, as near to their potential targets as possible. These groups were poised to move across the Channel as soon as forward areas had been cleared, to establish themselves at both temporary airstrips similar to the ALGs in England, and more permanent French aerodromes. Being able to operate from bases in France put tactical Thunderbolt groups that much nearer the fighting, individual aircraft often being but a few minutes' flying time from the front lines. The already legendary ability of the P-47D to absorb combat damage stood it in further good stead as the hazardous business of close support demanded an increasing number of sorties against heavy, concentrated ground fire.

Numerous Thunderbolts returned to base with large parts of the airframe blasted away by ground fire and engine cylinders not only wrecked but missing entirely. Somehow they continued to fly, got down and were repaired by the highly experienced personnel attached to Air Service Command. Pilots appreciated the fact their aircraft, crippled by combat damage, could probably protect them from further harm even if there was no choice but to crash-land into very solid ground objects!

Mid and late-war razorback Thunderbolts flying from forward

continental bases were outwardly very similar in appearance to aircraft that had first come to England to fly escort to heavy bombers. Apart from the 1943 change in the US national insignia, the fact that officially the AAF had decided to leave camouflage paint off new production aircraft (from February 1944) did not cut much ice with field commanders whose airfields remained within range of enemy aircraft. They appreciated that a coat of olive drab could mean the difference between losing a few machines to strafing *Luftwaffe* fighters or being given a few seconds' advantage in the air compared to the bright 'silver' ships which, with the sun's reflective help, could be seen for miles. It therefore became common for groups to continue to fly the older razorback P-47D models alongside the newer 'bubbletops', the tactical paint-work they adopted often being left to individual commanders or pilots. Certainly there were many pilots who flew P-47s in 'natural aluminium finish' without a second thought and they came to no harm.

In air combat good vision from the cockpit is vital and some P-47Ds were fortunate enough to get the RAF Malcolm hood. This frameless canopy section was adapted to fit in place of the 'greenhouse' hood universally fitted to all razorback Thunderbolt models, but it was in too short supply to keep up with demand. Republic had plans to rectify that situation, however.

Enter the bubbletop... Republic did not deem that the change from the razorback to a cut-down rear fuselage to take a clear vision canopy merited a revised designation and both sub types were known as P-47Ds. The precise confirmation of change was in the production blocks, those aircraft from the P-47D-25RE onwards having the teardrop or 'bubbletop' canopy.

Under the skin, early and late production P-47Ds differed

Hardly stirring the dust at an advanced landing ground, Thunderbolts of the 36th Fighter Group led by P-47 D-22 S/N 42-25984 of the 23rd Squadron, prepare for a sortie. This photograph was almost certainly taken at the group's airfield at Kingsnorth, Kent a facility that had been in operation since July 1943, time enough for grass under the pierced steel plank (PSP) to become established! The lack of underwing ordnance on the P-47s may indicate a training sortie.

considerably; in common with other manufacturers, Republic carried out a series of progressive modifications and improvements to its primary wartime design, largely as a result of combat reports from pilots and the company's own technical representatives. These largely anonymous individuals worked with operational groups in the field, putting in many hours of work, part of which was inevitably to sympathise with the occasional 'gripes' of the men who were risking their lives flying the company product. There were not too many of those, however.

Even when pitted against the skilled and battle-experienced *Experten* who led the *Luftwaffe's* western front and Reich-based fighter *Gruppen* and who enjoyed the benefit of fighting over their own territory, the sheer performance of the P-47 ensured that its pilots were given a fair chance in combat. At altitudes above 20,000 ft (6,100 m), the Thunderbolt's performance reached its zenith, whilst any attempt by a Bf 109 or Fw 190 to evade encounter by breaking away into a half-roll and dive was generally foiled by the superb dive acceleration of the P-47. Such acceleration even stood the test against the speed of the German Me 262 jet fighter and the reader will see evidence of this and how it was exploited to maximum effect in Chapter 14 of this book.

Once paddle-bladed propellers were fitted, the Thunderbolt enjoyed a faster rate of climb, thus offering no quarter to German pilots endeavouring to escape by that means.

By the time they were flying close support sorties right into Germany, the Ninth Air Force P-47 groups had gained some advantage over their colleagues in the Eighth who had first and foremost, flown bomber escort missions from the UK. This advantage was that of range. Ground attack sorties from continental bases were usually flown over more modest distances, and the P-47D really came into its own, with the advantage that it needed to give nothing away in terms of built-in firepower. Other types were rarely able to carry the offensive load of the P-47D. It goes almost without saying – for this was so common in the way that the air war actually developed – that the P-47 spent much of its time successfully flying the type of sortie for which it had not actually been designed.

FOUR

Oberst. Günther Lützow (seen standing in this photograph), would be instrumental in the "Mutiny of the Kommodores". By late autumn 1944, Galland was, in his own words, "barely tolerated".

MUTINY, DISMISSAL AND EXILE: THE CRISIS OF COMMAND

Der Grosse Schlag

Throughout the autumn of 1944, following the apocalyptic mauling that the bulk of the *Jagdwaffe* had received as a result of its hurried and badly managed deployment in the cauldron of Normandy, Adolf Galland had been working on an innovative gamble which had received the personal backing of both Hitler and Göring. In September 1944, using the short luxury of a halt in the extended Allied advance, he began working to create a "new" reserve of such strength that the *Jagdwaffe* would be in a position to send up "at least 2,000 fighters" against a major raid, with the intention of making an impact on the escort fighters as well as harrying the bombers from Sweden to Switzerland if necessary.

Galland was prepared to sacrifice four hundred aircraft and 150 pilots if 400-500 *Viermots* could be brought down in one massive operation or *Grosse Schlag* – "Great Blow". He began by pulling fighters back from the southern front and Austria of fighters, and reactivating two fighter units crewed by Italian volunteers to cover Italy. Practice manoeuvres were run through again and again taking into account all possible variations of approach flight the bombers might take and using the bloody lessons gained over the past seven months. Sufficient fuel was scraped together and stockpiled to cover 2,500 sorties and command infrastructure was revised. Intensive training had been given to both unit commanders and their crews so that any and all of the Western Front and Reich-based *Jagdgeschwader* could react quickly and efficiently to any one of the six general types of American raids that they might have to oppose.

Time after time, Galland had drummed the fact home to his unit commanders that they should avoid becoming confused at seeing so many German aircraft airborne at the same time – possibly as many as 2,000, a rare sight indeed. Several key airfields in the west had been allocated for use by the Reich based home defence units so that they could land if low on fuel and take-off again for a second mission and it was hoped that at least 500 fighters would make use of this opportunity. Now a massive force of fighters, the largest assembled by the *Jagdwaffe* in the West since 1940, stood waiting ready to clash with the bombers over the Reich itself. They were supplemented by further aircraft drawn from the three *Geschwader* based in Belgium and Holland, all of which had been briefed to attack the American fighter escort on their approach or return. Additionally, up to 100 nightfighters were on stand-by in Denmark and southern Germany to deal with any crippled B-17s or B-24s endeavouring to make for emergency landing points in neutral Sweden or Switzerland.

Finally, as fog and rain blanketed western Europe for the first two weeks of November, on the 12th of the month, Galland announced to the *Luftwaffe Führungsstab* that his carefully conserved fighter reserve was ready to attempt the *Grosse Schlag*.

All that was needed was a break in the weather. Galland waited, but it never came.

Hitler meanwhile, craving victory in the West – which, in the light of his planned new shock offensive in the Ardennes, seemed so possible now – could ill afford to allow the bulk of his airpower to lie dormant on airfields in the Reich waiting for something to happen against which it seemed the *Luftwaffe* could do little anyway. Galland's theories of conservation and promises of success seemed hollow and unreliable. In Hitler's mind, Galland was just stalling and afraid. The reserves, which, admittedly, he had most diligently built up, could better be deployed in regaining the initiative in the west by supporting the land offensive which, in turn, could drastically alter the military and political situation in Germany's favour by driving an invincible armoured wedge between the Allied armies and thrusting through the heavily forested hill country of the Ardennes towards the key sea-port of Antwerp. In embarking upon such an ambitious and audacious attack, Hitler hoped also that he could trap the American First and Ninth Armies around Aachen, thus at least, eliminating the threat posed to the Ruhr and subsequently allowing him to draw on the Western Front for vitally needed men and material with which to counter the next big Soviet attack in the east. This decision for Adolf Galland, when it came, was a shock.

In his private diary of 1945, Galland wrote: "In mid-November (1944), I received orders to prepare the fighter units held in reserve for a great defensive battle in the West and to train them accordingly. In reality, it was impossible to fulfil this order due to the poor training of the pilots and the lack of fuel needed for further training. It was only in early December that I was informed about the forthcoming Ardennes offensive. The hopeless situation in the East made it impossible to even dream of an offensive in the West. But at this time, I was barely tolerated anyhow... I failed to understand how such a large number of fighters were to be accommodated on the inadequate airfields in the West. The true intentions in the West were only made known to me at the beginning of December. I was gravely concerned for the following three reasons:

1. An offensive in the West was senseless, but it was an absolute necessity in the East.
2. I knew that the insufficient training and lack of experience of the unit commanders meant failure of the *Jagdwaffe's* efforts.
3. The *Grosse Schlag* thus became an impossibility."

To what extent Galland voiced his fears at this time or whether they were listened to if he did, is not clear. In any case, events were rapidly overtaking him and by the second half of November 1944, his position and influence were beginning to be deliberately undermined by moves designed to pass power into the hands of those considered by both Hitler and Göring to be more capable, dynamic and dedicated. The first such move came on 15 November 1944 when *Generalmajor* Dietrich Peltz was propelled from his position as commander of the now virtually unemployable IX. *Fliegerkorps* to take command of II *Jagdkorps*. In such a position, Peltz theoretically held tactical control of the entire *Luftwaffe* fighter force on the Western Front and was therefore well placed to direct fighter operations in support of the Ardennes offensive.

Peltz approached his task with radical speed and determination, overturning whatever policy of meeting mass with mass in the air that Galland had laid down, at least in the area of II. *Jagdkorps*. The *Führer's* wishes were to be carried out and the fighter arm would, for the duration of the offensive at least, apply itself to supporting the ground forces over the Ardennes, essentially a task for which it had not, under any circumstances been trained. But whatever knowledge of fighter command Peltz was lacking was made up for by the appointment of *Oberst* Gordon Gollob as leader of the Special Fighter Staff for the Ardennes offensive, reporting directly to Peltz. Gordon Gollob was one of the most highly decorated and combat-

Right: Almost certainly taking part in Galland's intended Grosse Schlag operation would have been aircraft of JG 26, the unit he led in more victorious times. Here Fw 190D-9s of 7. Staffel taxi out from their wooded dispersal points at Nordhorn, autumn 1944.

Below: These B-24 Liberators of the 458th BG, 2nd Bomb Division, Eighth Air Force seen here at their home base of Horsham St. Faith in England, could have been one of the targets for Galland's proposed Grosse Schlag. During the autumn of 1944, they were one of many heavy bomb groups attacking strategic targets across the Reich.

experienced officers in the ranks of the *Jagdwaffe* and the man who, driven by ambition, would become one of Galland's most vociferous critics and ultimately engineer his dismissal as *General der Jagdflieger*.

Born of Scottish descent in Vienna in 1936, Gollob became the first of the German *Experten* to score 150 confirmed aerial victories, all but six of which were achieved over the Russian front and nine of which he claimed in one day, an accomplishment which earned him the award of the Diamonds to his *Ritterkreuz*, third only behind Mölders and Galland. His operational career spanned a total of 340 missions in which he flew twin-engine Bf 110 destroyers in Poland and Norway. Converting to single-engine fighters, he joined II./JG 3 on the Channel Front where he was heavily engaged against the RAF and later went with that unit to Russia where he became its *Gruppenkommandeur*.

In December 1941, following his award of the *Ritterkreuz* and as a response to his numerous innovative suggestions for technical improvements to the Bf 109, Gollob was removed from operations and transferred on a temporary assignment to the *Erprobungsstelle* Rechlin. Returning to southern Russia in May 1942, and on Galland's recommendation, he took command of JG 77 where he rapidly notched up his score to 100 victories, becoming the *Jagdwaffe's* highest scoring fighter pilot in August of that year by reaching 150 confirmed victories. The Diamonds were awarded to him by Hitler personally.

His exploits became legendary all along the Russian front but on Galland's instructions, he was moved to the west in October 1942 where he was made responsible for tactical fighter command in north west France. Here, once again, Gollob applied himself diligently and creatively. In April 1944 however, as a result of apparent "disciplinary and operational" reasons, Galland transferred him yet again to his own personal staff where he was to represent the *General der Jagdflieger* in matters concerned with the development of jet aircraft projects. Here, so it seems, Gollob began to cause Galland problems, mainly as a result of his lack of understanding of jet-powered capability.

"I appointed him to my staff and entrusted him with full responsibilities for the preparation and planning for operational employment of the Me 262 and Me 163." Galland later recalled. "Gollob did not tackle the task to my satisfaction. He was interested only in the purely technical aspects, neglecting ground organisation, the training of air and ground crews, setting up a communications network and the formation of operational units. This caused considerable friction between Gollob, myself and my staff. In the end, I had to monitor his work in detail and check whether my orders were being executed. Gollob did not like this at all. I therefore transferred him to the *Kommando der Erprobungsstellen*. He swore to take revenge on me and my staff! To this end, he teamed up with Peltz etc. to have me removed from my post, believing that I was too influential."

This rapid deterioration in relationships between the *General der Jagdflieger* and one of the most agile, experienced and innovative, if not forceful officers on his staff, was to prove instrumental in promoting the growing sense of decay and

Oberst Gordon Gollob – a skilled, diligent and creative fighter commander, who ultimately worked to bring about Adolf Galland's downfall.

spiritlessness that seeped through the senior echelons of the *Jagdwaffe* command in late 1944.

Into the Wilderness

Operation *Bodenplatte* was the infamous and ill-fated brainchild of Dietrich Peltz and it was a plan conceived of desperation. Supported by a desperate and probably despondent Göring, Peltz had decided that the best way in which to offer support to the armoured thrust through the Ardennes was to neutralise Allied tactical airpower in one concerted knock-out attack where it was at its most vulnerable – on the ground. By using the element of surprise, Peltz had logically concluded that such an attack would both incur minimum casualties and consume the least amount of fuel as against the alternative of long running costly dogfights over the front against numerically superior enemy formations. Though originally intended to coincide with the launch of the ground offensive, the weather frustrated this plan and the operation was deferred despite the commencement of the Ardennes offensive. However, on 14 December, Peltz briefed the stunned western based *Geschwaderkommodoren* on his plans. At first light, under complete radio silence on a day when the meteorological conditions were considered favourable and guided by Ju 188 pathfinder aircraft, virtually the entire strength of the *Luftwaffe's* single-engine fighter force on the Western Front would be deployed in a low-level hit-and-run operation mounted against eleven key Allied fighter airfields in Belgium, Holland and north-eastern France. The six component *Geschwader* of 3. *Jagddivision* would attack the British 2nd TAF bases in northern Belgium and Holland whilst the three *Geschwader* of the *Jafü Mittelrhein* would strike at the American fields of St.Trond, Le Culot and Asch. In the south, JG 53 under the control of 5. *Jagddivision* would attack Metz.

Curiously, the *General der Jagdflieger* was absent from this briefing; instead he learnt about the preparation for the attack on the airfields "...by pure chance".

"I was only briefly informed about this operation during the pre-mission briefing at II. *Jagdkorps*." Galland recalled. "I had no part whatsoever in its preparation, briefing or execution."

Finally, at dawn on the 1 January 1945 and at the first suitable break in the weather, German fighters from 33 *Gruppen* left their forward bases and roared in tight formation towards the Allied lines. History has proven that the operation was a disaster and marked the end of the German daylight fighter force's period as an effective weapon on the western front. Though complete surprise was achieved and moderate successes gained at Eindhoven (where two Canadian Typhoon squadrons were virtually destroyed), Brussels and St.Denis-Westrem, the attacks on Volkel, Antwerp and Le Culot were nothing short of catastrophic. In many cases the German formations failed to even find their allocated targets whilst elsewhere they fell as victims to their own *Flak* or became lost or collided. Altogether 127 British aircraft were destroyed with 133 damaged and 185 personnel killed or wounded; it was, without doubt, an unexpected and painful blow but *Bodenplatte's* effect on long-term Allied tactical operations would be negligible. For the beleaguered and strained *Jagdwaffe* however, the cost was much higher. In total, 151 pilots were killed or reported missing, including three *Geschwaderkommodore*, 6 *Gruppenkommandeure* and 10 *Staffelkapitäne* with a further 63 pilots taken prisoner.

In the Ardennes, hampered by terrain and weather, starved of fuel and meeting firm Allied opposition, the German ground assault had faltered and stopped having penetrated 112 kilometres (70 miles) at its deepest point but still far short of Antwerp. *Feldmarschall* von Rundstedt proposed that the offensive be abandoned but Hitler refused. By 30 December, the last German attempt to close the Bastogne corridor had failed and *General* von Manteuffel had publicly abandoned hope of any further offensive action. Initiative had been lost. Hitler ranted.

At his Berlin headquarters, appalled by the irreplaceable losses incurred in the West as a result of *Bodenplatte* and aware of the growing plots to oust him from his position as *General der Jagdflieger,* Adolf Galland prepared for the worst. "It was quite clear to me that only a radical disbanding of the fighter units would ensure the survival of what still remained. This, however, was not something to be discussed. Göring did not see me anymore, neither was I invited to meetings. My influence on the *Jagdwaffe's* further affairs was nil. Only the *General der Jagdflieger* Staff allowed me and some of my collaborators, to participate, since our co-operation was needed. Before December was out, I approached the *Luftwaffe* Chief of the General Staff (Koller), requesting further instructions. I also asked him to support my request for my return to operational service at the front."

This initial request was ignored and instead a dangerous new dimension began to emerge, instigated, so it would seem, by Galland's new and bitter rival, Gordon Gollob. "After I had taken him to task very seriously," Galland explained to the Americans in May 1945, "He began to put out feelers, turning on the one hand to the bomber men and on the other to Himmler in order to be able to threaten me with the SS. He volunteered a lot of information to the SS too. He also attacked my private life. I discovered this by the fact that the SD and the *Abwehr* were put on to me. He, himself, employed similar methods and smuggled people into my staff who spied on everything. It was a marvellous piece of organisation, a magnificent plan, intended first to oust me from my post and they succeeded after the atmosphere around me became so poisoned..."

Precisely why, in December 1944, Gordon Gollob allegedly approached the *Reichsführer*-SS Heinrich Himmler about his ailing relationship with Adolf Galland, his mis-employment and the crisis existing within the *Luftwaffe* is not clear . What is clear, however, is that by this time, Himmler's position as the "...the most powerful man in the Third Reich" and chief of possibly the most feared organisation in the world, was still secure. Certainly, his power base had now expanded by extending SS interests into areas far beyond their normal police, internal security, intelligence and *Waffen*-SS military jurisdictions. Since the summer of 1944,

Reichsführer-SS Heinrich Himmler.

Himmler had taken effective control of the V-2 rocket production and deployment programme and the SS now co-ordinated all attacks against the British Isles. The *Reichsführer* had also just relinquished his post of "Supreme Commander Upper Rhine" – in which he bore command responsibility for the hastily assembled *Volkssturm* and Replacement Army divisions based along the western frontier of the Reich from the Swiss border to the Saar – in order to be closer to the *Führer* at his *Adlerhorst* headquarters at Bad Nauheim, near Frankfurt.

There can be little doubt that Himmler would have welcomed and courted an opportunity to expose and exploit the cracks and dissent now spreading through the senior command of the *Jagdwaffe* in order to exert his influence and power in matters over which he yet had no say. Furthermore, Himmler's relationship with Göring was becoming tetchy, probably due largely to Göring's own fear of the SS Chief's knowledge of the criticisms levelled against the *Luftwaffe* and how he might use them. Hanna Reitsch, the accomplished female test-pilot, observed the rumour-mongering at this time: "Complaints against Göring came from all possible sources and usually found their way to Himmler's desk. Through Himmler, I became acquainted with many of these. Often they begged Himmler to take control of the *Luftwaffe* himself or at least to impress Hitler with the stringent need of replacing Göring. These were sent to Himmler because it was known that of the "big four" he was the only one who would at least read such complaints; a thing that had long been impossible with the others, least of all with Hitler, as all such information was short-circuited long before it reached his desk."

Gollob's seemingly justified criticisms of the *General der Jagdflieger* were the perfect entrée for SS intervention. Galland was to become both the target of the SS and Göring's scapegoat.

His relationship with Göring now at an all time low, the last two months of 1944 were to become a dark time for Galland. As he recalled: "Gollob contacted the SS, getting as high as Himmler, whom he told that the *Luftwaffe* did not employ him properly and that the affairs of the *Luftwaffe* required thorough investigation. Since I had obstructed the *Jagdwaffe's* development, I should be dismissed without fail. Himmler then put all this to Hitler, who, during one of the daily situation conferences spoke most disparagingly about me. The preconditions for my dismissal had thus been created."

"Things were gradually made impossible for me," Galland explained to his interrogators after the war, "It was a very slow job, engineered by the man who wanted to usurp me from my post for reasons of private hatred and envy. With this aim in view and having started the ball rolling by contacting Himmler, he was able to get some pull. Whenever the SS or Himmler were mentioned to the *Reichsmarschall*, he ceased raising objections."

With Galland and Gollob now being used as political pawns by Himmler in his discussions with Hitler, events were now rapidly overtaking Göring's ability to control them. The stakes were becoming dangerous and too high. Caught in this cleft of a dilemma, Göring stalled for time and asked Galland to produce a report on his opinions of Gollob. "This report," wrote Galland in his private diary, "which I believe to have been clear and unbiased was then given to Gollob, a method that speaks for itself. Gollob then stepped up his machinations against me. In November, I had discovered that all my telephones had been tapped. Officers, newly attached to my staff were supposed to provide Gollob with material against me. Various clues made the SD's intense interest in me, quite obvious. I was warned to keep away from certain of my private friends who were known not to harbour such positive feelings about the Party. Meanwhile, a struggle for my job went on behind my back, particularly between Peltz, Herrmann and Gollob. Göring had gone to the West and these gentlemen were queuing up in his office! The situation appeared ridiculous to me and I sent a request to Göring to relieve me of my post and after a short furlough, allow me to serve at the front. Göring then discussed my relief with Hitler, saying that he was, as yet, undecided about my successor. Hitler thereupon stated that Himmler had proposed Gollob for the job. Göring, however, did not really want Gollob since various people had spoken badly of him. But now that the *Führer* himself had made the decision, Göring had to go along with Gollob."

So it was that between Christmas 1944 and New Year 1945, during the course of a "one-sided" two and a half hour telephone call, Göring carefully spelt out to Galland the reasons why he would have to go. "Göring tried to blame me without really having a clear opinion on any of the matters himself. " Galland recalled in his diary, "Amongst other things, he reproached me for having a negative influence on fighter tactics, a lack of support and failure to enforce his orders, for having created my own empire in the *Jagdwaffe*, having a wrong staff policy, removal of people I did not like and that it was my responsibility for the bad state of the *Jagdwaffe*.

I was not permitted to say a word in my defence, though the tone during the discussion was moderate. At the end, Göring expressed his gratitude, saying that after my leave, he would appoint me to an important position within the leadership. I said that this was not acceptable since under no circumstances would I want to be in a leading position now that the *Jagdwaffe's* collapse was imminent. I again requested to be employed operationally with the Me 262, not as a unit leader, but simply as a pilot. A decision was supposed to be made during my leave."

Generalleutnant von Massow, in command of *Luftwaffe* Flying Training, spoke aptly of this occasion in May 1945: "To have sacked Galland, who really is an incredibly able man, was one of the last big mistakes the leaders of the *Luftwaffe* made. In my opinion, Galland was the cleverest man we had in the *Jagdwaffe*. The last of our brains had been frittered away..."

With no choice left but to abide by Göring's order, Galland left for his enforced period of leave "...embittered, depressed and without any definite plan for the future."

A Meeting in Berlin

On 19 January 1945, acting on an unprecedented, risky and courageous initiative, a small delegation of discontented and highly decorated senior *Luftwaffe* fighter commanders confronted *Reichsmarschall* Hermann Göring at a pre-arranged meeting held at the *Luftwaffe* officers club in a snow covered Berlin.

The unrest and depression which had been simmering for months within this clique of officers was attributable in the main

to the increasing levels of abuse being heaped upon the weary and strained pilots of the grossly outnumbered and undertrained *Jagdgeschwader* by their Commander-in-Chief who now threw them regularly and without adequate preparation into bad weather operations. It was also born of what this select group felt was the criminal misuse of the Me 262 and its allocation in increasing numbers to the newly formed *Kampfgeschwader (Jagd)* units established by Peltz as fighter units comprised mainly of speedily retrained bomber pilots. These sentiments were further fuelled by the distrust which had accumulated of Göring's small inner circle of young, ambitious advisers – mainly men from the Bomber Arm – who now more and more seemed to be influencing the *Reichsmarschall's* decisions.

But it was perhaps the clumsy and insulting way in which the "Galland affair" had been handled that provoked the most outrage amongst this group and led, in January 1945, to one highly experienced and respected officer taking the matter into his own hands. Born in Kiel in 1912 to a distinguished military family, *Oberst* Günther Lützow was descended from the old Prussian family of the same name, the warriors of Fehrbellin and Rossbach being amongst his ancestors, whilst at the other extreme in his lineage stood men of the cloth. Lützow's family had provided him with an education that had been directed more towards theology than military life, but the events of his youth inevitably steered him towards service life and the *Luftwaffe*. After service with the *Legion Kondor* during the Spanish Civil War in which he scored the first ever recorded victory in the Bf 109, the war in Europe saw him fly as *Kommodore* of JG 3 in both the Battle of Britain and in Russia and as such he was able to gain first hand experience of front-line leadership and the development and refinement of air tactics. He became only the second *Experte* to achieve 100 victories and was awarded the *Ritterkreuz* with Oakleaves and Swords. Following a period as Galland's *Inspekteur der Jagdflieger*, he then commanded the 1. *Jagddivision* from November 1943 until March 1944 where he assumed overall command for day and nightfighter operations in north western Germany and the Low Countries. By January 1945, he was commanding the 4. *Fliegerschuldivision*, responsible for the training of new fighter pilots. Recognised by many as being one of the most outstanding field commanders in the *Luftwaffe*, Galland has described "Franzl" Lützow as "...an irreproachable, courageous and straight talking man."

And it was Lützow who would become known as the principal architect and self-appointed spokesmen behind the so-called "Fighter Pilot's Mutiny" (sometimes referred to as the "Revolt of the *Kommodores*").

Accompanying Lützow as the chief protagonists in the crusade for moral and strategic justice were a glittering array of some the *Luftwaffe's* finest fighter aces and front-line commanders – *Oberst* Johannes "Macki" Steinhoff (176 victories, previously *Kommodore* of JG 77 and now *Kommodore* of the newly formed Me 262 fighter wing, JG 7 at Brandenburg-Briest), *Oberst* Hannes Trautloft (57 victories, recently appointed as *Kommandeur* of 4. *Fliegerschuldivision*), *Oberst* Gustav Rödel (98 victories, no longer commanding JG 27 but about to take up new appointment as *Kommandeur* 2. *Jagddivision*), *Oberst* Edu Neumann (13 victories, *Jafü Oberitalien*), *Oberst* Günther *Freiherr* von Maltzahn (68 victories), *Major* Hans-Heinrich von Brüstellin (a Staff Officer on Galland's Fighter Defence Staff) and Hauptmann Hugo Kessler, (Galland's personal aide and also on the Fighter Defence Staff) .

Throughout the first half of January 1945, a series of covert and highly venturesome meetings had been engineered by the members of the clique in an attempt to make their feelings of unrest known. Bearing in mind the results of the failed attempt to assassinate Hitler in July 1944 and the swift and brutal way in which that "conspiracy" had been dealt with, to even contemplate an expression of discontent with Göring's leadership can, at this time, only be considered as courageous, if not desperate. But the way to Hitler was not easy and all of the meetings, including an extremely dangerous one with a high ranking SS official, failed to achieve the desired result, namely to bring about a meeting at which the conspirators would force upon the *Führer* the issue of replacing Göring and to exonerate themselves from the wrongful accusations being levelled at them for the failure of the aerial defence of the Reich.

Eventually, however, following an audience with the officers concerned, *General der Flieger* Karl Koller, the *Luftwaffe* Chief-of-Staff, saw fit to warn Göring that attempts had been made to reach Hitler by "...using services outside the *Luftwaffe*". In his memo to Göring late on 17 January, he advised the *Reichsmarschall* of the "increasing depression... the feeling of deep bitterness" prevailing in the *Jagdwaffe* and the reasons for it – the continual accusations of cowardice, Galland's dismissal, the lacking of confidence in the direction of operations, strategic deployment, personnel policy and general leadership at senior command level." In conclusion, he implored the *Reichsmarschall* to grant an audience with the group "...in order to clear the air."

Göring yielded, though the fact that this meeting had been covertly engineered by using the offices of his Chief-of-Staff and, even worse, by involving his bitter rivals, the SS, meant that Göring's mood was typically hostile and unreceptive; he had grown tired of the seemingly endless complaints which his fighter pilots levelled at their machines and the high command and of the hollow excuses they offered for failing to stop the Allied strategic air offensive which now threatened to bomb the Reich into destruction.

Undeterred by Göring's enmity the conspirators reported to the *Haus der Flieger* on Leipzigerstrasse in Berlin where they gathered around a round table in a small conference room and waited for the arrival of the *Reichsmarschall*. It was an awesome assembly; Lützow, Steinhoff, Trautloft, Neumann and Rödel as well as *Oberstleutnants* Hermann Graf, (*Kommodore* JG 52 and holder of the Diamonds to the *Ritterkreuz*), Helmut Bennemann (*Kommodore* JG 53), Josef Priller (*Kommodore* JG 26), Fritz Aufhammer (*Kommodore* JG 301) and *Major* Gerhard Michalski (JG 4). By the end of the war, collectively, these pilots had accumulated nearly one thousand enemy aircraft shot down. Galland's presence had not been requested.

Lützow had been elected to act as the group's spokesman and as such now held "...a comprehensive proposal incorporating the *Jagdwaffe's* demands". The demands contained in this document were effectively the same as had been presented to Koller two days earlier, but at the top of the agenda was the diabolical

Oberst Günther Lützow

treatment of Adolf Galland.

As the meeting commenced, Lützow rose to his feet and began by demanding the right to uninterrupted speech and then, point by point, summarised the group's grievances; Galland's needless dismissal, the accusations of cowardice, the creeping influence of commanders with no fighter background, the requirement for the correct (concentrated) deployment of forces with which to attack the Allied bomber threat, the immediate availability of all Me 262s and the reserve bomber pilots of the IX *Fliegerkorps* for deployment on fighter operations.

Predictably, Göring's reaction to the demand of the conspirators was one of anger, gross indignation, scorn and disgust. He harboured no sympathy with his insolent and defeatist *Experten*. Tossing the "Points for Discussion" aside, he vented his fury at Lützow; the *Jagdwaffe* would *not* receive the Me 262 – the bomber arm would get it because they knew how to use it. As for Galland, an officer who Göring begrudgingly respected, it was time that he was replaced – he was in need of "rest and relaxation". In Göring's opinion, all that such representations achieved was to waste time and undermine morale. But, as Steinhoff recalls in his memoirs, Göring did not intend to let the matter rest at that:

"Lützow was standing behind his chair, staring at Göring with a look almost of hatred... "What are you after, Lützow – do you want to get rid of me? What you've schemed up is full scale mutiny... That's enough! I don't wish to hear any more! You're all mad and I propose to treat you accordingly. You! Lützow! For an officer you have an incredible conception of your duty as a soldier..." Placing his fat hands on the table, he pushed back his chair and stood up. His face was crimson. "Lützow... I'll have you shot!" And with a final, lordly sweep of his gold-beringed hand that condemned us all outright he rampaged out of the room, followed by his dazed clique."

In a state of fury and outrage, Göring was swift to mete out appropriate punishments. Within hours, arrest warrants were sent out for both Galland and Lützow. As an example to the rest, Lützow was ordered to vacate his post as *Kommandeur* IV. *Fliegerschuldivision* and leave the Reich within 48 hours. At Göring's instigation, he was to be suitably banished and removed from any place in which he may provoke more trouble – the first victim of the phenomenon that became unofficially known as *"Reichsverbannung"*! Italy was considered to be sufficiently far away and it was to a hill top headquarters in Verona to which he travelled by train that night to take over as *Jafü Oberitalien*. Lützow was in exile, unable to leave Italy or to receive any visitors who may have been considered subversive.

Steinhoff too, was made redundant and for Galland, as he graphically recorded in his diary, the situation was fast becoming intolerable: "Next morning, I was ordered to report to the Chief of Personnel. I was informed that Göring was furious about the events in the *Jagdwaffe,* assuming that I had inspired them. I was to take immediate action to calm tempers and opinions. When I stated that I had no influence whatsoever on these things, I was

MUTINY, DISMISSAL AND EXILE

ordered to leave Berlin within twelve hours, not to leave the place where I was to spend my furlough and be ready for immediate recall. Göring had a telex sent to all fighter units, relieving me of my post in a quite spiteful manner and appointing *Oberst* Gollob as my successor. Peace was thus superficially restored. My staff, who were deeply attached to me, quickly disintegrated. Those who remained continued to stand by me or rather, by my policies. Gollob, initially, did not want to keep anything of the "old spirit" but was incapable of any productive work. I am not going too far in accusing Gollob of a feeling of hate and revenge towards me and my former staff. His first activities involving them were entirely directed towards collecting material against me with which he hoped to bring about my downfall. I was told that for two weeks he was busy playing one person off against another and finally reporting to Göring that he was incapable of taking charge of the staff in its present alleged corrupt state, demanding a court martial to investigate the situation. Göring agreed on the spot and ordered the *Luftwaffe's* supreme judge and two senior judges to start an investigation into the conduct of my aide, my Chief of Staff and against me. Like me, both gentlemen were sacked and sent on leave. Gollob participated personally and intensively in these investigations. The accusations which were frantically collected in from everywhere, reflect on the characters of their originators in such a degrading way that I cannot repeat them here. I am not aware of the charges raised against me by the SD. However, it was quite clear that my political views were considered suspicious and it was reported that I thought the situation hopeless."

In late May 1945, whilst in Allied captivity, *Generalfeldmarschall* Erhard Milch spoke bitterly of this situation to a number of fellow senior officers: "Gollob conducted an enquiry on Göring's orders while Galland was still in his job, as a result of which Galland was suspended from his post. They told the *Führer* that Galland was a dirty scoundrel, besides which as *General der Jagdflieger*, he had been a complete failure, particularly so, since the management of the *Jagdwaffe* was beneath contempt. The *Führer* entirely agreed... and then Galland's nerve broke... They had a scapegoat for everything..."

Though the pressure on Galland was now unfairly overwhelming, there was to be no let-up and the sense of persecution and isolation was crushing. Whilst on his enforced leave, members of the *General's* staff kept him informed of the events taking place in Berlin. We return to Galland's personal recollections:

"During my leave, those officers still supporting me, kept me up to date by telephone about developments concerning the investigations being conducted against me. There was no doubt that I was to be brought down by all and any means. I broke off my leave and returned to Berlin. My aide was arrested and remanded in custody at a Berlin prison. My car was seized outside my apartment and my movements and telephone were placed under surveillance. My batman was interrogated in a most disgraceful manner, yet I was not interrogated at all, apparently so that my only chance to confront the evidence mounted against me would be in court. However, I was kept very well informed about the game. Göring had been informed twice about the investigation's progress, Gollob being present on both occasions. He was the instigator, while Göring made the most of the situation, because:

i) He wanted to expose me following the alleged *Jagdwaffe* mutiny.
ii) He was able to accuse me of being responsible for the *Jagdwaffe's* collapse after 1 January 1945 and arraign me before a judge thus directing attention away from himself
iii) He had come to hate me since I had rightly predicted the collapse

Meanwhile, my situation had become extremely awkward. I decided that I would not present myself to a judge who, in passing sentence, would only follow Göring's orders. The alternatives, however, would only incriminate me still further. These were:

a) To make myself available to the judge
b) To desert, asking for justice and protection from the enemy
c) To use my pistol

Alternative (a) has been covered; (b) was out of the question since I would have been pronounced guilty without further ado and my parents and brother held accountable. I decided therefore, on (c)

Conspirators (from left to right): Obersts. Gustav Rödel, Günther Freiherr von Maltzahn and Johannes Steinhoff.

43

but only once I had established that there was no longer any chance of making an appeal to anybody of any influence. I determined however, to take the conspirator responsible and any such desperate action on my behalf, with me."

Depressed, perhaps suicidal, Galland talked to his friends. The same night that he returned to the capital, a sympathetic female colleague of his who lived nearby – an anti-Nazi divorcee with connections in the film industry – decided to take action and at great personal risk contacted the one man who she knew still held considerable power and influence with Hitler *and* who would fight for Galland's reputation; Albert Speer, the level-headed Armaments Minister. Awakened in the early hours, Speer listened to the woman's story and found himself appalled. Instinctively, he immediately contacted Hitler to protest and was astonished to find the *Führer* unaware of the way in which Galland – a war hero, whatever else he might be guilty of – was being treated. Equally astonished and despite it now being the middle of the night, Hitler contacted the SD. Wheels began to move and significantly, only hours later, Galland received two telephone calls from the RSHA intended to "reassure" him. This first was from SS *Gruppenführer* Heinrich Müller, the notorious and rabid anti-Semitic head of the *Gestapo*. The stocky, peasant-bred Bavarian who had personally authorised the dispatch of thousands of Jews to Auschwitz, advised Galland that there had been a "mistake" and that an SS officer would be assigned to him first thing in the morning to ensure his personal safety. The second caller was Müller's immediate and even more brutal superior and head of the RSHA, the scar-faced SS *Obergruppenführer* Ernst Kaltenbrunner. Kaltenbrunner, too, spoke smoothly and quickly of "errors" and "misunderstandings"; "...people with whom up to now, I had nothing to do, thank God." wrote Galland later.

Early the next morning, Galland was ordered to report to the Reichs Chancellery to meet the *Führer*. When he arrived however, he found that Hitler, recently returned to Berlin from the *Wolfschanze,* had been detained elsewhere and he was sent to meet Hitler's *Luftwaffe* adjutant, *Oberst* Nikolaus von Below. Von Below apologised on behalf of the *Führer* and advised Galland that Hitler had personally arranged to drop all charges against him. "The scandal was obviously causing great concern." Galland recalled, "The investigations were dropped immediately, my aide freed but transferred to the paratroops with immediate effect."

Von Below then gave Galland another piece of surprising but most welcome news. As he explained: "I was to set up a unit to prove that the Me 262 was a superior fighter and that it could be operated efficiently as a fighter. To some extent, this notion was already outdated because both Nowotny and JG 7 had proved this to be the case already but, of course, he (Hitler) was never well informed about the present state of affairs because he, himself, had been the one who had given orders curtailing any fighter activity – many, many of his decisions were based on false information. The third order was that I was to report to Göring who would give me further details about the establishment of this unit."

On 23 January 1945, as an act of

formality and finality, and in a somewhat revealing communiqué, the *Reichs-marschall* officially advised all *Luftwaffe* command staffs as well as every fighter *Staffel* and fighter training unit of Galland's dismissal and his successor's appointment:

Orders regarding the Jagdwaffe

Generalleutnant Galland has been dismissed from his post following several years service as General der Jagdflieger, in order that he may once again be deployed in command once his health has been restored. I wish to express my sincere thanks to Generalleutnant Galland for services performed on behalf of myself, for the German Jagdwaffe and for the Fatherland. With untiring zeal in both operations and administration, Generalleutnant Galland has fulfilled the aims of the Jagdwaffe.

In place of Generalleutnant Galland, I have appointed Oberst Gollob to safeguard the duties of the General der Jagdflieger. I expect that the Jagdwaffe will support Oberst Gollob with its full support and energy. It should be remembered that it is neither the organisation nor the man that is important but only the goal that is common to us all – the regaining of air supremacy over German territory.

We are in the most difficult and most decisive hours of this war. In many places, the Volkssturm has been called up for national defence; all Germans – down to the very last man – are taking up arms. The German Jagdwaffe will not stand back behind these men – but rather inspired by a holy fire, will sacrifice everything for the cause that is right, alert and conscious in battle.

Göring

As a weary but elated Galland journeyed to Karinhall, Göring's sprawling country estate on the Schorfheide, the noise of guns rumbling in the east was clearly audible, for by now the Soviet winter offensive had forced a critical gap between the German armies assigned to defend East. With nothing to stop it now, the Red Army had swept across the River Oder north west of Oppeln. Bombs continued to fall on the Reich; since the New Year, the American Eighth Air Force, working in co-operation with RAF Bomber Command, had been systematically hitting synthetic and crude-oil refineries. In trying to intercept the American raids against industrial and fuel targets in northern and central Germany on the 14th, the *Jagdwaffe* lost 107 pilots killed or missing with another 32 wounded. Tank and aircraft factories, benzol plants and the railway network – marshalling yards, repair shops, junctions, bridges and also road traffic bottlenecks – were subjected to ceaseless attacks by the US Tactical Air Forces. For the *Jagdwaffe,* losses amongst the four *Jagdgeschwader* left for Reich defence following a major transfer of units east, were rising to nearly 30% of sorties flown, while victories gained amounted to less than 0.2% of Allied strength.

Galland addresses a conference on fighter defence in 1944. Within months he would be dismissed as commander of the Jagdwaffe.

FIVE

JAGDVERBAND 44 'THE GALLAND CIRCUS'

By late January 1945, the *Luftwaffe* was able to boast a total of seven *Gruppen* equipped wholly or in part with the Me 262 and intended for use as either day fighters or fighter-bombers. A further two *Gruppen* had been established to co-ordinate further conversion of redundant bomber-pilots on to the jet in accordance with Peltz's and Gollob's restructuring of the IX. *Fliegerkorps'* assets. The composition of this still largely untested miscellany of jet units was as follows:

JG 7

III./JG 7 had been established at Lechfeld in mid-November 1944 as the initial stage of development of what was intended to be the first jet fighter *Geschwader*, with its flying and ground personnel largely being drawn from the remains of the ill-fated *Kommando Nowotny*. By early

January 1945, with the *Gruppe* now up to its intended strength of forty pilots, the 9., 10. and 11. *Staffeln* were moved to their respective operational bases at Parchim, Oranienburg and Brandenburg-Briest. However, whilst pilot availability may have been acceptable, aircraft availability was painfully lacking with only 19 Me 262s being recorded as on strength on 19 January. The ultimate command of the *Geschwader* was also in a state of metamorphosis with *Oberst* Johannes Steinhoff being replaced as *Geschwaderkommodore* in mid-January as a result of his involvement in the "mutiny" against Göring. His place was taken by *Major* Theo Weissenberger.

Successes at this stage were still frustratingly elusive though there had been cause for cautious optimism on the sporadic occasions when the jets did successfully intercept Allied aircraft.

A pair of Me 262 A-1as of JG 7 at Brandenburg-Briest being fitted with experimental 21 cm WGr. air-to-air mortar tubes as used to varied effect by piston engined aircraft in the defence of the Reich. The aircraft in the foreground is believed to have been that of Major Rudi Sinner, Gruppenkommandeur III./JG 7.

The rest of JG 7 however was dogged by training crashes, lack of aircraft, inadequate airfield conditions and poor weather. It would not become truly operationally ready for at least another month.

III./EJG 2

In the autumn of 1944, the 10. *Staffel* of III./EJG 2 had been formed around the remnants of *Erprobungskommando* 262 at Lechfeld. The intention was to form a dedicated Me 262 operational training unit which would be able to offer pilots converting to the jet a comprehensive and thorough training programme. Initially, about fifty pilots were assembled from both fighter and bomber units and fighter school staffs and a selection was made of promising new pilots who were about half way through their Operational Fighter Training Pool syllabus. The new pilots in the training pools were given a pre-jet flying course which consisted of finishing their regular 20 hours flying time in conventional fighter aircraft with the throttles fixed in one position to reproduce a technical problem found in flying in the Me 262, the throttles of which were not to be adjusted in flight at high altitudes.

Upon arrival at Lechfeld, all pilots, both experienced and inexperienced, were given three days theoretical instruction in the operation and functioning of jet engines, the features and flying qualities of the Me 262, as well as some practice in operating the controls in a wingless training model. This introduction was followed by a course in the operation of conventional twin-engined aircraft. Pupils were given five hours flying

Below: "Red 13" was the personal aircraft of Heinz Bär, Kommandeur of III./EJG 2, the Luftwaffe's Me 262 operational training unit.
Right: Oberstleutnant Heinz Bär discusses the maintenance of his aircraft at Lechfeld, early 1945. He would later command JV 44.

time in the Bf 110 and Si 204 practising take-offs, landings, flight with the radio course indicator, instrument flying and flying on one engine. Upon completion of the course, the pilots returned to Lechfeld where they were given one more day of theoretical instruction and then began conversion to the Me 262.

Practical instruction on the Me 262 began with half a day's exercise in starting and stopping the jet motors and taxiing. Flying instruction consisted of a total of nine take-offs as follows:

1. Thirty minutes of circuits with only two main fuel tanks full.
2. Same.
3. One hour aerobatics and aerial manoeuvring.
4. Ditto.
5. One hour high altitude flight to 9000 metres (29,500 ft).
6. One hour cross-country flight at 3600-4500 metres (11,800-14,760 ft).
7. One hour flying in two aircraft *Rotte* element, first with an instructor and then with another student.
8. Same.
9. Gunnery practice, firing all four MK 108s at ground targets. First approach without firing and four other approaches firing.

This was considered to be the absolute minimum with which to qualify a pilot for operational readiness on the Me 262. However, such training was severely restricted due to the shortage of the twin-seat training version, the Me 262 B-1, and even by the end of January 1945, III./EJG 2 recorded only three such machines on strength.

The unit was helped, however, by the appointment of *Oberstleutnant* Heinz Bär as its commander. Bär was one of the *Jagdwaffe's* most famous *Experten*. His service career stretched back to 1939, the year he scored his first victory in the west. Concluding the Battle of Britain with seventeen confirmed victories, he then flew in Russia with JG 51 and within two months had chalked up a total of sixty kills. The award of the *Ritterkreuz* came in July 1941 followed by the Oakleaves in August, a month which saw him down six Soviet aircraft in one day.

Leaving Russia in 1942, he was given command of JG 77 in the Mediterranean where he flew over Sicily, Malta and North Africa, claiming another 45 victories and gaining the Swords to the *Ritterkreuz* despite contracting a punishing bout of malaria and being stricken by gastric ulcers. Ill and exhausted by endless combat, Bär returned to Germany for a period of convalescence before embarking on a long, hard stint as one of the foremost operational commanders in the Defence of the Reich. In some quarters, his reputation was that of a "hard man" and as one *Luftwaffe* airman was heard to say: "Actually, from what one has heard about Bär, he was a tough who was avoided as much as possible by the officer corps. There must have been some fellows who behaved arrogantly – young airmen – and he must have given them hell."

of attrition against the Allied tactical air forces as they struggled to provide badly needed air-support to the German armies battling in the west, but with their bases continually under attack from RAF Tempests, against whom only the Me 262's speed was the saving grace, and with shortages of fuel and bombs, this was difficult. The *Geschwader* had calculated that 65 tons of J2 fuel were needed to train just one pilot. Operations were mainly directed against targets in the Liège, Antwerp, Nijmegen, Volkel and Eindhoven areas as well against enemy troop concentrations resulting from the failed airborne assault at Arnhem.

But many of KG 51's former Ju 88 and Me 410 pilots now assigned to fly the Me 262 found it a difficult and challenging task, unfamiliar as they were with the strange new engines and consequently losses grew.

Also in existence at around this time were a pair of hastily formed training *Gruppen*, established in order to commence fighter cross-training of former bomber pilots attached to units of Peltz's IX.*(J) Fliegerkorps* and a solitary Me 262 equipped nightfighter *Kommando* though this small unit was still awaiting delivery of the new two-seat Me 262B-1a/U1 nightfighter variant.

Ground crew attach an SC 500 bomb to a Wikingerschiff bomb rack beneath an Me 262 A-2a of KG 51 during the winter of 1944.

Due to his well known outspokenness, Göring saw fit to "demote" him and his first posting in Germany was as a "humble" *Staffelkapitän* then *Gruppenkommandeur* in JG 1 before moving on in mid-1944 to take over JG 3. His personal score of enemy aircraft rose to over 200 machines and of his final tally of 220 at the war's end, 21 would be four-engined kills.

Despite the application of Bär's usual energy to the leadership and organisation of III./EJG 2, throughout December 1944, the number of pilots undergoing training at Lechfeld increased dramatically in proportion to the instructors – a total of 135 trainee pilots for only 28 instructors, though the ratio of aircraft to pilots was even lower.

KG(J) 54

The first elements of a former bomber *Geschwader* to convert over to the Me 262 in the fighter defence role, *Stab* and I./KG(J) 54, had just about concluded their elementary operational training at Giebelstadt. The original KG 54 had a long and glorious history, its Ju 88s seeing action in Norway, France, over England in 1940, Russia, the Mediterranean and against the British Isles again during Peltz's *Steinbock* campaign in early 1944.

Initial delivery of the Me 262s to the newly designated KG(J) 54 commenced without too many problems and by 19 January, when the pilots had received approximately six hours individual familiarisation on the Me 262, 16 jets belonging to the *Stab* and I. *Gruppe* took off on the first of three formation exercises. Unhappily, all three exercises flown between 19-23 January had been dogged by technical problems and pilot errors which, in turn, had resulted in a number of abortive take-offs and crashes. II./KG(J) 54, at Kitzingen, was still forming up.

KG 51

Perhaps of all the Me 262 units operational by the end of January, KG 51 was the most tactically effective and 'blooded'. Since November 1944, when I./KG 51 had absorbed *Kommando Schenk*, the *Geschwader*, by now under the command of *Oberstleutnant* Wolfgang Schenk was operating two *Gruppen* of Me 262 bombers. Throughout the gloomy autumn of 1944, KG 51's jet equipped *Gruppen* were engaged in an intense campaign

BATTLE OVER BAVARIA

This then, was the composition and state of the *Luftwaffe's* Me 262 fighter and fighter-bomber strike force in late January 1945, the time when *Reichsmarschall* Göring called his sacked fighter general to Karinhall to ask him to form what was to become one of the most mythical yet curious fighter units in military history, hailed in some circles as *"The Squadron of Experten"* whilst labelled in others as *"A Flying Sanatorium"*.

In fact, now installed as *General der Jagdflieger* and still unaware of what Göring was about to propose to Galland, it had been Gollob's intention to dispatch the disgraced Galland to the east, and possibly oblivion, by placing him in charge of one of only two Fw 190-equipped *Staffeln* left to defend the northern sector of the Eastern Front. Mercifully for Galland however, this transfer was not to take place.

At Karinhall, Göring endeavoured to ladle yet more accusations on Galland on the strength of the SD's investigations. According to Galland he was denied the opportunity to defend himself on this occasion. Unaware of von Below's dialogue with Galland at the Reich Chancellery in Berlin, Göring also offered his hollow reassurance that it had been *him* who had arranged to drop all the charges levelled against Galland; "...a bare lie," Galland recorded later in his diary.

Then came the real reason for the meeting. Galland recalls: "He further told me that the *Führer* had agreed to my request and had withdrawn the order grounding me. I was to set up a small unit to demonstrate that the Me 262 was the superior fighter that I had always claimed. A small unit only in *Staffel* strength was to be organised, since any more than that would not be possible. I would have to find the aircraft myself. I was to submit my proposals to him. He told me that *Oberst* Steinhoff whom he had dismissed and whom he had called a "sad case", could be made available and that *Oberst* Lützow would be available immediately, if I wanted him. The unit would not be under the command of any division, corps or airfleet – I was to be totally independent. However, there was to be no contact between the new unit and any other fighter or jet unit. Nor would the *General der Jagdflieger* have any powers over my new unit. I was happy about my new assignment and rather amused at the strange situation of commanding a *Jagdstaffel* as a *Generalleutnant!*"

Göring also instructed Galland that although he was not, under any circumstances, permitted to include his name as part of the unit's name, (perhaps an indication that Göring knew perfectly well that Galland still had "pulling power" throughout the *Jagdwaffe*), its title would be his decision. As he stood in Göring's study, Galland decided upon "JV (*Jagdverband*) 44" – the "44" partly standing as a cynical reference to the fateful year of 1944 which saw the decay in both the *Jagdwaffe* and his own position, partly as a numeric link to the first fighter unit he had ever commanded and partly as a play on the words, in German, which referred to the *Führer* – and though Göring approved the title, he was not, of course, aware of Galland's reasoning.

Galland took his leave and returned to Berlin, finding himself quarters in Kladow, a small village on the banks of the Havel. Here he began the first tentative steps to establish his new unit.

With Galland gone less than a week, however, Gollob went energetically about his new assignment, an "inheritance" which he found "...depressing enough".

A P-51D Mustang of the 317th Squadron, 325th FG from the US Fifteenth Air Force over Europe in early 1945. Göring admitted that such aircraft were "... practically doing training flights over Bavaria" by this time.

On the 29 January, at a meeting in Berlin and in an effort "...to avoid the *Reichsmarschall's* suggestions", Gollob briefed representatives of his staff and the various technical departments on his proposals for the radical reform and expansion of the *Jagdwaffe* based upon the uniform conversion of all fighter and bomber units to the Me 262. A total of 499 machines were 'delivered' to the *Luftwaffe* in December with a projected production of 700 due in February and with this in mind, Gollob authorised the immediate redesignation of the majority of those bomber units attached to IX. (*J*) *Fliegerkorps* into Me 262 conversion units. Additionally, Gollob also directed that the dedicated conventionally equipped Reich defence fighter units, JG 300 and JG 301, should also be immediately converted to the Me 262. If all went according to plan and production levels continued unabated, such reform would lead to the creation of a new, super fast, all weather air defence force and would lead to quick conversion without the need for time-consuming blind-flying training, a quality in which the bomber pilots were already skilled. Gollob did acknowledge however, the "psychological" disadvantage of putting aside the fighter units in favour of the bomber units As such, JV 44, so far, did not figure at all in Gollob's thinking, if indeed, he was even aware of what Galland was now doing.

But however creative Gollob's drive for the expansion of the jet fighter arm was, the reality of events was fast overtaking his intentions. Throughout January and February 1945, P-38, P-47 and P-51 fighters and fighter-bombers of the Ninth Air Force and French First Air Force ranged freely across the Rhine, attacking railway lines, marshalling yards, road junctions, troop and armour concentrations, supply depots, fuel installations and almost anything that moved. On one day alone, 23 February, XIX TAC's fighter-bombers flew more than 500 sorties and accounted for more than 2,300 tanks, armoured vehicles, rail cars and motor vehicles destroyed or damaged. Under American interrogation in early June 1945, Göring expressed his concern at what was a weakly defended southern Germany, already placed in jeopardy by prowling fighters and bombers from the Fifteenth Air Force operating from bases in northern Italy. He admitted that "...Mustangs were practically doing training flights over Bavaria", and that consequently he had decided to recall

Galland in an attempt "...to stop this nonsense."

On 10 February 1945, OKL ordered *Oberst* Gollob to reorganise the Fw 190 equipped IV./JG 54 as II./JG 7 with the fourth *Staffel* of this *Gruppe* being allocated to Galland as the basis for his "independent" *Jagdstaffel* which would subsequently be incorporated into JG 7.

This order, in its exact form, never seems to have been carried out, although a fortnight later, on 23 February, Galland did meet with *Oberstleutnant i.G.* Ruhsert to discuss his tentative requirements for the establishment of his *Jagdstaffel*. These seem to have been accepted in principle by Ruhsert for the next day he discussed them with *General* Koller who then officially sanctioned, with "immediate effect", the establishment of *Jagdverband* 44 at Brandenburg-Briest.

Galland had personally chosen Brandenburg-Briest, an airfield situated some 50 kilometres (31 miles) to the west of Berlin for logical reasons. As a designated jet base it was both equipped with heavy *Flak* defences and well located for the aerial defence of Berlin. Furthermore, the *Gruppenstab* of III./JG 7 under *Major* Erich Hohagen was resident there as well as the 11. *Staffel* both of which drew their aircraft from a nearby Me 262 collection depot.

At this stage, the number of aircraft to be allocated to JV 44, though "..to be supplied with all speed" was to be kept to a level considered to be in accordance with "self-supporting operations... as absolutely neccesary." Galland was to draw his flying personnel from those made available to him through consultation with the *Luftwaffe* Personnel Office, whilst ground personnel were to be channelled to him from 16./JG 54 and III./EJG 2. As with JG 7, JV 44 was to be tactically subordinate, in all respects, to *Luftflotte Reich,* though, as a mark of his autonomy, Galland was accorded the "disciplinary powers" of a *Divisions-Kommandeur.*

On 25 February, Galland submitted his completed proposals for the organisation of JV 44 to the Quartermaster of the *Luftwaffe* General Staff. Galland's intention was to create a single totally "self-supportive" *Jagdstaffel* with a nominal strength of 16 Me 262s and 15 pilots, supported by a *"Gruppenstab"* equipped with a further 7 aircraft and meteorological, administration and medical personnel. The unit would also be backed up by its own motor transport and signals section as well as an aircraft and weapons servicing company.

Six days later however, after due consideration by the *Luftwaffe Organisationsstab,* Ruhsert communicated with Galland to the effect that his proposals for the composition of JV 44 would need to be revised by excluding the Meteorologist and Weapons Technician from the *"Gruppe kommandeurstab"* and by cutting back on the entire motorised vehicle fleet, although the originally requested field cars, motorcycles, bicycles and trailers would be allowed to remain.

Though the author has found no documentary indication as to why this reduction in unit composition was ordered, it can only be presumed that this was due simply to the chronic shortage of manpower, vehicles and fuel affecting the entire *Luftwaffe* at this time. In a curious paradox however, the *Organisationsstab* authorised an increase in the number of aircraft allotted to the JV 44 *"Gruppenstab"* from a proposed 7 machines and 7 pilots to 16 aircraft and 15 pilots, thus effectively creating *two* Staffeln of equal size.

JOHANNES STEINHOFF

Born 15.9.1913. in Bottendorf, Saxony. "Macki" Steinhoff was considered to have been one of the greatest leadership personalities of the German Fighter Arm. A graduate in philology from the University of Jena in 1934, he intially joined the German Navy for officer training, but transferred to the Luftwaffe in 1936, rising to become *Staffelkapitän* of 2./JG 132 at Jever by 1938. The outbreak of war saw him flying as *Staffelkapitän* of 10 (*Nacht*)./JG 26, a hurriedly organised night-fighter unit, soon converted back to its day fighter role and based around the Baltic sea-ports. In this capacity, in December 1939, Steinhoff's obsolescent Bf 109Cs engaged RAF Wellington bombers attempting to attack German warships at Wilhelmshaven. Steinhoff shot down one bomber and his fellow pilots claimed another five, thus mounting one of the earliest organised daylight bomber interceptions of the war.

Steinhoff led 4./JG 52 through the Battle of Britain and was later appointed *Kommandeur* of II./JG 52 seeing service on the Russian front where he was awarded the *Ritterkreuz* for his 35th victory on 30 August 1941. A year later he scored his 100th victory (31 August 1942), receiving the Oakleaves to his Knights Cross two days later, by which time his score had already risen to 101 victories. His 150th victory came on 2 February 1943. The next month saw his transfer from Russia to North Africa, where he took over as *Kommodore* of JG 77. He led the Bf 109s of this unit from Africa, through the maelstrom of Sicily and over Italy and for the first time against American heavy bombers and their escort fighters, against which his own personal score continued to accumulate. He was awarded the Swords to his *Ritterkreuz* in late July 1944 in recognition of his 167th confirmed victory. Returning to the Reich, he was given command of the first Me 262 *Geschwader*, JG 7.

Johannes Steinhoff flew a total of 900 operational missions and is accredited with 176 confirmed aerial victories, of which 148 were scored in the east and six were four-engined.

"Bring a jet with you..." recruitment and training

Having obtained authorisation to proceed with the establishment of a fighter unit – in *whatever* shape or form – Galland now moved back into Berlin from Kladow and began to hunt for pilots. One of the first he turned to was his friend, the "disgraced" "Macki" Steinhoff, now placed in cold storage after his part in the "mutiny" and following his replacement as *Kommodore* of JG 7 by Weissenberger. With at least some experience on the Me 262, Galland intended to appoint Steinhoff as "Head of Training". Steinhoff had just returned to the Reich after having been caught trying to make an unofficial visit to Lützow in Verona and upon his arrival in Berlin was instructed to report to Galland at Brandenburg-Briest. As he wrote in his memoirs, he needed no urging. In building up the unit from scratch, there was much to keep Galland and Steinhoff busy. While Galland searched for pilots, Steinhoff grappled with the task of establishing the ground support infrastructure, a job which, in itself, apparently presented problems:

"It was my third posting in Brandenburg in five years of war. This time, it was not as the commander of a fighter group, but rather as a kind of "maid-of-all-work"... We threw ourselves into the task with the same spirit and enthusiasm that had characterised the early days of the *Luftwaffe* though the early days of *Jagdverband* 44 were far from being days of plenty. Our transport, for example, consisted of a single jeep and my tiny 90cc DKW motorcycle, which I had contrived to get assigned to us. My old unit, JG 7, was stationed on the same airfield, but they had orders from Galland's successor not to lift a finger to help us. For the most part they just ignored us, though there was the occasional smile of condescending sympathy for the "mutineers". (One or two of my former comrades looked as if they had a sneaking admiration for us, but they were probably under pressure not to show it. The vast majority of those who saw us pottering about the airfield, training busily, thought we were quite simply mad).

The general however, had influential friends, and we soon found ourselves on the receiving end of a swelling supply of equipment, aircraft, spares and weapons. We even got a second jeep. JG 7 asked for my motorbike back, so I buzzed cockily across the airfield on it and told them they could..."

At first, Galland turned discreetly to JG 7 in the hope that his name might attract one or two requests for transfers but found, much to his annoyance that Gollob had blocked that avenue. As Galland explained: "I selected Brandenburg-Briest as a base for the unit with excellent help from JG 7 as long as my own means were not sufficient. But Gollob expressly forbade JG 7 to help me and intervened, using Göring, with the aim of blocking the transfer of any pilots to me. The formation was so delayed that I lodged a complaint with the Chief of the *Personalamt* about this covert sabotage."

There is no doubt that the very fact that Galland had been allowed to form his own unit was a source of considerable irritation to the new *General der Jagdflieger*. "JV 44 was forbidden to influence other units in any way at all," Gollob wrote, "The unit was not placed under the command of the *General der Jagdflieger*, but rather its basis was formed by Galland, Steinhoff and (later) Lützow... The consequences as far as personnel were concerned were that a number of our best pilots and unit commanders were removed from their regular units because they were assigned to JV 44 or were joining it of their own free will."

In this account, Gollob makes no reference as to who the "best pilots and unit commanders" were. Nevertheless, this argument continued well into the post-war years. In 1984, Galland told a British researcher: "Gollob did everything to cross and counter-act

In his capacity as commander of 4. Fliegerschuldivision, Oberst Hannes Trautloft secured several former fighter instructors for Galland's unit. Trautloft is photographed here earlier in the war when he was Kommodore of JG 54. The "Grünherz" – "Green Heart" – emblem on the Bf 109 behind him also contains the emblems of I., II. and III./JG 54.

my wishes and proposals. Therefore, because of this and other reasons – mostly because of lack of communication – not all the pilots I wanted to have for JV 44 showed up at Brandenburg-Briest."

Conversely, Gollob reiterated his point of view to an American researcher two decades earlier when he wrote: "At exactly the moment when Galland and everyone else in the *Luftwaffe* knew that, above all, there was a shortage of experienced formation leaders, this gentleman didn't shrink away from requesting for himself – without exception – the Aces. He only got the ones I let him have and a few that he "organised" himself by roundabout means.... The list of pilots which Galland compiled for "his" JV 44 when he was no longer *General der Jagdflieger* was a *wish* list. What do you think would have happened had I pulled all of these experienced formation leaders out of their units to put them at *Herr* Galland's disposal? It was for that reason, that in many cases, I refused and so he got only a part of the nominated pilots and formation leaders, among them those who, unfortunately, were in disgrace – or those who, for other reasons, could not or did not wish to remain with their units..."

One formation leader and *Ritterkreuzträger* who fell into the latter category and who was offered the opportunity to join JV 44 by Gollob was *Major* Wolfgang Späte. Until March 1945, Späte had commanded JG 400, the only unit to fly the volatile Me 163 *Komet* rocket-powered interceptor operationally. However, lacking both the specialised rocket fuel needed for their engines and suitably trained pilots, JG 400 had been wound down. Späte, one of Germany's best known pre-war glider pilots and with more than 90 victories to his name, gained mainly in Russia where he had flown with JG 54, temporarily found himself redundant.

As he recalls: "Gollob, as successor to Galland, telephoned me and asked how I wished to be employed from then on. When I explained that I wished to defend my Fatherland by flying the Me 262, he said "Okay – JG 7 or JV 44?" I decided to go to JG 7. I chose JG 7 because I knew they had sufficient aircraft, enough fuel and the *Geschwaderkommodore*, Theo Weissenberger, was a friend of mine from the time when we both participated as glider pilots in the soaring competitions on the Wasserkuppe long before the war. It was also widely known that JG 7 had achieved considerable successes. I thought it would offer me the best opportunity to engage myself in the final defence of our country. On the other hand, I held a deep respect for Galland and the opportunity of flying with a unit under his guidance was tempting. I admired Galland, not least, because having been unjustly "fired" by Göring, he didn't withdraw, offended and moaning into some snail shell. Rather, he built up a flying unit, the size of a *Staffel*, went to the front and defended his country to the very last day. That was exemplary!"

And so it was, that as the "official" vetting on the transfer of pilots to the infant JV 44 began to take effect, Galland was forced to simply "spread the word" about what he was doing at

ERICH HOHAGEN

Born 9.1.1915. Erich Hohagen was regarded as one of the *Jagdwaffe's* true front-line veterans having accumulated several thousand hours flying on about 60 different types and having flown continuously on the Channel Front in 1940 during which time he was accredited with 10 victories. In Russia he was wounded on numerous occasions and returned to the west later in the war to take up command positions with JG 2 and JG 27 in the defence of the Reich. Of a total of 55 victories gained from over 500 missions, 13 were four-engine bombers. Following one air battle over the Western Front in the autumn of 1944, Hohagen was forced to belly land his stricken fighter in a small field. Aircraft and pilot ploughed into a bank and Hohagen had smashed his head on the aircraft's reflector sight. A surgeon later replaced a piece of his skull with plastic and pulled the skin back together. Even so, as Steinhoff later recalled, "...The two halves of his face no longer quite matched." Supposedly recovered from his wounds, Hohagen was posted to III./EJG 2 at Lechfeld in late 1944 where he began to convert onto the Me 262 prior to taking command of the embryonic III./JG 7. Still troubled by headaches however, as a direct result of his many wounds and thus considered unfit for service by the Staff of the *General der Jagdflieger* and the Personnel Office, Hohagen had been returned to hospital near Berlin from where Galland and Steinhoff had plucked him for operations once again.

Brandenburg-Briest. Some pilots *did* transfer to the unit following Galland's telephone or telex request, but these were not, by and large, the legendary *Experten* that he had hoped for, but rather those pilots recovering from wounds or instructors who had spent a considerable period of time with the various schools units and who had thus not been exposed to combat for weeks or even months on end. Others were fresh out of the training schools, sent to join Galland by his former colleague, *Oberst* Hannes Trautloft, who now, conveniently, controlled one of the fighter training divisions.

As Galland recalled: "With the situation deteriorating daily, I was expecting to be accused of intentionally delaying the formation and operations of my unit, something that would have been very dangerous for me. However, it was not very long before Göring ordered that my unit's strength must reach its full complement. Meanwhile, Trautloft, who had taken over the 4. *Flieger-schuldivision* from Lützow, helped me enormously by transferring combat experienced fighter instructors from his training schools. News about events at Brandenburg-Briest spread quickly through the *Jagdwaffe* and an increasing number of accomplished fighter pilots

asked to join my unit. Most of them arrived without the consent of the Personnel Office."

Two of the first such officers and *Experten* to be acquired "unofficially" were the recently hospitalised but long-experienced combat veterans, *Ritterkreuzträger, Majors* Karl-Heinz Schnell and Erich Hohagen. With so many adversities to contend with, the presence of two such well known and respected aces as Schnell and Hohagen alongside him must have proved a real boost to Galland. Following them, came Steinhoff's former wingman and adjutant from the time he had commanded JG 77 in Italy, *Leutnant* Gottfried Fährmann. Fährmann had proved himself a capable fighter pilot shooting down at least one Mustang and one Lightning over Italy in the summer of 1944 as well as being shot down himself during an attack on a formation of B-25s in July 1944 after which he returned for duty unscathed. A former Ju 88 bomber pilot also joined JV 44 at this time, *Leutnant* Blomert, whose stint at the nearby *Fluglehrerschule der Luftwaffe* – the Flying Instructor's School – was approaching an end and whose knowledge of blind flying, twin-engine handling and asymmetric flying would be a bonus in the training of pilots converting to the Me 262.

One of the first non-commissioned pilots to be transferred "officially" to JV 44 however, through agreement with the Personnel *Amt*, was twenty-one year old *Unteroffizier* Eduard Schallmoser and his career with the unit from its inception at Brandenburg-Briest to its surrender in Austria ten weeks later, is very representative of many of the young pilots who passed through it at one time or other between February and May 1945.

Very often, transfer, by whatever means, to an Me 262 unit, represented the pinnacle of a flying career and with the growing realisation that the end of the war was only a matter of weeks away, many were grateful for the experience to simply savour the exhilaration of flying the ultimate fighter aircraft of the time as were the pilots of the already established Me 262 units. An unexpected reprieve from yet more hospitalisation and the opportunity to fly with JV 44 were viewed with considerable favour by Erich Hohagen: "I had only received one week's training on the Me 262 at Lechfeld, as far as I remember, but I was very proud and honoured to fly it since I was still suffering from a head fracture that had occurred one month before. It was the absolute fulfilment of my flying career and I knew for sure that, at that time, no further enhancements could be made. It was the biggest step since the Wright brothers flew an aircraft

KARL-HEINZ SCHNELL

Born 10.1.1915. in Essen, "Bubi" Schnell had flown with distinction as both *Staffelkapitän* and *Gruppenkommandeur* in III./JG 51, seeing action initially with II./JG 51 during the French campaign and the Battle of Britain. With his service in Russia, Schell accumulated a total of 72 victories during the course of approximately 500 missions. He was awarded the *Ritterkreuz* on 1 August 1941 following his 29th victory. As a result of wounds sustained over the Eastern Front however, he had been posted back to Germany to take command of the fighter school unit, JG 102, though his wounds regularly caused him problems and when Steinhoff arranged his transfer to JV 44, it was from a hospital.

EDUARD SCHALLMOSER

Born in Aying, Bavaria in 1923, Eduard Schallmoser first became captivated by flying with the *Flieger-Hitlerjugend,* the glider sports association of the *Nationalsozialististisches Fliegerkorps* in 1938 and, like so many of his generation, avidly pursued his love of silent flight for another three years during which time he gained his A, B and C proficiency certificates in model building, fieldcraft, workshop duties and physical fitness. In May 1941, whilst still a boy, he officially joined the *Luftwaffe* as a member of the 3. *Fliegerausbildungsregiment* at Klagenfurt where he embarked on the standard course of fitness training, medical examination, infantry training and sport. In December of that year he progressed to a *Flugzeugführer-Anwärter-Bataillon* at Seyring bei Wien where he received instruction in radio communication and navigation. In February 1942, as part of the standard wartime *Luftwaffe* flight training programme, Schallmoser began his basic pilot's training at the *Flugzeugführerschule A/B 112* at Böblingen near Stuttgart where he commenced what would be a two and a half year flying training course (aerobatics, instrument training, formation flying and cross country) during which he would be fortunate enough to accumulate more than five hundred hours on a variety of types including the Klemm 35, Focke-Wulf 44, Bücker 131, Heinkel 51, Arado 96, Caudron C445 and the Junkers 34. Additionally, in May 1944, the young Schallmoser spent a short time at the *Nachtjagdschule* Altenburg where he was given a brief introduction to the Bf 109 E in preparation for deployment as a *Wilde Sau* free-ranging nightfighter pilot.

By October 1944 and eagerly awaiting transfer to either a day or nightfighter unit flying in defence of the Reich, Schallmoser concluded his initial training by transferring to the operational fighter training unit 6./JG 101 and then 7./JG 112 where his *Staffelführer* wrote of his pupil:

Intelligent and fit. Very talented. Open and knowledgeable person. Is very interested in becoming a fighter pilot.

A spell at 12./*Ergänzungs-Jagdgruppe* 1 at Weidengut/Breslau followed in November 1944, where he familiarised himself on the Bf 109 G, F and the rare T variant in which he gained 1.5 hours flying time. Upon conclusion of his course at EJG 1 on 21 November 1944, Schallmoser's *Staffelkapitän* was pleased with his pupil's achievements; he wrote:

His take-offs and landings are faultless. He is fully conversant with the Bf 109. His combat flying capability is good. He is quiet and confident in formation flying. The result of his aerial gunnery: average. Recommended for fighter group. (Me 262)

So it was that, instead of being posted to a conventional day (or night) fighter unit, Schallmoser was sent instead to III./EJG 2 at Landsberg to begin operational training on the Me 262. It is relevant, here, to note the pattern and composition of the actual flight training given at III./EJG 2 for a future jet pilot:

11 **December 1944 to 6 January 1945: (Landsberg)**
Familiarisation on Si 204 and Bf 110
(20 take-offs/2 hours)

13 **January to 2 March 1945: (Unterschlauersbach)**
Familiarisation on Me 262

Circuits	-	3 take-offs/1.5 hours
First flight	-	1 take-off / 30 minutes
High altitude (12,000m)	-	2 take-offs/ 2 hours
Navigation	-	1 take-off/ 45 minutes
Formation flt	-	1 take-off/ 30 minutes

As with his earlier training, his instructor at Lechfeld was very satisfied with Schallmoser's abilities:

A big, tall man with quiet mannerisms; open and honest in character. Considerable operational awareness. In his circle of comrades, he is well liked. Promises to make a good fighter pilot. Trained up to A/B standard and possesses strong emotions about flying. Converted on to Si 204 and Bf 110 with no problems whatsoever. Take-offs and landings very consistent. Flies single engine like a model. Precision landing is good. Strongly recommended for the Me 262.

With the successful completion of his Me 262 training, Schallmoser received his posting to JV 44 on 2 March 1945 and the next day he travelled to Brandenburg-Briest.

Eduard Schallmoser (left) with a fellow pupil during flying training in the winter of 1942/43.

heavier than air. Basically there was no similarity in flight characteristics compared to other aircraft I had flown and though it was easier to handle on the piloting part, things were much more critical on the flight safety side of things. For example, the engines could have been improved and better fatigue resistance built in. I also felt that the hydraulic system was insufficient and that there would have been benefit from the installation of dive brakes."

Despite the enthusiasm shared for the Me 262 by most of the unit's pilots, during the first weeks of formation at JV 44 and despite Steinhoff's efforts as "Head of Training", conditions were even more primitive and many of the pilots arriving in early March 1945 were nowhere near as fortunate as either Hohagen or Schallmoser in receiving at least *some qualified* training on the jet fighter. Indeed, one officer sent to Galland as a potential Me 262 pilot had not even served in the *Jagdwaffe* and thus had no fighter training or experience at all!

Unteroffizier Johann-Karl "Jonny" Müller was an experienced ground-attack pilot but, like Hohagen and Schnell, had been hospitalised from 15 October 1944 until 25 January 1945 as a result of wounds incurred whilst flying Fw 190 fighter-bombers on the eastern front. At the time Müller had been flying as escort on a number of occasions to the legendary *Stuka* ace, *Oberst* Hans-Ulrich Rudel. Having been wounded, Rudel personally recommended that, once recovered, Müller should go to JV 44 which was now known to be forming, though quite why Rudel should make such a suggestion to a fighter-bomber pilot remains unclear, especially since it must have been recognised that the transition from Fw 190 fighter-bomber to Me 262 jet fighter at such a late stage in the war would present some challenging adjustments!

Nevertheless, Müller reported for duty with JV 44 at Briest on 3 March 1945. Here he joined the curious assortment of unwanted *Experten* and *Ritterkreuzträger* and their solitary, freshly trained jet pilot, Eduard Schallmoser. Also gathering at Brandenburg-Briest at this time were the growing number of redundant fighter instructors, most of them former combat seasoned pilots themselves whom Galland had been able to secure for his *Verband* with the assistance of Trautloft and who would form the "backbone" of the unit. By early 1945 the majority of the A/B and C training schools were being disbanded and thus the need for instructors had diminished considerably. Nevertheless, these pilots would have been trained in instructing on blind flying and in instrument courses and were thus ideal for JV 44's needs. *Ofw.* Reckers came from JG 101, *Lt.* Roth from JG 102, *Ofw.* Haase from JG 105. One such instructor who was ordered to report to JV 44 at this time was twenty eight year-old *Oberfeldwebel* Rudolf Nielinger who came from JG 103 and though he arrived at Brandenburg-Briest in an Fw 190 on 11 March 1945 somewhat startled to find that he was to go operational on the Me 262, his service career typifies the individual levels of valuable operational experience that Galland was now amassing.

Meanwhile, Steinhoff had begun training in earnest by placing Blomert and two other instructors from the *Fluglehrerschule der Luftwaffe*, *Fw.* Otto Kammerdiener and *Fw.*

Meissner in charge of elementary navigational and twin-engine training flights. Possibly with the assistance of Trautloft and Blomert, Galland was able to secure the services of at least four twin-engine Siebel 204Ds from the *Fluglehrerschule der Luftwaffe* which were then put to good use around Brandenburg-Briest mainly for the purposes of practising twin-engine take-offs and landings, using the radio course indicator – the *Zielvorsatzgerät* 16, navigation and instrument flying and flying on one engine.

For these tasks, the Si 204 was a sturdy and very suitable workhorse. Evolved originally for DLH from the pre-war Fh 104A Hallore five-seat light transport and powered by two 600 hp Argus As 411 twelve cylinder engines, it was built both at the SNAC works in France as well as by the Aero

JOHANN-KARL MÜLLER

Johann-Karl "Jonny" Müller was an experienced *Schlachtflieger* – ground-attack pilot – who started his operational career with IV./SKG 10 in Normandy in April 1943. The following month from the *Gruppe's* base at Caen, he took part in a series of daring, low level "nuisance" raids mounted against random targets along the south-eastern coast of England. Whilst flying these missions, "Jonny" crash-landed on at least two occasions in France but was able to walk away from his wrecked Fw 190s unharmed. Later, in the summer and autumn of 1943, he saw intensive action over Sicily and Italy until October 1943, when, as part of a general restructuring of all dive-bomber, ground attack and fast bomber units, IV./SKG 10 was redesignated II./SG 10. By December of that year it had transferred to the southern sector of the Russian front where it operated as a component unit of *Luftflotte* 4. Here in the early autumn of 1944, Müller flew Fw 190s as escort on a number of occasions to the legendary *Stuka* ace, *Oberst* Hans-Ulrich Rudel, *Gruppenkommandeur* of III./SG 2 which was engaged in meeting the Soviet advance across the Hungarian plains. Following Müller's hospitalisation from 15 October 1944 until 25 January 1945 as a result of wounds incurred whilst flying Fw 190 fighter-bombers in the east with II./SG 10, Rudel personally recommended that, once recovered, he should go to JV 44. Nevertheless, following a brief posting to the Aircrew Assembly Depot, *Frontfliegersammelgruppe Quedlinburg*, Müller reported for duty with JV 44 at Brandenburg-Briest on 3rd March 1945.

and BMM factories in Czechoslovakia. *Luftwaffe* interest in the Si 204 centred around it being a replacement for the Fw 58 *Weihe* as the standard blind-flying, navigation, radar and radio trainer for the *Flugzeugführerschulen*. Normally unarmed, but capable of accommodating five trainees as well as a crew of two, it was generally considered to have been a very pleasing aircraft to fly.

To all intents and purposes, the first month of JV 44's operations was spent absorbed by the routine, if not hurried, process of training. Fortunately, apart from the usual restrictions on fuel, training proceeded without any incident. As Galland recalls: "What we really did in Brandenburg was just to get familiar with the aircraft, taking off and landing, that was all and

BATTLE OVER BAVARIA

To the Army Air Force chiefs and crews of B-17 Flying Fortresses operating deep into Germany, the Me 262 represented a deadly new adversary which for a time, gave cause for concern. But the relative obsolescence of the B-17 became almost an asset as the German jet pilots found the speed differential difficult to cope with – they had a scant few seconds to slow down enough to match the Fort's low speed for a fatal burst of cannon fire. Here B-17Gs of a 1st Air Division group (probably the 379th), flying at around 220-230 mph (354-370 kph) unload their bombs on another target.

To the Army Air Force chiefs and crews of B-17 Flying Fortresses operating deep into Germany, the Me 262 represented a deadly new adversary which for a time, gave cause for concern. But the relative obsolescence of the B-17 became almost an asset as the German jet pilots found the speed differential difficult to cope with – they had a scant few seconds to slow down enough to match the Fort's low speed for a fatal burst of cannon fire. Here B-17Gs of a 1st Air Division group (probably the 379th), flying at around 220-230 mph (354-370 kph) unload their bombs on another target.

Me 262s, came from 6:30 to 7 o'clock, low to level, resulting in the entire tail section of one B-17 being shot off.

Of a total of 37 machines committed, JG 7 lost three pilots killed with one badly wounded and five aircraft sustained heavy damage. But this was an acceptable price to pay and proved Galland's theory that, if used correctly in a fighter role, a small force of Me 262s could inflict devastating damage.

Nevertheless, with the growing threat of prowling Allied fighters mounting sweeps on the jet airfields, Galland's immediate priority was to obtain some Me 262s with which to equip his own unit and provide some back-up to JG 7. Frustratingly, delivery of factory fresh jets was proving to be extremely slow. It still seemed as if priority was being given to JG 7 – an understandable situation given that this unit was achieving successes whilst Galland was still trying to scrape together more competent pilots, a task made difficult by the restrictions imposed by Gollob. By the afternoon of 14 March however, the first recorded flight in an Me 262 by JV 44 was made from Brandenburg-Briest by *Ofw.* Nielinger, flying "White 3", who was airborne for 25 minutes on a familiarisation flight.

On 18 March 1945, upon the instigation of *Generalmajor* Josef Kammhuber, Görings personal "Plenipotentiary" for Jet Aircraft, OKL ordered that *Jagdverband 44 "General Galland"* was to become operational with a strength of twenty aircraft as soon as possible. As a result of the directive, more aircraft began

Steinhoff looked after that side of things."

By now, the collection depot at Briest was allowing regular deliveries of aircraft to JG 7 which was beginning to make encouraging headway against the bombers. In the three days between 18-20 March, the *Geschwader* flew no fewer than 11 sorties, including a mission on the 18th against the Eighth Air Force in which 28 Me 262s made contact with a formation of bombers and its fighter escort on course for Berlin, destroying 13 aircraft in all and damaging another six. Eighth Air Force Intelligence wrote of the attacks made against the 1st and 3rd Bomb Divisions:

Two bombers were lost by 1st Division in the target area... The jets launched their attacks from out of contrails and aggressively pressed home against the last two groups, in one instance to within 50 yards (46 metres). Several concentrated attacks were made by two to four jets – others attacked singly. Jets made skilful use of superior speed and though escort fighters engaged, only one jet was claimed damaged... Me 262s made strong attacks on 3rd Division bombers from west of Salzwedel to Berlin; attacks, though not continuous, were skilful and aggressive, contrail cover being used to good effect; six bombers were lost to these attacks. Initial attack was on the low squadron of the second group in the column, which squadron at the time was strung out and in poor formation. Four Me 262s in a formation similar to that used by P-51's came out of clouds from 5 o'clock low, closing from 75 yards (68.5 metres) to point-blank range... Second attack, by three

JG 7 – defenders of Berlin.

54

RUDOLF NIELINGER

Rudolf Nielinger had commenced his flying training in December 1939 as a young *Unteroffizier* with *Fliegerausbildungs-regiment* 31 at Posen where he accumulated nearly 180 hours of basic flying skills on a variety of types including Fw 44s, Fw 58s, Bü 131s, Go 145s, Ar 66s, Ar 96s and Kl 35s. The following November, with his basic training completed, he was posted to the *Jagdfliegerschule* Stolp-Reitz on the Baltic coast where he graduated onto the Bf 108 and Bf 109 E and on which he embarked on basic fighter training and formation flying.

In March 1941, he received his first operational posting when he was assigned to *Hptm.* Josef Fözö's II./JG 51 which was re-equipping at Mannheim after its tour of duty on the Channel front. Nielinger's first taste of operational flying came very soon when he flew Bf 109 E's for 4. *Staffel* out of Mardyck against the RAF over north west France and England until May of that year at which time the *Gruppe* was moved back to Dortmund in preparation for the invasion of Russia. II./JG 51 was immediately heavily committed against the Soviet air force, operating as one of the component units of *Luftflotte* 2's II *Fliegerkorps* acting in support of Army Group Centre's drive on Moscow. It was over Russia that Rudolf Nielinger, flying the Bf 109 F, would accumulate his first 18 victories in a series of virtually non-stop offensive patrols and ground attack and Stuka escort operations lasting throughout the remainder of 1941 and up to the autumn of 1942.

In early November 1942, converting to the Bf 109 G-2, he was transferred away from Russia along with the rest of II./JG 51 – now under *Hptm.* Grasser – for Tunis in North Africa as reinforcement intended to tackle the Allied fighter units covering the enemy advances following the recent British and American landings in French Morocco and Algeria. Nielinger arrived in Africa having survived 280 missions over Russia.

Success was quick to come to Rudolf Nielinger in Tunisia and he scored his first victory over the Allied air forces when he shot down a Bristol Beaufort bomber north west of Bizerte only three days after arriving in Africa. He would not score again for six months. Meanwhile, the aerial battle over Tunisia intensified as the Allies drove east and crossed the frontier until bad weather finally halted their advance. For the remainder of the year and in appalling weather conditions, the pilots of II./JG 51 found themselves defending their airfield and the harbour at Tunis and escorting the Ju 52's that brought in vital supplies for von Arnim's hard-pressed *Heeresgruppe Afrika*. Nielinger found himself pitted against British bombers escorted by droves of Spitfires as the Eighth Army pushed against the Mareth Line in March 1943.

On 20th April 1943, II./JG 51 fled for Sicily pursued by Spitfires and in May they moved again, this time to Sardinia where Nielinger scored his 20th and final victory, over a Curtiss P-40, before leaving the island in September for a brief sojourn in the Reich. In January 1944, he rejoined his *Gruppe* in Italy where it was now flying ground attack escort missions over the Anzio beach head, but at the end of that month he

was taken seriously ill, probably as a result of his service in Africa, and once again returned to Germany.

Rudolf Nielinger achieved the following confirmed victories:

1.	25.06.41	SB 2	- near Cyjanie, Russia
2.	03.07.41	DB 3	- Khuravitch, Russia
3.	31.07.41	I-16	- Kritschev, Russia
4.	09.08.41	Pe-2	- Ielnja, Russia
5.	22.08.41	I-16	- NW of Ielnja, Russia
6.	25.08.41	DB 3	- South of Gomel, Russia
7.	25.08.41	SB 2	- South of Gomel on Stuka escort, Russia
8.	29.10.41	I-16	- West of Tula, Russa
9.	05.12.41	Pe-2	- near Bogalitchava, Russia
10.	18.02.42	J 61	- Tchern, Russia
11.	05.08.42	Pe-2	- ENE of Dugino, Russia
12.	05.08.42	Yak 1	- ESE of Subtzov, Russia
13.	22.08.42	Il-2	- NE of Kritchina, Russia
14.	23.08.42	Il-2	- SW of Koselsk, Russia
15.	23.08.42	Il-2	- SW of Koselsk, Russia
16.	27.08.42	Il-2	- ENE of Orel, Russia
17.	14.09.42	Il-2	- NW of Rzhev, Russia
18.	14.09.42	Il-2	- NW of Rzhev, Russia
19.	17.11.42	Bristol Beaufort	– NW of Bizerte, Tunisia
20.	21.05.43	Curtiss P-40	– NNE of Villacidro, Sardinia

Following a period of recuperation, Nielinger was assigned as an instructor at the fighter training wing, JG 103 based on the Baltic coast around Stralsund and Greifswald. Here, his responsibilities were to train desperately needed new fighter pilots in the tried and tested *Rotte* and *Schwarm* formation concepts using an assortment of old Bf 109 E's as well as the more modern Fw 190. It was a relatively uneventful period, with the exception of a lucky escape from a failed Bf 109 G-4 from which he baled out over his old training field of Stolp-Reitz.

However, by early 1945 the majority of the A/B and C training schools were being disbanded and thus the need for instructors had diminished considerably. Nevertheless, these pilots would have been trained in instructing on blind flying and in instrument courses and were thus ideal for JV 44's needs. So it was that *Ofw.* Nielinger received orders to report to Galland's *Verband* and he arrived at Brandenburg-Briest in an Fw 190 on 11 March 1945 somewhat startled to find that he was to go operational on the Me 262!

A smiling Rudolf Nielinger (right) in the cockpit of a Fw 44 trainer at Goslar, November 1940 at the completion of his training.

KLAUS NEUMANN

Born in Wettin/Saale, twenty-one year old Klaus Neumann had first seen service with the *Luftwaffe* in 1943 and had been presented with the *Ritterkreuz* as a *Feldwebel* by Hitler personally in December 1944 upon the occasion of his 31st victory and for his work as a pilot with IV.(*Sturm*)/JG 3 where had shot down at least nineteen four-engine bombers in the defence of the Reich, becoming one of the acknowledged "specialists" in that field. Prior to that he had flown in the east with 2./JG 51 as an NCO pilot being accredited with 12 victories against the Soviet air force. In January 1945, this young but highly competent *Experte* was transferred to a staff position with JG 7. Neumann recorded approximately 200 operational missions from which he was accredited with 37 victories in total, of which 12 were claimed in the east. He was posted to JV 44 in March 1945.

FRANZ STIGLER

Franz Stigler was a veteran fighter pilot who had fought a long, hard war flying 480 combat missions with II./JG 27 over Africa, the Mediterranean, Sicily, Italy and in the defence of the Reich. He had amassed 28 confirmed victories exclusively in the Bf 109, 17 over the desert and 5 gained against four-engine bombers over Italy and Austria. He had himself been shot down on seventeen occasions, baling out six times, the rest successfully crash-landing or

ditching. In early 1945, he was posted to III./EJG 2 at Lechfeld for eight weeks to undergo standard conversion onto the Me 262. His transfer to JV 44 came in March 1945.

FRANZ STEINER

Described as "...a passionate flier", Czechoslovakian born Franz Steiner underwent operational training on the Bf 109 at schools in Austria and East Prussia in April 1939 before being posted to JG 27 in the late summer of 1940, with whom he flew in the Balkans and North Africa. Posted back to Europe in early 1942, he joined JG 1 and was almost immediately moved to Trondheim in Norway as part of *Kommando Losigkeit*, a special short-term unit formed from pilots of JG 1 and intended to offer air protection to certain vessels of the German *Kriegsmarine* seeking shelter on the Norwegian coast and in the fjords following Adolf Galland's famous "Channel Dash" operation to free them from their enforced ports in France. Returning to Germany, Steiner continued his duties with JG 1 until the summer of 1944 when he spent a brief spell as a fighter instructor with an *Ergänzungsgruppe* in Märkisch-Friedland. He then transferred to JG 11 where he flew Fw 190s in the defence of the Reich claiming an impressive tally of 5 B-17s, 4 B-24s, 1 P-38 Lightning and 1 B-26 Marauder destroyed. Ordered to JV 44, March 1945.

to trickle in to the unit from the Briest collection depot and following Galland's instruction, they began to apply a simple consecutive code-numbering system to their aircraft, with the individual white numbers being applied on the fuselage between the cockpit and the *Balkenkreuz*. "All the Me 262s that we took over at Brandenburg at that time were factory finish," Galland recalled, "We had no time for painting fancy things on them... I had white numbers painted on the fuselage, that's all. Simple and easy to recognise for inexperienced pilots. There were no other markings – there was no time."

Small numbers of experienced fighter pilots were still arriving at Brandenburg-Briest. Czechoslovakian born *Feldwebel* Franz Steiner had come from JG 11. Steiner, however, like so many others, was eager to fly the much vaunted jet fighter and his move to JV 44 gave him the opportunity. As he recalls: "I was selected by *Generalleutnant* Galland in person after a short conversation with him. Exactly what criteria I had to make him keep me and send others away, I don't know. For me, the most important thing was to fly this "legendary bird". Conversion onto the Me 262 at Brandenburg-Briest didn't give me any problems, though I never once saw an instructor fly with anyone despite there being a two-seater available. *Oberst* Steinhoff just gave me a few prior instructions and then told me to take off on my first flight! I have to say that flying the Me 262 was the high point in

my flying career. Whenever you first got off the ground and had attained height and speed, you couldn't help but feel a sense of absolute elation and wonderment. In my view, the only weak point was the engines. Engine failure during take-off which, unfortunately, was all too common, almost always meant certain death for a pilot. You would have felt safer with rocket-assisted take-off. In flight, especially in a shallow dive, you had to adjust for the sensitivity of the engines too much."

The unit received a further boost in late March 1945 with the arrival of two more accomplished and battle-hardened fighter pilots, the *Ritterkreuzträger Fahnenjunker-Oberfeldwebel* Klaus Neumann and *Leutnant* Franz Stigler. Coincidentally, despite their admirable service records, both these pilots had been forced to leave their previous units as a result of altercations with their commanding officers. "I finished my training at Lechfeld having flown the Me 262 only once." Stigler recounted. "I then went over to EJG 1 for a short spell. The training there was very rudimentary and I made a stupid remark about it and had to leave. In the meantime, word had got out that Galland was forming a new jet unit at Brandenburg so I called him from Lechfeld and asked whether I could join him – after all, I had just been trained to fly the Me 262! He said: *"Sure, no problem, glad to have you. Just bring a jet with you."* So I went over to the jet manufacturing plant at Leipheim and tried to get hold of an Me

262. I said I was under instruction to collect the aircraft for JV 44, but they had never even heard of the unit! Anyway, by that stage, things were in such turmoil that I managed to secure the aircraft and I then flew direct to Brandenburg-Briest. I didn't do much when I got there though because the unit was in the process of getting organised and we were left well alone..."

The Allied and Russian advances into the Reich were now threatening to split northern Germany from the south. By late March 1945, the Americans, British and Canadians were across the Rhine. To the east, Gdynia, Danzig and Königsberg were all under siege by the Red Army, whilst further south in Hungary, Esztergom on the eastern bank of the Danube, north of Budapest, was surrounded, ensnaring thousands of German troops.

The Americans too were continuing to pulverise jet airfields and production centres in the south. Since January, following a directive by General Spaatz and Air Marshal Bottomley, German jet aircraft production centres had ranked as a joint number one priority target for the Allied strategic air forces alongside oil refineries and storage installations. With a view to offering some defence for the vital manufacturing centres in the south, Koller ordered Galland to transfer JV 44 to Lechfeld. Galland however was uncertain about the wisdom of this instruction. Without authorisation and leaving Steinhoff nominally in charge at Brandenburg-Briest, he motored south alone in his BMW sports car on a lightning tour of the jet airfields in Bavaria. There was only one base which Galland considered suitable for JV 44 – München-Riem. Despite being a both a major transit airfield for units arriving from the east as well as a gateway for Italy, it was still a large field, well-prepared and in good condition. Galland made his decision and drove back to Brandenburg.

Meanwhile, training had been continuing without much interruption, though, as far as is known, only one combat sortie was flown by JV 44 from Brandenburg when, whilst on patrol with Neumann and Blomert, *Oberst.* Steinhoff shot down a Soviet Il-2 Shturmovik ground-attack aircraft near Strausberg to the east of Berlin.

Upon his return to Brandenburg on or around 28 March, Galland immediately began arrangements for the transfer of JV 44 south to München. Contacting Kammhuber once again to arrange the necessary transport, he received some encouraging information; Koller had ordered that IV./KG 51, now based at Riem and Erding and responsible for training volunteer pilots from all IX.*(J) Fliegerkorps* component units onto the Me 262, should hand over all its aircraft to JV 44 upon its arrival at Riem in order to provide a significant defence force for the jet manufacturing industry. This meant, hopefully, that the unit could be brought up to a more significant strength and that, as such, more pilots would be allocated to it. If this were to happen, then the experience of the various fighter instructors now attached to Galland,

would prove highly valuable.

On or around 29 March, a "full-sized goods train" left Berlin for the journey south to München-Riem. On board were members of the ground crew together with as much vital equipment as Galland, Steinhoff, Schnell and Hohagen had been able to gather together from the supply depots, in order to ensure smooth operation of the unit upon its arrival in Bavaria – technical equipment, spare turbines, weapons, tow tractors, support vehicles and flying gear. It is unlikely that the full flying complement of JV 44 exceeded 20 pilots.

Adverse weather over most of eastern and southern Germany, bringing multi-layered cloud, light showers and poor visibility, prevented transfer on the 30th. The next day, 31 March, OKL recorded that a total of 9 Me 262s had been delivered direct from the factories to *Jagdverband* 44 of which one machine was undergoing repair. Six more were unserviceable as a result of enemy action – probably bombing raids or fighter sweeps mounted against Brandenburg-Briest. Another two were expected to arrive from the training units. Comparatively, and as an indication of how irrelevant JV 44's efforts were considered by the High Command, JG 7 had been allocated a total of 333 Me 262s. Altogether, 79 of its aircraft were serviceable as of 31 March with a total of 204 aircraft lost to either enemy action or other causes.

With his meagre force ready to depart, Galland decided to assign only half of his *Verband's* strength – Steinhoff, Fährmann, Hohagen, Stigler, Neumann, Steiner and Nielinger – to ferry JV 44's jet fighters direct from Brandenburg-Briest to München-Riem. Galland, accompanied by some of the remaining pilots, would fly south by Siebel. It is not believed that Karl-Heinz Schnell was able to fly the Me 262 because of his wounds and the author has, to date, found no evidence to suggest that he flew to Riem. It is possible therefore that Galland placed him in charge of the land transfer along with Meissner.

At dawn on 31 March, Steinhoff and his wingman, Gottfried Fährmann, took off, leading the first formation of JV 44's Me 262s to the south. They would be followed later that day, at 17:40, by a second formation led by Klaus Neumann.

At 16:10 that afternoon, Si 204 BD+DZ, formerly of the *Fluglehrerschule der Luftwaffe* and piloted by Kammerdiener, took off from Brandenburg-Briest en route to Altenberg south of

Possibly taken at Brandenburg-Briest in late March 1945, this photograph shows one of JV 44's principal training aircraft "Red S" as flown by "Jonny" Müller, Rudolf Nielinger and Franz Steiner. Me 262 "White 6" – also flown by Steiner – can be seen parked alongside.

Leipzig on the first stage of its journey to München-Riem. Kammerdiener was accompanied by a new but welcome recruit to JV 44; *Lt* Hoffman, an experienced Me 262 instructor, had arrived from Lechfeld where he had served with III./EJG 2 under Heinz Bär. BD+DZ arrived at Altenberg at 16:55 that afternoon and, after a one hour refuelling stop-over, flew on to München-Riem arriving at 18:20 that evening, where it immediately began to unload its consignment of vital signals and communications equipment.

At 06:25 the next morning, 1 April 1945, another Si 204, (BU+PB), took off from Brandenburg-Briest piloted by *Oberleutnant* Blomert and carrying Galland, Müller, Schallmoser and more of the unit's equipment.

München-Riem Arena for Battle

JV 44's land and air transfer to Bavaria proceeded relatively smoothly with only one recorded problem when *Ofw.* Rudolf Nielinger and his *Rottenführer,* Klaus Neumann, were forced to land at an intermediate field due to a faulty turbine on Nielinger's Me 262. By 1st April, the rest of the unit was at München-Riem and Galland and Steinhoff once again began the task of bringing

the *Jagdverband* up to full operational status as soon as possible.

There had been an airfield at München since 1909 when the Zeppelin airship *Viktoria Luise* successfully landed on what was then the exercise ground at Oberwiesenfeld in a northern district of the city. Two years later, the aviator Hellmuth Hirth won the 50,000 Mark Kathreiner Prize for a 540 kilometre long distance flight in a Rumpler Taube from Oberwiesenfeld to Berlin in 5 hours 51 minutes and from then on aeronautical activity in München began to increase dramatically. In 1920, the first regular passenger and cargo air service commenced between Oberwiesenfeld and Frankfurt-Rebstock followed by the introduction of further routes in 1921 to Nürnberg, Leipzig, Bremen and Augsburg and the München-Konstanz route. Zürich, Vienna, Budapest, Innsbruck, Bad Reichenall, Regensburg, Salzburg and Stuttgart were added as destinations between 1924-25 with 8,747 passengers recorded as transiting München-Oberwiesenfeld in 1925. By 1930, and with aid from the *Reichsverkehrsministerium,* considerable redevelopment had taken place including a new departures hall, new technical site

In a panoramic shot taken by the USAAF in June 1945, an assortment of abandoned Luftwaffe aircraft including at least four JV 44 machines are lined up close to the compass swinging base in front of the bombed out airport buildings at München-Riem.

and workshops and new electrical and optical equipment for night landing. The investment paid off and by 1932, München-Oberwiesenfeld saw 15,759 passengers use its facilities.

But by the late thirties, industrial and commercial expansion in the city of München demanded a larger more accessible aerodrome and in 1936, the *Reichsluftfahrtministerium* agreed to a project proposed by the City authorities to develop a tract of open farmland nine kilometres (5.5 miles) east of the main city, at a point one and a half kilometres (1 mile) south east of the villages of Riem and Feldkirchen, north of Haar. The RLM appointed Professor Dr.-Ing. Sagebiel, architect of the modern aerodromes at Berlin-Tempelhof and Stuttgart-Echterdingen, to design the new field to be known as München-Riem. All three aerodromes would share the same oval shaped landing ground design, with the

Ju 90s of Deutsche Lufthansa operated from München-Riem throughout the war.

longest axis running approximately east to west. Both the departure and arrival halls as well as the control tower at München were contained in one vast continuously curving structure located close to the airfield's northern perimeter, whilst to either side of this building were located various workshops and stores. The airfield itself was comprised of a well drained grass surface with gravel subsoil. The east-west axis measured 2,011 metres (2,200 yards) whilst the north-south axis spanned just over 1,500 metres (1640 yards). Two broad "starting platforms" made of concrete lay at each end of the east-west axis, each one measuring some 320 metres (350 yards).

The new "Münchener Flughafen Riem" opened officially on 1 September 1939 but Germany's attack on Poland that day delayed the transfer of many services previously running out of Oberwiesenfeld. In October of that year however, the Alpine route – Berlin-Stuttgart-Venice-Rome – was opened.

Throughout the war, München-Riem operated as both a transit airfield for a multitude of *Luftwaffe* units arriving from- or going to the east and south as well as a "hub" for the German airline, *Deutsche Lufthansa (DLH)* which, from 1941, operated direct non-stop services to Berlin, Venice, Zürich and Lyon from the airport. Later, in the winter of 1944, as a result of heavy Allied air attacks on the airfield at Stuttgart-Echterdingen, *DLH* transferred its Berlin-(Stuttgart)-Barcelona-Madrid-Lisbon service to Riem and this continued to operate right through to the cessation of hostilities in May 1945. Additionally, *DLH* maintained large engine repair workshops at Riem in which work was done for both its own machines and those of the *Luftwaffe*.

By April 1945, when JV 44 arrived at Riem, the aerodrome had been converted to accommodate and operate *Luftwaffe* personnel and aircraft. An underground fuel store had been constructed close to the largest of the two main hangars, the rear of which contained nine workshops. The second hangar was located next to the motor transport depot. Airfield personnel were quartered in an extreme western section of the sprawling semi-circular building, originally designed by Sagebiel as a hotel for passengers. Ammunition storage pens were built close the main München-Muhldorf road from which was gained access to the airfield.

Aircraft could be sheltered in up to 35 large, purpose built blast pens located off the north and south perimeter roads and for airfield defence three heavy *Flak* emplacements had been built to the south west of the field with twelve more for light *Flak* scattered to the north, east, south and west, though what condition both these and the blast pens were in by April 1945 is questionable.

More importantly, the runway could accommodate the take-off distance of 1,850 metres (2,023 yards) needed by an Me 262 with a full fuel load and underwing armament of 24 R4M 55 mm rockets.

As Galland remembers: "At München-Riem, we really had to speed things up in order to become operationally ready and it was both our firm determination as well as our passionate desire to do so. *Oberst* Steinhoff was a pillar of strength to me and he pursued preparations to become combat ready with considerable energy. The task of getting all the transport ready which would carry our crews was handled brilliantly."

In such matters, Galland and Steinhoff were assisted by several experienced *Luftwaffe* personnel. *Major* Werner Roell, an acclaimed former Stuka pilot, helped with the establishment of communications and the ground support infrastructure. *Hauptmann* Werner Gutowski, a former *Geschwaderadjutant* in Steinhoff's old wing, JG 77, in Italy, came to act as the unit's "adjutant". Arriving from Berlin, Gutowski swiftly began setting up the *Verband's* operations room in what had once been the classroom of rambling 19th century evangelist children's home in the village of Feldkirchen some three kilometres (2 miles) to

Günther Lützow talks with Oberst von Maltzahn and Oberst Hannes Trautloft in the courtyard of JV 44's operational headquarters at Feldkirchen, mid-April 1945. The Feldkirchen Children's Home located three kilometres east of München-Riem became JV 44's Gefechtsstand – operational headquarters.

WERNER GUTOWSKI

An experienced fighter pilot and staff officer, Werner Gutwoski was the perfect choice as "adjutant" for JV 44; he had flown combat missions over the English Channel with JG 52 in the summer of 1940 before taking a place on the *Geschwaderstab*. Later he had commanded a fighter training *Staffel* (3.(Erg.)/JG 52) in East Prussia before that unit was redesignated 9./JG 1. Gutowski joined JG 77 from III./JG 11 and saw service as a *Staffelkapitän* and *Geschwader-Adjutant* in Italy before being returned to the Reich in mid-1944 to take up a position on the *Stab General der Jagdflieger* where he became an adviser to Galland on matters pertaining to fighter deployment. But when Galland was removed, Gutwoski found that he had too many "differences of opinion" with Gollob and he became one of the first of Galland's former staff to be axed. Gollob sent him to JV 44 .

WERNER ROELL

Born 8.2.1914. at Ailly-sur-Noye in France, *Major* Werner Roell was a veteran *Stuka* pilot who had flown nearly 500 missions over the Balkans, Crete and Russia with St.G 77. Whilst serving in the Crimea in 1942, Roell had distinguished himself by sinking the light cruiser *Molotov*, an accomplishment which earned him the *Ritterkreuz* in May 1943 after having flown 440 sorties against the enemy. 1944 saw him leave Russia for a posting as *Inspektionschef* of the *Luftkriegsschule* Bug auf Rügen where he lectured on dive-bombing tactics before being transferred again, late that year, to the staff of the jet aircraft "plenipotentiary" *Generalmajor* Josef Kammhuber. Following Galland's visit to him in March, Kammhuber had decided to send Roell to München in order to begin preparing the airfield for the arrival of JV 44 . As Roell remembers: "Having been posted onto Kammhuber's staff, I became one of a team of officers who were representatives of the *General-major*. We were sent to all the different jet units to ensure that there was sufficient co-operation at unit level – that there was commitment at a time when the war situation had become extremely critical. For my part, I was sent to München-Riem where I was placed in charge of organising and helping with communications and the ground infrastructure specifically for Galland's fast new jet fighters, although at that time, I did not know Galland personally. We had our hands full from the start since there were regular bombing raids against Riem airfield and the craters had to be flattened out each time..."

HERBERT KAISER

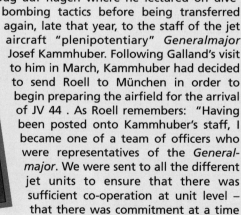

Born 16.3.1916 at Jessen, Saxony, Herbert Kaiser was a veteran NCO pilot with combat experience gained from nearly 1,000 missions flown on virtually every front and whose operational career had commenced in 1938 when he flew under the command of his young *Staffelkapitän*, Johannes Steinhoff in 2./JG 132 at Jever. From there he spent a brief time flying Bf 109 B's with *Trägergruppe* 186 which was being prepared as a carrier based fighter group in readiness for the completion of the *Kriegsmarine's* aircraft carrier, the *Graf Zeppelin*. However, when this project was scrapped in 1939, the *Gruppe* was integrated into III./JG 77 with which Kaiser flew successively in Poland, the West in 1940, Rumania, Greece and Russia. In October 1942, III./JG 77 was moved to North Africa where he shot down five aircraft (P-40s and Spitfires) but was severely wounded. A short spell as a fighter instructor in the south of France followed in January 1943 as well as the award of the *Ritterkreuz* in recognition of his 53rd victory, but Kaiser was soon reunited with III./JG 77 for the defence of Sardinia and Italy, where he shot down another four enemy machines. In January 1944, Kaiser was transferred yet again, when he received orders to join III./JG 1. He fought in Normandy and on 6 August, his Bf 109 was attacked over Paris by a Spitfire. Though Kaiser managed to bail out of his burning fighter, his right leg became entangled in his parachute and he collided with the rudder. Suffering from multiple fractures to the right thigh, he was hospitalised in France and Germany until the end of February 1945 when he was transferred to Bad Wiessee to await a posting. He had scored 68 victories but as a result of his wounds, flying an aircraft such as the Me 262 with JV 44 was to prove impossible. Instead he would assist in the unit's ground control.

the east of the airfield. From one of the great windowless walls hung a large blackboard with a box for sponge and sticks of chalk, whilst from another hung a vast glass panel beneath which was a detailed operations map of southern Germany and Austria The surface of the glass was divided into a grid of squares around the cities of München, Augsburg, Regensburg and Nürnberg, each one labelled in red crayon. The rest of the building was given over to the unit's stores, vehicles and as accommodation for some of its key personnel.

Gutowski was assisted in his task by another former JG 77 pilot, *Ritterkreuzträger* and acquaintance of Steinhoff's, *Fahnenjunker-Oberfeldwebel* Herbert Kaiser whom Galland and Steinhoff had coaxed out of the *"Jagdfliegerheim"* – a convalescence centre for wounded and mentally strained fighter pilots known as *"Haus Florida"* at Bad Wiessee, a well known spa resort on the shores the Tegernsee. Together with Gutowski, Kaiser would direct JV 44's operations from the ground at both the Feldkirchen operations centre and Riem itself, Kaiser engaged in the actual tactical direction of the jets in the air, whilst Gutowski handled liaison with the various command staffs and organisations as well as making sure that the ground support organisation at Riem was functioning efficiently.

Galland quartered himself in a nearby forester's lodge, whilst his pilots and ground crews billeted themselves with various families living in and around the villages of Feldkirchen, Salmsdorf and Haar.

SIX

The men of the 34th Squadron, 17th BG line up in front of one of the unit's Marauders at Barksdale Field near Shreveport, Louisiana, 8 August 1942. At this time, the unit was being strengthened almost daily with the arrival of new personnel and Barksdale – known fondly as the 'Country Club of the Air Corps' – offered good accommodation, a Post Exchange, the amenities of a city close at hand and, most importantly, good food!

Toujours Au Danger – Ever Into Danger
THE 17th BOMBARDMENT GROUP

Having won undying fame by flying B-25 Mitchells from the deck of the carrier Hornet to bomb Tokyo in April 1942, the 17th Bombardment Group (Light) henceforth changed tack. Despite the fact that it had also been the first AAF unit to operate the B-25, the powers that be decreed that the 17th exchange its Mitchells for Marauders. It consequently became a B-26 unit 'for the duration'. and comprised the 34th, 37th (previously the 73rd), 95th and 432nd (previously the 89th) Bomb Squadrons.

Able to trace its lineage back to combat in the First World War, the 17th Bombardment Group was the oldest medium bomber unit in the Army Air Forces and had been activated as the 17th Pursuit Group in July 1931 at March Field, Riverside, California. It became an Attack Group in 1936 and a Bombardment Group in 1939. Although its official badge and motto was not approved until 1934, it became proud of its subsequent unofficial nickname, *'Daddy of Them All'*, the origins of which lay in the unit's service in Sardinina when a member of the group painted a rather provocative sign. The sign was located at the entrance to Poretta airfield and served as reference to the fact that the 17th was divided time after time to form the nucleus of new groups. This infuriated men from other groups based on the island!

In November 1942 aircrews of the 17th, led by Group CO Lt Col C.D. Sluman, flew fifty-seven new B-26B-1s and B-2s east across the South Atlantic ferry route, via the Caribbean, Brazil and Ascension Island, bound for North Africa. The first crews arrived at Accra in late November and proceeded to their operational airfield at Telergma, Algeria.

The 17th Bomb Group became part of the Twelfth Air Force, a very welcome backup to the 319th, the original Marauder group in the Mediterranean Theatre of Operations, which had had some very rough early missions. In common with other units of the Twelfth, the 17th adopted tail numbers for aircraft ('plane in squadron') identification, plus red as a group colour. These distinctive markings were in direct contrast to the RAF-style fuselage code letters and tail markings used by the Ninth Air Force based in the UK and later on the European mainland.

Flying the 'short wing' B-26Bs, the 17th flew its first combat mission on 30 December, a six-ship strike on Gabes airfield in southern Tunisia of which five machines were from the 34th Squadron. Flak and fighters reacted to put holes in five aircraft and cause two B-26s to crash-land on return although none were lost. The Gabes defences claimed the first 17th Group B-26 shot down during a return raid on 31 December when fire from a Bf 109 exploded one machine from the 432nd Squadron. Crews thereafter proceeded to build up experience in a difficult theatre of war. There were too few aircraft for the two groups to constitute a strong medium bomber force and each was handed a variety of targets including anti-shipping missions. Other targets were at Sfax, La Hencha and Sousse, the latter's marshalling yards being a prime target as they were well utilised by the Germans.

In conformity with original AAF doctrine for the Marauder, the 319th Group had begun operations with low level target approaches, whilst the 17th adopted both low and medium altitude (between 7,000 (2,133 m) and 10,000 (3,048 m) feet in the MTO), the latter proving to be marginally safer. All Marauder crews began an intensive period of combat 're-evaluation' to use a range of new tactics designed to increase mission effectiveness and minimise losses to ground fire.

The 17th had not enjoyed an outstanding combat debut, having lost 12 aircraft in 16 missions during January 1943. Combat attrition was partly made up by aircraft passed on by the 319th BG which had had an even rougher entry to combat. The latter group was stood down for a rest in February, leaving the 17th as the only Marauder group in the MTO. Shortly before that, on 7 February, the unit had flown a successful twenty ship mission to Elmas aerodrome in Sardinia during which, according to the mission report, the " ... complete area was covered by bombs, ... fires started in fuel dump, hangar and plane areas. Ammunition dump believed to have been destroyed." A number of Bf 109 fighters and Ju 52 transports were also destroyed. By this time the 320th Group had arrived in the theatre, as had three groups of B-25s. With a fourth Mitchell unit due to arrive in March, the MTO medium/attack bomber force which included the A-20s of the 47th Bomb Wing, was poised to support the RAF in finishing German and Italian military ambitions in North Africa.

Support missions were flown by the 17th Group to prevent the Germans exploiting the American disaster at Kasserine, a task that had been achieved by 24 February. El Aouina airfield, which harboured numerous Luftwaffe transport aircraft, was parafragged by the 17th's Marauders on the 24th. The cost was three B-26s shot down by flak.

Accidents did, inevitably, happen: B-26B-10 (S/N 41-18320) of the 432nd Squadron, 17th BG photographed at Djedeida, Tunisia on 26 September 1943, having bellied-in during landing. The aircraft had served with the squadron since May. A little later the same day, the first rains came since the 17th had arrived in Tunisia in June.

On 1 March an attack on rail and road bridges at La Hencha cost two aircraft but the important junction was destroyed by 500 lb bombs. Thereafter airfields, supply lines and shipping targets occupied the men of the 17th, who ran the full gauntlet of flak and enemy fighters. Gabes, which held less than fond memories for the crews, was removed from the target list when Allied troops captured it on 29 March. Roads, railways and Axis airfields on the Cape Bon peninsula now occupied the 17th as the Allies continued to make significant gains on the ground. Sfax fell on 10 April and within days the Axis armies had been pushed into north east Tunisia, the US and British armies from the west having linked up with Montgomery's Eighth Army driving up from the south.

With the 320th back in the line and flying its first mission on 22 April, the 17th finally had some support and the two Marauder groups continued pressurising Tunisian targets, airfields becoming something of a 17th Group speciality. April however was modest in terms of missions, with only six flown but by the end of the month, the total combat record to date had risen to 53 missions, 595 tons of bombs dropped and eighteen crews lost. Thirty-four B-26s had been lost to strength since operations began.

The 17th moved to a new Algerian base on 10 May. It headed north east to Sedrata, north of Montesquieu. By then the 17th had received the more capable B-26B-10, the 'big wing' Marauder with significantly boosted performance. Crews needed all the help they could get to operate safely from Sedrata, which had been built by Army engineers and was somewhat lacking in facilities – but the worst aspect from the viewpoint of aircrews, was the runway surface. Peppered with small stones, it was constantly overlaid with sand and dust which coated engine parts and made every landing and take off quite hazardous. The 6,000 ft (1,828 m) runway was reassuringly long although the land fell way from the strip on three sides – in short, Sedrata was not voted the place for a long stay by the 17th!

William D. Baird, a former gunner with the 34th Squadron remembers: "Watching a take-off from Sedrata was rather

Taken at Telergma, Algeria in early 1943, the smoking remains of a B-26 of the 319th BG with which the 17th shared facilities, lie off the runway shortly after dawn. The luckless Marauder had been rammed and set on fire by a P-38 Lightning fighter-bomber which had crashed on take-off. A 500 lb bomb carried by the Lightning exploded.

spectacular. The planes would drop out of sight at the end of the runway. then, several minutes later, they would reappear far out over the valley and already forming up. Once in a while, if a take-off was aborted too late, the plane would skid to the end of the runway and disappear down the slope at the end. One good thing – an abortion didn't delay the take-off of the next plane!"

Having materially helped drive the Axis out of Tunisia the 17th participated in the reduction of Pantelleria. Starting on 18 May, the group pounded the island's defences under Operation Corkscrew. Sicilian and Sardinian targets were also attacked during this period and on the 21st, the war diary of the 34th Squadron recorded: "... With the utmost determination we again went out after Decimomannu Airdrome, this time with the 34th out in front. The results were good and further bombing of this target will not be necessary for some time." Four days later, Col C. Ross Greening took over command.

Becoming part of the provisional 2686th Bomb Wing in May, the 17th joined with the 319th and 320th plus the P-40s of the 325th Fighter Group to operate in combined strength, the first mission as a wing taking place on 6 June. More bombs fell on Pantelleria from the bays of 17th Group Marauders before the garrison surrendered on the 11th. With hardly a pause, the group flew missions to targets in Sicily in preparation for the Allied invasion codenamed Husky.

Airfields nearer to their targets were available in Tunisia and on 24 June the 17th moved 100 miles (161 km) north east to Djedeida. That proximity the Americans quickly realised, meant civilisation – trees, water and pyramid tents. The latter came courtesy of the AAF but they vastly improved the living conditions of group personnel.

It was 3 July before the group mounted its first sorties from the new base; Millis landing ground in Sicily was the target and one B-26 failed to return. German fighters usually reacted vigorously to any attacks on their airfields and the Marauder force sometimes had its work cut out to minimise losses to this cause. When Allied troops went ashore on 10 July the B-26s flew a large scale mission, primarily to help isolate the battlefield. To keep the *Luftwaffe* on the ground the group put thirty-seven B-26s over Trapani/Milo airfield on the 11th. Flak and fighters in abundance could not prevent American high explosive falling on aircraft and barracks and despite the presence of German interceptors, no Marauders were shot down. Holed badly, two aircraft of the 34th Squadron reached base fit only to be scrapped, and three men were fatally wounded out of the seventeen crewmen hit by flying steel during the action.

With Allied fighters based in Sicily the mediums could be sent further afield, to targets in Italy. On a raid on 17 July the group lost Col Greening. Co-piloting a Marauder leading a strike on Naples for the first time, Greening apparently bailed out with the rest of the crew before his crippled B-26 crashed on the lower slopes of Mount Vesuvius. The new group CO from 18 July was Lt Col Robert A. Zaizer who took over in time for the unit's 100th mission, on 27 July.

The losses of earlier months were mercifully absent in August, the group completing fifteen missions with all aircraft returning. Not that things were dull; gunners were credited with destroying thirteen enemy aircraft. By the end of the month the provisional 2686th Wing had become the 42nd Bombardment Wing (Medium).

Military targets for the 17th now included those in Florence, Venice and Rome, which required pinpoint accuracy to avoid peripheral bomb damage to priceless museums and relics. More mundane was the pounding of roads, railways, bridges and waterways to prevent as many German troops as possible escaping

Two pictures showing B-26C-15 (S/N 41-35177) Uden-Uden's Oil Burner *a well-known and battle-scarred ship of of the 34th Squadron, 17th BG in 1943 and also a supreme example of the Marauder's toughness. The aircraft took a direct flak hit in the left-hand engine whilst commencing a bomb run on the Roccasecca River Bridge in Italy on 30 December 1943. Despite a serious reduction in power and loss of manoueverability, the pilot, 2nd Lt Robert R. Bennett of Toledo, Ohio, managed to keep the aircraft on course, drop his bombs on the target and fly for a further two hours on one engine over water and through bad weather to return. For his "consummate mastery of the aircraft, his steadfast devotion to duty and his consistent calm efficiency in the face of concentrated AA fire", Bennett was awarded the Distinguished Flying Cross. T./Sgt Al Hurt, the crew chief responsible for the aircraft, who was also aboard on that mission, is seen standing in front of his charge. The* Oil Burner's *luck held until 8 June 1944 when it was taken off strength to become a "war weary".*

A trio of Marauders from the 17th BG showing off various examples of nose art. Top: B-26C-45 (S/N 42-107539) SAN ANTONIO ROSE of the 95th Squadron. Probably photographed whilst at Poretta, Corsica, this aircraft was taken on strength in mid-October 1944 and was still flying at the end of the war. Centre: Flamboyantly painted yet evidently battle-tested B-26C-10 (S/N 41-34892) MODERN DESIGN was a "hand-me-down" aircraft from the Ninth Air Force given to the 34th Squadron, 17th BG in late 1944 whilst at Rouvres en Plaine. The ship survived the war intact. Bottom: Typically rugged and showing signs of heavy usage, this is B-26C-45 (S/N 42-107784) of 432nd Squadron, RITA B – BLOOMFIELD, N.J.. This ship was taken on to the 17th BG's strength on 19 January 1945 at Rouvres en Plaine, but was lost over Germany on 26 April 1945, possibly as a result of fighter attack.

from Sicily with sufficient war materiel to continue the fight. This could not realistically be achieved by air power, but enemy strength was nevertheless reduced by the mediums' efforts.

With early production models giving way to improved B-26B, F and G models, combat in the MTO continued to provide ample evidence that the Marauder was rugged enough to withstand the enemy's worst. A number of 17th Group aircraft, complete with impressive bomb logs, went home for war bond tours to emphasise the point. All B-26 bases had witnessed mission returnees torn by numerous flak hits and flying without far larger chunks of airframe than anyone had thought possible. The 17th gained a new CO on 14 September when Maj Donald J. Gilbert took over from Col Zaizer but the 'view from above' was not so positive. On 6 October the group was stood down, ostensibly for R & R and training but there were rumours that performance, particularly in bombing accuracy, needed significant improvement. All squadron COs were also changed, with a view to injecting a new impetus into the 17th and an intensive programme of formation flying, practice bombing and gunnery was conducted throughout the month. The 17th was back in the line by the 30th.

Another base change saw the 17th's Marauders flying from Villacidro in Sardinia from 8 December – after the airfield's most dangerous bomb craters, some made by the group itself, had been filled in. Terrible weather had seen many missions from Djedieda scrubbed or completed with disappointing results. Winter also brought rain – far too much of it. Airfield dispersals flooded and bombers had to take it mighty easy during taxiing and take off. The diarist of the 34th Squadron recorded for the 15th December: "... No mission today. Runway is peeelenty wet!" – and again on the 16th: " ...The men are pretty well settled in their bivouacs and are chewing their nails and waiting for the weather to clear and the field to dry up so they can again send their greetings to *Der Führer.*" Though mission effectiveness may have suffered a little, the 17th, with new skills, soon hit such targets as Grosseto and Cassino.

Railways and bridges began to figure more prominently and these small, difficult targets would continue to attract a torrent of Allied bombs, so vital were they to German military operations in Italy. Such targets were hit non-stop by the 17th in the eight-day period 23 – 30 December, with maximum effort and few mechanical difficulties.

January was marshalling yards, some bridges and leaflet drops. "Nickelling", the USAAF term for 'paper raids' involved dropping pamphlets over a wide area. Soon more serious work was involved. On 22 January Operation Shingle, the landings at Anzio, went ahead. Support by the Marauder force was but part of a massive Allied air effort to ensure the troops on the ground secured a bridgehead and to ward off *Luftwaffe* attacks aimed to ensure they would fail. The 17th flew 24 missions during the month. Cassino absorbed many bombs despite few positive signs of German occupancy of the monastery. Rubble piled up and the Fifth Army still could not take the massive natural barrier of Monastery Hill. Aerial bombing soon became counter-productive. Little movement was made as the enemy made good use of the available cover, thoughtfully provided by Allied aircraft. And to cap it all the Germans then counter-attacked at Anzio. Marauder crews were called upon to drop frags and demolition bombs from low level, right in front of Allied troop positions. This they did on two occasions.

February saw the first 'natural metal' B-26s flying missions with the 17th. Although they stuck out 'like sore thumbs' the

A well-known but nevertheless dramatic picture depicting a 95th Squadron Marauder seconds after being hit by Flak in the starboard engine over Toulon in August 1944. The blades of the shot-away engine are still spinning and the wing fuel tanks have ignited. The aircraft crashed into the city. There were two survivors. The diarist of the 34th Squadron recorded: "The thorn in our sides, those hot gun positions near Toulon harbor... one of the hottest the 17th has tackled in a long time..."

group seemed not to apply field camouflage as other units did, probably because unit commanders felt it didn't matter that much or indeed that paint in the necessary quantities was simply as scarce as everything else in the MTO at that time! There were signs of a general improvement, however.

The spring of 1944 saw the red-tailed Marauders of the AAF's oldest bomb group over Rome, Florence, Vezzano and Cassino town. MAAF's massive strike reduced the town to rubble on the 15th, concurrent with the far-reaching Strangle campaign against German transportation routes – all of them, by whatever means, were to be hit again and again until the enemy defence lines were broken. In time, it would be done.

A turnaround in fortunes now brought the 17th the accolade of best bombing record in the 42nd Wing, many of its efforts

being against those infernal bridges. Spanning crossing points relatively few Italians, much less Americans, had ever heard of, they took on a brief importance during the spring and summer of 1944. Airmen were not for understandable reasons, always convinced that their efforts were assisting the army troops fighting a world away from their own. They could not see the Germans forced to improvise to get a few pounds of supplies to the front when many tons were needed or those small breaches in the line when the enemy ran out of everything and gave up half mile of ground. But small gains would all add up, eventually – and air power was the key to success.

Strangle ended on 11 May to give way to Diadem. Little changed for the Marauder crews; mediums were required to carry on pounding rail and road links, troop concentrations and strong points. German radar-directed guns were given a man-made snowstorm in the form of 'Chaff' on 23 May when the 17th's aircraft dropped the bundles of tin foil for the first time. Weather conditions in Italy continued to hamper operations and the bombers were stood down, sometimes for days on end.

Rome fell on 5 June 1944 – and the event was immediately overshadowed by the landings in Normandy the following day. The war in Italy went on. Diadem finished on 22 June with the Germans eighty miles north of the Eternal City. On the 29th the 17th Group flew its 300th mission, to ammunition dumps at La Spezia. Then came news that a new operation, Dragoon, the invasion of southern France, would require the services of the 17th. Night mission training commenced with the squadrons meanwhile achieving an admirable 74% in bombing accuracy for the month of June. 'Mallory' sorties helped knock out rail bridges, six of them spanning the River Po, in northern Italy. This partly prevented the Germans getting supplies from Austria and elsewhere through the Brenner Pass, Mallory Major which

Rouvres en Plaine airfield, home to the 17th BG from November 1944 to June 1945. Despite the bleak winter landscape of January 1945, Dijon the nearby capital of Burgundy apparently offered the men of the 17th – "... theatres, clubs, bars, sightseeing and women in abundance." Note the bomb craters and approximately 80 aircraft parked around the damaged airfield buildings.

followed on 12 July, concentrating on the Po bridges. All 22 of them were hit in six days of medium bombing by B-26s and B-25s.

Col R. O. Harrell succeeded Col Gilbert as CO on 21 July 1944. The day before, the 17th Group commander had gone down in a Marauder over the Po Valley after an attack on Ostiglia rail bridge. It had been Gilbert's 94th mission. Only three other aircraft was lost by the group in 28 missions during the month of July.

Dragoon became a reality in August. The 17th bombed Levens road bridge in southern France on the 2nd, and finally brought it down with two more raids up to the 4th. Italian airfields and bridges occupied the group for the next few days and on the 11th the 17th's aircraft were over Hyères on the Riviera coast. Guns near St Tropez and at Toulon were hit on the 12th and 13th respectively, with St Tropez again on the 14th. There was little enemy opposition to *Dragoon* and on 15 August, the invasion force went ashore. The B-26s of the 17th smothered German gun positions around Hyères with fragmentation bombs. A record 11 missions were flown by the group, 89 sorties in all without loss.

The 17th kept up the pressure on the enemy gun positions, Chaff as well as bombs successfully neutralising the amount of fire

Captured on film by a photographer/gunner in a neighbouring aircraft, B-26C-45 (s/n 41-07798) GORGEOUS BETTY (aircraft nearest camera) and another unidentified Marauder of the 95th Squadron, 17th BG both wearing a virtually all-over natural metal finish, pass over another burning target moments after bomb release, Germany, 1945. GORGEOUS BETTY survived the war having notched up ninety missions.

able to reach the bomber formations. But the Toulon guns would be remembered by participants as one of the toughest targets they had ever attacked. As the B-26s were still operating from Sardinia the rapid advance of Allied forces through southern France soon put potential targets out of range. The mediums returned to their old hunting ground in Italy. More records were made as the group flew almost daily, the aircraft and personnel loss rate being kept low although the period was not known for its milk runs. Such was the accuracy achieved by the mediums that bombers could

obliterate enemy positions only a few hundred yards from Allied soldiers. During September, without any noticeable change of pace, the 17th was alerted to again move base, this time to Corsica.

Poretta was the 17th's new home from 22 September. Small and surfaced with PSP, this Corsican base required the Marauders to be lightened in order to get off safely in the 6,000 feet of available runway. Targets remained those in northern Italy, the 17th revisiting the Po Valley bridges during this period. Crews found few permanent spans in use but the Germans had created temporary crossings. These were duly bombed but they usually had heavy flak defences and the group was obliged to continue to count the cost in wounded men and patched aircraft.

Marauders shot down on operations or totally lost to group strength to all causes remained in low, single figures. But personnel casualties on some 'rough missions' could be surprisingly high and despite the fact that if seven men out of seventy in a ten-strong B-26 force meant that only a (low) ten per cent had been wounded, at squadron or group level, that price was always reckoned to be too high.

That November the 17th became part of the 1st Tactical Air Force, in company with the 320th Group and French B-26 units. More 319th aircraft were passed to the 17th when the former re-equipped with Mitchells and the 1st TAC moved from Corsica to bases in the south of France, Rouvres-en-Plaine near Dijon in the case of the 17th. It was to remain there until the cessation of hostilities.

As the pincers closed on Germany 1st TAC Marauders shared missions with their Ninth Air Force colleagues. Attacking an increasingly small area of territory still held by the Germans, the medium bombers of three AAF tactical air forces – 1st TAC, Ninth and Twelfth Bomber Commands – could bring a massive weight of firepower on what remained of the Third Reich. The 17th Group's final missions were directed by its last wartime commander Col Wallace C. Barrett, who took over on 20 March. That the 17th Bomb Group crews were exposed to exactly the same dangers as other units which had operated in Europe was occasionally shown by increasing attention from the *Luftwaffe* fighter force. Such interceptions culminated for the 17th in the Me 262 attacks by JV 44 in the spring of 1945.

While Marauder losses to jets were mercifully low, for the few eye witnesses, what these 'new generation' fighters could do to conventional medium bombers with advanced weapons, had a sobering effect. It made crews realise, however fierce their loyalty to the B-26, that the days of piston-engined bombers were suddenly numbered.

The 17th flew 598 missions during the Second World War, the last on 1 May 1945 when the B-26s used Shoran – short range radar and navigation – equipment to place their bombs accurately on the German garrison holding out on the Ile d'Oleron, an island off Bordeaux. Within a week the Germans had capitulated and the war in Europe was finally over.

In June 1945 the 17th occupied Hörsching in Austria before moving to France in the autumn, en route for the USA. The move was completed by late November, inactivation taking place on the 26th.

SEVEN

Vincamus Sine Timoris – Without Fear We Conquer
THE 323rd BOMBARDMENT GROUP

As the second of the original four Army Air Force groups to fly the Marauder in Europe, the 323rd was activated on 19 June 1942 at Columbia Army Air Base, South Carolina before firstly moving to MacDill Field, Florida followed by a return to South Carolina in October 1942 to the Myrtle Beach Bombing and Gunnery Range airfield. Its component squadrons, the 453rd, 454th, 455th and 456th, trained with B-26s for almost a year – including a stint at Baer Field, Fort Wayne, Indiana where there were frustrating delays whilst the unit's Marauders were undergoing modification in New York – before making a phased move to England between April and June 1943, on assignment to the Eighth Air Force. Making its new home at Earls Colne in Essex, the 323rd, under the command of former West Pointer, Col Herbert B. Thatcher, made its combat debut on 16 July. Led by Col Thatcher, the group sent sixteen B-26s to bomb Abbeville marshalling yards.

Given that Allied air war policy, as defined at the January 1943 Casablanca conference, was first and foremost the destruction of the *Luftwaffe*, this target was something of a mystery to the 323rd crews. They all knew the fate of the 322nd Group on its first mission earlier in the year so everyone assumed that a target hopefully offering low-key German reaction would be less costly. Nevertheless, many participants were sceptical that they would survive this 'baptism of fire' in an aircraft that had garnered a less than enviable reputation.

They needn't have worried. Abbeville's close proximity to the French coast would mean minimum time over enemy territory and the target run-in would be brief. And the presence of 18 squadrons of Spitfires gave as much reassurance of good protection as most bomber men needed. Bombs were dropped from 11,500 ft (3,505 m) , the Marauders taking 20-25 seconds to complete their runs over the target at an indicated airspeed of 190 mph. German reaction was indicated by flak bursts – and fighters – although the escort kept German interceptors well away from the bombers. There were no B-26 losses although ten aircraft were damaged and one man was wounded.

Bad weather forced a break in operations until 25 July when the group was cleared to hit the coke ovens at Ghent with 18 aircraft. Attacks on airfields plus one more to destroy coke ovens, occupied the 323rd's initial month in combat, the first aircraft loss being gratifyingly deferred until the tenth mission, to Poix aerodrome on the 31st during which both heavy flak and Fw 190s were encountered. Overall, the bombing results had been satisfactory.

With the successful combat debut of a second B-26 group, the small medium bomber force of Eighth Air Support Command began developing its combat tactics. Medium altitude bombing appeared to achieve good results and so was adopted as standard procedure. Evasive action during the target run-in also became an integral part of Marauder missions, this to confuse the aim of the German *Flak* gunners.

Combat naturally brought incidents and these included individual crews having to fly severely damaged ships back to base which really tested the resilience of the Marauder. A case in point occurred on 2 August, when the 323rd despatched 31 B-26s to hit the *Luftwaffe* airfield at Merville. Pushing on through a lethal curtain of *Flak* which damaged several machines, the bombers made it to the target where Lt. James Davis aircraft, *Miss Emily*, took a direct hit in the cockpit which tore huge holes in the side of the aircraft and sent it into a spin. Despite extensive damage to both aircraft and crew, Davis was able to return safely to base. Other ships came back on one engine and on occasion, returned home with a full bomb load. Neither feat had previously been thought possible by the anti-B-26 lobby, so crews of the 323rd thus helped reinforce the positive view that Marauders would remain an integral part of the Allied air arsenal.

Marauder bombing results improved steadily in the intervening summer and autumn months. The 323rd could regularly despatch 36 aircraft and put 54 on the line for a 'maximum effort', the first of which took place on 9 September. The group actually struck three briefed targets that day, one of them being coastal defence guns. As part of Operation Starkey, the rehearsal for Overlord the following year, such strikes indicated how the battle order for the Allied air forces on D-Day would eventually look.

So encouraging were the bombing figures for the B-26 that when the tactical US Ninth Air Force was formed in the UK on 16 October 1943 it was more or less built around the four original groups of Marauders assigned to the Eighth Air Force. Formed to ultimately support Allied armies in the field when Overlord was a reality, the Ninth had much hard flying ahead of it.

The 323rd was affected by the weather again in October, only seven missions being possible during the month. November saw some improvement, with twelve flown, including two maximum efforts of 54 aircraft each. Targets included the first 'Noballs' and aerodromes at Tricqeville, Montdidier and St Omer. On the 5th, the location for the Marauders' bombs was Mimoyecques. Unknown to the crews at the time, this was the site for the so-called V-3, long range guns built into subterranean tunnels and designed to bombard London. This and subsequent air raids prevented the weapon from ever being used.

During November Col Wilson R. Wood, former commander of the 454th Squadron, took over the 323rd and during the pre-invasion phase the group was briefed to attack so many Noball sites in France that it adopted the nickname 'Wood's Rocket Raiders'. Wilson Wood was to continue at the helm of the 'white tails' until early in 1945.

The German flying bomb launch infrastructure was severely damaged by operations conducted by the Marauders of the 323rd BG.

There was some concern that Noball targets were absorbing so much of the Marauder groups' time that other important targets were being neglected. The trouble was that nobody knew how effective Crossbow operations were – only that it was vital to strangle the flying bomb offensive before it started. Consequently the 323rd and other B-26 units continued to bomb Noballs when the weather permitted. As an example of the effort expended, every target for the white tails in January 1944 was a Noball. Analysis of the group's mission log for February reveals that of 36 assigned targets, 29 were "Noballs". In 20 missions the 323rd despatched an average of eighteen aircraft per target, the number rising to thirty-seven B-26s for a double mission (two sites) to La Glacerie on the 7th.

Major-General John O. Moench, USAF, (ret) was a pilot with the 323rd BG at this time. He remembers: "The V-1 sites were pretty damned well-defended – but that depended on how you count and how black your sky became. A dozen 88 mm guns was not unusual – sometimes a lot more. They were not like the Ruhr numbers we had to fly, but often the sites were located in proximity to some heavily defended targets, the fire of which could not be avoided going in or coming out."

The group's 100th mission milestone was reached in February which saw 36 missions flown, positive indication of how the pace was hotting up. In March the V3 site was again hit by the 323rd and the group rounded out the month with a satisfying 'revenge' mission to Ijmuiden on the 26th. Fifty-four Earls Colne Marauders helped make up a 380-strong B-26 force otherwise composed of aircraft from the 322nd and 394th Groups, which together with some A-20s, dropped over 700 tons on the notorious power station complex.

Roads and marshalling yards were again featuring in the 323rd's mission briefings by late March, the return to more typical fare of Ninth Air Force B-26 groups confirming the successful conclusion of the anti-V-1 offensive. German rail transport too had taken a beating from medium bomber strikes; from being in a position to run 100 supply trains a day through

France in April, the interdiction campaign had by the end of May reduced this to a meagre 20. There was no way that this was enough. But maintaining such pressure presented the American groups with their own problems – they began to run seriously short of 2,000 lb (907 kg) bombs, the ideal 'bridge breakers'.

A quartet of pre-D-Day missions was laid on. Then the big day dawned – 6 June 1944 – and the 323rd was briefed for another four missions within that historic 24 hours. Three of these were to pound beach defences and the last was to hit a rail junction at Caen. Immediately afterwards, the white tails added the weight of their bombs to assist Allied troops attempting to break out of the German-fortified town of St Lô.

There followed a period 'in the doldrums' as the 323rd was not called upon to fly another mission for the first seventeen days of July. Weather was again the main cause of the stand-down which left crews frustrated, a fact compounded by frequent missions (night as well as day) being scheduled and then scrubbed. Low cloud and rain persisted and even training flights, which served to break the monotony, could not be safely laid on. During this period one crew took off nine times and immediately 'went on instruments' eight times!

The B-26s of the 323rd BG became recognised as valued specialists at bombing "Noball" sites and aerodromes in north west France during the first half of 1944, which were regarded as "pretty damned well-defended". Here, white tailed Marauders of the 456th Bomb Squadron release their bomb loads on another target.

Finally the weather cleared enough for the 323rd to fly its next combat mission on 18 July. This was a 36-ship support effort to help break the German resistance at Caen, two boxes of eighteen aircraft each box releasing a total of 550 tons of bombs immediately east of the city known as the Demouville Defended Area in USAAF nomenclature.

The concentration and indeed weight of high explosive dropped by Allied aircraft on Caen had no precedent and it was at the time the greatest concentration of bombing in history. Despite that fact the Germans subbornly held out, defying Dempsey's British Second Army to take the city.

The 323rd was again hampered by the weather and only on the 22nd was a successful mission possible. Even this entailed PPF bombing through 10/10th cloud on pathfinder signal – but at least the *Luftwaffe* did not appear, the inclement conditions effecting single-engined fighter operations even more than those of medium bombers.

With considerable persuasion from the air, the Germans were slowly pushed back. Operation Cobra, marred by a number of 'short' bombings which killed friendly troops, nevertheless succeeded in shattering organised resistance at Caen. By early August Patton's Third Army was racing headlong through France, the Americans having broken the German defence at St Lô, with the British Second Army preparing to finally take Caen, a slow process. Overhead the Ninth was continuing to smash bridges to wreck any organised enemy retreat. The 323rd had hit the Nay railway bridge north of Nantes on 24 July and the Mantes-Gassicourt spans on the 25th.

That the bridges were vital to the Germans was shown by the *Flak* reaction which usually succeeded in reaching the mediums' altitude and wounding crewmen even if on a good day it did not kill anyone or shoot a single bomber down. It had long been rare for the B-26s to return home without damage, however minor.

By August the 323rd was preparing to move from England to A-26 Lessay in France. This initial move took place on the 26 August and within the month the group was travelling again to A-40 Chartres, on 21 September. The first B-26 night missions were flown from these forward French airfields during August, primarily to neutralise enemy batteries around the port of St Malo. Finding few problems in flying the B-26 on unfamiliar night operations, the group continued these during the month to knock out German fuel and ammunition dumps.

In September the 323rd was briefed to attack enemy positions holding up the capture of the important naval base at Brest. Despite being briefed four times in three days for this mission with it being scrubbed as many times, when the Marauders were able to go to work, the results were good. On one day the Group dropped 70 tons of bombs on the Brest strong points. During the latter part of that month, the white-tailed Marauders shifted their combat area to eastern France where targets were pounded in support of Allied troops advancing on the Siegfried Line fortifications.

When the Battle of the Bulge broke on the Western Front in December 1944, the 323rd attacked part of the German transportation network used to bring reinforcements into the Ardennes region, so vitally important to von Runstedt's Panzer offensive. The group won a Distinguished Unit Citation for operations during the week of 24-27 December, one of the most critical periods of the German 'eleventh hour' surprise attack. Rail bridges and enemy strong points around Nonnweiler, St.Vith and Houffalize were hit. These were maximum effort strikes which, with the clear weather, were conducted in the face of heavy flak and many aircraft suffered damage. By the 27th, many of the 323rd's crews had flown five missions over the course of four or five days.

With the 'Bulge' finally straightened and the front stabilised, the Allied drive into Germany gained a new momentum. For its part the 323rd flew interdiction missions into the Ruhr and bombed a variety of communications targets. From 14 February the white tails group was commanded by Col Rollin M. Winingham, formerly of the 397th Bomb Group.

To support the last Allied air offensive in Europe the 323rd had moved to A-69 Laon/Athies and thence to A-83 Denain/Prouvy, the latter base being occupied on 9 February 1945. The final combat sorties were flown from Denain on 25 April and by the German surrender, the group had flown a grand total of 318 missions. The 323rd was based at R-77 Gablingen, Germany from 15 May.

A B-26 (S/N 43-34118) of the 455th Squadron, 323rd BG waits on its pierced steel planking dispersal, probably in France, 1944. Such planking allowed Engineer Aviation Battalions to construct useable advanced airfields in less than two weeks.

EIGHT

B-26B 7I-F (s/n 295903) HARD TO GET *makes its bomb run against a target in France, 1944.*

We Win or Die

THE 344ᵗʰ BOMBARDMENT GROUP

Activated at MacDill Field, Florida on 8 September 1942 as a B-26 replacement training unit, the 344th Bomb Group, comprising the 494th, 495th, 496th and 497th Bomb Squadrons, was awarded the title "The Hottest Outfit to Ever Leave MacDill Field" as a result of the drive and enthusiasm shown by the unit during its initial training. In July 1943, the 55th Bomb Wing further commended the group in noting a high standard of devotion to duty, maintenance and engineering as well as a zero flying accident rate for nearly five months. After a year spent at Lakeland, Florida, the 344th moved to Stansted Mountfichet, Essex in February 1944 staging via the "Southern Route" – Puerto Rico, British Guiana, Brazil, Ascension Island, Liberia, French Morocco and Cornwall. By the time the group prepared to move overseas, it was on its sixth commanding officer, Col. Ronald F. C. Vance. Part of the second batch of B-26 groups that had originally been scheduled to join the Eighth Air Force, the 344th went straight to the Ninth and immediately began training flights over England, familiarising itself with navigational matters before embarking on combat missions.

As the first combat group to arrive in the UK with Marauders devoid of much of their camouflage paint, the 344th took the unofficial name 'The Silver Streaks'. It was the sixth B-26 group to join the Ninth Air Force and, on 6 March, undertook its first mission, striking Bernay St. Martin airfield suffering slight damage to four aircraft and experiencing *Flak*. Spirits were

buoyant when, following its second mission the next day, a commendation for "... a job well done" was received from the commander of the 99th Bomb Wing

Throughout the spring of 1944, the 344th BG flew missions against targets on the standard tactical target list – airfields, bridges, marshalling yards, V-1 sites, coastal defences and many others in France, Belgium and Holland. Throughout this time, the group's B-26s took a considerable hammering from German Flak; on the 23 April mission to the Heuringhem V-1 site in France, no fewer than 28 of the 37 ships dispatched were damaged, three of which required fourth echelon repair. One aircraft was lost at the target. On another mission on 10 May mounted against the Mons marshalling yards, 25 out of 38 machines came back with battle damage and eighteen days later during a raid on the Amiens yards, 23 were damaged and one lost out of a force of 37 aircraft dispatched. Despite this punishment, the Group would fly Marauders in combat with success for 14 months.

The 344th's D-Day targets were coastal batteries at Cherbourg, which proved particularly tough nuts to crack. The Marauders, with a white tail triangle as a group marking, were part of a 486-strong maximum effort by the B-26 force on that historic day. An overcast forced many of the bombers down to below 5,000 ft (1,524 m) to make their runs along the beaches and with the bad results of the early low level Marauder missions

Above: Photographed post-D-Day, with its standard invasion stripes standing out against the clouds, this is B-26-B-50 (S/N 42-107683) of the 497th Squadron, 344th BG. The aircraft, piloted by Lt L.R. Powers, would later take part (Box 2, 1st flight, No.5 position) in the 24 April 1945 mission to Schrobenhausen which would encounter an attack by Me 262s of JV 44.

Below: In what would become an all too familiar sight to both German personnel employed to guard bridges and supply dumps in France as well as to native French railway workers, a formation of Marauders from the 344th BG (494th Squadron) heads out to another tactical target in France.

B-26B-50 coded 7I-D of the 497th Squadron, 344th BG heads across the English Channel en route for another tactical target in France, circa March-May 1944. This aircraft, piloted by Lt Riley V. Woodruff, would meet JV 44 (Box 2, 1st flight, No.1 position) on 24 April 1945.

in mind, some men felt they would not see the day out. Fortunately the German defenders had easier targets than the fast medium bombers and losses were very light. Accompanying crews were however shocked to see one 344th machine explode as the result of an attack by an Fw 190, one of the few sorties into the invasion area the *Jagdverbände* managed on 6 June. Throughout the rest of June 1944, the group's B-26s supported the seizure of the Cotentin Peninsula and the British thrust against Caen.

For flying an intensive round of sorties against troop concentrations, supply dumps, a bridge and railway viaduct at St Lô during the period 24-26 July, the 344th received a Distinguished Unit Citation. The group continued to attack bridges with some success during the Allied breakout from Normandy and to hinder the German forces of Army Group B encircled at Falaise. Some target variety was given to the crews when they were briefed to hit ships and strong points in and around the harbour at Brest during August and September.

On 30 September, after a seven month residence during which the group had engaged the enemy in a total of 148 missions, the 344th departed Stansted and moved to A-59 Cormeilles-en-Vexin, France, which was to remain its base until almost the end of hostilities. Cormeilles was a mess, having been subjected to sabotage by the departing Germans. Though the runways were serviceable, a considerable amount of work was needed to keep them in good repair. Furthermore, storage areas previously used by the Germans had been blown up and with the onset of autumn conditions were very muddy. However, within two days after arrival, the group was operational, testimony to the efficiency and dedication of the unit's personnel. Now flying over considerably shorter ranges than had been possible from the UK, the 344th was able to maintain constant pressure on the Germans. The group's B-26s bombed rail lines, bridges, fortifications, supply dumps and depots in France and during October-November extended its reach to similar targets in Germany. Col Robert W. Witty took over group command on 8 November following Vance's posting to the 99th Bomb Wing. Vance had been decorated with the DFC a month earlier for his

B-26C-45 (s/n 42-107666) / Y5-F named BARRACUDA of 495th Squadron, 344th BG receives repair to its port engine nacelle following battle damage sustained over France in 1944. The machine later flew under 2nd Lt F.L. Choate to Schrobenhausen on 24 April 1945 (Box 1, 1st flight, No.3 position) coming up against JV 44's jets.

courage and leadership on operations. Witty's tenure saw a flexible and effective style of command.

During the winter, the German offensive in the Ardennes was materially helped by appalling weather which kept Allied tactical aircraft on the ground for days on end. As with other medium bomber groups, the 344th pitched in as soon as the weather cleared to blunt the German offensive in the 'Bulge'. It mounted an attack on the bridge at Mayen and though enduring a savage attack by German fighters, it emerged from the mission unscathed. Despite the poor weather in December, the 344th flew more missions that month than it had in November.

Sorties in support of the Ardennes counter-offensive occupied the 344th until January 1945. Missions throughout December tended to be close support for ground forces as opposed to direct tactical support, involving strikes against enemy defended towns, supply depots and troop concentrations. The nature of these had changed little although they were now located in Germany rather than France and were if anything, even more heavily defended. Some losses to *Flak* continued to accrue. As the territory held by the enemy contracted, the mediums were given some targets that were of a more strategic nature and for the 344th these included oil storage tanks.

Despite a successful run of operations, the 344th BG, like many other groups, experienced its fair share of bad luck and drama. On 15 December 1944, a Marauder piloted by Capt. Curtis I. Seebaldt, the Group Control Officer and the intended lead operational aircraft for that day, came down during take-off. With its gear just swinging up, the right engine failed and the aircraft settled on the runway. Fortunately, Seebaldt and his crew were able to exit the Marauder. Four minutes after abandoning ship however, the sixteen 250 lb bombs on board exploded, destroying the aircraft, with blast from the explosion smashing windows up to two miles away.

All in all though, casualties and battle damage for the closing month of 1944 were comparitively light and the group ended the year having completed 183 missions.

There was a bad start to 1945, when, on New Year's Day, the B-26 piloted by 2nd Lt. Robert R. Chalot of the 497th Squadron and carrying two 2000 lb general purpose bombs, crashed on the runway during take-off and exploded, killing four members of the engineer rescue squad. Despite the flames however, the crew were extricated from the wreckage.

More losses occured on the February mission to the Euskirchen bridge when five Marauders were shot down and another 21 damaged, the highest number for some months. Thirty-one personnel were listed missing and another six wounded.

Throughout the first half of March 1945, bridges, marshalling yards and road junctions were the main targets.

Moving to A-78 Florennes/Juzaine in Belgium on 5 April, the 344th assisted the final drive to put the remnants of Third Reich territory into Allied hands by hitting marshalling yards at Celle, Saalfeld, Anchorsleben, Zwickau, Tubingen and Juterbog all with excellent results, often despite haze and clouds. The 25 April mission to Erding airfield was to be the 344th's last. In just over a year of combat the Silver Streaks had flown 266 missions.

With the war over, the group occupied Schleissheim in Germany during September 1945. One of the B-26 groups that was not obliged to immediately relinquish its aircraft, the 344th laid on a number of demonstration flights and proceeded with crew conversion training on the A-26 Invader. The 344th was also one of the few ex-Marauder units that was in position to become part of USAFE. Marauders remained on hand for some time even after a number of crews had completed their training on the new attack bomber; the 344th could well stake another small 'claim to fame' by being the last AAF combat group to fly the B-26.

The group remained in Germany until February 1946, having the previous December been redesignated the 344th Bombardment Group (Light). The latter part of this designation was further confirmation that the unit had re-equipped with Invaders, for under post-war re-classification of army aircraft, the A-26 had become a light bomber, and previously-designated heavies such as the B-29 were classed as mediums.

In the meantime, remaining air and ground echelons rotated home until the 344th became one of many Second World War groups that made only a 'paper' transfer home, minus 'personnel and equipment'. It was formerly inactivated in the US on 31 March 1946.

You can't teach an old monkey new tricks, but it might just fix your engine... With monkey(!) wrench clasped firmly in hand, "Jocko" – a mascot believed to have been picked up by a crew of the 344th BG when they stopped for fuel on an island en route to England from the USA – goes to work on an expensive piece of aeronautical machinery somewhere in Europe.

Paws For Thought

Andrea Rochell,

07919647642
07893937200

Hatley

A warning to bold Luftwaffe fighter pilots as applied to a P-47D of the 313th Fighter Squadron, 50th Fighter Group in France 1944.

Master of the Sky
THE 50th FIGHTER GROUP

Comprising the 10th, 81st and 313th Squadrons, personnel of the 50th Fighter Group began arriving in the European theatre on 5 April 1944 from the AAF Fighter Command School and the AAF School of Applied Tactics in Florida. The unit had been activated at Selfridge Field, Michigan on 15 January 1941 and originally designated the 50th Pursuit Group.

Commanding the group was Col William D. Greenfield, who had assumed the position while the unit was in the US. He was to lead the 50th through its early months of cross-Channel operations from Lymington, Hampshire, which began on 1 May. Flying razorback-model P-47Ds, the group was soon carrying out dive-bombing missions as the date of the invasion approached.

The 50th's base at Lymington was one of the temporary airfields known as Advanced Landing Grounds (ALGs). Set up primarily to accommodate the influx of AAF tactical units prior to the invasion, the ALGs were an inspired idea - although some of them proved to be a little less than resilient with seven ton Thunderbolts continually pounding the pierced steel planking strip runways.

The 50th was one of three groups that went operational on 1 May, along with the P-47-equipped 404th and P-38-equipped 370th Groups.

Tactical fighters were needed in France as soon as the invasion had proven to be a success and ALGs could be established on the other side of the Channel. As the first troops ashore established a bridgehead in Normandy, the 50th prepared to move. An airfield site identified as A-10 at Carentan was selected and in mid-June the Thunderbolts flew in, ready to begin combat operations under IX Tactical Air Command control, from the 25th of the month.

Earlier, on 7 June, Lt Billy Bryan had been credited with the 50th Group's first aerial victory. Three days later the invasion-striped Thunderbolts ran into Bf 109s and in the resulting combat three enemy fighters and one P-47 went down. In total, sorties from Lymington had netted the group six enemy aircraft - for the loss of six Thunderbolts.

By 16 August, the 50th Fighter Group was operating from A-17 Meautis on the French coast. The group's fighter bombers continued to fly numerous sorties in support of the advancing armies, largely free from interference from the Luftwaffe. But on the 26th Deputy Group Commander Frank E. Adkins shot down two Bf 109s over the Elbeuf area to make him an ace, these victories being added to three he had previously scored in the Pacific flying P-40s and Airacobras.

Following the push across France, the 50th occupied A-47, the AAF designation for Orly, one of the main Paris airports, on 4 September. By 15 September the group had moved on once again, to A-69 Laon/Athies. Yet another change of base was made by the autumn of 1944 when Y-6 Lyon/Bron became home to the 50th. Flying operations began from there on 28 September. The 50th's final base in France was A-96 Toul/Ochey, which it used from 3

BATTLE OVER BAVARIA

November 1944, the month that Col Harvey L. Case took over as group commander. By that time the 50th's Thunderbolts had acquired the red nose cowling recognition band denoting attachment to the 1st Tactical Air Force and for the last seven months of the war, officially starting on 1 November, the group was part of this combined American-French force established primarily to support the US Seventh Army. It was this army that had landed in southern France as part of Operation Dragoon on 15 August 1944 and was by the autumn, pushing up into the Strasbourg area.

As the war drew to a close, the *Luftwaffe* more actively engaged US aircraft on certain days, although the response to bomber and fighter sorties could rarely be predicted with any certainty. Nor could the very real threat posed by German jet interceptors be accurately measured. Combating enemy aircraft was in any event a peripheral duty for the Ninth's Thunderbolt groups, for their primary task remained that of ground attack. Consequently the 50th did not, in common with other tactical Thunderbolt units, expect to run up a high toll of aerial victories although all the groups invariably shot down a few enemy aircraft during their combat period. However, the appearance of Me 262s during the spring of 1945 brought about a change in tactics. Medium bombers had for some months been only indirectly escorted by fighters owing to the decrease in *Luftwaffe* activity and overall Allied air superiority as Germany's ability to continue the war was slowly but surely destroyed. But when the Me 262s demonstrated their ability to shoot down American mediums - and any other type - with consummate ease if pilots pressed home their attacks, fighter escort once more became essential. That is how the 50th and other tactical groups found themselves flying bomber escort during the last months of the war. Not that their primary ground attack work was neglected, far from it. For the 50th Group, continuing prowess in close support was reflected in the award of a Distinguished Unit Citation for generally excellent work during the period 13-20 March 1945 when the Allies were heavily engaged in penetrating the defences of the Siegfried Line.

"Razorback" P-47Ds of the 81st Fighter Squadron, 50th Fighter Group seen here dispersed at Carentan airfield in France shortly after the invasion. In the foreground is S/N 42-25904 2N-U Lethal Liz II. Tactical groups of the US Ninth Air Force spearheaded the Allied invasion of the continent in 1944, the Thunderbolt becoming one of the most widely operated fighter and ground attack types.

Taken at Toul/Ochey, one of the six French bases from which the 50th FG operated, this view shows P-47D-26 42-28229 Juicy Luicy, the personal mount of Capt. Philip M. Savides, receiving attention from the ground crews, the man on the wing feeding fresh .50 in ammunition into the trays for the four machine guns with a drop tank in the foreground.

Two Fw 190s fell to the guns of Lt Col Robert D. Johnston, CO of the 81st Squadron, on 9 April. These victories, claimed over the Crailsheim area, were numbers five and six for Johnston who thus became an ace, the second and last pilot of the 50th Group to be so honoured.

On 25 April, the 50th was involved in a major action when it was briefed to attack a number of airfields south of Munich. For its contribution to this mission, the group won its second DUC. The following day the group was briefed to escort 1st TAC Marauders of the *Armeé de l'Air* and was called in during the mission to assist AAF B-26s under attack by Me 262s of JV 44. One pilot of the 10th FS shot at and hit the Me 262 piloted by none other than Adolf Galland (see Chapter Sixteen).

During one year of combat the 50th's pilots had had relatively little opportunity to clash with the *Luftwaffe* but by the end of the war they had scored 63 confirmed aerial victories. The additional 'probable' and 'damaged' claims added up to seven and 25 respectively.

As to the share of confirmed kills, the squadrons ended the war with the 81st emerging as the top scorer with 30, the 313th had 21 and the 10th was credited with 12. Airfield attacks had added an unknown number of enemy aircraft destroyed on the ground.

The 50th Fighter Group flew the P-47D for the duration of its combat operations in the ETO and in common with the other units of the Ninth, had all but relinquished its razorbacks in favour of bubbletop models by the time hostilities ceased. Late model D-27s and D-30s were being used in 1945, some of them employing tube-launched rockets and napalm in addition to the standard range of Thunderbolt ordnance - .50-cal ammunition and bombs.

Squadron decorations for war service included the 10th FS being cited by a Belgian Army Order of the Day for the period 6 June to 30 September 1944 and a DUC for combat in the ETO from 13 to 20 March 1945 and specifically, air actions over Germany on 25 April 1945.

With peace the 50th Fighter Group occupied Giebelstadt and then Mannheim to undertake a brief period of policing Germany in the weeks following the capitulation.

TEN

Colonel Ray J. Stecker (left), commander of the 365th Fighter Group – the Hell Hawks – from D-Day to war's end, inspects a Group emblem.

Hell Hawks

THE 365th FIGHTER GROUP

nother Ninth Air Force group that flew the P-47D for the duration of its service in the Second World War, the 365th Fighter Group had the 386th, 387th and 388th Squadrons assigned. Taking the collective nickname 'Hell Hawks', group personnel arrived in the UK in December 1943 from Richmond Army Air Base, Virginia where it had been activtated in May of that year. The group took up residence at the newly-completed airfield at Gosfield, Essex. In command was Lt Col Lance Call who had taken over in May. Razorback Thunderbolts, 25 aircraft per squadron, arrived in January 1944 and the group flew its first missions on the 22nd of that month. This was a partial bomber escort shared with the 361st FG, Eighth Air Force and flown by the tactical group owing to the urgency attending the Argument directive to

destroy the German fighter force, both at front line and production level, prior to the invasion of Europe.

It was not a very satisfying debut in combat for the participating pilots; by turning for home a little early, the Hell Hawks missed all the action, which was marked with intense fighting and heavy Allied and German losses. A second escort was flown on 24 February and again the 365th missed combat, briefed as it was to provide withdrawal support to the bombers. England's winter weather invariably intervened to disrupt

P-47 Thunderbolts of the 388th Fighter Squadron, 365th Fighter Group, dispersed at Chièvres, Belgium during the winter of 1944/45. Seen here is a replacement P-47D-28 in natural metal finish contrasting with camouflaged 'razorback' Thunderbolts. The 365th, the 'Hell Hawks', was pitched into the Ardennes fighting and materially helped wreck von Rundstedt's last ditch offensive.

mission planning and by the end of February the Hell Hawks had flown but six missions. In the meantime a number of pilots who had been temporarily attached to other groups to gain experience, returned to Gosfield to 'spread the word' on combat in the ETO. All first-hand accounts were eagerly seized upon by pilots who had yet to encounter the enemy.

At last, on 2 March, the Hell Hawks pilots came home flushed with stories of combat with the *Luftwaffe*. Another escort mission had seen the bombers picked up in the vicinity of Bastogne in Belgium. When the heavies were attacked by a substantial force of Fw 190s, the 365th pilots did their level best to protect the 'big friends'. Despite the claims of six Fw 190s, the grim price of war took the edge off the victories. Only one P-47 had gone down but the first loss experienced by a group new to combat was always deeply felt.

Prior to Overlord the *Hell Hawks* flew south west to the ALG established at Beaulieu in Hampshire, Lance Call continuing to lead the group.

The 365th was one of the first groups of P-47s to make the move across the Channel and it was flying from A-7 Axeville by 29 June. Three days previously group leadership had passed to Col Ray J. Stecker. Progressively moving up to A-12 Lignerolles, A-48 Bretigny, A-68 Juvincourt, A-84 Chièvres/Mons and A-34 Metz/Frescaty as the Allied front line pushed forward, the Hell Hawks' P-47s cut a swath of destruction as the liberation of France from German domination moved towards complete realisation.

The 365th was part of the Allied tactical effort to stop von Runstedt's breakout through the Ardennes 'bulge' during which, in common with other groups it benefited from target guidance provided by US ground radar.

By early 1945 the last German offensive in the West had been contained and the 365th operated from A-78 Florennes/Juzaine from 30 January. Ground attack operations preoccupied the unit's pilots on a day to day basis but they flew with the comforting knowledge that should the Luftwaffe appear, they had an aircraft equal to most situations.

As was generally the case with other tactical fighter groups, relatively little air combat was actually recorded by the 365th and Maj James E. Hill of the 388th FS who had shot down two Fw 190s on 21 October 1944, probably gave little thought to adding the three more enemy aircraft necessary to make him an ace. But on 18 April 1945 he nailed three Bf 109s. However, tougher adversaries were about to cross the path of the Hell Hawks pilots in the shape of *Luftwaffe* jet fighters (see Chapter Fourteen).

The 365th Group had been cited for a DUC for destroying 'numerous enemy fighters over the Bonn-Düsseldorf area' on 21 October 1944 and a second DUC was awarded for operations four days before clashing with JV 44 when on 20 April the group attacked various airfields, military transportation and ammunition dumps. In addition the group was awarded the Belgian Army Citation for its operations between 6 June and 30 September 1944 and the Belgian *Fouragers* for the period 16 December 1944 to 25 January 1945.

Lt Col Robert C. Richardson III took over as group CO on 26 April and he was to see the unit through to the end of war and to lead until some time afterwards. Suippes in France was the last overseas base, the 386th moving in on or about 29 July 1945. The 387th and 388th Squadrons were in place by the 30th.

Looking resplendent and formidable in its virtually all metal finish, this is P-47D (s/n 42-27275) of the 388th Fighter Squadron, 365th Fighter Group, probably photographed at the forward airfields of either Lignerolles, Bretigny or Juvincourt in France, 1944. Production of the aircraft was financed by war bonds raised by the employees of the Republic Aviation Corporation.

A photograph probably taken at the same time as the one shown on page 77 showing P-47 Thunderbolts of the 388th Fighter Squadron, 365th Fighter Group, dispersed at Chièvres, Belgium during the winter of 1944/45.

Despite the indisputable superiority of Allied airpower by late 1944, the 365th Fighter Group and other units were given local protection in the form of American AA units which were well able to tackle most "nuisance" raids the Luftwaffe may have attempted. Here, Capt. George W. King of the 386th Fighter Squadron taxies a bombed-up P-47D close to a pit for a light quadruple gun mount at Chièvres airfield in Belgium. The Luftwaffe did hit the 365th at Metz on 1 January 1945 when the defences could not prevent 22 of the group's Thunderbolts from being destroyed.

PART TWO BATTLE

BATTLE OVER BAVARIA

OTTO KAMMERDIENER

Born 23 July 1921, Altona, Hamburg. Otto Kammerdiener went through standard *Luftwaffe* pilot training commencing shortly after the outbreak of war in November 1939 with 3./*Fliegerausbildungsbataillon* 13 where he embarked on the usual course of fitness training, medical examination, infantry training and sport, followed by a stint at 1.*Techische Kompanie, Fliegerwaffentechische Schule (See)* Bug/Rügen (lit. Naval Aviation Weapons School) from January 1940. Between April and August 1940, he was with the respective cadet companies of the 6. *Fliegerausbildungsbataillon* 26 at Heiligenhafen and the *Flugzeugführerschule (See)* Pütnitz or Marine Pilot Training School, where it seems he was destined for a career within the maritime arm of the *Luftwaffe*. Several of these schools had been established around the pre-war testing stations on the Baltic coast. Then, in December 1940, *Gefreiter* Kammerdiener was transferred to the *Flugzeugführerschule* A/B 119 for basic pilot's training in aerobatics, instrument training, formation flying and cross country. Promoted to the rank of *Feldwebel* from *Unteroffizier* on 1 April 1943, in July of that year another transfer took him to the *Fluglehrerschule* – or Flight Leader's School – at Quedlinburg, followed by a further move in August 1944 to his first qualified capacity as an instructor at the *Fluglehrerschule der Luftwaffe* at Brandenburg-Briest. Eight months later on 11 March 1945, he joined JV 44.

THE BATTLE OVER BAVARIA – APRIL 1945
Known major interceptions against USAAF B-26 Marauder formations by JV 44.

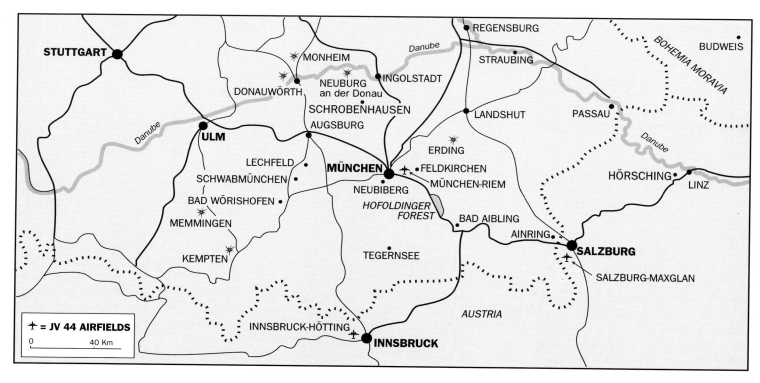

20.04.45.
B-26 Marauders of the 323rd Bombardment Group (M) over Kempten and Memmingem.

24.04.45. a.m.
B-26 Marauders of the 17th Bombardment Group over Schwabmünchen

24.04.45. p.m.
B-26 Marauders of the 322nd and 344th Bombardment Groups south east of Monheim.

25.04.45.
B-26 Marauders of 323rd Bombardment Group over Erding.

26.04.45.
B-26 Marauders of 17th Bombardment Group over Neuburg an der Donau.

ELEVEN

In Walter Krupinski's view the Me 262 was "a flying dream"; this picture shows JV 44's Me 262 W.Nr. 111745 'White 5' at München-Riem.

1-20 APRIL 1945
A FLYING DREAM

"A Flying Dream"

On the night of 1 April 1945, Adolf Galland and Johannes Steinhoff visited the Haus Florida Luftwaffe recuperation centre at Bad Wiessee. As we have seen, it was from here that they took Herbert Kaiser for service with JV 44. However, besides Kaiser, they secured at least two more pilots for the unit. One was the well known *Ritterkreuzträger, Hauptmann* Walter Krupinski. With more than 1,100 missions to his name, 197 confirmed aerial victories, having been five times wounded, baled out on four occasions as well as having undergone numerous crash landings, Krupinski's accomplishments typified those of the many legendary young *Experten* who found fame and glory whilst fighting over the Russian front between 1941-1944, though by March 1945, Krupinski had effectively been made redundant by the continual regroupings and redesignations of the various *Luftwaffe* fighter *Geschwader*. Again, as with Kaiser and Gutowski, Krupinski was very well known to Steinhoff, having flown as his wingman over Russia, but now, with no prospect of a satisfactory posting, he had determined to sit out the remaining weeks of the war in comfort and safety at the *Jagdfliegerheim.*

Krupinski had been at Bad Wiessee less than a week when he received his two surprise visitors. They made him an offer which he could not refuse: "When at the beginning of 1945, I had flown the "long-nosed" Fw 190 D-9 and then, later, the Me 262 for a month with JV 44, I realised that we had much better aircraft than the old, brave Bf 109. But it would be true to say that the high point of my flying career was that last month of the war at München-Riem on the Me 262 with Galland and Steinhoff. Everyone knew that in reality the war was nearly over, but that with the Me 262 a flying dream had become a reality. It would have been the night of 1st April 1945. Steinhoff and Galland turned up completely unexpectedly at the recreation centre. I thought they were still up in the north at Brandenburg-Briest – I'd heard about this unit Galland had formed. In fact they had flown their aircraft down to München-Riem that day and had come straight to Bad Wiessee. Steinhoff grinned and asked me; "*Graf* – (that was my nickname from the old days) – *how would you like to fly the Me 262?*" I was astonished and made these big eyes and immediately said "*Yes!*"

Krupinski's "training" on the jet fighter began in earnest early the next morning – 2 April 1945 – at München-Riem. A lone Me 262 was hauled out onto the concrete start platform on the western edge of the airfield. Steinhoff was the instructor. Krupinski remembers: "The next morning I was sitting in the cockpit of an Me 262 at München-Riem. I had a hell of a bad head – the result of too many drinks the night before! Steinhoff was standing on the port wing. He was laughing and said: "*The most difficult thing with this type of aircraft is to start the engines. I'll do that for you."* There was no reading any books or anything like that. There was no "training programme". He just gave me some basic information – enough to get started. *"It's very tricky."* he said. *"On take-off, you need a very long time until you get airborne. Don't do anything in a hurry. On landing, it's the other way around – you can't get the speed back down to a normal landing speed. She's fast – very fast!"* Actually, I found that taking off in the Me 262 was fairly easy because the nose wheel rolled nice and smoothly, but the problem – as Steinhoff had said – was that the engines didn't accelerate and bring up speed fast enough. You needed the whole length of the airfield before you reached an adequate take-off speed. At München-Riem, the strip we used was about 1,100 metres (1,202 yards) long and only after about 1,000 metres (1,093 yards) did you have the lifting speed to come off the field. Anyway, I prepared myself for take-off; I closed the canopy, threw a quick glance over the instrument panel – brakes off – and slowly, like a lame duck, the bird began to roll. But then the end of the runway, as I predicted, came towards me very quickly. A glance at the speed indicator told me I was moving at 200km/h. Pulling gently at the stick, I got into the air. No drag and she climbed swiftly. Landing-gear up. Throttle lightly back to 8,000 rpm. I climbed and the speed grew and grew: 350 – 400 – 500 – 600 km/h – there seemed no end to its speed. Still I climbed. The bird flew on – it was fantastic! Nothing like the Bf 109. For my first roll in the climb I used only ailerons, moving with lightning speed; neither rudder nor thrust were needed and at 6,000 or 7,000 metres (19,685/22,965 ft) I levelled out, the speed slowly approaching 900 km/h (560 mph). So there I was, flying on my first mission – though, I suppose it was more of a solo transition flight really."

Krupinski headed south towards the Bavarian Alps. Then, as he swept over the Tegernsee and the *Jagdfliegerheim* at Bad Wiessee, he heard his radio crackle into life. It was the controller at Riem with a warning of enemy aircraft.

"The first thing I did was to fly over the recreation centre," Krupinski recalls, "Just to show them that I was flying again! At the same moment our reporting centre was announcing over the radio that there were some Lightnings over Innsbruck – *"Come back to the field immediately... Return to Riem!"* Anyway, I thought to myself that the distance from Bad Wiessee to Innsbruck wasn't very far – *I'll just take a look."*

Nearing the city, Krupinski immediately spotted the distinctive twin-boom shape of the American fighter-bombers. Approaching them at 900 km/h (560 mph), he lined the first one up in his sight. His positioning was perfect and at just over 7,500 metres (24,600 ft), he closed in. Krupinski continues: *"This is a nice idea – I thought to myself – I'll get one on my first mission! I* managed to get one of the Lightnings in my sights and held him there whilst I sat on his tail chasing him over Innsbruck. But the moment I thought – *Perfect – I've got him, I'll shoot.... Whoosh! I* was away! Over and above them – much too fast. I watched the fire from my four MK 108 cannon disappear into the blue. It was just the same as in the early days against the Russians when they flew those old biplanes, like the I-153 and the I-16 Ratas and we flew the Bf 109 – there was such a difference in speed and you had to compensate."

The Fifteenth Air Force recorded that on 2 April 1945, a single Me 262 approached an "escort flight" of Lightnings at 12:55 at 7,600 metres (25,000 ft) over Innsbruck, but that it did not attack.

"It was time I headed for home," Krupinski concluded, "München-Riem soon appeared below me and my speed began to decrease. Pulling back on the stick I slowly brought my approach speed down to about 300 km/h. The power of the engines however, was frightening. The aircraft was jerky and tail-heavy. I'd had my "training" but due to the events of the last hour, I'd completely forgotten what I'd been told! The strip came up to meet me. I didn't dare touch the throttle. Landing gear down –

landing speed at 230 km/h, going down to 200 km/h. Then the flight was at an end and as I came off the runway, I saw Johannes Steinhoff standing there laughing. From the expression on his face, it was as if he was asking *"No?"* and in my thoughts, I answered *"Yes, this is the bird. We must have more of these... fast."*

Later that day, having spent the past forty-eight hours stranded at Unterschlauersbach awaiting repairs to his Me 262 "White 7", *Ofw.* Nielinger finally took-off at 18:40 landing at München-Riem twenty-five minutes later.

"Jagdverband Galland" – Operational

As the pilots of JV 44 acquainted themselves with their new aircraft and their new base, elsewhere, the commanders of the German *Jagdwaffe* – composed mainly now of the officers constituting Göring's *Kindergarten* – began to influence jet fighter operations. Frustrated by the seemingly wasted effort in forming JV 44, its drain on resources (which, it was considered, could be far better utilised elsewhere) and by its lack of any quantifiable success, on 3 April 1945, *Oberst* Gollob prepared a three page report addressed to Göring and the OKL entitled *"Jet Operations in the Fighter Sector"*. In the third paragraph of this document, Gollob commented that:

"Jagdverband 44 has not achieved anything so far, although it does have a number of very good pilots. Furthermore, JV 44 adopts other operational methods which detract from those that are commonly accepted. It is proposed to disband the unit and to deploy its pilots more purposefully with other units."

Two photographs depicting Me 262 W.Nr. 111745 'White 5' parked on the perimeter road at München-Riem, this aircraft being one of the most photographed of JV 44's Me 262s and flown variously by Uffz. Eduard Schallmoser and Uffz. "Jonny" Müller.

The beginning of April 1945 saw the first seeds of decay in any form of coherent fighter defence leadership being sown. Command was already fragmented and competitive. In one quarter, from the headquarters of the IX.*(J) Fliegerkorps* at Treuenbrietzen, *Generalmajor* Peltz was consolidating his position as commander of all of the bomber units now struggling to familiarise themselves with the Me 262 fighter, directing these units in the aerial defence of Austria and Bohemia-Moravia. Peltz's feelings at this time are made clear from an intercepted radio message dated 3 April:

"Peltz... reports work on many airfields not being carried out with necessary energy. Half of the working day of 12 hours is wasted as a result of Allied air raids. Work is to be started before first light, any rest to be taken during main raid period and work resumed at night. Divisional commanders to report if this arrangement not practical or if repair of runways and tracks takes too long. Unit commanders to report to the Division or to Peltz personally if work is not carried out by the station commander in the spirit of this order."

For its part, JV 44 had not been made subordinate to Peltz but was, instead, to report to 7. *Jagddivision.*

Despite the duplication and disorder at command level, jet operations in both the north and the south of Germany continued unabated if not without some difficulty. Early in the morning of 4 April, a force of 30 Me 262s drawn from the now much depleted *Stab,* I. and III./JG 7 prepared to take off from their bases at Parchim, Lärz, Burg and Brandenburg-Briest to intercept a daylight raid of 1,400 B-17s and B-24s from the US Eighth Air Force enroute to bomb targets across northern Germany. Of this German force, nine aircraft were compelled to drop out of the mission before take-off due to mechanical and technical problems and another three machines returned early before engagement. Things were made worse by the fact that

WALTER KRUPINSKI

Born in Domnau, East Prussia in November 1920, Walter Krupinski spent the latter part of his youth employed by the *Reichsarbeitsdienst* before being discharged a few days after the outbreak of war in 1939 to take up a place at the famous *Luftskriegsakademie* at Berlin-Gatow where he underwent the standard course of basic military and flying training. Following the conclusion of fighter pilot training in Vienna in October 1940, where he had been schooled on a variety of types including the He 51, Ar 68 and Bf 109 B and D, he was transferred to his first operational posting at 6./JG 52 a unit based at the time at several locations throughout Holland and Belgium. Krupinski had started what was to become a long and highly successful association with the *Geschwader*.

However, his first encounter with the enemy proved a failure when he and his squadron colleague, *Leutnant* Gerd Barkhorn (of whom we shall hear more later), took off from their base at Ostend and chased a lone Bristol Blenheim across the Channel. Despite exhausting their entire supply of ammunition, neither pilot was able to hit the elusive RAF reconnaissance machine and eventually the two Germans were forced to turn for home. It was an inauspicious start for two pilots who between them would eventually notch up nearly 500 kills. Lack of luck continued to dog the young Krupinski throughout his entire posting on the Channel Front and though he subsequently flew thirty missions over England and frequently came into contact with RAF Spitfires and Hurricanes, deficient gunnery skill robbed him of any success.

With the German invasion of Russia, Krupinski finally scored his first kill late in 1941 against a Red Air Force long range DB-3 bomber south of Leningrad. By the end of that year, his tally stood at just 7 kills, but following a short rest in Germany in early 1942, the tide of fortune was to change. Returning to Russia having worked hard to improve his shooting qualities, Krupinski quickly increased his personal score to 66 enemy aircraft destroyed and in May 1942 he was awarded the *Reichsmarschall's* Honour Goblet. With a rapidly increasing score, more decorations were quickly showered upon him; August saw the award of the German Cross in Gold followed two months later by the *Ritterkreuz*. By October 1942 Krupinski had shot down various types of YAK's and LaGG's as well as several Pe-2 and Doulgas Boston bombers, Il-2 *Shturmoviks* and Il-4s.

Wounded and hospitalised, Krupinski then spent three months as a fighter instructor in France before returning to Russia on 15th March 1942 as *Staffelkapitän* of 7./JG 52 at Taman on the Kuban bridgehead. Now he seemed unstoppable, scoring eleven victories in one day on 5th July 1943 and achieving his 150th kill on 12th October. Many pilots flying under him were also attaining staggering scores, including the young *Leutnant* Erich Hartmann. The following day – 13th October, with his 154th victory, Krupinski brought 7./JG 52's total victory tally to 1,000. His experiences in Russia are, today, still etched indelibly in his memory, particularly since it was not all "duck shooting".

"Of the five *Geschwader* in which I flew, " Krupinski recalled to the author, "I have no doubt that it was JG 52 that left the greatest mark on me. During my time with the *Geschwader*, I was wounded three times, baled out of burning aircraft twice and made so many crash landings I've lost count – including one in a minefield! However, a lot of books state that I have 198 victories but this is not quite true. About five or six years ago, I went to the *Bundesarchiv-Militärarchiv* in Freiburg and studied some documents relative to JG 52. In these documents I found one of my *Abschußmeldungen* and on it was a big stamp from the *RLM* – *Not Valid! Not sufficient witnesses.* The reason was as follows; we were over Zaporozhe close to the Dnieper River on our "victory-rich" retreat. I was flying with my wingman when we suddenly came upon a formation of twelve to fifteen LaGG's and Airacobras and a fierce dogfight ensued. We became separated and my wingman disappeared and then slowly, one by one, the Russians headed for home until I was left flying around in circles for about fifteen minutes with the last of them. I did my best to get the better of him but he was very good. Finally, I guess he got low on fuel and he had to break off the engagement by baling out. I returned to base but at that time you couldn't report a victory unless you had a witness. A little later a man came up to me from a unit which was based nearby. It was one of those special units that listened to enemy radio transmissions and he was one of those Germans who had been born in Russia which was why we had him there. He said: *"We know about your victory!"* I was amazed. I said: *"What?"* He then explained: *"We were listening to the Russians by radio and picked up their own report of the incident! It is confirmed!"* So I asked him to write a report and then I went to my *Gruppenkommandeur*, *Major* Günther Rall and asked him if there was anything we could do but he said it would involve a lot of paperwork Eventually, I persuaded him to speak with Dieter Hrabak, the *Geschwaderkommodore*,. Hrabak said: *"Let me ask the Fliegerkorps what their opinion is."* So he spoke to *General der Flieger* Kurt Pflugbeil who simply told me to send in *another* report so that he could look at the matter. So, I re-wrote my report giving all the details and then, years later, I found it in the *Bundesacrhiv* as not valid! From that day on, my "official" score is 197 – not 198!"

Krupinski left JG 52 and Russia in March 1944 to return to the Reich and take up command of the 1. *Staffel* of JG 5 which had now returned from the Far North for Home Defence duties. After scoring another four kills with JG 5 and having been awarded the Oakleaves to the *Ritterkreuz*, he was transferred again, this time as *Gruppenkommandeur* of II./JG 11 based at Hustedt, near Celle. With the Allied invasion of June 1944, the *Gruppe* was one of those rushed into the

VORLÄUFIGES BESITZZEUGNIS

DER FÜHRER
UND OBERSTE BEFEHLSHABER
DER WEHRMACHT
HAT

DEM Oberleutnant Walter Krupinski

DAS EICHENLAUB
ZUM RITTERKREUZ
DES EISERNEN KREUZES

AM   2. März 1944   VERLIEHEN.

Hauptquartier d.Ob.d.L., DEN   26. April   1944
Der Chef des Luftwaffenpersonalamts

Generaloberst

Walter Krupinski's citation for the award of the Oakleaves to the Knight's Cross dated 2 March 1944 in recognition of 177 confirmed aerial victories and 1,000 missions. At this time, he had just returned from the east to take command of I./JG 5 in the defence of the Reich.

His penultimate transfer came in early October 1944 when he was posted to *Oberstleutnant* Josef "Pips" Priller's JG 26, taking command of III. *Gruppe* equipped with Bf 109s. It was to be a fateful posting made worse by a long, cold autumn of attrition with the whole of JG 26 deployed along the German-Dutch border and pitted against the Spitfires and Typhoon fighter-bombers of the British 2nd TAF. The weather over north-west Europe hampered operations and the *Jagdwaffe,* still reeling from the devastating effect of *Bodenplatte,* was starved of fuel, outnumbered and exhausted.

Krupinski recalls: "I was at the time *Gruppenkommandeur* of III./JG 26, Galland's old *Geschwader* and we were in the north of Germany at Plantlünne, near Lingen. "Pips" Priller had just been appointed *Inspekteur-Jagdflieger West;* he was now responsible for all the fighter units in the north. At that time – March 1945 – it had become very clear that due to pilot and aircraft availability as well as the fuel situation, the *Geschwader* could not support four *Gruppen* any longer and Priller decided that one would have to be disbanded. My *Gruppe* was the so-called "high cover fighter group" and it was decided that it would be this Third *Gruppe* which would be broken up. Priller bade me farewell but as a gesture of goodwill, ordered me to go down to Lechfeld to ask Bär who was commanding III./EJG 2, if and when my *Gruppe* could convert to the Me 262. That was the official instruction. I drove down to Lechfeld early next morning in one of those little wood-burning cars – there was simply no petrol left anymore and I arrived there about lunch-time the next day. I went straight to Bär, whom I had known for a long time before and said: *"Hello! I've come to ask when I can bring you my pilots from III./JG 26 and convert over to the Me 262?"* Bär found that very funny and burst out laughing. He said: *"Look, I have a hundred pilots who would like to convert to the Me 262!"* There was no way that Bär could accommodate us – no chance at all. He needed months to convert the pilots he already had, let alone us. So, I shrugged and left. I decided to go down to Bad Wiessee where we had our fighter pilot recreation centre and finish the war there where I could still enjoy a few drinks and some good food."

However, within days, Krupinski was flying with JV 44.

cauldron of Normandy operating from makeshift strips at Beauvais and Mons-au-Chausée on low-level ground support missions against the advancing Allied armies. Krupinski went on to claim another fourteen Allied aircraft destroyed, including nine of the dreaded American P-51 Mustangs as well as some four P-47 Thunderbolts before his own Bf 109 exploded in mid-air. Miraculously, Krupinski survived but was once again hospitalised.

"I flew over 1,000 missions and scored more than 190 victories in the Bf 109," Krupinski remembers, "flying the E, F, G and K variants and for many years I considered this machine to have been the best that the *Luftwaffe* had to offer. The fastest of the breed was definitely the F-4 which I flew mainly in Russia, whilst over the Reich, I flew the Bf 109 K-4 with methanol injection as a high altitude fighter meant to protect our Fw 190 "heavy fighters". But, in spite of all the many upgrades, the later Bf 109 variants were always lame ducks, limited by the many "lumps" in their profile, something which no longer fitted into the "old shirt"".

The Luftwaffe recuperation centre at Bad Wiessee, known as Haus Florida.

Cherokee Indian chief, one of several American Indians serving with the 323rd.

To the south, meanwhile, JV 44's operations were being conducted at an altogether more sedate pace with only one known patrol being flown by the unit on 3 April when a *Rottenflug* comprising *Lt.* Fährmann accompanied by *Uffz.* Schallmoser flying Me 262 "White 5" took off from München-Riem at 17:55 on a patrol over the city. They returned 20 minutes later having made no contact with the enemy. Whether or not JV 44 had, by this stage, actually taken on the aircraft of the disbanded IV./KG 51 is also unclear, though it seems unlikely.

The 4th was equally quiet, with Johannes Steinhoff using the opportunity to continue with his "training programme". Those pilots still unacquainted with the Me 262, such as Franz Steiner and "Jonny" Müller were seizing this period of relative calm to continue their conversion training. Steinhoff himself had, by now, began to form mixed opinions about the Me 262. As he recalled after the war: "Naturally, the flying qualities of the Me

Above left: The Jumo 004 jet engine was susceptible to turbine blade fatigue caused by high operating temperatures and faults in the induction system. Above right: A rare view taken from the cockpit of an Me 262 in flight.

those aircraft leaving Parchim had to do so under attack from P-47s and P-51s, just some of the 850 Allied fighters sent to escort the bomber formation and which had gathered around the airfield waiting to 'bounce' any jets that might appear. Despite this, JG 7 managed to drive through the escort and hack down seven *Viermots* using cannon and rockets. But by the end of the day, Weissenberger was forced to report that five of his pilots had been killed or missing and three were wounded; 23 jets were battle damaged or in need of repair. The *Geschwader* was now finding it difficult to cope.

USAAF medium bombers had by now begun to encounter the German jets. The 323rd BG was attacked for the first time by Me 262s on a mission to the Crailsheim marshalling yards on 4 April, losing one aircraft. Aboard this Marauder was the son of a

"I've always wanted to do this!": Uffz. Eduard Schallmoser playfully brandishes a spade behind a fellow pilot's head on the perimeter track at München-Riem, April 1945. The three pilots wear typical very late war flying leathers – issued in abundance to JV 44 – and have been hard at work digging "one man foxholes", a primitive form of protection intended for pilots evacuating their aircraft on the ground in the event of being caught in an Allied air attack. Schallmoser's Me 262 W.Nr. 111745 "White 5" can be seen in the background.

JV 44 – München-Riem
April 1945

Another view of JV 44's Me 262 "White 5".

Uffz. Eduard Schallmoser (fourth from left) together with other JV 44 pilots and local ground staff gather off the perimeter road close to the western start platform, München-Riem, April 1945. The main control buildings at Riem can be seen in the background.

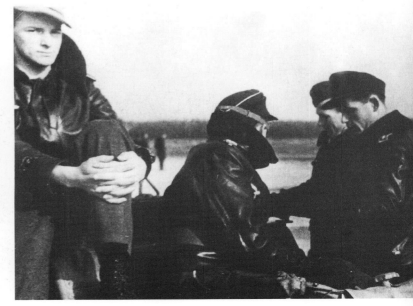

A group of JV 44 NCOs in discussion around a Kettenkrad half-track at München-Riem, April 1945. Eduard Schallmoser is to the far left of both pictures.

A Lockheed P-38L Lightning of the 37th Fighter Squadron, 14th Fighter Group taken in Italy in late 1944/early 1945 shows off its business-like form. It was one such aircraft of the 14th, which Uffz. Eduard Schallmoser of JV 44 shot down over Höhenlinden on 4 April 1945.

particularly during violent manoeuvres: oil pressure controls, as used on modern jets, were then unknown. Similarly, though their absence nowadays is also unthinkable, we had to do without dive brakes and this considerably limited our manoeuvrability particularly as regards loops and turns... In order to reduce speed, it was neccesary to reduce power, which again, at high altitude, could lead into a compressor stall. The other weakness was the Junkers 004 turbines. Their blades could not withstand the temperatures sometimes reached and this, together with faults in the induction system, often caused them to burn up. The life of these engines was therefore only 20 hours and the accident rate was high."

262 were influenced by the high wing loading and the low thrust. We needed a 1,200 metre (1,312 yard) runway and the acceleration after take-off was slow, so that during the first few minutes, the aircraft had to be nursed. At cruising speed – something over 800 km/h – the Me 262 handled well, except that the controls needed much force,

Left: Major Erich Hohagen at the controls of an Me 262. He witnessed Schallmoser's attack on William Randle's P-38 Lightning.
Below: Clad in typical late war flying gear, Uffz. Eduard Schallmoser (far right) and other pilots walk past Me 262s "White 5" (W.Nr. 111745) and "White 6" at München-Riem, April 1945.

There had been a blip of excitement during the morning of 4 April, when *Uffz.* Eduard Schallmoser embarked upon the first incident in what was to become a very personal but highly dangerous trend in attacking enemy aircraft. Airborne from Riem at 11:00 as part of a *Rotte* with Fährmann, Schallmoser encountered a group of P-38 Lightnings twenty minutes later immediately due west of Riem over Höhenlinden flying reconnaissance at an estimated 9,500m. Approaching through the heavily overcast conditions with incredible speed and still unfamiliar with the capabilities of the Me 262, Schallmoser

A B-17 Flying Fortress of the 379th BG over England. The 379th flew more sorties and dropped a greater bomb tonnage than any other bomb group in the Eighth Air Force during the Second World War.

attacked from head on but was unable to roll away in time and rammed one of the American aircraft. *Major* Erich Hohagen recalled Schallmoser's story: *"Uffz.* Schallmoser was still not familiar with the fire control system in the Me 262 and on this mission he attacked a squadron of 12 Lightnings. Approaching with high closing speed, he manoeuvred to the correct firing range but used the wrong switch and as nothing happened he looked down into the cockpit to check. Looking up again, he realised that he couldn't avoid collision with one of the enemy fighters and clipped its tail with his starboard wing. The aircraft became unmanoeuvrable and crashed, though the pilot escaped."

It is very probable that the Lightning pilot was 2nd Lt. William Randle from Missouri flying P-38L, serial number 44-25761 of the 49th Fighter Squadron, 14th Fighter Group attached to the Fifteenth Air Force and based at Triolo in Italy. Randle's aircraft formed part of the reconnaissance escort flight which was patrolling the area.

Another pilot in the formation, 2nd Lt. Robert J. Slatter, observed: "At 11:20 hours flying at Höhenlinden, Germany, 15,000 ft (4,572 m), I sighted an Me 262 making a pass on our leader and his wingman, Lt. Randle, from six o'clock low. He came up from a 45 degree angle. When I saw the jet, I called to the leader to break twice. The jet was closing in very fast and as the leader broke left, I saw the complete tail assembly of Lt. Randle's plane come off. His plane yawed to the right and went down in a flat spin. I broke above the jet and did not see Lt. Randle bail out. Approximately three minutes later, I saw a chute floating down at 1,000 ft (305 m). I also noted that his plane burst into flames as it hit the ground."

The two German pilots headed back to Riem, Schallmoser fortunate in the fact that his machine had sustained only light damage and *Luftflotte Reich* was able to report that evening that two Me 262s of the *"Jagdverband Galland"* had been operational over southern Germany destroying one enemy reconnaissance machine without loss.

The war situation now facing Germany was becoming more critical day by day with lines of communication increasingly being placed at risk, fuel supply almost exhausted and hopelessly inadequate land and air forces pitted against an overwhelmingly strong enemy. The gravity of the hour was now undeniable, even to the most fanatic and seemingly oblivious members of the Nazi leadership. Hitler had now hidden himself in a concrete bunker, deep below and behind the Reich Chancellery in Berlin together with Bormann and the dwarfish Goebbels. Elsewhere, Göring had broached the subject of conducting a negotiated peace settlement with the Western Allies. But both Göring's prestige and that of the *Luftwaffe* had, in the eyes of the leadership, sunk to an all-time low.

In the west, the American First and Ninth Armies had completed their encirclement of Model's Army Group B in the Ruhr. The Allied armies were now advancing at up to 80 kilometres (50 miles) per day into Germany and nearly 20,000

Johannes Steinhoff (centre) seen here at München-Riem with his wingman, Lt Gottfried Fährmann (right). The two pilots engaged B-17s of the 379th BG on 5 April 1945. One of the heavies was shot down by JV 44, but Fährmann was forced to bale out of his jet because of engine failure. His parachute became tangled in trees and he was cut down by local civilians.

German troops were surrendering daily. Churchill now publicly opined that the war in Europe would be over within two months at the very most. To the east, the Red Army was in control of the Hungarian oilfields, thus depriving the Reich of its very last source of petroleum and consequently its ability to wage war. Russian troops were fighting in the suburbs of Vienna.

On 5 April, following an *Alarmstart* order and in what was probably its first operation against the *Viermots*, JV 44 sent up a formation of five Me 262s just after 10:30 to intercept an incursion by more than 1,000 Eighth Air Force heavy bombers operating against various transport and airfield targets in southern Germany. Led by *Oberst* Steinhoff and his wingman, *Lt.* Fährmann, this formation also included *Hptm.* Walter Krupinski and *Ofw.* Rudolf Nielinger flying Me 262 "White 8", though the identity of the fifth pilot is not known. Flying on a north easterly course from München-Riem, the Me 262s made contact with B-17s of the 1st Air Division over Straubing, shooting down one Fortress of the 379th Bomb Group using what were later described as "unaggressive and uncoordinated tactics" before Fährmann, troubled by engine failure, was himself shot down by the fighter escort, apparently managing to bale out over the Danube. The remaining Me 262s broke off their engagement and returned to Riem, landing seconds after a flight of Mustangs had strafed the field. With only one of his four 30 mm MK 108 cannon functioning, Steinhoff was able to damage one before they flew off. Fährmann landed by parachute in some trees close to the river.

Meanwhile, cut down from the trees by some local farmers and taken to a neighbouring farmhouse, the luckless Fährmann was interviewed by the mayor of the nearest village who then contacted Riem by telephone to report his presence and safety. Fährmann later endured a painful journey back to Riem in a motorcycle sidecar, arriving shortly before dawn the next morning.

On 6 April, JV 44's strength stood at 18 Me 262s with only seven machines considered serviceable, in one of which, ("White 3"), Jonny Müller was airborne between 11:35-12:45 when he made a patrol from Riem.

Weather restricted operations for the American medium bomber forces and only two groups were able to operate; Douglas A-20 Havocs from the 410th BG hit marshalling yards at Gottingen, Herberg and Northeim while one Marauder group, the 394th, carried out a leaflet dropping mission. But the next day, 7 April, 269 mediums of the 9th Bombardment Division dropped bombs on marshalling yards at Gottingen and Northeim in central Germany, with four aircraft sustaining damage.

At least one JV 44 pilot managed to bail out of a defective Me 262 successfully. Ofw. Leopold Knier clad in the familiar late-war leather flying jacket worn by many JV 44 pilots seen here unharmed after baling out over München-Riem, mid-April 1945. He apparently walked back to the airfield after having landed safely!

On the afternoon of 8 April, Otto Kammerdiener of JV 44, flying on his first operational patrol in an Me 262, was bounced by American fighters near Riem and his aircraft "White 8" was damaged in the right turbo unit, forcing him to land at 16:44 with only one engine operational.

The mediums were back again that day, when a force of 477 aircraft, from the 9th Bombardment Division dropped 843 tons of bombs on marshalling yards and oil storage facilities during the morning. But there was a price to pay; two bombers were lost and another 44 damaged. The 323rd BG lost one B-26 with another 14 damaged. However, Marauders from the 387th, 394th and 397th BGs went to Nienhagen where the raid on the local oil refinery was so succesful and spectacular with smoke at the target so dense that several formations had to make repeated bomb runs to ensure the required results. During the afternoon, the Division returned again with 144 mediums attacking a communications centre at Sonderhausen.

Above and inset opposite: 9 April 1945: "White tail" B-26 (S/N 43-34344) RJ-H piloted by 2nd Lt Lloyd E. Weinberg of the 454th Squadron, 323rd BG over the Naumberg ammunition and vehicle depot. In these dramatic shots, T./Sgt Robert M. Radlein flying in a neighbouring aircraft, has captured RJ-H just before and just as it releases its load of 500 lb bombs.

The next day, 9 April, operating conditions at Riem worsened considerably when six of JV 44's Me 262s were damaged by fragmentation bursts during a heavy American raid on the southern districts of München including the airfield during the late afternoon. A force of 228 B-17s of the Eighth Air Force's 3rd Air Division escorted by nearly 200 P-51s – part of a much larger force attacking jet airfields throughout southern Germany – dropped 550 tons of bombs on the airfield during a fifteen minute pass. Several buildings in the vicinity of Riem, Gronsdorf and Haar were either destroyed or damaged as was the road to Feldkirchen, whilst on the airfield itself, the control tower, administration and accommodation buildings were hit by high explosive and incendiary bombs. The main hangar and two adjoining hangars were badly damaged by incendiaries and large stretches of the perimeter tracks and taxi-ways were hit by high explosive bombs. The ammunition dump was left burning and the north and south dispersal areas torn apart by high explosive, incendiary and fragmentation bursts. The bombs claimed the lives of six personnel with another 50 wounded. The main east-west runway was hit several times and left pitted with craters.

Miraculously, ten minutes after the bombers had departed Riem at 17:20, the unit managed to scramble at least one of its jets when Me 262 "White 5" flown by *Uffz.* "Jonny" Müller pursued the home-bound Allied formation. Müller returned safely just over 40 minutes later (18:03) without having been able to achieve any success.

Elsewhere, Marauders from the 322nd, 323rd BG and 394th BGs attacked an ammunition dump at Naumberg during the morning, leaving the target burning and heavily damaged. That afternoon, the Marauders of the 323rd and 344th BGs joined forces with Douglas A-26 Invaders of the 409th BG and A-20 Havocs of the 410th BG to decimate the marshalling yards at Saalfeld.

Throughout southern Germany, the effect of the Allied raids on other jet airfields and the units based on them, had been devastating. At Schleissheim, a major airfield to the north of München, the attack had left 15 killed and the accommodation and administration buildings, runway, hangars, dispersal points, vehicles and M/T sheds heavily damaged. At Landsberg, 700 HE bombs had killed eight personnel and obliterated the runway. At

Oberpffafenhofen, six aircraft had been destroyed and another 15 damaged with four hangars, the runway and several buildings left badly damaged. It was the same story at Fürstenfeldbruck, Memmingen, Leipheim, Saalfeld and Lechfeld where not only the runway had been damaged but also the important rocket-boosted Me 262 *Heimatschützer II* and *IV* prototypes hangared there. Even worse was the story at Neuburg an der Donau, the home field to III./KG(J) 54 where in the space of twelve minutes, 65 B-17s with heavy fighter escort bombed runways and dispersal and take-off points.

The Americans had by now perfected their lethal art and as Galland himself recalled in May 1945: "For the people on an airfield, the most unpleasant attacks were the ones in which they used small fragmentation bombs; they caused incredible damage to the aircraft, vehicles and equipment – everything on the airfield was destroyed. However, these small bombs didn't render the airfield useless. You could land on them again – even with fighters – once some of the fragments had been cleared. The craters didn't even need filling up as they were shallow. Attacks with heavy bombs didn't affect the aircraft on the airfield as they caused relatively little damage, even when they exploded quite near. The danger was not so much the bombs themselves as the rubble, stones, fragments and things of that sort which were thrown up by the bombs. They penetrated the aircraft. The craters made the airfield useless and then it was a question of how much man-power and machinery we had to clear the place up. There was a definite lack of construction machinery such as tractors, dredgers and bulldozers with which to fill in the craters. If before a raid – or even better – immediately afterward, a few (American) fighter-bombers had attacked what machinery we had, they could have put us out of action completely. Things could have been made even worse by making combination attacks – first, a rain of light bombs followed by heavy bombs to destroy the runway and dispersal area. They did that at Riem; I was there when they laid a bomb carpet – not just one, but eight of them – that shook us. Then they also dropped sticks of incendiaries and we couldn't quite cope with that. The saying was

An American reconnaissance photograph from April 1945 clearly showing the oval layout of München-Riem airport. The main airport buildings, hangars and workshops are visible to the northern edge of the field, whilst to the western edge is the expanse of one of the starting platforms where JV 44 established its dispersal. The unit's jets were usually parked along the perimeter track connecting the start platform with the airport control buildings. Careful examination of some of the aircraft positioned off the southern perimeter track in the main area of bomb craters reveals them to be Me 262s.

that the American fighter-bombers would even attack a stray dog!"

At Lechfeld too, the jet training *Gruppe*, III./EJG 2, with a mere 12 serviceable Me 262s on strength under the redoubtable *Major* Heinz Bär, had only that morning signalled a warning to General Kammhuber to the effect that training was now being constantly hampered by air-raid alerts, requesting the immediate transfer of at least one *Staffel* to Hörsching in Austria so that training could continue uninterrupted in some form. The *Gruppe* was already low on qualified instructors and its rail-wagon fuel tankers were now hidden away in nearby woods. However, when the *Viermots* arrived shortly after 17:30 that same day, they damaged the runways and several buildings yet, miraculously, destroyed only one jet fighter and damaged another.

In response to such crippling attacks by the USAAF, the

Luftwaffe was forced to conduct a radical reorganisation of its jet fighter force. Upon the express orders of Göring, Peltz, as commander of IX. *(J) Fliegerkorps*, was now given control of the jet bomber *Geschwader*, KG 51, which was now to halt all operations pending orders for transfer and further deployment from Peltz. Peltz was also planning to transfer elements of III./JG 7 to München-Riem where they could operate alongside JV 44, a timely decision, since on 10 April, the USAAF relentlessly bombed Brandenburg-Briest as one of a clutch of jet airfield targets in northern Germany, leaving heavy damage to buildings, the runway, several hangars and the repair centre as well as destroying three Me 262s and killing or injuring 14 personnel. In attempting to deal with this attack JG 7 lost 27 aircraft, making it the blackest day in the *Geschwader's* history.

Enemy fighter attack was now a hated but regular occurrence at München-Riem and on 10 April, three Me 262s were destroyed and another three damaged during a low-level strafing run by P-51s from the 353rd FG. In response, "Jonny" Müller flying in Me 262 "White 5" scrambled from Riem at 10:32 to engage a flight of P-47 Thunderbolts patrolling over Augsburg. Müller shot down one of the American fighters over the city and returned to Riem at 11:38. Müller's victim was probably from the Ninth Air Force's 36th Fighter Group. Later that day, OKL noted that of a total of 13 Me 262s delivered to JV 44 direct from the factories, eleven had been destroyed by enemy action, with another machine lost due to "other causes".

OKL was now deeply concerned at the level of attrition. The same day they signalled *Luftwaffenkommando West* :

Available jet and rocket airfields are being neutralised by strong Allied fighter forces thus impeding the landing of our own units after operations. Alternative landing facilities are therefore of decisive significance.

The problem was to be compounded by the fact that, after 9 April, there was a marked increase in American medium bomber activity over southern Germany, brought about partly by the rapid disintegration in German resistance in the area of the US First and Third Armies and partly because of an Allied fear that the Nazi leadership was planning to create a so-called "Alpine Redoubt" – a desperate last-ditch defence in the mountains of Bavaria and Austria. Emphasis was now placed on attacking supply depots, motor transport, rail junctions, tank factories – *anything* that might be considered of assistance to the Germans in building up their forces in the mountains. München-Riem – with three quarters of its main hangar, control tower, accomodation and administrative buildings gutted or wrecked from the 9 April attack – was still considered a prime target.

The Gathering of the "Experten"

For the next week, München-Riem airfield was bombed and strafed again and again. On 11 April hundreds of Allied heavy and medium bombers raided transportation targets throughout southern Germany – Regensburg, Landshut, Nürnberg,

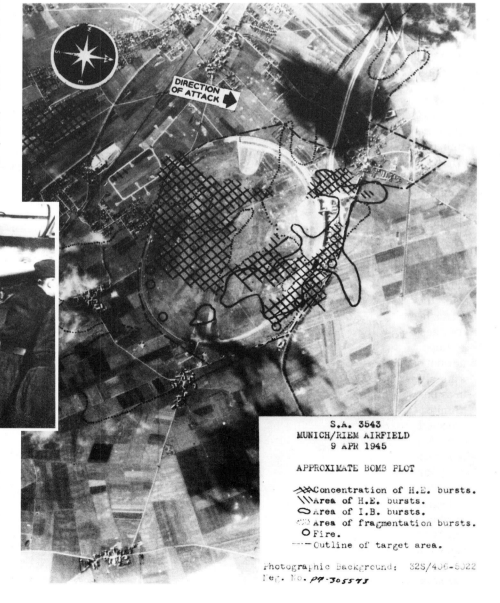

Carpet of bombs: A self explanatory photograph of München-Riem taken shortly after the 9th April attack by the US Eighth Air Force and showing the scale of devastation effected by the bombers.
Inset: Mechanics and pilots hand-push an Me 262 A-1a to shelter, München-Riem, April 1945. The pilot walking beside the aircraft is probably Ofw. Leopold Knier. Note the unusual size of the black "8" on the nose of the aircraft.

S.A. 3543
MUNICH/RIEM AIRFIELD
9 APR 1945

APPROXIMATE BOMB PLOT

Concentration of H.E. bursts.
Area of H.E. bursts.
Area of I.B. bursts.
Area of fragmentation bursts.
Fire.
Outline of target area.

Mid April 1945 saw an increase in American medium bomber activity over southern Germany. The Marauder units were briefed to attack German supply and munitions depots, transportation, marshalling yards and bridges. Here, B-26s of the 496th Squadron, 344th BG head out to or return from just such a mission.

Ingolstadt, Donauwörth, Obertraubling (where 1,200 HE bombs fell on the airfield alone). More than 1,000 fighters flew escort and sweeps against road and railway targets around Bayreuth, Nürnberg, Stuttgart and Ulm.

The Americans approached München shortly before 13:00 in two waves, commencing bombing at heights of 6,000-7,000 metres (19,685/22,965 ft). One wave struck the eastern districts of the city whilst the other bombed the south and the nearby airfields including Riem. Unterpfaffenhofen, Plannegg and Germering suffered most, with many houses destroyed and a large fuel installation – probably at Krailling – set ablaze.

The 9th BD despatched 678 medium bombers to marshalling yards at Aschersleben, Bernberg, Köthen, Rendorf and Zwickau. Ammuntion and storage facilities were targeted at Bamberg and Naumberg. When the Marauders of the 323rd BG accompanied by Havocs from the 410th BG hit Bernberg, they left 12 rail lines cut, rolling stock destroyed, service buildings wrecked and 60 per cent of the yards unusable.

The British came again on the night of the 13th when 25 RAF Mosquitoes mounted a nuisance raid, bombing random targets across the city.

For the handful of exhausted pilots now attached to JV 44 , it was a testing time. With many of their aircraft destroyed as a result of the continuous raids, there was little hope of embarking on any effective retaliation. In a somewhat out-of-character move, Gollob pressed Kammhuber to allocate a further 12 Me 262s to the *"Jagdverband Galland"* as soon as possible.

Amidst this chaos and confusion, JV 44 received three unexpected but welcome additions to its ranks during the first half of April, when, firstly, the famous twenty-six year old *Ritterkreuzträger Major* Gerd Barkhorn – one of the highest scoring Russian front aces – joined the unit having recently relinquished command of JG 6. Barkhorn was followed by the "disgraced" Günther Lützow who arrived at München-Riem soon after leaving the post of *Jafü Oberitalien* at Verona and having personally requested and obtained approval to join Galland's *Jagdverband* from none other than the man who had angrily banished him to Italy in the first place, *Reichsmarschall* Hermann Göring.

The only known former nightfighter pilot to join JV 44 at this time, and yet another *Ritterkreuzträger*, was *Major* Wilhelm Herget who had been trained to fly the Me 262 early in 1945 but also become acutely saddened and sickened by horrific scenes he had witnessed in a slave labour factory whilst serving on the staff of the *Sonderkommission Kleinrath*. Later, he was to play a key role in the story of JV 44.

Thus it was that by mid April 1945, commanded by Adolf Galland, who was assisted by two such dedicated and highly decorated officers as Günther Lützow and Johannes Steinhoff and with fellow *Ritterkreuzträger* Gerd Barkhorn, Willi Herget, Karl-Heinz Schnell, Klaus Neumann, Walter Krupinski, Erich Hohagen and Herbert Kaiser, JV 44 was now gaining a reputation as one of the most esoteric units in the *Luftwaffe*, if not for its tactical effectiveness then at least for its legendary members. In some quarters it was already being dubbed the *Staffel der Experten* – "Squadron of Aces", though it was also widely known that several members of the unit had either fallen foul of Göring, had been expelled from their previous units because of insubordination or were combat-seasoned veterans declared unfit for conventional front-line posts due to the severity of their wounds. Whatever the case, there had been nothing like it before.

Galland now set about revising the command structure of his expanding unit and he asked *Oberst.* Lützow, now his Ia and "adjutant", to draw up an *Arbeitsplan* of responsible officers. Under Lützow's tentative plan, Steinhoff was to be placed in charge of flying operations assisted by Hohagen as Technical Officer and Schnell as officer in charge of airfield repair and renovation. Reporting to Lützow would be *Hptm.* Montanus, a radio and communications expert and *Hptm.* Vollmer, a reserve officer, who apart from being designated to keep a track of JV 44's victory tally was also the owner of a cigar factory which kept Galland supplied with his favourite brand. *Hptm.* Kessler, Galland's personal adjutant from his days as *General der Jagdflieger* and who had, by now, also arrived from Berlin, performed his customary role with *Hptm.* Sprotte, another reserve officer, reporting to him on matters pertaining to motor transport whilst *Major* Barkhorn oversaw the operations of the

Verband's little fleet of Si 204 courier and liaison aircraft.

In principle, JV 44 was still an autonomous unit and not required to report officially to any regional fighter command. Indeed, there is evidence to suggest that at command level, it was still not totally clear "who" or "what" JV 44 was! In many respects, this was probably just as well, since the critical war situation was now wreaking havoc with channels of communication, often resulting in the issuing of conflicting orders as competing commands sought to gain control of the scattered and badly depleted units still operating in the defence of the Reich.

In many cases, the epicentre of this confusion appears to have been at the headquarters of Peltz's IX. *(J) Fliegerkorps* still operating out of Treuenbrietzen but imminently to relocate to Prague. With both the eastern and western fronts now so close to its bases and suffering from a virtually annihilated ground organisation, operating conditions for the component *Gruppen* of

On 11 April 1945, hundreds of medium bombers hit transportation targets throughout southern Germany, inflicting yet more damage on an already crippled and beleaguered enemy infrastructure.

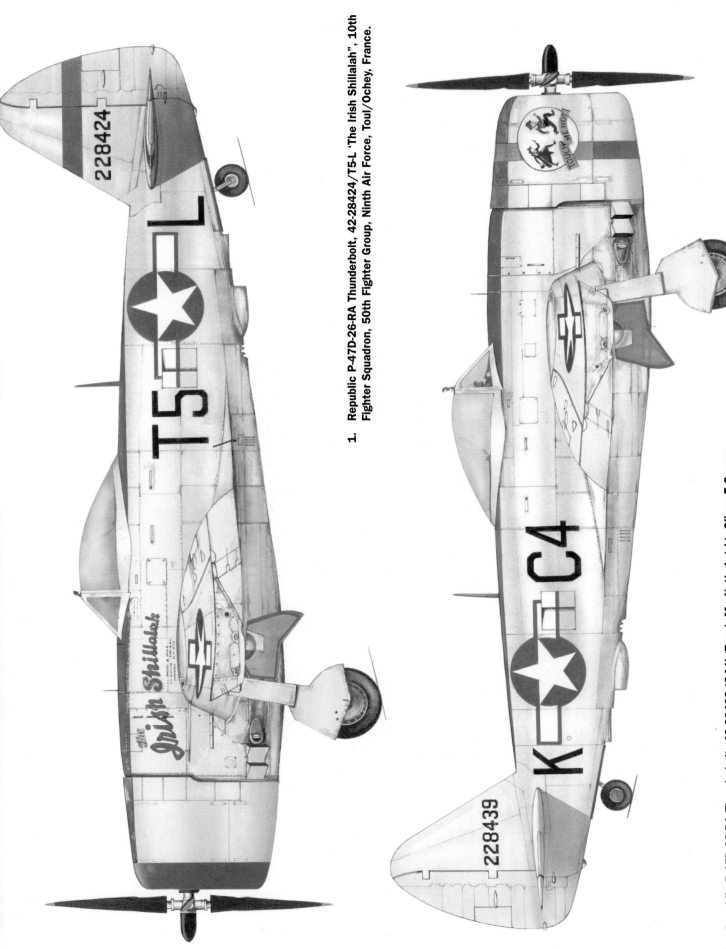

1. Republic P-47D-26-RA Thunderbolt, 42-28424/T5-L 'The Irish Shillalah", 10th Fighter Squadron, 50th Fighter Group, Ninth Air Force, Toul/Ochey, France.

2. Republic P-47D-28-RA Thunderbolt, 42-28439/C4-K 'Touch Me Not', 1st Lt. Oliven T Cowan, 388th Fighter Squadron, 365th Fighter Group, Ninth Air Force, Aachen, Germany.

97

3. Martin B-26G-25-MA Marauder, 44-68132/ WT-A, 456th Bomb Squadron, 323rd Bomb Group, Ninth Air Force.

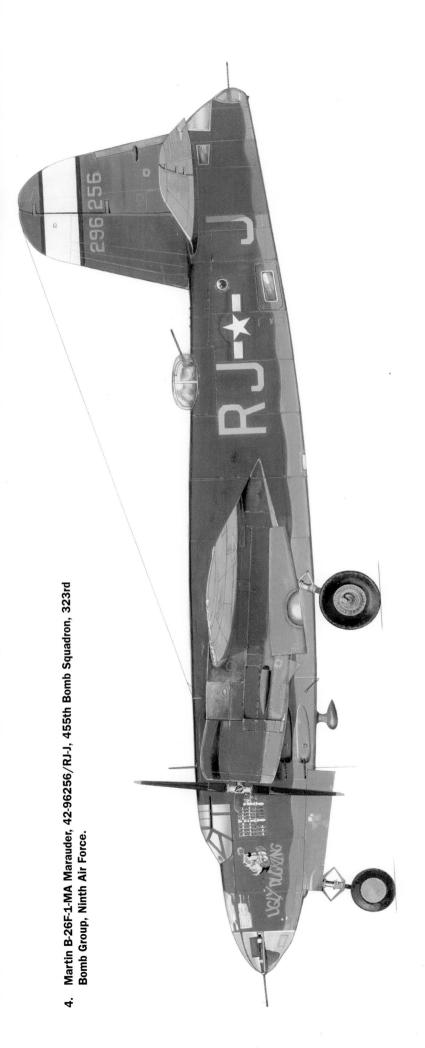

4. Martin B-26F-1-MA Marauder, 42-96256/RJ-J, 455th Bomb Squadron, 323rd Bomb Group, Ninth Air Force.

5. B-26 Marauders of the 344th BG taxi-out at the start of a mission to Cologne in February 1945.

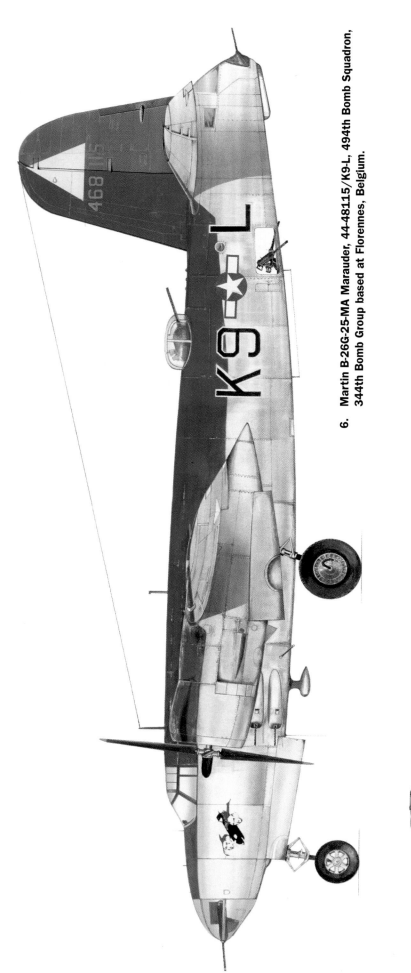

6. Martin B-26G-25-MA Marauder, 44-48115/K9-L, 494th Bomb Squadron, 344th Bomb Group based at Florennes, Belgium.

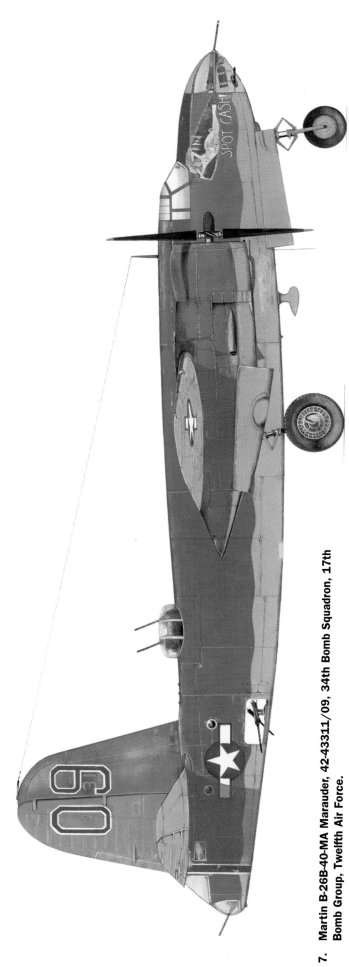

7. Martin B-26B-40-MA Marauder, 42-43311/09, 34th Bomb Squadron, 17th Bomb Group, Twelfth Air Force.

8. Martin B-26C-45-MO Marauder, 42-107729/17, 34th Bomb Squadron, 17th Bomb Group, Twelfth Air Force.

9. Me 262A-1a W.Nr. 111745, 'White 5', Jagdverband 44.

10. Me 262B-1a (W.Nr. not known), "White S", Jagdverband 44, (probably formerly EJG 2).

11. Me 262A-1a/U4 W.Nr. 111899, Jagdverband 44.

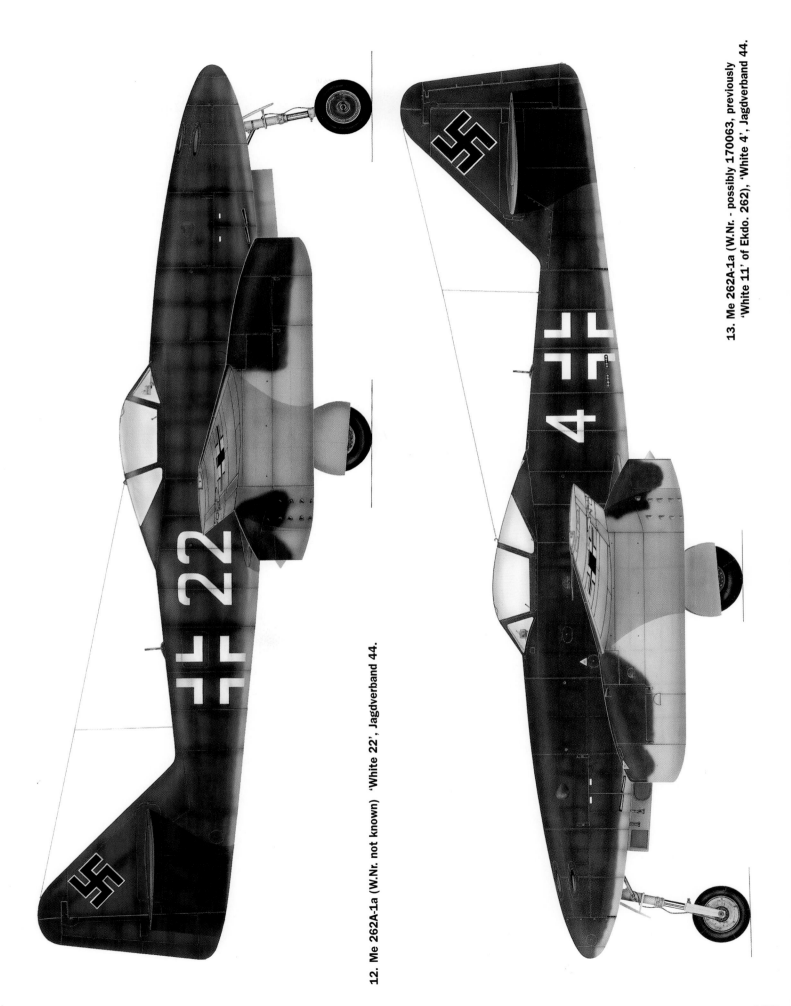

12. Me 262A-1a (W.Nr. not known) 'White 22', Jagdverband 44.

13. Me 262A-1a (W.Nr. - possibly 170063, previously 'White 11' of Ekdo. 262), 'White 4', Jagdverband 44.

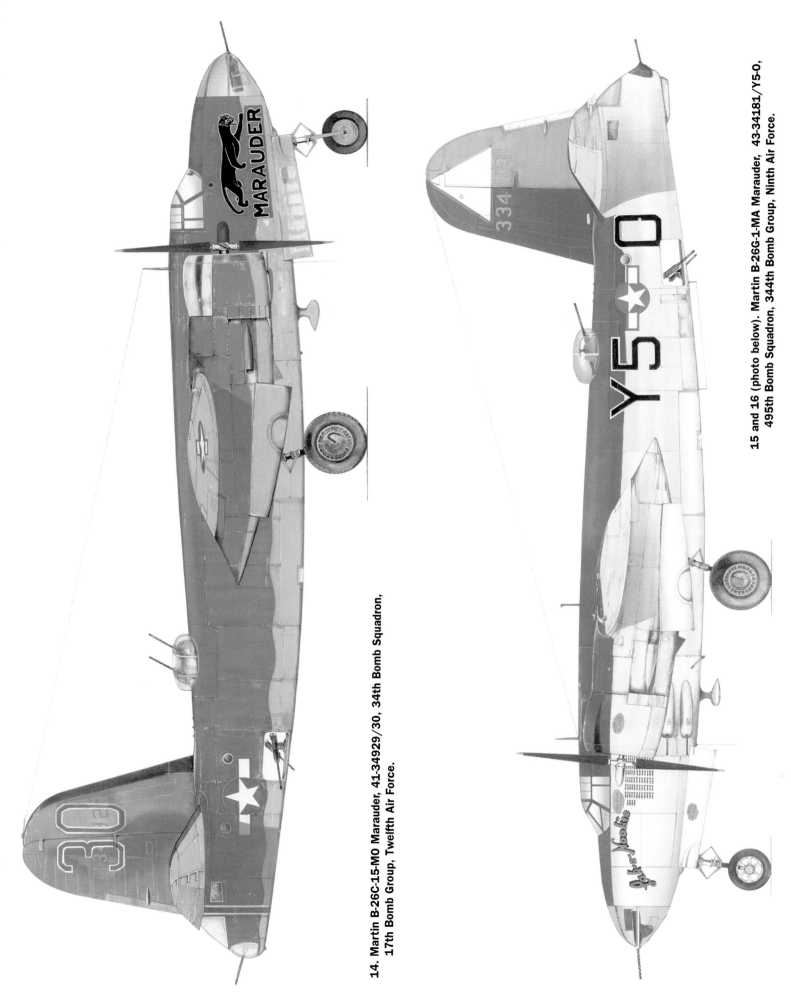

14. Martin B-26C-15-MO Marauder, 41-34929/30, 34th Bomb Squadron,
17th Bomb Group, Twelfth Air Force.

15 and 16 (photo below). Martin B-26G-1-MA Marauder, 43-34181/Y5-O,
495th Bomb Squadron, 344th Bomb Group, Ninth Air Force.

17. Martin B-26B-45-MA Marauder, 42-95771/37, 37th Bomb Squadron, 17th Bomb Group, Twelfth Air Force.

18. Me 262A-1a (W.Nr. not known) 'White 1 and S', Jagdverband 44.

19 and 20 (photo below). Me 262A-2a W.Nr. 111685, "9K+FH", Jagdverband 44.

21. Me 262A-2a W.Nr. 111712, Jagdverband 44.

WILLI HERGET

A native of Stuttgart, born in June 1910, Willi Herget, known affectionately as *"der Kleine"* (lit. *"Titch"*) on account of his 1.7 metre (5.5 ft) stature, was Germany's fourth highest scoring nightfighter *Experte*. He had entered the still embryonic *Luftwaffe* in December 1936 having developed his flying skills in a series of privately financed flying lessons. Upon the outbreak of war, Herget joined the Bf 110 equipped II./ZG 76 as a *Zerstörer* pilot flying successfully during the Battle of Britain and by the end of 1940 he had accumulated fourteen day victories (mainly Spitfires and Hurricanes) before transferring to the nightfighters and joining NJG 3 in 1941. Later, in 1942, via a short posting to NJG 1, he was appointed *Gruppenkommandeur* of I./NJG 4 at Frankfurt equipped with Bf 110, Do 217 and Ju 88 nightfighters. By June 1943, when the RAF Bomber Command night offensive against the Ruhr and Hamburg was at its zenith, Herget was awarded the *Ritterkreuz* by the then commander of the nightfighter arm, *General der Flieger* Kammhuber upon the occasion of his 30th victory.

But perhaps his greatest success came on the night of 20 December 1943, when Bomber Command launched an attack on Frankfurt and during which Herget downed eight bombers in 50 minutes. One of his victims that night was claimed using only four rounds of ammunition. In this attack, he had manoeuvred his Bf 110 below the targeted Lancaster and using the engine exhaust as a guide, waited until he could see the reflection from the exhaust in his mirror before opening fire.

The Oakleaves to the *Ritterkreuz* were awarded by Hitler during a much-publicised ceremony on the Obersalzberg in April 1944 to mark his 63rd victory

On 2 January 1945, Herget was transferred away from operational duties and attached to the staff of the *Sonderkommission Kleinrath*, a special investigative body set up under *Generalleutnant* Kleinrath, the commander of the 1. *Jagddivision* at Döberitz. The *Sonderkommission* had been instigated by Albert Speer's Armaments Ministry and charged with eliminating bottle-necks in the test-flying and delivery schedules of newly manufactured aircraft. The *Sonderkommission* included at least four travelling missions, each briefed to conduct investigations into conditions at the major flight testing centres.

For his part, Herget was appointed head of the mission dealing with the flight testing of the Me 262 and a few days after his appointment he set out on an inspection tour accompanied by his three-man staff comprising a representative from Messerschmitt, and his former *Gruppe*

technical and fighter control officers from NJG 4. Together, they systematically visited the production and testing facilities at Schwäbisch-Hall, Leipheim, Memmingen, Lechfeld and München-Riem. The prime objective of Herget's team was to reorganise each centre's production timetable in such a way as to increase both output of the badly needed jet aircraft and flight testing. During his tour, Herget was able to increase the rate of testing to a small extent by making adjustments in meal times and in the hours of work. It was also arranged that test-flying should take place in weather conditions previously considered unsuitable and special arrangements were made by Herget's officers for flying to continue even during air raid alerts.

Herget subsequently discovered that one of the major contributory factors to the "bottle-neck" in Me 262 production lay in the unsatisfactory level of output from the wing assembly plant at Leonberg which amounted to only 150 sets per month as against a scheduled output of 750. Herget decided to investigate this situation personally and, exceeding his authority, visited the Leonberg factory close to his home town of Stuttgart. What he saw there repulsed him; a large number of the workers employed at the plant had been drawn from concentration camps and were so weak from hunger and exhaustion that they often fainted at their posts on the assembly lines. Herget complained in the strongest possible terms to the SS official in charge of the slave labour but was simply told that adequate food supplies and the transport to move them had been refused by "higher authorities".

Herget duly reported this worrying state of affairs to Kleinrath, who immediately travelled to Oberammergau to meet with Messerschmitt personally. Messerschmitt seemed horrified by what Herget had discovered and sacked the Leonberg factory manager on the spot. However, this course of action had little effect and so, appreciating the critical importance of increasing Me 262 production, Kleinrath next reported the matter directly to Göring. Göring, in turn, communicated with the Armaments Ministry. The only result of this intervention however, was that Herget was severely reprimanded for interfering in matters "... in which he had no concern" and was forbidden to set foot in any Messerschmitt factory again, with the additional implication that he would be far better off employed on operational duties.

Depressed and disillusioned, the nightfighter ace duly returned to what he was best at and visited the Lechfeld test centre on 5 April 1945 to carry out trials with the Me 262 A-1a/U4, a new variant equipped with the long-range Mauser 50 mm MK 214 cannon (see Chapter 15 for details).

JG 7 on their airfields around Berlin steadily deteriorated to the point of becoming untenable, prompting Peltz to assert his authority and grasp control of the jet fighter *Geschwader* in an attempt to integrate it into his *Fliegerkorps*.

Meanwhile, from his base in Berlin, Kammhuber was mindful of the ever decreasing supply of fuel and ordered the "...utmost economy" in the use of J2 fuel. *"Aircraft are not to taxi*

to dispersal areas under own power," Kammhuber dictated, *"Unit commanders to be instructed under threat of court-martial."*

On 14 April, two of JG 26's veteran *Staffelkapitäne, Leutnant* Georg Kiefner (1./JG 26) and *Oberleutnant* Alfred Heckmann (5./JG 26) were ordered to travel to München-Riem to join JV 44. Both had flown the "long-nose" Fw 190D-9 in combat over Holland against the British 2nd TAF and "Fred" Heckmann had

GERHARD BARKHORN

Born 20.3.1919 at Königsberg in East Prussia, Gerhard Barkhorn had been awarded the Swords to his *Ritterkreuz* with Oakleaves in recognition of his 250th aerial victory and a career that started during the Battle of Britain and which subsequently spanned more than 1,000 missions, predominantly in the east where he had flown as *Gruppenkommandeur* of II./JG 52. Like his fellow JG 52 pilot, Walter Krupinski, Barkhorn was, by many standards, a "slow starter", not scoring his first kill until his 120th mission in July 1941. From then on however, his rise to the very top of the *Luftwaffe* score table was meteoric. The Oakleaves to the Ritterkreuz came in January 1943 following his 120th victory. He ended the war as the second highest scoring fighter pilot in the history of air fighting with 301 confirmed aerial victories, second only to Erich Hartmann. Barkhorn's accomplishments over Russia were legendary, but a momentary lapse of concentration during the summer of 1944 almost proved fatal. Overcome by fatigue from continuous combat and flying on his sixth mission of the day, Barkhorn was bounced by a flight of Red Air Force Airacobras, suffering severe wounds to his right leg and arm. A four month spell in hospital ensued after which, he returned to JG 52 for a brief period engaging in the defence of Hungary. In January 1945, Barkorn was posted to take over the Reich defence unit, JG 6, at Posen, as a result of its previous *Kommodore* being shot down during Operation *Bodenplatte*. But recurring problems from his earlier wounds continued to plague Barkhorn, preventing him from fully converting to the "long-nosed" Fw 190 D-9 and, like Krupinski, he found himself recuperating at Bad Wiessee until word of JV 44 reached him.

(presumably south Germany) operated against B-26s" that day. Certainly, Marauders were in operation that day, when "white tails" of the 323rd visted Kempten ammunition depot, a target well within range of JV 44's Me 262s, but all of that group's aircraft returned without harm having left Kempten ablaze. However, one B-26 of the 387th BG was lost that day. Mediums from the 9th Bombardment Division also attacked targets at Gunzenhausen, Wittenburg and Zerbst.

Also on the 16th, a formation of Fifteenth Air Force P-38 Lightnings dive-bombing a bridge on the Walchensee 65 kilometres (40 miles) south of München, was attacked by 5 Me 262s. The Me 262s made one pass, forcing the Lightnings to jettison their bombs and then pulled away. There were no claims and no losses on either side. It is possible that these jets were from JV 44 .

The notion that R4M rockets were now being used by JV 44 is given credence in a signal sent from the *"Fliegerführer Transport"* the same day allocating two He 111s to collect a consignment of R4M rockets from Lübeck-Blankensee for movement to München-Riem.

As part of a wide-ranging operation against several key *Luftwaffe* airfields, the USAAF attacked München-Riem at 13:26 on the 16th, when 11 Mustangs made a low-level sweep across the field destroying 17 aircraft and damaging another eight. How many of JV 44's prevailing strength of 23 Me 262s were damaged, if any, is not known. Other airfields attacked included Erding, Bad Aibling, Neubiberg, Mühldorf, Landau and Straubing. A total of 62 aircraft were destroyed with a further 53 damaged on these fields alone.

On the evening of 16th also, a confident General Spaatz dispatched a personal message to his Air Force commanders, Doolittle and Twining, from his headquarters at Reims:

Oblt. Alfred Heckmann.

"The advances of our ground forces have brought to a close the strategic air war waged by the United States Strategic Air Forces and the Royal Air Force Bomber Command. It has been won with a decisiveness becoming increasingly evident as our armies overrun Germany. From now onward, our Strategic Air Forces must operate with our Tactical Air Forces in close co-operation with our armies..."

On 17 April, JV 44 was in action against medium bomber incursions over southern and south-west Germany, targeting yet more marshalling yards, oil storage facilities and motor transport and ordnance depots. At 13:34, *Generalleutnant* Galland led a formation of seven Me 262s probably including Steinhoff, Fährmann, Krupinski, Stigler,

been awarded the *Ritterkreuz* in September 1942 as recognition of the 50th of his eventual 71 victories, the first of which he had scored as early as June 1940. He had flown with JG 3 during the advance into Russia and had then been employed as a fighter instructor before being transferred to JG 26 in January 1944. It is likely that Galland hoped to use these pilots to assist in establishing an airfield protection *Staffel* at Riem. However, though both men set out on the journey from JG 26's bases at Stade and Sülte en route for Riem, they were only able to get as far as Lechfeld before the war ended.

One pilot who did manage to reach Riem was *Ritterkreuzträger, Oberleutnant* Hans Grünberg, formerly *Staffelkapitän* of 1./JG 7, who joined JV 44 on or around 17 April. Arriving in München from his former base near Prague, he met General Kammhuber who was visiting the city. Grünberg must have expressed his doubts about the effect JV 44's operations were having on the overall conduct of the air war, for Kammhuber responded frostily: *"Do you want to go on flying or join the infantry?"* Grünberg conceded and reported to Galland who undoubtedly found his presence at JV 44 a fillip, though within days Grünberg was shot down over Bavaria.

During the day before, some sources claim that a formation of JV 44 aircraft led by Galland and equipped with the new 55 mm R4M air-to-air rocket was operational, Galland claiming two B-26 Marauders with rockets, possibly of the 322nd Bomb Group, which was known to have lost two machines. This assertion is supported by ULTRA intelligence decrypts which note that a formation of 14 Me 262s of "...an unidentified command

Oberst Günther Lützow and Oberst Johannes Steinhoff, two of the Luftwaffe's finest fighter pilots and unit commanders, discuss operational matters outside JV 44's dispersal hut, München-Riem, mid-April 1945. Right: Designed and manufactured by Askania and Carl Zeiss, the EZ 42 gyroscopic gunsight proved unpopular and ineffective with JV 44's pilots. They soon abandoned it.

HANS GRÜNBERG

Born 8.7.1917. at Gross-Fahlenwerder in Pommerania, "Specker" Grünberg had originally flown with JG 3 in Russia where he had commanded 5. *Staffel* and where, in more than 500 fighter and ground attack missions, he had baled out four times and accumulated 61 of his eventual 82 victories. He was awarded the *Ritterkreuz* in July 1944 following his 70th victory. A cool, level-headed officer who had performed extremely well in the Me 262 conversion course at Lechfeld, he subsequently became a competent jet pilot and tactician, shooting down five enemy bombers whilst with JG 7 before joining JV 44 briefly in mid-April 1945.

Schallmoser and Nielinger, to intercept an incoming bomber formation, most likely B-26 Marauders from the 17th and 320th BGs who were bombing the Altendettelsau ammunition dump, west of Nürnberg, that afternoon. The jets were directed to proceed by the Feldkirchen control centre on a northerly course, Ansbach – Rottenburg – Nürnberg. Problems plagued the operation from the start. *Ofw.* Nielinger flying "White 12" was forced to turn back after twenty minutes on account of a landing gear defect.

Approaching the enemy formation, *Uffz.* Schallmoser flying "White 10" found that the newly installed gyroscopic EZ 42 gunsight malfunctioned and was useless. Undeterred, he flew into the midst of the *Bomberpulk* only to discover that his guns were jammed. Returning for a second pass, the guns "unjammed" themselves just in time and Schallmoser was able to record hits on one of the P-47 escorts, but not without sustaining damage to his own aircraft. Return fire from the Thunderbolt left a large hole in the canopy, though Schallmoser himself was miraculously unharmed.

A gunner from the 34th Squadron, 17th BG, S/Sgt. James A. Valimont of Williamsport, Pennsylvania was badly wounded when the tail section of his B-26 was shot away during an

Above: From mid-April 1945, General Spaatz signalled that with the "strategic" air war having been "won", the job was to be finished by "tactical" air power. The Marauder groups were more than capable of carrying out the task.

Left: A typical scene at a Marauder airfield in France, in this case of Cormeilles-en-Vexin, home of the 344th BG from October 1944 until the last four weeks of the war. This photo shows B-26C-45 (S/N 42-107666) \ Y5-F BARRACUDA *of the 495th Squadron, at its dispersal.*

Drama at München-Riem
Steinhoff crashes

"aggressive" jet attack and his left leg was was severely cut by flying fragments. With just the framework of the tail remaining intact, and according to a subsequent DFC citation, Valimont "...resolutely manned his guns and on the next attack so badly damaged the fighter aircraft that the attack was diverted without further action."

Luftwaffenkommando West reported that *Jagdverband* 44 had accounted for one enemy aircraft shot down, with another probable. JV 44 is also reported to have lost one machine, though the identities of pilot and aircraft are unknown.

As a result of these initial problems with the EZ 42 however, most of Galland's pilots simply locked the new sight so that it functioned like the old fixed reflector sights.

JV 44 persevered; and yet 18 April 1945 saw some of the most widespread operations yet mounted by the Eighth, Ninth and Fifteenth Air Forces over central and southern Germany. 760 B-17s and B-24s from the Eighth Air Force escorted by as many fighters pounded railway targets at Rosenheim, Traunstein, Passau, Straubing and Plattling. The Fifteenth Air Force struck at similar targets in the Prague-Pilsen area, whilst for nine hours between 10:00-19:00, B-25 Mitchells and B-26 Marauders from Ninth and Twelfth Air Forces visited fuel dumps and railway installations around Ingolstadt, Unterhausen, Ulm and Oldenburg. The crumbling remains of the Reich's rail network were being set ablaze.

Against this massive armada, JV 44 was only able to muster a force of six Me 262s which were readied to take-off to intercept incoming bombers during the morning. The day had started like any other, as Johannes Steinhoff recalled:

"We drove round the perimeter road, noting that our unit had meanwhile grown into a respectable fighting force. The ground crews, working non-stop, had repaired, refuelled and reloaded the aircraft and dispersed them around the field with the aid of special track-laying motorcycles.

The squadron's mess area was a masterpiece of improvisation, consisting basically of a table and a few rickety chairs set up in the middle of a patch of weeds and undergrowth. A field telephone stood on the table. The pilots lounged in deck-chairs sipping coffee out of chunky Wehrmacht cups. Saucers of thin red jam and a stack of damp army bread covered some of the cup rings on the stained table top and provided our sustenance. The morning was very chilly, with several strata of light cloud obscuring our view of the Alps.

For the thousandth time we sat down to endure the agony of waiting before a scramble. No one felt like talking, so we sat in silence. The road that ran past the airfield fence was deserted. Looking west, one could see the greyish silhouette of the roofs and churches of München – an unreal, shadowy mass, as if the city was dead and abandoned."

The mess area Steinhoff describes was located to the edge of München-Riem's western starting platform. The JV 44 pilots' only accommodation was a small army-style *Feldhütte* erected close to the end of the brick wall that skirted this side of the airfield and near to the hard standing where the unit's Me 262s were parked, having been towed from their concrete blast pens by trusty semi-tracked *Kettenkrads*. The flimsy *Feldhütte* was a familiar sight to many of the unit's pilots who had seen service on forward airstrips in Russia; groundcrews were able to assemble them in less than two hours. Meals for the pilots were

Trying out the new garden furniture?: Pilots of JV 44 gather outside their humble Feldhütte at München-Riem, mid April 1945. L-R: unknown, unknown, Hptm. Walter Krupinski, Oberst Günther Lützow, Oberst Johannes Steinhoff, unknown, Uffz. Eduard Schallmoser, Lt. Klaus Neumann, Hptm. Waldemar Wübke, unknown. The flare pistols on the table were used to alert ground crews of an imminent take-off.

brought out from the kitchens at Feldkirchen by motorcycle.

Sometime after 13:00, having received updated information from Feldkirchen on the progress of the incoming raids, Galland decided to scramble six jets to intercept the bombers, this formation in turn being broken down into two three-aircraft *Ketten*, the leading element to be led by himself, the second by Steinhoff. As Gottfried Fährmann yelled across to the ground crew who were busy digging slit trenches, to ready the Me 262s, the six pilots prepared themselves – a final check of the course and maps, a last gulp of coffee, a last chance to urinate behind the *Feldhütte*, perhaps subdued smiles and murmurs of "good luck" from those pilots not detailed to fly. Then, wearily, the pilots began to walk to their jets. There was little talk of tactics, since Galland had already briefed his pilots time and time again to go straight for the bombers.

"My Me 262 was parked in front of the high wall that bordered the airfield to the west." Steinhoff wrote

The instrument panel of an Me 262 A-1a. The Revi 16B gun sight can be seen in its folded position to the top right of the photograph; in this position, landing visibility was improved. To the centre is the fusing panel for an external bomb load with switches for options for a diving attack or level attack. The arming panel for the nose-mounted cannon is to the left, located below the blind flying panel.

in his memoirs, *"I ran quickly around her once before getting in. I ducked under the wing and felt the rockets with my hand; I pulled back the slotted flap out of the leading edge, letting it spring back with a loud clack... Once in the cockpit I wriggled around on the parachute until I found the right position, hitching myself up with both hands on the cockpit rim. It always took me a minute to get comfortable. The seat was adjustable to bring one's eyes exactly on a level with the sight. I slipped on my shoulder straps and waist belt... then buckled my helmet under my chin. I picked up the oxygen mask. Meanwhile my eyes had flashed over the instruments. I set the altimeter for barometric pressure, moved the ailerons with my feet, checked the rudder with the control stick and switched on the radio. I was ready."*

One by one, the aircraft began to roll from the hardstanding onto the start platform ready to take-off towards the east as per customary procedure. In the first element were Adolf Galland, newly promoted *Leutnant* Klaus Neumann and *Oblt.* Franz Stigler. In the second element were *Oberst* Johannes Steinhoff, *Hauptmann* Walter Krupinski and *Leutnant* Gottfried Fährmann. This small combat formation, was, without doubt, one of the most formidable and distinguished assemblies of *Luftwaffe Experten* ever to ready itself for action; four of the six pilots were

18 April 1945 saw some of the most widespread activity yet mounted by the American medium bomber force over Germany. The 17th BG was briefed to bomb Schussenried airfield. Here, Marauders of the 17th pull away from a target they have left ablaze.

Ritterkreuzträger, whilst five of them had accounted for nearly 550 victories between them. Furthermore, at least three of these aircraft (Galland, Steinhoff and Neumann) carried racks of twelve R4M rockets under each wing to supplement their MK 108s.

Walter Krupinski told the author: "On take-off, we used a close formation because it was the easiest and safest way to come out of Riem. We had to lift off very fast because of the continuous risk of enemy fighters above the field or very near to it. Close formation with four aircraft however, was a bit tricky, first of all because the grass strip at Riem was not that wide and secondly – and I witnessed Steinhoff's accident when I was positioned to the left of his aircraft and Fährmann to the right – if you tried to take-off with four aircraft and something went wrong, it would have been terribly difficult to get away. As a result, we stuck to three aircraft formations."
Johannes Steinhoff wrote later:

"I saw the General stick his right hand out of the cockpit and wave it in a circle. A mechanic started the little motors at the front of the turbines and the turbines fired and began to hum.

Temperature normal, air pressure normal, close cockpit, taxi into position. I had only to turn the aircraft into the wind and the flag lined runway stretched away before me. The General's flight moved off with turbines screaming, their exhaust rocking my Me 262 quite violently. The penetrating smell of kerosene filled the cockpit. When the three shapes had disappeared in a towering cloud of dust and fumes, I eased the throttle forward and took my toes off the brake pedals. With a gentle shudder, the aircraft began to move...

The heavy jet rolls along the grass with painful slowness. All my tanks are full... She's too heavy, I thought half unconsciously. The field was extremely bumpy and uneven; the previous day's bomb carpet had made innumerable shallow craters that had been filled in in a somewhat makeshift fashion...

I saw the General lift out of the dust cloud in front of me and retract his undercarriage. At that moment the silhouette of his Me 262 began to wander to starboard; my machine was changing direction, although, having reacted automatically, I was already countering with the rudder...

In the final third of my take-off run I reach nearly 200 kph (124 mph) when suddenly the left wing drops. The airplane starts to yaw... I lose my left gear. I lose direction. My speed doesn't increase and is not enough to get airborne. The road at the end of the airfield looms closer. I know now that a crash cannot be avoided due to the heavy load...

When the undercarriage hit the embankment, the Me 262 reared up as if caught by one of those hard gusts of wind that you get on a hot summer's day. The shock was not cruel and final, not the death smash of an elegant and extremely vulnerable masterpiece of technology against a

solid obstacle. Instead, it was as if the aircraft were making a desperate attempt to lift off into its element in spite of everything – although the last, muffled blow had ushered in its final destruction; crashdown, fire, explosion!"

Walter Krupinski was following at speed a short distance down the runway on Steinhoff's port side. He remembers: "What I saw is very easy to explain; I saw that Steinhoff's port wing dropped. We'd had an air attack the day before and there was a lot of metal and debris scattered all over the field, fragments of enemy bombs and so on. He got a flat tyre – of that I'm absolutely certain. He came very near to me – dangerously near, only metres away. I pulled back on the stick and became airborne and I flew right over his aircraft. By that time it had not yet exploded, but by the time I had gained speed and began to climb and turn, I looked back and saw the explosion."

Klaus Neumann was already in the air, flying as part of Galland's *Kette*: "I was already in the air, but I looked back and saw this exploding aircraft. I thought *"That's it – Steinhoff's burning"*."

Steinhoff: *"Catapulted high into the air, the stricken bird dragged itself through several more seconds of existence. Shortly before the impact, my hands flew instinctively to the shoulder harness. I tugged so violently on the straps*

Johannes Steinhoff listens to an update from the war-room at Feldkirchen. L-R: unknown, Hptm. Walter Krupinski, Hptm. Werner Gutowski, Oberst Günther Lützow, Oberst Steinhoff, Lt. Klaus Neumann, unknown, Uffz. Eduard Schallmoser, unknown.

that my body slammed back against the seat. Then, all of a sudden, everything seemed to grow still. There was only the hissing of the huge flames. As if in slow motion, I saw a wheel go soaring through the air. Metal fragments and bits of undercarriage flew after it, spinning very slowly. Wherever I looked was red, deep red.

Grasping the sides of the cockpit, I pulled myself up until I was standing on the parachute. I had got my feet over the cockpit rim when the rockets started exploding under the wings. They skittered over the field and went off with a hellish bang. Taking great leaping strides, I ran out along the wing to escape from the flames. And when I emerged from the inferno and my straining lungs filled with fresh air, I sank to my knees as if under the impact of a mighty blow... I managed to get to my feet and as I stumbled a few steps farther everything went black: my eyes had swollen shut. I became aware of piercing pain in my wrists where the flames shooting through the cockpit floor had burned off the skin between my gloves and the sleeves of my leather jacket..."

"He tried to fly the aeroplane off the runway," Galland recorded in his diary, "but it dropped down again, crashing onto the road forming the airfield's eastern boundary. The whole plane caught fire almost immediately and then somersaulted, coming to rest about 100 metres (328 ft) further on in a field. "Macki" managed to jump from the burning wreck with severe burns to his head and arms – only a man with his agility could react so promptly."

The remaining five Me 262s continued their mission, though there is no documentary evidence to suggest that any successes were scored against the American bombers or even that JV 44 made contact with them that day. All five aircraft returned to Riem safely however and upon landing as Walter Krupinski remembers, first thoughts were for Steinhoff: "When I got back, the first thing I did was ask a mechanic where Steinhoff's body was. I was certain that he was dead – it had been a really big

Below: This photograph, taken by a USAAF photo-reconnaissance group in June 1945, shows the grass runway at München-Riem looking towards the eastern dispersal area and the hamlet of Salmsdorf. Steinhoff probably crash-landed in the dispersal area.

explosion. I immediately went over to Oberföhring Military Hospital and right then he didn't look too good at all."

Werner Roell also visited Steinhoff at Oberföhring shortly after the horrific crash. "They had put him in an underground ward and his whole head and both wrists were wrapped in bandages. There were just three holes for his eyes and mouth – I didn't even know it was him! I went onto the ward and said *"Where's Oberst Steinhoff?"* A voice answered *"I'm here!"* I walked over and asked him – *"How are you doing?"*. He said – *"Fine."* – which, of course, meant *"Miserable"*! But he was a very brave man in that respect."

Steinhoff had been saved by the sectionalised design of the Me 262 in which the pilot was contained in the *Führerraum Wanne*, the self-contained metal subassembly which held the instrument panel and electrical controls, stick and rudder, throttles, seat, battery and rear cockpit section and which in instances such as those described above, was intended to break free on impact.

Steinhoff's crash resulted in a reorganisation of JV 44 's "command structure". Erich Hohagen took over from him as the *Jagdverband's Einsatzchef*, whilst Franz Stigler filled Hohagen's previous position as Technical Officer.

The Me 262 was still proving a difficult aircraft to master for many of the pilots now attached to JV 44 – even the recognised *Experten*. Steinhoff had observed that Lützow, out of combat for more than two years, was wary of the unfamiliar jet fighter. Even Gerd Barkhorn encountered problems with the aircraft and developed a well-known dislike for it. Sometime between 19-27 April and in the last of only two operational flights in the Me 262, Barkhorn's starboard Jumo engine failed and he was forced to break off an attack on an American bomber formation and return to Riem. Crippled by a significant loss of speed, the lone, damaged jet became vulnerable to the bombers' Mustang escort, some of which pursued him towards München. Slipping through cloud and mustering as much speed as he could, Barkhorn approached a clearing in some woods and prepared for a crash-landing. His intention was to have the canopy already pushed open in order to facilitate a swift escape from the dying jet once it had come to rest on the ground, having already taken the precautionary measure of releasing his seat harness during his descent. But in bringing the Me 262 down onto the uneven ground, the plan rudely backfired, for the landing proved much rougher than anticipated and the lurching motion caused the canopy to slam down on Barkhorn's neck.

"It was a pilot's mistake," Galland recalled, "He touched down too late with too much speed." But the second highest scoring fighter pilot in the *Luftwaffe* had narrowly avoided being decapitated and within twenty four hours he was back inside a hospital.

Meanwhile, also on the 18th, JV 44 was reinforced by the arrival at München-Riem from Neuburg an der Donau of the Me 262s of *Hptm* Werner Brandau's 4./KG(J) 54 which had been ordered (presumably by a reluctant IX.(J) *Fliegerkorps*), to hand

The smouldering remains of Johannes Steinhoff's Me 262 lie on the grass at the eastern edge of Riem, close to the little hamlet of Salmsdorf, 18 April 1945.

all its remaining jets over to Galland's unit before transferring its entire personnel to II./KG(J) 54 at Fürstenfeldbruck, though this latter unit was already aircraft-less. At the same time, the dissolution of this famous *Kampfgeschwader* continued with the entire III./KG(J) 54, also at Neuburg an der Donau receiving orders to hand over its aircraft to JV 44 and thereupon cease functioning as an operational flying *Gruppe*. An advance detachment of Me 262s allocated to JV 44 from this unit left Neuburg the same day and headed for the transit field at Erding where having landed they were almost immediately subjected to an attack by Marauders which resulted in nearly all the aircraft being destroyed.

The next day, with III./KG(J) 54 virtually annihilated, OKL issued instructions for the further use of what remained of the *Geschwader*. The ground elements of II./KG(J) 54 were to remain at Fürstenfeldbruck for eventual incorporation into the now severely depleted JG 7, whilst the ground staff of the Third *Gruppe* were to transfer to Neuburg an der Donau to Erding pending "...incorporation into depleted jet units (JG 7 or JV 44)".

JV 44 was operational again on the 19 April, despatching three Me 262s to intercept some of the 550 Ninth Air Force Marauders attacking transport targets in southern Germany. It is possible that JV 44's "victims" were B-26s of the 322nd Bomb Group which had just bombed its secondary target for the day, the railway bridge at Donauwörth. The jets attacked, in what would be their customary style against the Marauders, from the rear. They immediately drew fire from the bomber gunners as well as the P-47 escort. Such an encounter indicates both the psychological impact the jets must have had on the mediums' crews and the difficulty the Germans had in assessing the true capability of the Me 262. According to German records, one bomber was shot down and another probably destroyed without loss. In reality, two Marauders were damaged. On the American side, the three jets were later interpreted as "eight to ten Me 262s".

B-26 Marauders of the 17th BG flying in formation; by late April 1945 this was a dreaded and despised sight over southern Germany.

"Pneumatic hammers": the installation of four MK 108 30mm cannon in the nose section of an Me 262.

TWELVE

JV 44
TACTICS AND WEAPONRY

"The Pneumatic Hammer"
The MK 108 30 mm Cannon

The offensive armament of the standard Me 262 A-1a, as fitted to aircraft belonging to JV 44, consisted of four nose-mounted 30 mm MK 108 cannon. The prime benefit of this weapon, used profusely by the *Luftwaffe* for close-range anti-bomber work over Europe from early 1942 onwards, lay in its simplicity and economic process of manufacture, the greater part of its components consisting of pressed sheet metal stampings. In many ways, the MK 108 was considered to have been a masterpiece in weapons engineering, not only saving precious materials but also hundreds of man hours on milling machines and precision grinders.

With the advent of massed American daylight bomber formations bristling with concentrated defensive firepower, the need arose for a long-range, heavy calibre gun with which a German pilot could target specific bombers, expend the least amount of ammunition, score a kill in the shortest possible time and yet stay beyond the range of the defensive guns. It was a virtually impossible requirement and yet the MK 108 almost achieved this, though the RLM rejected Rheinmetall's first proposal on the basis that German

fighter pilots were considered by Udet, the *General-luftzeugmeister*, to all be crack-shots easily capable of shooting down the heaviest bomber with 20 mm calibre weapons at extended ranges!

First designed in 1940 by Rheinmetall-Borsig, as a private venture, the MK 108 was a blow-back operated, rear-seared, belt fed cannon, using electric ignition, being charged and triggered by compressed air, though once installed into any aircraft, there was no method of adjustment for harmonisation. One of the most unusual physical features of the gun was its extremely short barrel earning it the type-name *Kurzgerät* (lit. "short apparatus")

Firepower: the MK 108 cannon with 30 mm incendiary and high explosive shells.

which gave it its low muzzle velocity of between 500-540 metres (1640/1770 ft) per second with a maximum rate of fire of 650 rounds per minute. The weapon was subsequently integrated into the later variants of the Bf 109 and the Fw 190 A-8 where it quickly earned a fearsome reputation amongst the *Sturmgruppen* and the Allied bomber crews who dubbed it the "pneumatic hammer."

A total of 60 rounds was fed by means of a disintegrating belt from an ammunition can mounted above the gun. On release of the sear, the bolt travelled forward under the action of two driving springs. A projection on top of the bolt then passed through the ring extracting a round and forcing it into the chamber, firing the round while the heavy bolt was still moving forward. After firing, the empty cartridge case reseated itself in its link. Ejection was performed by means of pawls activated by camming grooves cut into the top of the bolt. The new round then slipped into position using the same process. Neither the barrel nor the receiver moved in recoil, the entire force of the firing process being absorbed by the rearward motion of the bolt against driving

Bemused USAAF officers inspecting the shell-blasted remains of a B-26 Marauder tail gun area and horizontal stabliser. This was the kind of damage that could be inflicted by as few as one or two well-aimed rounds from an MK 108.

springs which acted as buffers against recoil. Subsequently, no locking mechanism was needed since by the time the fired round had overcome the inertia of the massive bolt, the projectile had left the barrel and the pressure had dropped.

Adolf Galland had mixed feelings about the gun installed in JV 44 's Me 262s: "Firstly, it was constructionally speaking, extraordinarily easy to install four MK 108s into the aircraft. Secondly, it was good to have a gun which solved all our problems; that is to say – a gun which had a rapid rate of fire and great destructive effect, although there was the disadvantage of an insufficiently flat trajectory. Then there were other snags; the guns were not that much good when you were banking because the centrifugal forces arising from banking ripped the belts. Of course, they didn't rip if you didn't fire! But these teething troubles were easily sorted out by a well-trained ground crew."

Two basic types of shells could be loaded into the MK 108; the 30 mm high explosive self-destroying tracer type "M-Shell" designed to cause blast effect and the 30 mm high explosive self-

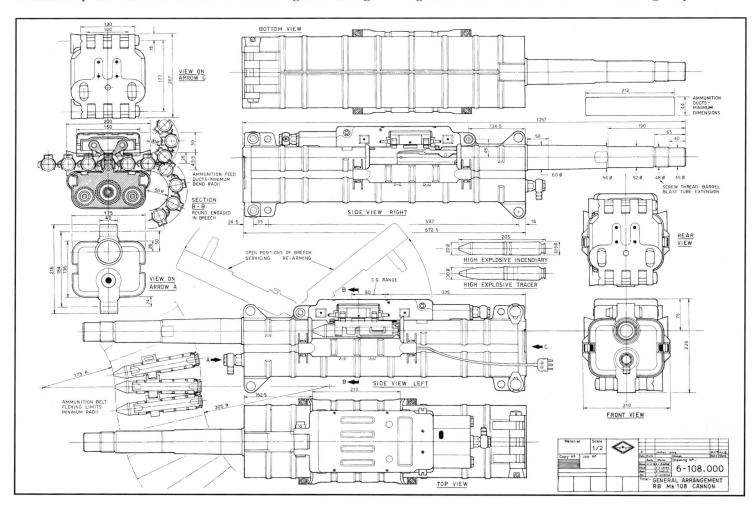

destroying incendiary shell intended to cause both a blast and incendiary effect. German weapons and ballistics technicians had decided that the maximum destruction to an enemy aircraft could be created by causing the largest possible explosive effect in its interior but that this in turn was dictated by the size of the enemy aircraft and by the quantity of explosive that could physically be placed into a projectile. The thicker the shell wall, the more energy was needed for the destruction of the shell itself and thus, less energy remained for the destruction of the target by the ensuing explosion. This theory led to the development of the "Mine Shell" which combined a minimum thickness in shell casing with a maximum load of explosive. Using such ammunition, the entire enemy aircraft could be regarded as the "target area", it making no difference where the hit was actually made. As such, with "Mine Shells" a fighter pilot had an inherently greater chance of scoring a kill.

Following tests carried out at the Rechlin experimental centre, it was discovered that five hits from a 30 mm "M Shell" carrying 85 g of explosive were needed for the destruction of either a B-17 Flying Fortress or B-24 Liberator.

Conversely however, incendiary shells were also considered an extremely potent form of ammunition but only really effective when targeted at fuel tanks. In such a case, therefore, the vulnerability of an enemy aircraft could be measured by the area/size of its tanks. However, a certain degree of penetrative force was still needed in order to break through the airframe or any protective armour carried by the target without breaking up and igniting until actually striking the fuel. To overcome this problem, the 30 mm incendiary shell was fitted with a hydrodynamic fuse which activated only when making contact with a fluid.

"Just a Whisper"
The R4M air-to-air rocket

In early April 1945, a new dimension was introduced by JV 44 into the air war being waged against Allied bombers over southern Germany and Austria – the R4M air-to-air rocket. For many months, German ballistics engineers had recognised that the installation of rockets would become "indispensable" as the introduction of more and more fixed armament into single fighter aircraft became increasingly difficult, combined with the corresponding increase in defensive firepower of USAAF bomber formations.

Below: The 55mm R4M air-to-air missile shown here in its two basic operational variants, fitted with an armour piercing warhead and below, with a high explosive warhead as also used by ground forces.

Luftwaffe armourers load a 21 cm air-to-air mortar shell into its launch tube fitted to a Fw 190 fighter operating in the defence of the Reich. The weapon's substantial blast effect was intended to break up USAAF bomber formations but in fact it was largely inaccurate and success was negligible.

Throughout the latter half of 1943 and into 1944, several fighter units deployed in the defence of the Reich had been equipped with the primitive and hastily converted tube-launched, spin-stabilised Army mortar shell, the 21cm *Werfer-Granate* in an attempt to break up bomber *Pulks* by the weapon's considerable blast effect. But the weapon was largely inaccurate and successes had been negligible, with only isolated impact being made on a tightly formed bomber "box". The only plausible alternative was for a fighter formation to attack a bomber *Pulk* simultaneously firing batteries of rockets carried either in underwing racks or in nose mounted "honeycombs", with which a dense "fire-chain" could be created which would be impossible for the bombers to avoid. In June 1944, the *TLR* put forward a requirement for an electrically fired, fin stabilised weapon whose warhead would contain sufficient explosive to destroy a four-engine bomber in one hit. Four weeks later, a powerful consortium of companies, each with individual responsibility for different components was formed and led by the Deutsche Waffen und Munitions Fabrik (DWM) Research Institute of Lübeck.

Below: The component parts of the R4M rocket with the fins to the main body extended.

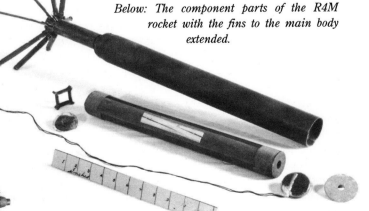

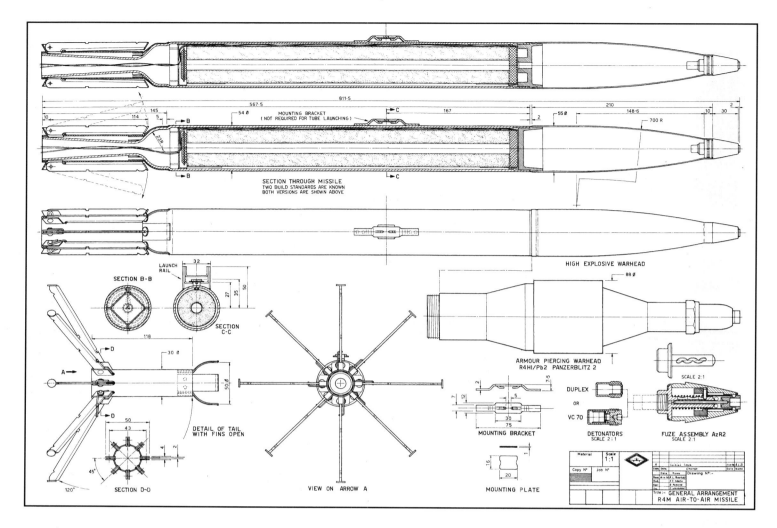

This consortium duly presented the *Chef TLR* with a proposal for an 814 mm long, 55 mm calibre rocket with a warhead containing 520 g of HTA explosive and ignited by an AZR 2 detonator, all bearing a weight of 3,500 g. The rocket was intended to be launched against aerial targets from a range of 800 metres (875 yards) and stabilised by eight fins which would open automatically by aerodynamic drag immediately after launching.

The proposal was received favourably and the designation "R4M" (*Rakete 4 kg* (8.8 lb) *Minenkopf*) applied. Firing trials took place at the end of October 1944 on the Strelná firing range at the Westin works of Brünn AG and at Heber at Osterode. However, the *Erprobungsstellen* at Rechlin (which had conducted the first air launches in December) and Tarnewitz both judged that the missile was still unsatisfactory as a result of the poor standard of manufacture of some individual parts. By the end of January 1945, once some initial burn-out problems had been solved, a general re-working of the rocket, incorporating various aerodynamic and warhead refinements was conducted.

In its final form, the R4M appeared as an unrotated, rail or tube-launched, single venturi, solid fuel propelled, multi-fin stabilised missile, with the warhead contained in an exceptionally thin 1 mm sheet steel case enclosed in two pressed steel sections welded together and holding the Hexogen HE charge. The missile bore a high charge weight to case weight ratio.

From the Me 262, it was intended to launch the R4M from wooden under-wing racks, mounted by four screws and positioned outside of the engines, with the connections between the launch rack and the wing surface faired in to counteract the

possibility of air eddies as much as possible. The standard launch rack – known as the EG.-R4M – was designed and manufactured by Kurt Heber of Osterode and measured approximately 700mm in length with each rocket being fitted with sliding lugs so that it could hang freely from the guide rails. Prior to loading into the rack, seven of the R4M's eight fins were held in a folded-down position by binding them with spring-steel wire made with spherical or similarly thickened ends. The wire ends were then crossed and the eighth (free) fin pressed down to hold the other seven in place. Each rocket was then loaded from the rear of the rack with the eighth fin held in place by the rail securing the wire binding. The rocket was pushed along the guide-rail until the rear sliding lug was arrested by a notch in the rail. At the back of each rail was a terminal contact block connecting the ignition wires which hung down close to the socket. Once fired, the eighth fin was designed to spring free which, in turn, released the binding wire thus allowing the remaining seven fins to open, a process which commenced at about 400 mm from the rail and finished once the rocket had flown approximately 2.5 metres (8 ft).

As many rails as desired could be fitted together to make one launch rack by means of transverse connection, with a gap of 65 mm between each rail, though it was usual to carry a maximum load of 12 R4M's under each wing of the Me 262 using a 21 kg (46 lb) rack. It was calculated that the loss of speed incurred to an Me 262 as a result of a Heber launch rack being fitted was approximately 16 km/h.

On 5 April 1945 the testing and evaluation unit, *Jagdgruppe* 10

When fired, it was both safer and more effective if the rockets were loosed in salvos, in order to avoid an excess build up of gas in any one place. Furthermore, once an R4M had left its rails, the diameter of the open fins measured 240mm, this dictating that only every fifth rail could be discharged at any one time.

Interviewed by the British, Johannes Steinhoff recounted the R4M's potency when deployed by JV 44: "The new armament was rockets... The great advantage of these was that though their speed only slightly exceeded that of sound they could be let off 1,100 metres (1,205 yards) away from the target – and from this range continued until they represented a field of fire of over thirty metres (98 ft) by fourteen metres (46 ft). This meant that by releasing all his rockets at once against a close formation of bombers, a pilot couldn't miss! We had, at last, the means not only of combating these hitherto almost unassailable formations, but of destroying them. And the escorting enemy fighters, shocked at these tactics, could do nothing about it. Two bombers would be hit, lose control, collide and disappear together downwards. Then another pilot's rockets would be released, another two bombers would collide and the whole formation would be thrown into indescribable confusion. Over Nürnberg, over Augsburg, over the Alps, we were clawing them out of the skies, almost without risk of retaliation. But – and it is a big "but" – it was five minutes to twelve, in other words early April, before we got the rocket armament and then only enough to equip a few aircraft."

Nevertheless, the R4M had arrived just in time, for JV 44's "honeymoon" period at München-Riem was at an end.

Two views of a standard battery of twelve R4Ms fitted to an under-wing launch rack on an Me 262 A-1a of JG 7.

which had been carrying out operational trials with the rocket in conjunction with Messershmitt Augsburg, was ordered to arrange to supervise the equipping of JV 44 with R4Ms and launching racks. They must have moved swiftly, for the next day a "Re-equipping Detachment" from JGr. 10 arrived at München-Riem having made the long journey by air from their base at Redlin with enough launch racks and missiles to equip twenty aircraft.

Galland recalls: "On the Me 262 we could mount the R4M outside of the turbines under the wings, twelve on each side with little aerodynamic disturbance. They were fired over a switch relay in 0.03 seconds of one another and aimed in exactly the same way as the MK 108 with a natural dispersion of about 35 square metres (377 sq. ft). But on account of the arrangement of the rockets, a shotgun like pattern was made creating a rectangle around the bomber. The war head was a 55 mm HE shell filled with Hexogen and one hit – any hit – no matter where scored, sufficed to destroy a four-engined bomber. The loss of speed from the Me 262 as a result of mounting the R4M was insignificant. The RPs were mounted with an upward inclination of 8 degrees and fired at 600 metres (656 yards) at which range they had the same ballistics as the MK 108... When you fired them, you just heard *sssssshhhh....* Just a whisper."

Indeed, this phenomenon was probably the result of the high velocity of 240 atü (kp) with a burning time of 0.8 seconds and stemming from a propelling charge of 815 g which gave a maximum velocity of 540 metres (1,772 ft) per second once a rocket had been fired. Ground crews and armourers were warned to position the rocket carefully in its guide rails in order to ensure that the gas jet was allowed to escape unhindered without causing blast to any parts of the aircraft's fuselage, since the accumulation of gases in any slots or hollow spaces could have led to explosion.

Tactics

Whatever the reason behind a pilot joining Galland's "break-away" unit of jet fighters between February and April 1945, as we have seen, without doubt, the main attraction for many was the eleventh hour chance to fly one of the most technically advanced operational aircraft in the world. For some, transition from conventional piston engine fighters such as the Bf 109 or Fw 190 – types which many pilots had flown without a break for six years – to the new super-fast jet powered fighter came relatively easy; for others, it proved to be a more difficult and perplexing task. But as if learning to master this new dimension in powered flight within the shortest possible time and amidst conditions of absolute chaos was not enough, then to learn to use it as an offensive weapon in combat conditions against a numerically superior opponent was even harder. It is a credit to the skill, dedication, perseverance and courage of these young German airmen that, under such circumstances, operations were flown at all.

Oblt. Franz Stigler, a dedicated Bf 109 pilot remembers the difficulties experienced in the transition to flying combat missions in the Me 262: "I flew a few operational missions in the Me 262 – about seven in all, all from München-Riem with JV 44. I never flew combat missions out of Brandenburg – things were not too eventful there. Before that though, I'd flown 450 combat missions with JG 27 in Africa, over the Mediterranean and in the

Defence of the Reich. I'd shot down two B-17s and had myself, been shot down so many times, I lost count, so I considered myself to be fairly experienced. But when we got the Me 262, we had to learn all over again. To be honest, there were no tactics. We just took off and did what we had to, although we usually flew in twos and threes. We hit the bombers in loose formation, from the front, firing all the way in. We were so fast but the controls were so sluggish at speed you really had to concentrate. And when we got there, we found that we couldn't dive at a bomber formation from the front effectively. If, for example, we came in from the front at 15-20 degrees, we came in so fast the aircraft started yawing – we couldn't hold it steady. It was so fast and with our speed there was little chance of shooting accurately, so instead, we eventually had to change our approach to come in from behind and below."

As ever though, Galland worked hard and pragmatically to develop the neccesary tactics with which to ensure success against the bombers as well as keeping his pilots alive, but he too recognised that there were certain factors connected with handling the Me 262 which had to be borne in mind and which were inescapable. As he explained to a USAAF interrogation officer on 23 May 1945: "In principle, the tactics of an Me 262 formation, irrespective of what they were opposing, were determined by the flying qualities of the aircraft. First, there's the high speed, secondly, there's the rather small banking performance which is connected with the high speed and thirdly, there is the very limited ability to compare acceleration with conventionally engined aircraft. By acceleration, I mean the capability of going from limited speeds to high and vice versa. The Me 262 needs plenty of "elbow room" in both cases – ie; it takes more time to both increase and reduce speed. For formation flying, this means that flying in battle formation is a little more difficult than it is for conventionally engined aircraft; it demands rather more experience because keeping position cannot be done as in conventional aircraft, in other words, by means of a throttle lever – but instead, position must be kept by means of sideward movements, – ie; by shortening flight direction or by swinging out and increasing the distance covered. In any case, it is wrong to give up the one element of superiority the jet aircraft has, namely, speed, particularly as picking up speed again takes longer than in conventionally engined aircraft."

JV 44 was rarely able to muster more than sixteen serviceable Me 262s for any one day, whilst operational capability for any one sortie was even lower - as few as five or six machines. Here, a JV 44 Me 262 A-1a receives fuel on the starting platform at München-Riem, April 1945. Note fuel feed hose and valve connected to the aircraft.

"In addition, is the fact that the degree of efficiency in all jet-propulsion units increases with gathering speed, whereas with decreasing speed, it declines in geometrical progression even more. The best illustration of this is that the acceleration power of a jet propelled aircraft on the ground is considerably less than that of a less powerfully engined aircraft. All Me 262 tactics were subordinated to these principles and their effect on formation flying. All movements carried out by a formation or a single aircraft in aerial combat have to be conducted in a far more rigid, "straight line" style than those of ordinary aircraft. The banking dogfight as such is not suitable to the jet fighter unless there is a situation where the aircraft are banking against one another. In such a case the same conditions apply for both aircraft."

Official immediate post-war documentation indicates that it was rare for JV 44 to have more than sixteen Me 262s *serviceable* for any one mission, though examination of other documentary records reveal that, in reality, the average number of aircraft actually *operational* on any one mission was much lower – closer to five or six or even fewer. With such extreme numerical inferiority, it should be remembered that the prevailing and restrictive tactical doctrine laid down by Göring in February 1945 to the effect that the prime role of the jet fighter was to attack bombers rather than tackle their escort fighters, to a great extent impeded effective tactical employment of the Me 262 and thus, success.

Galland and Steinhoff had observed that the large turning radius and slow acceleration of the Me 262 made the old *Kette* element of three aircraft, rather than the more traditional and commonly adopted four aircraft fighter formation, the *Schwarm*, much more practical and versatile. The *Kette* was also preferred by the pilots of JV 44 as a result of the Me 262's lack of manoeuvrability which made maintaining formation in a larger element extremely difficult.

As Galland recalled: "The *Kette* appealed to us because on our runways, which were basically all 60 metres (65 yards) wide,

The three aircraft *Kette*

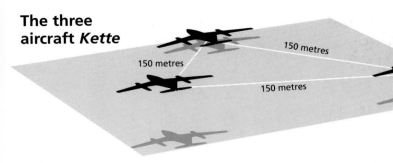

150 metres

150 metres

150 metres

three aircraft could take-off side by side simultaneously, whereas a fourth aircraft couldn't have got on the runway and would have had to have taken-off later after quite an interval of time. It would then have had the difficulty of establishing contact with the rest of the formation. Therefore, we reverted to the *Kette* formation with slightly less intermediate spacing than we would have flown with conventionally engined aircraft – about 100 metres (109 yards) when climbing and thereafter in level flight, about 150 – 180 metres (164/196 yards). These reduced intervals make it easier for the formation to keep together. Assembling after take-off only works providing the following aircraft takes-off very quickly afterwards, a thing which is not so easy for jet fighters owing to their unwieldiness on the ground. A formation of several *Ketten* next to one another is simply the "Vic" formation in which one has one *Kette* flying in front, one *Kette* to the right and one to the left. There's sufficient space between the *Ketten* to allow each *Kette* to move and manoeuvre freely, in other words, a good 300 metres (328 yards). Other *Ketten*, also in "Vic" formation, fly at a higher altitude so that they provide mutual cover. In the *Kette* itself, aircraft are generally staggered below or behind each other, but not above each other owing to the range of vision of the Me 262; when passing above, you lose sight of the leading aircraft and it can be difficult to find it again. Only when diving, when one puts the nose down steeply, must a formation leader let the rest of the formation know his intentions. In such a case, one can then pass overhead and then bank in."

Once formed up, Galland would rely on *Egon* procedure to lead his jet formation towards the Allied bombers. Once visual contact was made with the bomber *Pulk*, one group was selected as target and the jets manoeuvred behind it so as to mount their attack from the rear. Getting into a satisfactory attack position however, was often difficult due to the great speed and turning radius of the Me 262 and decisions regarding the attack had to be made quickly and often at great distances from the target, from where it was difficult to correctly assess the bombers' range, course and altitude.

Galland: "The actual attack on an enemy bomber formation presented the following difficulties; one: because of the high cruising speed of a jet formation, which generally speaking was about 750 kph (466 mph) (and 550 kph (342 mph) when climbing), it was relatively difficult to tell the exact direction of the approaching bombers. The reason for that was that one was not carrying out an observation from a fixed point but was dashing through the air at such a pace that it was difficult to establish the relationship between the progress of the target and one's own direction. It *could* be done, but it needed a hell of a lot of practice. For that reason,

the graduation of curves that one had to fly when positioning for an attack made things fairly difficult. The second difficulty was to get right behind the target – say about 1,000 metres (1,093 yards) – at an angle of approach of zero degrees, as seen from the side. It generally happened that one approached at an angle anyway. That wouldn't have mattered, providing one had a gyro sight which worked well, but if you hadn't got that, then you noticed how all the inexperienced pilots fired behind the target. The third difficulty, of course, was that owing to the very high speed, it was difficult to score a sufficient number of hits in the time available – in other words, to shoot well."

Galland continues: "My pilots were authorised to fire from 600 metres (650 yards). They were also permitted to fire a short burst before that if they noticed that they were being fired upon by the bombers. But the actual effective fire should have commenced from 600 metres (650 yards). For that purpose we made marks on our sights and when, for example, a B-17 was within those marks, it meant the range was at 600 metres (650 yards). We also fired our

A page taken from Otto Kammerdiener's aircraft recognition manual showing the Martin B-26 Marauder and classifying it as a "Bomber" and "Torpedo Aircraft", though it was more well known to the Germans as the Haifisch or "Shark". Kammerdiener claimed two Marauders shot down whilst serving with JV 44.

USA

Kampfflugzeug, Torpedoflugzeug
Martin B-26 C, D Marauder

1. **Verwendung:** Kampfflugzeug, Torpedoflugzeug (USA)
2. **Besatzung:** 6 Mann
3. **Spannweite:** 19,8 m   4. **Länge:** 17,7 m
5. **Bewaffnung:** 12—13 MG. 12,7 mm. Neuerdings Heckstand mit Doppel-MG. 12,7 mm, ähnlich der B-17 G
6. **Größte Bombenlast:** 2,2 t bei 800 km Eindringtiefe
7. **Höchstgeschwindigkeit:** 495 km/st in 4,3 km Höhe
8. **Marschgeschwindigkeit:** 320 km
9. **Größtes Fluggewicht:** 16,8 t
10. **Dienstgipfelhöhe:** 7,5 km
11. **Einsatzhöhe:** 0—4 km
12. **Größte Eindringtiefe:** 1000 km mit 1 t Bomben

24

Taken during the 323rd BG's mission to the Memmingen marshalling yards on 20 April 1945, this detail from a remarkable photo shows the effect of a JV 44 attack against a Marauder formation. Visible just below B-26 S/N 44-68132 is a flight of four white-tailed Marauders, one of which has just been hit by cannon or rocket fire and is burning.

rockets at that range... We often hit two bombers with them in one go. The Me 262 could only count on success in attacking formations of heavy bombers if they were able to approach in fairly close formation and not if they approached at great distances apart. The *Kette* had to at least remain at one height; a clear-cut allocation of targets had to be made and the whole *Kette* had to fire simultaneously in order to make the defensive fire of the bombers disperse. During the final 1,000 metres (1,093 yards) of approach, the Me 262 should have been moving at a speed of at least 850 kph (528 mph), as otherwise we would have been "money for jam" for the escort fighters and their air superiority. Sometimes though, it wasn't neccesary to fly that fast and that made everything considerably easier. However, that increased the pressure on the steering gear to a great extent and you had to trim a great deal and so during that last 1,000 metres (1,093 yards) you had to hold the control column with *both* hands in order to be able to control the aircraft. That meant that the actual attack was made from a distance of 1,000 metres (1,093 yards) and that you needed *at least* 2,000 metres (2,187 yards) to get into the right position for an attack"

"In attacking, you didn't approach at the same height as the bombers, but you banked and dived to below the bomber level and approached from that level, rising when the distance was about 1,000 metres (1,093 yards), reaching the correct height at 600 metres (650 yards); from 1,000 metres (1,093 yards) to 600 metres (650 yards) you didn't merely rise but shifted your position a little. From 600 metres (650 yards) onwards, you *had* to fly in a perfectly straight line whilst starting your offensive fire. When you were 150 metres (165 yards) away at the latest, you had to turn away. If you had approached to within such a short range you had to turn away above the bomber whatever happened; on *no* account could you afford turn away from the bomber while still directly behind thus exposing your belly as then it was almost certain that you would have been hit. But, if you had approached to within 200 metres (220 yards), there was

Marauder tail gunners were often the first to bear the brunt of JV 44's rear mounted attacks. Shown here are the results of a similar attack made against B-26B IDIOT'S DELIGHT II of the 322nd BG by Fw 190s on 27 August 1943.

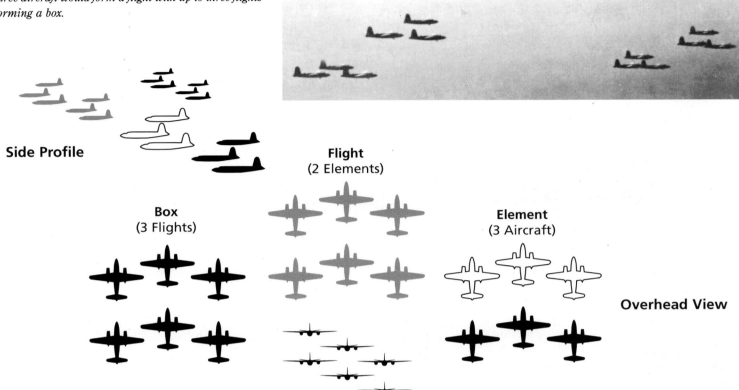

B-26 Marauders of the 17th BG illustrate a text-book box flight formation offering, according to a Ninth Air Force manual, "flexibility, compactness and firepower". In theory, in assembling for an attack, two elements of three aircraft would form a flight with up to three flights forming a box.

Side Profile

Flight
(2 Elements)

Box
(3 Flights)

Element
(3 Aircraft)

Overhead View

Frontal Profile

STANDARD NINTH AIR FORCE
B-26 MARAUDER BOX AND COMPONENTS

| 2 Boxes | = | 1 Group |
| 2 or more Groups | = | A Formation |

only one way out and that was to turn away as close as possible, passing *over* the whole bomber formation. In any case, it was dangerous to turn away by flying underneath, as pieces of shot-down bombers, men baling-out, jettisoned bombs or burning aircraft flew straight into your face or into your turbines."

To be on the "receiving end" of an attack by Me 262s was terrifying. S./Sgt. Bernard J. Byrnes was an armourer gunner flying B-26 Marauders with the 432nd Squadron of the 17th Bombardment Group. As such, he manned the twin .50 calibre Browning machine guns in the top turret and on 26 April 1945, witnessed at first hand an attack by Galland's jets. He had initially trained on the B-17 Flying Fortress, but just before he received his overseas posting, he was transferred to B-26 Marauders since there was a requirement for air gunners in the medium bomber squadrons. Byrnes remembers: "I liked the B-17 but I am very

S./Sgt. Bernard J. Byrnes, a B-26 armourer gunner with the 432nd Squadron, 17th BG: "If the Germans had put those jets in the air sooner, it would have been very bad for us."

glad I went onto the B-26; they were a fine plane to be in during combat. However, those Me 262s were one terrible fighter to have to deal with. They came in so fast, that you hardly had any time to lead them before they were on you using those four heavy calibre cannon. A normal fighter range of fire was about 300 yards and from a medium bomber like the B-26, we could fire with some accuracy out to about 600 yards, so we had a little advantage. But with the Me 262, they came in so fast, it was point-blank firing. You had no advantage of range. If the Germans had put those jets in the air sooner, it would have been very bad for us."

Providing sufficient ammunition and speed remained, the jets were able to pass on to another bomber group within the

View of a predator: an Me 262 streaks past an American bomber formation.

same formation and attack it in a similar manner, though if speed had been lost, then a second attack was often dangerous in the presence of escort fighters. If these were encountered, then a shallow dive usually enabled the Me 262s to regain enough speed outdistance all Allied fighter types.

However, though the speed of the Me 262 was undoubtedly a tactical advantage and the cannon and rocket aramament was formidable, the Martin B-26 Marauder proved a tough adversary for the pilots of JV 44. Indeed, on 14 May 1945, Galland told his American captors that of all American bombers he had confronted in combat, the one "...he would least enjoy to attack," was the B-26

Adolf Galland told American interrogators that the B-26 Marauder was the bomber "... he would least enjoy to attack." Flying in tight formations, they were "... very difficult to approach" and had "... a devastating firepower."

Marauder. Galland's interrogator recorded that "...He (Galland) stated that the B-26s usually flying in very tight formations were very difficult to approach. He found through hard experience that they had a devastating fire-power."

THIRTEEN

20 APRIL 1945
THE END OF THE UGLY DUCKLING

"Junkyard Fugitive"

April 20, 1945: Adolf Hitler's fifty-sixth birthday was marked by an Allied heavy daylight raid by 800 Eighth Air Force bombers against rail targets in the Berlin area. The RAF would follow that night, despatching 76 Mosquitoes in six separate raids on the capital. The Red Army was only some 16 kilometres (10 miles) from the north-eastern outskirts of Berlin and the city shook with the impact of continuous Russian shelling. News came that Nürnberg had fallen to the Americans with 17,000 German soldiers taken prisoner.

In the south, and by adopting such tactics as described previously, JV 44 was able to bring down three B-26 Marauders and damage another seven from a Ninth Air Force formation comprising the 323rd, 394th and 397th Bomb Groups despatched to bomb the marshalling yards at Memmingen.

The 48 aircraft of the 323rd BG, lead by Captain Lewis S. Caldwell, were formated into three 'boxes' comprising eight six-plane flights following a course out of their base at Denain-Prouvy which would take them across the Rhine and straight into Bavaria. The crews of the 323rd had reason to be cautiously optimistic; as we have seen, operations over the past few weeks had gone relatively well with an "affordable" level of casualties and the bombing in April against marshalling yards, oil refineries and ordnance depots across southern Germany had been extremely successful.

We join the mission, with 1st Lieutenant James L. Vining, a native of Louisiana and a pilot of a "borrowed" B-26F-1 (42-96256) "J" for Jig *Ugly Duckling* flying with 455th Bomb Squadron embarking that morning on his fortieth combat mission: "Having flown the last previous mission a couple of days earlier – a milk run to the same area – we should not have been scheduled for the mission on the 20th." Vining remembered. "However, despite the good news and Patton's arrival in Czechoslovakia, the inimitable "powers that be" decided on an "all out effort", requiring every available plane that could possibly be airborne. Thus my crew was made ready for this unnecessary strike. Following a routine briefing, during which Intelligence confirmed that all German aerial resistance had collapsed, an eventuality developed which – in retrospect – seemed to presage the ultimate tragedy that at the moment appeared so remote. Due to a shortage of planes in our squadron and in order for us to provide a proportionate share of crews, a sister squadron "loaned" us the ship assigned to my crew. It was a standard, if macabre, jest that a borrowed plane was usually the worst in the lender's inventory. Among the numerous defects gradually discovered in this particular junkyard fugitive, the immediate and most critical was a malfunctioning bomb release!"

Ugly Duckling had, in fact, been borrowed from the 454th Bomb Squadron. Her usual crew was commanded by 1st Lt Harold C. Day and her radio operator/waist gunner was T./Sgt

Robert M. Radlein who had been flying with her since November 1944. Radlein was one of six brothers serving in the American forces during World War Two and 20 April saw him embarking on his 39th and final operational mission of the war, one that was to provide him with a "very exciting finale" to his combat flying. He recalls: "Our usual crew aircraft had the name *Ugly Duckling* and a Donald Duck type duck painted on the left nose fuselage. The right nose was inscribed *"The Mighty F"*. The standard joke was that it meant "4F" which was a draft category for a person unfit for military service. 256J had a reputation for aborting or not even getting off the ground at all! However, our crew never had any trouble with it and when we did fly it, it always went to the target and back. Other crews were not as fortunate."

The 455th Bomb Squadron's heavily burdened ground crews worked hard to fix *"Ugly Duckling's"* latest problem and Vining's borrowed aircraft was finally able to start its engines about thirty minutes later than the scheduled take-off time, making it the last of the Group's machines to depart rather than the third as originally planned. The Group quickly assembled and crossed the Rhine south west of Stuttgart on course for southern Germany almost immediately running into a heavy and unexpected screen of *Flak*.

On the ground, JV 44's control room at Feldkirchen had picked up the bombers' approach and the unit duly dispatched a force of around 15 Me 262s from Riem, formed into individual *Ketten*, between 10:30-11:00 to intercept. *Uffz.* Eduard Schallmoser flying "White 11" was airborne at 10:38 and, guided by

Left: 1st Lieutenant James L. Vining, 455th Squadron, 323rd BG on leave in Brussels, early April 1945.
Below: B-26F-1 (S/N 42-96256) RJ-J UGLY DUCKLING *of the 454th Squadron, 323rd BG photographed at its dispersal probably at Laon-Athies, France, early 1945.*

B-26B-30 (S/N 41-31918) RJ-R Can't Get Started of the 454th Squadron, 323rd BG photographed by Robert Radlein whilst in flight on a mission to bomb the Kempten ammunition depot, 16 April 1945 and piloted by 1st Lt Dale E. Sanders. The 323rd was able to report that "... many hits were obtained in the area and large fires were started in a number of buildings." Four days later, Me 262s of JV 44 would shoot Can't Get Started from the skies above Memmingen. Sanders and other members of the crew were posted missing.

Feldkirchen, flew quickly towards incoming bomber formation.

Vining remembers: "We approached the IP at Kempten in standard boxes (2 and 2/3) but as we turned, the flights dispersed in order to hit the target by single flights in trail. Thus my flight was the last to turn to begin the bomb run. We were at 12,000 feet (3,660 metres) and in the turn we started getting light flak (20 and 40mm) which was possible because we were only about 4,000 feet (1,220 metres) above the highest terrain. As we rolled out of the turn onto a 4-minute bomb run I heard from my tail gunner the now dreaded words: *'Fighters coming in from the rear!'*."

Flying elsewhere in the 323rd BG's formation was Robert Radlein in 1st Lt Day's replacement B-26G: "On 20 April, we were assigned to fly in the number 4 position behind box leader, Major (Arthur E.) Smith, our squadron commander and I was sitting back in my waist position fat, dumb and happy not thinking about much of anything really because nothing was happening. I really wasn't aware of Me 262s being in the area. The plot unfolded when I glanced out of my window at our number 6 plane on our left wing and I noticed that the tail gunner was burning out his barrels firing at something and apparently frozen on the trigger. At first, I thought he was probably just clearing his guns, so I didn't think too much about it. But he never stopped shooting – he just wouldn't let up. I thought, *Hell, that guy must be shooting at something.* So I stuck my head out of the left waist window – which I always kept open in case I had to bale out – to see what he was shooting at and just then I saw two of the P-51 escorts flashing across our tail. They too seemed to be burning out their barrels because there must have been six feet of flames out in front of their wings. I thought, *Hell, they're shooting at something too!* "

It was just after 11:00 and JV 44's Me 262s were flying west in line astern in loose *Ketten* at between 3,350-4,000 metres (11,000-13,125 ft). Sighting the American aircraft in clear skies over the Kempten-Memmingem area and identifying them as B-26 Marauders, Eduard Schallmoser flying in the vanguard of the German strike force, readied himself for an attack. At that moment, the bombers were still flying in a deliberately tight formation in order to increase the density of their defensive firepower and to prevent the jets from breaking up the individual elements. But as Schallmoser made his rearward approach

towards the enemy formation at speed, he suddenly found his cannon jammed as a result of an ill-timed stoppage in the loading mechanism and for a split second his concentration was diverted. Uncannily similar events to those which befell the young German pilot on 4 April, were about to unfold.

As the first *Kette* closed in on the Marauders – cannon blazing – from 6 and 7 o'clock low, the tail gunners began to open up in reciprocation. But the initial impact of the jets' speed combined with the fire from their lethal MK 108s was devastating. First to be hit – some fifteen seconds before "bombs away" – was B-26B-30 (No. 41-31918) coded RJ-R *Can't Get Started* of the 454th Squadron flying in number three position, lead flight, box one piloted by 1st Lt. Dale E. Sanders from Glendale, California. Cannon fire had hit the port-side engine and it was smoking badly.

The awful realisation of what was happening was beginning to dawn on Robert Radlein: "By now, I figured something must have been happening so I looked out of the right waist window to see what everyone was shooting at – fortunately, I had my gun stationed out of the right window – and right then, this Me 262 appeared, right up alongside of us, three o'clock level, about 100 yards out, flying to all practical purposes in formation with us.

T./Sgt Robert M. Radlein, 454th Squadron, 323rd BG was Ugly Duckling's usual radio operator/waist gunner. On 20 April 1945, he flew in a replacement aircraft and witnessed at first hand the JV 44 attack. Radlein is seen here in 1945 prior to a training flight and wearing routine flight clothing with his headset snapped to his parachute harness.

Taken in March 1945, a month before she would be lost over Kempten, Bavaria, another photo of B-26F-1 (s/n 42-96256) RJ-J Ugly Duckling of the 454th Squadron, 323rd BG, this seen time parked on pierced steel planking at Denain-Prouvy, France with a protective tarpaulin over her cockpit and nose section. Note that ground personnel have over-painted the aircraft's nose-art and name .

Inset: The tarpaulin now removed, members of B-26F-1 (s/n 42-96256)) Ugly Duckling's ground crew pose for a shot in front of their charge at Denain-Prouvy, March 1945. From left: Sgt. Joseph P. Frawley, Cpl. Robert A. Guyton and S/Sgt. Kenneth A. Knowles (crew chief). The men's mud-caked boots are indicative of what conditions at Denain-Prouvy were like at this time.

my gun jammed. I cleared the jam in about two or three seconds, but by that time, he was gone."

"Just about then, our top turret gunner, S./Sgt. Edmundo Estrada, started firing. He had just raised his guns straight up and was shooting at an Me 262 passing overhead. He yelled *"I got him! I got him!"* – because he had seen all kinds of metal and debris come flying past our aeroplane. Estrada was convinced he had hit the jet, but unfortunately the pieces of metal that he had seen had come not from the German fighter but from our Number 3 aircraft piloted by Lt. Sanders which was flying on Major Smith's left wing. I looked out of my left waist window at Sander's plane as it started to drop away from the main formation and was able to see the entire radio compartment. The fighter attack had stripped away all the metal from the top of the wing, the radio man and navigator's compartment – I guess from just aft of the windows in the pilot's compartment and of course, one engine was also gone. I watched him falling out of formation and reached over to snap on my chest pack chute – things were warming up pretty fast and I figured that if I was going to have to bale out, I wouldn't do so without a parachute!"

Instantly I charged my gun and started firing. My gunnery training had taught me to fire short bursts of about ten rounds. I did it all automatically. I fired about five bursts, each of about ten rounds each – about fifty rounds in all – at the Me 262 and I watched my tracers lag behind his tail, which probably meant that I was punching holes somewhere in his fuselage. He pulled away and left and almost immediately another Me 262 pulled up into the same slot! I don't know what they had in their minds but it was giving me good target practice, so I fired off about two bursts at the second Me 262 – about twenty rounds – and then

As *Can't Get Started* began to drop out of formation, the bombardier was seen to salvo his bomb-load and escorting

An extremely dramatic photograph - and the only one of its kind known to exist - taken from aboard a 323rd BG B-26 depicting a pair of Me 262s of JV 44 in action against the group's Marauders over Memmingen, on 20 April 1945. One jet can be seen banking away to the rear of the low flight of bombers whilst immediately below B-26 44-68132 A-WT of the 456th Squadron can be seen the flight which the German pilot has just attacked from the commonly adopted 6 o'clock position. Careful study of the photograph reveals the disarray caused to the flight by the jets' attack and what appears to be at least one bomber trailing flames.

Me 262

Me 262

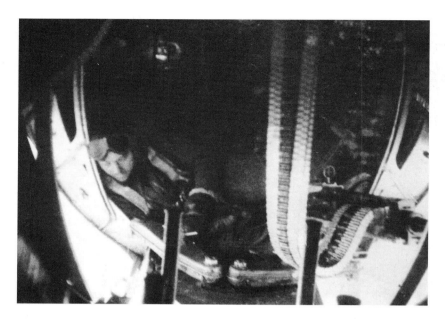

fighters reported seeing one parachute exit the aircraft which, astonishingly, was last observed by other Allied aircraft flying over northern Germany south of the Elbe river.

"Absolute Zero"

In James Vining's B-26 *Ugly Duckling*, Texan engineer/tail gunner S/Sgt. Henry P. Yates yelled his warning into the intercom and waited until the first jet was at 180 metres (200 yards) before firing, expending 200 rounds of 0.50 calibre ammunition at the oncoming German machine.

Vining: "In seconds, the first Me 262 zoomed by above number 4 and too close for comfort above number 1. Between fifteen and twenty seconds later the second jet followed the same path, only barely clearing the top of number 1. Just as quickly, the third jet zoomed in, barely clearing number 4 and I instantly knew that he could not go over number 1. There seemed to be no room for him to go under, so I braced myself for a horrible mid-air collision. However, he managed to nose down just enough to go under the right wing, running his rudder through the right propeller in the process, the prop slicing about half the rudder off."

Schallmoser's "White 11" had, in fact, struck the blades of 1st Lt. James H. Hansen's B-26 (No. 44-68109) which was leading its flight. As "White 11" began to flip over and drop through the American formation, pieces of its own debris trailing through the sky behind it, Vining's Armourer Gunner S/Sgt. Charles W. Winger fired a short burst and saw from his top turret that the jet closed to just 18 metres (60 ft) before passing away to the left in a steep dive and becoming "enveloped in black smoke".

"As if he were unsure of control of his craft," Vining recalled, "he eased downward and to the right, bringing him directly in front of my gunsight. The B-26 had two 50 cal. machine guns in pods on each side of the fuselage, fixed to fire straight forward for ground strafing purposes, though I am

eternally grateful that I never had to go on such a mission! With the jet in my gunsight, I automatically pressed the firing button on my control wheel and though I had never before fired these guns in combat, I had always kept them ready for action. I was somewhat amazed to see tracers indicating hits on his tail so I started following his direction in order to finish the job. But I shortly realised that doing so was taking me out of formation, so I ceased firing and moved back into my position, expecting a fourth jet to be closing in."

Schallmoser was also attracting fire from Hansen's top turret gunner – now at a distance of some 180 metres (200 yards) – and in the top turret of a Marauder flying in number 4 position, flight 2, box 3, Sgt. Edward S. Tyszkiewicz saw "...parts of the right wing" break away as the German jet dived away.

"I turned too late," Schallmoser wrote, "and rammed the Marauder which then fell away and crashed. Meanwhile, my Me 262 "White 11" was a complete loss and I was able, with my last reserves of strength to escape the aircraft by parachute and landed safely at my mother's home on the outskirts of Lenzfried-im-Allgäu."

Quite what the bewildered *Frau* Schallmoser must have thought as her son unexpectedly "...fell out of the clouds" and drifted into her garden on the end of a parachute can only be speculated on! Nevertheless, gathering his parachute under his arms and suffering from an extremely painful knee injury

The crew of 1st Lt James H. Hansen's 323rd BG B-26 (S/N 44-68109) M-WT miraculously avoided a catastrophe when Eduard Schallmoser's "White 11" hit the propeller blades of the bomber's starboard engine. The 455th Squadron Marauder suffered little damage and returned to base with all crew unhurt.

incurred when baling out of his aircraft, Eduard limped after his mother into the kitchen where he recounted to her the story of his air battle whilst devouring a large plate of freshly cooked pancakes!

Miraculously, despite Schallmoser's allegations that the American bomber "crashed", Hansen was able to nurse his rammed aircraft safely back to base without any casualties. "White 11" had hit the propeller of the B-26 in such a way that Hansen had not even needed to shut down his right engine since the blades had been evenly bent about six inches from their tips, causing no vibration. Schallmoser was later sent to hospital in Unterföhring, near München, for treatment to his knee where he would remain incarcerated until 25th April.

Back at 4,000 metres (13,125 ft), Tyszkiewicz had entered into a shooting match with another Me 262, firing 200 rounds from his guns as the jet climbed into the formation from 6 o'clock low, levelling out and firing from a distance of 900 metres (984 yards). The two aircraft continued shooting at each other until, at 180 metres (200 yards), the Me 262 passed to the right of the Marauder, pieces of its canopy and left jet nacelle breaking away as it disappeared from view at 3 o'clock apparently still under control. Elsewhere in the formation it was a similar story; the Marauder crews later reported that the speed of the German attack had created a confused picture with the majority of the jets closing into 180 metres (200 yards) before breaking away, although a few of the JV 44 pilots pressed home their attacks to "...absolute zero". Generally speaking though, on this occasion, the Americans considered that the jet attack had been "...uncoordinated" – "not systematic", not "planned".

Meanwhile, *Uffz.* "Jonny" Müller, his "White 15" laden with 24 R4M rockets, had taken off from München-Riem twelve minutes later than Schallmoser, at 10:50. Reaching Kempten, he made contact with the American bombers at 3,000 metres (9,850 ft) and fired his rockets into the formation of Marauders. The next few seconds are testimony to the deadly effectiveness of the R4M. The rockets hissed through the sky and two bombers began to plunge towards the earth.

Elsewhere, more Me 262s were now closing in on Vining's flight. He recalls: "In a fast glance over my shoulder, I saw a jet coming in out of a slight turn with muzzle flashes around the four 30 mm cannon in the nose – the fact that he was completing a turn may indicate that he was the number one jet returning for another pass. I turned my attention back to my position, tucking my wing closer to number 4 and at that instant a terrific blast went off below my knees and the plane rolled to the right. Sensing that my right leg was gone, I looked toward my co-pilot and while ordering him to take his controls, I noted that the right engine was at idle speed. So, in one swift arcing motion with my right hand, I hit the feathering button, moved to the overhead rudder trim crank and trimmed the plane for single engine operation and – just as rapidly – pressed the intercom button to order the bombardier to jettison the two tons of bombs. We were losing altitude at 2,000 feet (610 metres) per minute, which

Soon after baling out of his battle damaged Me 262 "White 11", Eduard Schallmoser poses calmly with his mother in the garden of his parents' home near München, 20 April 1945.

slowed to 1,000 fpm with the load gone."

The crew of Lt. M.S. Pietrowicz's B-26 flying alongside in number four position reported observing Vining's aircraft gradually drop out formation, flying on one engine and being attacked by enemy fighters but apparently still under control. Seeing the straggling bomber, a number of the JV 44 jets swung round for a second pass to administer the *coup de grace* while aboard the *Ugly Duckling*, Sgt. Winger continued firing at the "plethora" of jets that now attacked them, possibly damaging as many as four German machines. Eventually, the jets broke off their engagement and the battered B-26 somehow flew on.

A decision was subsequently taken to keep the aircraft airborne rather than bale out and with the co-pilot, Lt. James R. Mulvihill now flying the aircraft, the stricken bomber turned for home. Vining looked down to confirm the condition of his leg: "About three inches of my right ankle had been obliterated, leaving the foot dangling by a shred of skin perhaps 1/16th of an inch in width. The main artery was pumping volumes of blood into a wide pool covering the deck and already more than an inch deep. I decided to try to stem this flow by squeezing my leg above the knee which revealed to me the superhuman strength I had acquired. Silently, though, I resigned myself to my approaching death but resolved to do everything possible to save my crew. I held the flow to a trickle in this manner for the next ten minutes while directing the co-pilot and the gunners... I called the radio operator who manned the less strategic waist guns to come forward to render first aid. As he entered the radio/navigator compartment from the bomb bay, [S./Sgt. Newton C.] Armstrong saw the carnage on the flight deck and quickly snatched a headset, giving me the cord for a temporary tourniquet. Then he broke out the first-aid kit which contained a nice web belt tourniquet, sulfa tablets and powder, a morphine syringe and assorted bandaging material.

With the new tourniquet in place, I attempted to swallow a sulfa tablet but was unable to because the ground crew had failed to fill the water thermos and my throat was parched from loss of blood... Equally futile was any attempt to dust the wound with sulfa powder. In frustration, Armstrong offered to inject the morphine which I declined, assuming I would need it later if pain began. It was never used. Up to that point and for another fifteen minutes, I gave Mulvihill a complete verbal manual covering every contingency he could face in getting the B-26 back to *terra firma* in one piece. He had never flown the plane from the left seat or on single-engine and there were no brake pedals in his position. His performance that day should have been rewarded with more than the Distinguished Flying Cross which he was awarded for that action, but only learned about three years ago! Ironically, the gunners received no recognition."

Despite the blood-letting wreaked upon the lone B-26 by JV 44, Vining's aircraft had not yet seen the last of its ordeal, for a formation of Me 262s from I./KG(J) 54 from Prague-Rusin were also patrolling the München-Memmingem area between 10:54 and 11:23. Once again, as Vining vividly remembers, Yates shouted out a warning. "About ten minutes after the

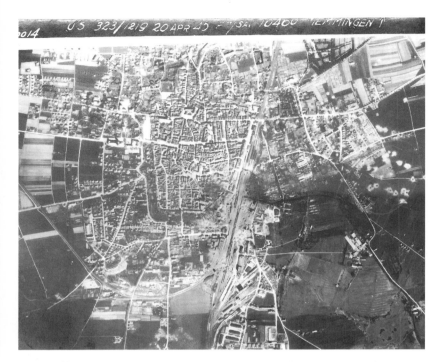

The effect of the 323rd BG's attack on the Memmingen marshalling yards are seen from these two strike photos. Bombs have hit the area immediately to the west of the yards.

aforementioned ministrations were completed, Yates in the tail turret once more gave us the blood-curdling news that jets were returning to attack, straight from the rear. Now fully aware that Yates would fire first, I quickly advised Mulvihill that, upon my signal in response to Yates' firing, he should make a ten degree turn into the dead engine, diving slightly to keep above stalling speed. Now my theory met the acid test. The jets came in precise trail about ten seconds apart – three of them. As planned and at my signal, Mulvihill turned and I witnessed each of the jets pass harmlessly some fifteen feet (4.5 metres) off my left wing. Holding my tourniquet with my right hand, I thumbed my nose

at each pilot with my left! As the third jet came alongside, I clearly saw him dump his stick and nose straight down. Looking over my left shoulder, I saw that two P-51s – from out of nowhere – had been able to overtake him at his slower attack speed. As he dove, the Mustangs rolled over in formation and dove at him on the angle. He never pulled out of that dive and I saw him splatter on the landscape. No one attacked us after that."

I./KG(J) 54 later reported that they had been unable to attack due to the "strong fighter escort screen", though no losses were recorded by the *Gruppe* that day. James Vining remembers that the P-51 presence "...was unique in my experience because it was the only sortie of my forty where we had a fighter escort (which may say something about the misinformation with which we started that day!)."

Some thirty minutes later as the crippled bomber flew over Stuttgart, Vining relinquished complete command of the aircraft to James Mullvihill and finally discarded his earphones and throat mike. Miraculously, the *Ugly Duckling* made it into Allied occupied territory, crash-landing into a camouflaged German tank trap at an abandoned airfield three kilometres (1.8 miles) east of Überherrn close to the French frontier. On landing however, S/Sgt. Winger, the armourer gunner, was killed when he was thrown against the side of the aircraft or its gun turret and T/Sgt. Wells sustained broken legs and injuries to his back when the bulkhead and door leading to the bomb bay collapsed upon landing and the aircraft split into four pieces.

"Jonny" Müller returned to München-Riem at 11:27.

James Vining survived the crash and was taken to a US military hospital in Metz. He was later awarded the Silver Star "...for gallantry in action against the enemy in aerial flight."

The JV 44 attack on the 323rd BG that morning had resulted in the loss of three bombers and one entire crew as well as seven further bombers damaged. Two Me 262s were claimed by Sgt. Edward S. Tsykiewicz, top turret gunner with the 323rd BG who was wounded in the jet attack and subsequently awarded the Silver Star and though no pilot losses are known to have been reported by JV 44, it is highly probable that a number of Me 262s were damaged.

The 323rd was up again in the afternoon, when together with Marauders from the 397th BG, it bombed the Nordlingen marshalling yards which were subsequently immobilised. One Me 262 appeared and made several passes at the group but did not fire.

Reinforcements

Elsewhere, the war situation was rapidly deteriorating to such an extent that even those at the very highest echelons of Nazi power were planning their escape from possible Russian captivity. In the early hours of 20 April, *Reichsmarschall* Hermann Göring had been one of the "loyal" inner circle to visit the *Führer* to extend his birthday greetings and used the occasion to venture a suggestion that he move south where he could be of more service to the Reich. Hitler ignored him but later that day, at the noon situation conference, the *Führer* decreed that he was splitting military control of what remained of the Reich into two. *Grossadmiral* Dönitz would take command in the north and Göring in the south. Göring finally sneaked out of Berlin for the

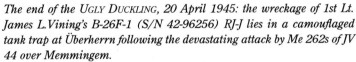

The end of the UGLY DUCKLING, 20 April 1945: the wreckage of 1st Lt. James L.Vining's B-26F-1 (S/N 42-96256) RJ-J lies in a camouflaged tank trap at Überherrn following the devastating attack by Me 262s of JV 44 over Memmingem.

relative sanctuary of Berchtesgaden at 01:20 on the 21st leaving an angry and beleagured *General der Flieger* Koller in command of the *Luftwaffe*. With demands being heaped upon him by a deranged *Führer*, Koller was faced with an increasingly difficult situation and he knew it. He wrote:

> "In spite of the continually narrowing and changing combat area, the Air Force encircled in a small pocket, surrounded on all sides by much stronger enemies – the greatest difficulties in the maintenance of communications and supplies – in spite of all this, everything that is humanly possible is being done. But decisive victories are no longer possible and the Luftwaffe will be completely dead in a few days."

Also aware of the inevitable end and at around this time, Adolf Galland called his pilots to the *Verband's* Feldkirchen control centre for a special briefing. He recalled to the author: "I assembled my pilots a week before the end at München-Riem and told them that the war was lost, the war was over but that we could continue flying as long as possible – not that we were in a position to change the military situation in any way. However, I only wanted volunteers – I was not ordering anybody to take-off anymore. So, in order that I knew that I was sending the right pilots into the air, I wanted to know which of them no longer wanted to fight. I offered them a guarantee that they would not be sent to

In late April 1945, Galland asssembled his pilots at München-Riem and offered them the option not to fly on operations if they did not wish to. Nearly all declined the offer and vowed to continue flying. Ofw. Rudolf Nielinger, JV 44, is photographed here at Riem, April 1945 and is seen clad in the typical late-war leather flying garb as issued to the pilots of Galland's Verband.

the front to fight on the ground and I think three pilots stated that they didn't want to fly. One was due to get married soon, another one had sick parents. All the others said *"We fight until the end."*

Klaus Neumann also remembers this briefing: "Galland called us together, made us form a line and said – *"For us, the war is over. Whoever wants to go home may do so. Please go now."* But no one did. We stayed together and we flew. We had nothing else to do. We couldn't win the war; we did it just to prove that the Me 262 was a fighter." With the continuing – and now unstoppable – drive by General Jacob L. Devers' US 6th Army Group into southern Germany in late April 1945, so the remaining Me 262 equipped units of the *Luftwaffe* still operating from airfields in northern Bavaria were forced to withdraw. At Lechfeld, which was now under direct threat, *Major* Heinz Bär had held out as long as possible. But by this time, forward American troops were only a few kilometres away and Bär, frustrated also by continuous attacks on the airfield, reluctantly took the decision to evacuate III./EJG 2.

BATTLE OVER BAVARIA

Heinz Bär had by now established himself as one of the *Luftwaffe's* leading jet fighter pilots having shot down a remarkable 13 enemy aircraft, most of them Mustangs and Liberators, in a little over a month whilst flying the Me 262 with III./EJG 2. On 23 April, he ordered his trainee pilots to transfer to Mühldorf, while he, together with his permanent staff and assigned pilots, went to München-Riem and reported to Adolf Galland. Here, they were immediately incorporated into JV 44. Bär brought with him a prototype variant of the Me 262, the A-1/U-5 (W.Nr. 112335) which he had flown since the middle of the month and which had been upgraded to carry a lethal weapons package of *six* 30 mm MK 108 cannon installed in the nose instead of the normal four.

With Steinhoff now in hospital, Bär's arrival at JV 44 together with his handful of experienced instructor pilots provided a much needed boost to the relatively small cadre of fully trained Me 262 pilots and also ensured the unit's mythical status in military aviation history, for never had so many legendary and highly decorated aces ever been associated with such a small unit in such a short time.

Also on the 23rd, after only two days at its new but heavily bombed airfield, I./KG 51 pulled out of Memmingem with all its aircraft and ground crews intact. The *Gruppe's* Me 262s, under the command of *Ritterkreuzträger* and former *Stuka* ace, *Major* Heinrich Brücker, flew direct to München-Riem and made its aircraft and pilots available to JV 44.

At 18:00, JV 44 was reporting a total of 12 Me 262s and five Focke-Wulf Fw 190 D-9/11s on strength, of which eight jets and just two Fw 190s were serviceable. These figures were supplemented in reality by the aircraft of the former III./EJG 2 which now had 16 aircraft at München-Riem of which 11 were serviceable. Documentary evidence also indicates that I./KG 51, which, as mentioned, had also just given up its aircraft to JV 44, was operating with 13 Me 262s of which seven were serviceable and it is possible that by this time, these too were at Riem.

By late April 1945, virtually the entire *Luftwaffe* jet fighter force was assembled on two main airfields – München-Riem and Prague-Rusin. Such a scenario presented the Germans with a new demand – that of protection from the ever growing, ever confident and thus ever bolder prowling Allied fighters and fighter-bombers which hawked around nearly every known operational *Luftwaffe* air base. The Me 262 was known to be at its most vulnerable when taking-off and landing, more so perhaps than

Heinz Bär, one of the Luftwaffe's leading jet aces, joined JV 44 in late April 1945.

conventional piston-engined aircraft due to the greater time and distance required for such a process as well as the time needed to engage in the more complicated task of starting the jet engines. For this reason, Adolf Galland meanwhile, had determined not to depend on or wait for, any orders from the High Command and began to set about establishing his own Fw 190-equipped *Platzschutzschwarm* or "airfield defence flight" to provide cover for his jet fighters.

Commanded by the highly experienced Russian front ace, *Leutnant* Heinz Sachsenberg, these, colourfully painted single seat piston-engined fighters endeavoured to provide air cover at Riem. As Galland explains: "The Americans were constantly observing our airfields and they attacked anybody who came out or who tried to get in, especially at München-Riem once they knew we were there and we lost some of our men that way. Sachsenberg was a good pilot and we felt safer when his aircraft were in the air. They surrounded the airfield – not in any formation – but usually just in pairs. We tried to get them into the air just as we took off and also when we came into land; we *tried* to do it, but often it didn't work because conditions were becoming impossible both on the airfield and in the air. Once up, they escorted us just around the airfield – once their undercarriages were up and they had climbed, it was time for them to come back."

Pilots of the "Würger Staffel" or "Butcher Bird Squadron", JV 44's semi-autonomous airfield protection and defence flight, posing for a photograph on the cowling of one of their Fw 190Ds at München-Riem, April 1945. The fast piston-engined fighters were intended to cover the jets during take-off and landing approach when they were at their most vulnerable.

FOURTEEN

THE LAST FLIGHT OF THE PRUSSIAN EAGLE

"I envy you, Galland..."

Hermann Göring arrived at his villa on the Obersalzberg from the inferno of Berlin on 21 April, weary but relieved that he had been able to get himself and at least a part of his precious art collection out of the capital and into the relative peace and tranquillity of the mountains. It was around this time that he met with Galland for the last time. Summoned to the Obersalzberg, the commander of JV 44 enjoyed a civil if slightly strained discussion with the *Reichsmarschall*. To Galland, Göring seemed "deeply depressed".

"Surprisingly," Galland recorded in his diary, "He received me with outspoken civility, requesting details about my unit's progress in reaching operational status, officially allocating Lützow to me and reluctantly agreeing that my premonitions regarding the employment of the Me 262 crewed by bomber pilots as fighters had been right. All this was somewhat incomprehensible to me and, in reality, what he meant to say was: *"Galland, you were right all along during our violent disagreements over the past few months."* Behind my back however, he persisted with his hostile attitude towards me until his eventual interrogation by American officers to whom he labelled me as his "best collaborator and adviser"."

The two men shook hands for the last time and, as Galland departed, Göring smiled and humbly confessed: "I envy you, Galland, for going into action. I wish I were a few years younger and less bulky... If I were, I would gladly put myself under your command. It would be marvellous to have nothing to worry about but a good fight, like it was in the old days." Galland left flabbergasted and returned to Riem.

Luftflotte 6 had now officially assigned JV 44's sizeable jet fighter force as being subordinate to *Generalmajor* Hentschel's 7. *Jagddivision* under which it was to operate in the air defence of southern Germany together with a handful of other single-engine day fighter and twin-engine nightfighter units based in the area.

To some extent, the pressure on these severely battered and depleted units, had been eased in mid-April by the decision by the Allies to divert the main thrust of the medium bomber campaign away from targets in southern Germany in favour of lending support to the offensive against German forces still holding out around the Gironde estuary in western France. But this respite was short-lived and it was not long before the Marauders returned in strength.

Clash over Schwabmünchen

For the American Tactical air forces, 24 April 1945 was a day of intensive operations mounted against various targets throughout southern Germany.

The sun catches the wings of a formation of Marauders of the 17th BG as they fly in perfect formation towards another target. On the morning of 24 April 1945, the group flew two missions involving five aircraft each to an ammunition depot at Schwabmünchen, but poor weather frustrated bombing.

In the morning, two formations of five B-26 Marauders each from the 17th BG rendezvoused with their Mustang escort over Nancy and attacked German ordnance installations at Schwabmünchen, south of Augsburg. The first was not able to drop due to bad weather and the second dropped without results.

Now, sixteen days after the group's second unit citation, JV 44 sent up a force of 11 Me 262s at 09:50 equipped with R4M rockets and led by *Oberst* Günther Lützow to intercept its bombers eight kilometres (5 miles) west of its assigned target. Galland wrote vividly in his diary: '"Franzl" became my closest friend in those last weeks; I shall always remember him as an outstanding example of a German fighter pilot – upright, courageous and cheerful. Having overcome some initial problems, flying the Me 262 operationally became his last great passion. On the morning of this particular day, leading a small formation, he had shot down a Marauder to the south of

Augsburg. Typically, however, he had been unhappy about not having been able to lead his echelon to a more successful attack against the enemy as planned."

Lützow's self-criticism was unfounded; the effects of what would be the first of two sorties flown by JV 44 that day, proved devastating as the crews in a three aircraft window flight embarking on the 17th's third mission of the day – flying apart from the other ships – were to discover. At precisely 10:02, just as the window flight was leaving the target and preparing to rejoin the rest of the formation, three of the Me 262s hit the bombers from behind in line astern closing in to 820 metres (900 yards) before they fired their rockets. It is probable that Lützow was accompanied in this first *Kette* of jets by *Fw.* Otto Kammerdiener, flying Me 262 "White 3", who now, with only seconds to go before the German fighters streaked through the Marauder flight and began to select a target.

In the main American formation, Sgt. Warren E. Young, an Engineer Gunner on board one of the 37th Squadron's ships, watched helplessly as the Me 262s came in. He remembers: "April 24th, we were attacked by jets for the first time. When I first saw the Me 262, he was coming straight for us from 5 o'clock high. I opened fire and in a matter of seconds he was overhead. I pushed the red high speed button on my turret to turn it so as I could fire on him again as he was flying away – but before the turret had completed its 180 degree turn the jet had gone. As I looked over the side of our plane, I saw a wing break off one of our bombers and then the plane went into a spin. From my gun position that was all I could see but I could hear the chatter on the intercom from the rest of my crew as to what they were seeing."

Young's fellow crew members were witnessing JV 44's R4Ms strike into the Marauder formation. One of the

Right: Closest of friends: Oberst Günther Lützow and Adolf Galland of JV 44 during a reflective moment at München-Riem, mid-April 1945.

Below: Seven of JV 44's jets are seen here on the western perimeter road at Riem, April 1945. The spire of the church in Riem village is visible in the distance behind the airport buildings. Because of its eleven week existence, few such photographs of the unit are known to exist.

With one wing shot away and the rest of the aircraft streaming flames, a "white-tailed" B-26, purportedly of the 455th BS, 323rd BG, plummets towards the earth whilst on a mission to a Noball site at Dannes in France, 5 February 1944. A similar fate befell STUD DUCK of the 17th BG whilst under attack from jets led by Günther Lützow on 24 April 1945.

first bombers to be hit – probably by the second jet – was the number 1 aircraft in the "window" flight, B-26C (42-107729) *Stud Duck* of the 34th Bombardment Squadron. Piloted on this mission by 1st Lt. Fred J. Harms, *Stud Duck* had been on the 17th's strength since early June 1944 and had flown a string of nearly ten perfect missions as a flight-leader aircraft by a different crew.

The other crews in the flight watched in horror as the R4Ms streak through the small formation and *Stud Duck* took a direct hit in its vertical stabiliser causing it to roll over to the right, narrowly missing the number 2 aircraft. Damage was also observed to the wing, waist position and aft bomb bay before the aircraft rolled away in a spin, disappearing into clouds with its wheels down and bomb bay doors open.

Aboard *Stud Duck*, only seconds after S./Sgt. Hal S. Brink the Armorer Gunner had called out the presence of enemy fighters, the impact of the blast from the R4M was so great that it forced the Engineer Gunner, S./Sgt. Edward F. Truver out of the aircraft. As he later wrote: "Nothing can be said except that right after we started shooting at the enemy planes there was an explosion which blew me out of my gun position and out of the plane. I happened to have my parachute on so I

Fw. Otto Kammerdiener of JV 44 claimed one Marauder shot down on 24 April 1945.

was able to come down safely. Upon reaching the ground, I landed just a short distance from our burning plane. I didn't see any other 'chutes while I was coming down and also the Germans who took me prisoner told me that I was the only one that got out of the plane. The others were all burned before the Germans who took me prisoner could get them out."

Stud Duck crashed approximately thirteen kilometres (8 miles) from the little town of Babenhausen, where Truver was later held prisoner. It was here, the day before the American 45th Infantry Division took the town and set him free, that a priest from a nearby village visited the shot-down airman. "According to him," Truver recorded afterwards, "he went to the wreckage of our plane after the fire was out and got the remains of several bodies and buried them near the scene of the crash. When I told him how many fellows were supposed to be in the plane, he returned to the scene but could find nothing that resembled what might be the remains of the remaining bodies."

Meanwhile, JV 44 returned from the morning mission having shot down at least one other Marauder from the 34th BS, B-26B (42-95786) *Skipper* piloted by 1st Lt Leigh Slates, as well as one of the Mustang escort. *Fw.* Otto Kammerdiener, flying Me 262 "White 3", claimed one of the bombers destroyed and one German pilot – an unnamed *Oberfähnrich* – was lost.

B-26 Marauder (s/n 42-107729) STUD DUCK of the 34th Squadron, 17th BG: JV 44's rocket-armed Me 262s shot it down during the attack led by Günther Lützow on 24 April. The force of the jet attack blew one of Stud Duck's gunners out of the aircraft. He survived.

B-26C-45 (s/n 43-34567) THE LADY LINDA of the 34th Squadron, 17th BG lost on the 24 April mission to Schwabmünchen. Though indistinct in this photo, careful study will reveal the words "The Lady Linda" beneath the muscical notes artwork on the nose .

The nose art on battle-veteran ship B-26B-50 (s/n 42-95987) YO-YO CHAMP, formerly of the 497th Squadron, 344th BG, latterly with the 34th Squadron, 17th BG, so named because of its legendary ability to always return from missions.

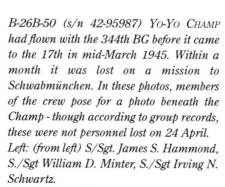

B-26B-50 (s/n 42-95987) YO-YO CHAMP had flown with the 344th BG before it came to the 17th in mid-March 1945. Within a month it was lost on a mission to Schwabmünchen. In these photos, members of the crew pose for a photo beneath the Champ - though according to group records, these were not personnel lost on 24 April.
Left: (from left) S/Sgt. James S. Hammond, S./Sgt William D. Minter, S./Sgt Irving N. Schwartz.
Right: (from left): F/O J.H. Roberts Jr., S/Sgt. James S. Hammond, F/O Bueford C. Holverson, S./Sgt William D. Minter, 1st Lt. Leroy P. Percy.

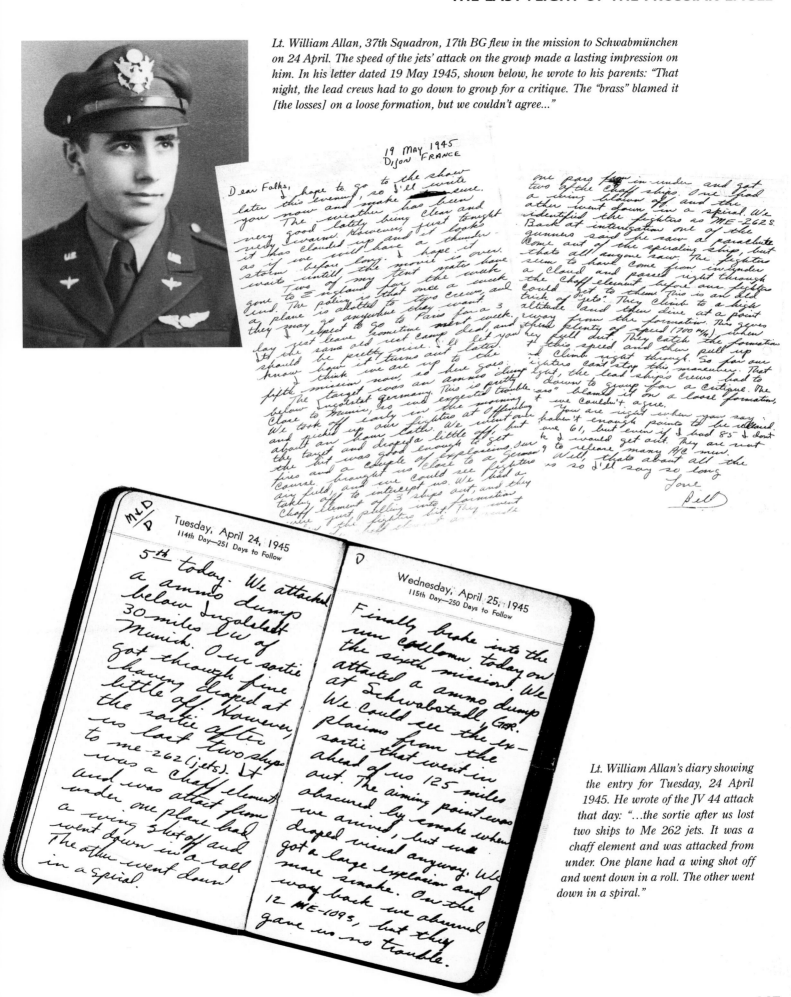

Lt. William Allan, 37th Squadron, 17th BG flew in the mission to Schwabmünchen on 24 April. The speed of the jets' attack on the group made a lasting impression on him. In his letter dated 19 May 1945, shown below, he wrote to his parents: "That night, the lead crews had to go down to group for a critique. The "brass" blamed it [the losses] on a loose formation, but we couldn't agree..."

19 MAY 1945
DIJON FRANCE

Dear Folks,

hope to go to the show later this evening, so I'll write you now and make sure. The weather has been very good lately, being clear and warm. However, just tonight it has clouded up and it looks as if we will have a thunderstorm before long. I hope it is over until the movie is over.

Two of my tent mates have gone to England for the week. The policy is that once a week a plane is allotted to two crews, and they want, and they may go anywhere they want. a plane. They expect to go to Paris for a 3 day rest leave sometime next week. It's the same old rest camp deal, and should be pretty nice. I'll let you know how it turns out later.

I think we are up to the fifth mission now, so here goes. The target was an ammo dump below Ingolstadt Germany, so close to Munich, and is expected trouble. We took off early in the morning and picked up our fighters at Offenburg about an hour later. We went over the target and dropped a little off, but the hit was good enough to get a couple of explosions, our Course brought us close to a German airfield, and we could see fighters taking off to intercept us. We had a chaff element of 3 ships out, and they were just pulling into formation when the fighters hit and made

one pass from in under and got two of the chaff ships. One had a wing blown off and the other went down in a spiral. We identified the fighters as ME-262s. Back at interrogation one of the gunners said he saw a parachute come out of the spiraling ship, but that's all anyone saw. The fighters seem to have come from in under a cloud and passed right through the chaff element before our fighters could get to them. This is an old trick of "jets". They climb to a high altitude and then dive at a point away from the formation. This gives them plenty of speed (700 m/h) when they pull out. They catch the formation at this speed and then pull up and climb right through. So far our fighters can't stop this maneuver. That night, the lead ship's crews had to go down to group for a critique. The "brass" blamed it on a loose formation, but we couldn't agree.

You are right when you say there haven't enough points to be released. We are 61, but even if I had 85 I don't think I would get out. They are not going to release many AFC men.

Well, that's about all the news so I'll say so long.

Love
Bill

Tuesday, April 24, 1945
114th Day—251 Days to Follow

M/D
/D

5th today. We attacked a ammo dump below Ingolstadt 30 miles w of Munich. Our sortie got through fine having dropped at little off. However, the sortie after us lost two ships to me-262 (jets). It was a chaff element and was attacked from under. One plane had a wing shot off and went down in a roll The other went down in a spiral.

Wednesday, April 25, 1945
115th Day—250 Days to Follow

D

Finally broke into the run codelumn today on the sixth mission. We attacked a ammo dump at Schwabstadt, Ger. We could see the explacions from the sortie that went in ahead of us 125 miles out. The aiming point was obscured by smoke when we aimed, but we dropped visual anyway. We got a large explosion and more smoke. On the way back we abound 12 ME-109s, but they gave us no trouble.

Lt. William Allan's diary showing the entry for Tuesday, 24 April 1945. He wrote of the JV 44 attack that day: "...the sortie after us lost two ships to Me 262 jets. It was a chaff element and was attacked from under. One plane had a wing shot off and went down in a roll. The other went down in a spiral."

In what is purported to be the last photograph taken before his disappearance on 24 April 1945, Oberst Günther Lützow walks pensively towards the starting platform at München-Riem accompanied by Adolf Galland.

"Like a Bat out of Hell..."

During the afternoon, the Ninth Air Force assembled a force of 256 medium bombers with fighter escort to mount attacks against targets in southern Germany. The first strike force, comprising Marauders of the 391st BG and A-26 Invaders of the 386th, 409th and 415th Bomb Groups, was assigned the (correctly) suspected jet base at Landau as its target, just under 100 kilometres (62 miles) north east of München and, at that time, the recently vacated home to the Me 262s of II./KG 51.

The second strike force, comprising 74 B-26s of the 322nd and 344th Bomb Groups from the respective Belgian airfields of Le Culot and Florennes/Juzaine, accompanied by forty-one A-20 Havocs of the 410th Bomb Group out of Juvincourt (a former jet airfield), was assigned as its target, an oil storage and supply depot located in woods at Schrobenhausen some fifty kilometres (31 miles) north west of München and which was known to be supplying fuel to German forces defending the approaches to that city as well as for the withdrawal into the so-called "Redoubt" enemy defensive area of extreme southern Germany and Austria.

Alerted by Feldkirchen to the incoming raid, JV 44 hurriedly scrambled a total of six Me 262s again led by Günther Lützow who had been briefed in Galland's absence by Heinz Bär and instructed to meet the bombers on a course bearing north-west from Riem for Schrobenhausen. However two aircraft from this formation aborted shortly after take-off either because of engine failure or mechanical problems. The remaining machines flown by some of the *Luftwaffe's* finest and most deadly *Experten* – Lützow, *Hauptmann* Walter Krupinski and *Leutnant* Klaus Neumann – all *Ritterkreuzträger* – and another unidentified pilot, flew on. On this occasion too, both Lützow's and Neumann's Me 262s were fitted with R4Ms.

In conditions of 9-10/10 strato-cumulus cloud with tops at 2,600 metres (8,530 ft), the 410th's Havocs ran into problems as they approached the target when the two pathfinder aircraft experienced simultaneous equipment failure. With visual bombing impossible because of the weather, the attack was abandoned and the formation turned away from the target area.

The remaining Schrobenhausen force flying in three boxes, about twenty minutes apart, was blessed with better luck and, assisted by their four PFF aircraft, the Marauders armed their bombs. As they did so, Lützow's four Me 262s were streaking up from the south across the Swabian Jura to catch them. At 15:27, just before the last element of bombers from the 344th BG was setting up to make its bombing run, the jets broke through the clouds at 7,000 metres (23,000 ft), diving to

Taken three days after the Schrobenhausen mission at Florennes, Belgium on 27 April 1945, this photo shows one of the aircraft which took part; B-26 S/N 42-107675 coded 7I-T SITTING PRETTY *piloted by Lt. D.R.Billing of the 497th Squadron, 344th BG. In this picture T./Sgt Finer and S./Sgt Mizelle haul a bomb trolley towards another waiting aircraft.*

According to certain group records, other losses incurred by 34th over the target included B-26C-45 (43-34567) *The Lady Linda* and B-26B-50 (42-95987) *Yo Yo Champ*, though this remains unclear. The former machine had been on the strength of the Squadron since January 1945 whilst the latter aircraft had only been taken on by the 34th the previous month from its prior employment with the 497th Squadron, 344th BG, Ninth Air Force. Ironically, this machine had been afforded the *"Yo Yo"* part of its name because of its legendary ability to always return from missions. However, though JV 44 claimed a number of both "confirmed" and "probable" Marauders on 24 April it has not been possible to conclusively ascertain whether *The Lady Linda* and *Yo Yo Champ* were shot down by jets or by Flak.

The crew of B-26G, K9-D, WILLIE THE WOLF (see inset) of the 494th Squadron, 344th BG photographed at the completion of their training at Lake Charles, Louisiana in October 1944 before departure to Europe. From left: Vincent R. De Courcy (pilot), Benedict Miller (co-pilot), I. Russo (bombardier, but replaced on 24 April mission by Walter R. Bennett), Andrew Navarette (engineer-gunner), Herbert L. Laport (radio-gunner), Norman G. Farley (armourer-gunner). Farley yelled a warning to his crew having seen a Me 262 climb behind WILLIE THE WOLF on 24 April 1945. He managed to fire some rounds before the jet turned and dived into the clouds.

3,350 metres (11,000 ft) to attack the Marauders' window flight south east of Monheim, one *Rotte* approaching from 6 o'clock level and breaking away low at 2 o'clock, the other attacking from 2 o'clock high, breaking away low from 6 to 8 o'clock.

Second Lt. R.M. Cello's B-26C coded Y5-S was one of three of the 495th Squadron's aircraft forming the window flight. Flying in number 1 position, the crew noted that the Me 262s "...made their first pass from low at 7 o'clock under the aircraft and broke at 2 o'clock level, turned and came from low at 1 o'clock, closed to 200 yards then fired to within 20 yards. One Me

262 came from pursuit curve and tail gunner opened fire at 600 yards. Gun jammed but fighter broke off at 500 yards."

Lt E.L. Johnson was pilot of the neighbouring aircraft in the number 2 position, B-26G coded Y5-2. He recorded: "Me 262 came from 7 o'clock below and passed under, breaking away at 3 o'clock. Did not fire. Returned from low at 1 o'clock, opened fire at 500 yards and closed to 50 yards. Broke away at 7 o'clock low."

Three of Johnson's gunners expended 450 .50 calibre rounds at the jet fighter until it "...turned on back and dove into clouds."

Sgt. Norman G. Farley was an armourer gunner manning the

Left: The Fall and Rise of K9-L: The original K9-L, B-26G THE FREDDIE DEES of the 494th Squadron, 344th BG probably at Cormeilles-en-Vexin, France in 1944. The aircraft was written off after bellying in. The nose art consists of a cartoon bomb flanked by the masks of Tragedy and Comedy.

Below: The replacement K9-L, B-26G, as yet unamed but bearing the same cartoon bomb and masks as the old aircraft.

tail guns on board a aircraft which had only been temporarily assigned to Lt. Vincent R. De Courcy's crew, B-26 coded K9-L of the 494th Squadron, 344th BG and flying as number 2 aircraft in the third flight, second box, off the right wing of the lead ship. Farley remembers the day clearly: "It was my thirtieth mission and it turned out to be my last. Our crew subsequently went on leave to Southport, England and the war ended before we returned to the group. However, I don't remember any mention of fighters in the area being made at the briefing before the mission. Shortly thereafter, I saw a plane which popped up from the clouds below us and started climbing towards us. I barely had time to cry out "...fighters!" before he was directly behind us in a climbing turn with his belly exposed to my tail position guns. I fired a few rounds and when he was slightly above us, he seemed to turn and dive for the clouds below us. At no time did I ever feel he was shooting at my plane. I *did* see some flames from his plane which I assumed were from his guns. I felt he was shooting at something above and to the right of my plane. Being in the tail position, I got a pretty good look, although a short one."

"I ordinarily flew K9-L except when it was down for maintenance. But I was flying aircraft K9-C that day." recalled Lt William P. Morton from Hazard, Kentucky, a pilot with the 494th Squadron, and in his own words a relative "latecomer" to the group, having joined it only at the beginning of the previous month. "I was in the number 6 position, third flight and near the target, I was absorbed in flying tight formation. I only recall the intercom conversation that some strange-looking fighters were shooting cannon fire at us. According to my gunners, they were well outside of the range of our .50 calibre guns. I then caught a glimpse of this object out of my left eye and it was moving like a bat out of hell..." (*Author's Note – See page 156)

K9-L's engineer gunner up in the top turret was Sgt. Johnny Quong. He was able to get a better look. "I saw, what seemed at first to be a twin engine B-26 straggler at a long distance, approaching at 6 o'clock." recalls Quong. "As it kept approaching, all the gunners saw it. It kept coming and then dived and broke off to the left. When it turned, I could tell it was not a B-26 but a smaller plane going like a bat out of hell. All the gunners started talking excitedly. *What the hell was that?* We were so excited that our pilot, Lt. W. P. Morton had to tell us to keep quiet after reporting to him what we had seen. We were being escorted by some P-47s which then began to chase this thing. None of us on Morton's plane fired a shot. We found out back in Florennes that the plane was a Me 262."

With the exception of the three window aircraft which were flying several thousand yards ahead and to the right of the main box, the Marauders promptly closed into a tight formation, with the two PFF aircraft, which had left the main body, quickly returning to the safety of the formation. The four German jets flashed below the bombers and disappeared into the undercast.

"We have visitors!" "OK... We'll be right down..."

Escorting the bombers that day were P-47 Thunderbolts of Colonel Ray J. Stecker's 365th Fighter Group, the "Hell Hawks". They had taken-off from their base at Fritzlar, south of Kassel, in three elements at twenty minute intervals so as to rendezvous with the individual bomber boxes heading for Schrobenhausen. The second element, comprising the 16 fighters of the 388th Fighter Squadron, took-off at 13:50 and was led by Major James

The "Morton" crew at Cormeilles-en-Vexin, France during spring 1945. From left to right: T.Sgt T.C. Schultz (tail gunner), F/O J.E Durham (bombardier), 2nd Lt.W.P. Morton Jr (pilot), 2nd Lt A.D. Reddrick (co-pilot), T./Sgt J. Quong (engineer-gunner), T./Sgt J.H. Mixon (radio operator-gunner). Both Morton and Quong sighted a JV 44 Me 262 and described it as moving "... like a bat out of hell."

E. Hill. The squadron was arranged with Hill leading Red Flight together with White Flight as low-cover for the bombers, while Captain Jerry G. Mast leading Blue Flight and 1st Lieutenant Oliven T. Cowan leading Green Flight formed the top-cover. They rendezvoused with the bombers at 14:30.

Shortly after rendezvous, the Group Leader of the 344th BG gave the warning of enemy fighters to Hill. 2nd Lt. James L. Stalter, piloting B-26G (No. 43-34181) coded Y5-O *Lak-a-Nookie* of the 495th Bomb Squadron and flying in number 6 position of the second flight, lead box of the 36-ship group formation, witnessed events: "My notes say that the Schrobenhausen mission was four hours long and we dropped by Pathfinder as a cloud layer beneath us prevented us from bombing visually. We had made our drop and were heading for home when I heard our Group Leader call the leader of our P-47 fighter escort, stating – *"We have visitors"*. The fighter leader's response still sticks in my mind. In a very, very slow Southern Texas drawl, he responded – *"OK... We'll... be... right... down...!"*

As the P-47s dropped down towards the target, one of the pilots in White Flight sighted and called in the Me 262s. Lt. Cowan, flying at just under 5,200 metres (17,060 ft) noticed the jets

Pilots of the 388th Fighter Squadron, 365th FG, relax by a lake used for gunnery practice near Kassel in 1945. Seen in the picture are two of the pilots who challenged Günther Lützow on 24th April; Major James E. Hill (sitting right) and 2nd Lt. Byron Smith Jr. (with sunglasses).

powering up through the bomber formation. Cowan, who had already shot down an Me 262 in February, instinctively slammed his P-47 into a dive and managed to bounce the German machines just as they were making their firing pass. Cowan targeted the outside jet and fired two short bursts, observing strikes, yet he could not match the German's superior speed. As Cowan explained to an American historian in 1982: "I recall thinking that my dive needed more speed and I became more aware of this as the damaged jet pulled away. At this point, I suddenly realised that I was really talking out loud to my plane to give more speed and then I wondered how much of this was on the radio. We had no fear of the German jets, because we could easily out-turn them. I am sure they had no fear of us, because usually they could leave us. Hence, we needed altitude for speed (diving) and a suprise element. With the jet's speed, they could hit fast and move on."

Cowan's dive however, did have the effect of splitting the JV 44 attack and forcing the German pilots to break up whatever formation they had. Meanwhile, on board *Lak-a-Nookie*, James Stalter watched the fighters whirl into action: "One Me 262 passed on our right and at our level at a very high rate of speed and in level flight. He was followed by a P-47 in close pursuit. While still within visual range, the Me 262 rolled over and did a split-S down into the cloud layer. The P-47 followed with the same manouever and disappeared from my view."

It is most likely that Stalter had observed Blue Flight Leader, Captain Jerry Mast chasing one of the jets. Stalter's radio gunner, Sgt. Edward J. Miller in his position at the waist guns where he would have had a view below and behind, also saw a P-47 "shoot down" an Me 262, though what he probably saw was the power dive chase developing between pilots of the 365th FG and one of the Me 262s.

A little over 600 metres (1,968 ft) above the last element of bombers, Mast glanced down and spotted one of the Me 262s veering away from Cowan before banking

Above right: 1st Lt Oliven T. Cowan and his crew chief, Sgt. Grabowski, in front of Cowan's personal P-47D TOUCH ME NOT at Metz, early 1945. Cowan was flying this aircraft when he encountered Günther Lützow on 24 April 1945.
Right: 1st Lt Oliven T. Cowan, 388th Fighter Squadron, 365th FG sits in the cockpit of his P-47 flanked by his ground crew.

to make another attack on the rear group of bombers from six o'clock low: "I split-S'd and went into a full power dive to cut the 262 off from the bombers." Mast recalled after the mission, "The pilot of the 262 saw me for he went into a steep dive before he had an opportunity to fire on the bombers."

Flying on Major Hill's wing in Red Flight was 2nd Lt. William H. Myers. He too saw the Me 262 and began to call its position to Hill. But when Hill suddenly banked sharply, Myers at first assumed that his squadron commander had also seen the jet. "Major Hill and I were alone near the bombers after the initial encounter with the Me 262s on that day and the entire squadron had become quite split up." Myers wrote in 1982, "I saw the Me

Above: In these pictures, B-26G (s/n 43-34181) Y5-O LAK-A-NOOKIE is seen in formation on an earlier mission from the cockpit of another B-26.

Left: 2nd Lt. James L. Stalter of 495th Squadron, 344th BG piloted B-26G (s/n 43-34181) Y5-O LAK-A-NOOKIE during the raid to Schrobenhasuen on 24 April 1945. He witnessed a P-47 of the 365th FG chasing Lützow's Me 262 into cloud.

Below: The crew of the 344th BG's LAK-A-NOOKIE on 24 April 1945 photographed during training at Lake Charles, Louisiana. From left to right: 2nd Lt. James L. Stalter (pilot), Lt. Robert Howk (co-pilot), Lt. Paul Mershon (bombardier/navigator), Sgt. David Phillips (engineer gunner), Sgt. Edward J. Miller (radio gunner), and Sgt. Alex Arzumanian (armourer gunner).

262 heading straight for us but I am not at all sure that Major Hill did. Someone said: *"I've lost him"* just as Major Hill began to bank sharply away. At that time I yelled: *"I have him,"* and headed straight for the Me 262. For some reason, he then went into a dive and I practically rolled onto my back trying to cut him off."

The airspeed indicator in Myers' Thunderbolt was reading more than 500 mph (805 kph) and the American pilot initially calculated that he could shoot the jet down the moment that it pulled out of its dive. "We continued to go nearly straight down until it became apparent that it was quite possible that neither one of us would be able to pull out of that dive. I later remembered that I had even fired my guns in the early moments, but it was a ridiculous effort since I was much too far away. Major Hill was able to observe the entire encounter from overhead and confirmed my activities. Neither of us ever saw or knew that Captain Mast was in the vicinity. This was quite possible because there would have been no way for Captain Mast to keep up with or close to the Me 262 if he was following him in a dive because he could not have the advantage I did in cutting the plane off. Captain Mast, therefore, could have been responsible for the initial manoeuvre which my presence would have forced continuance."

Mast's wingman, 2nd Lt. Byron Smith Jr., had followed his leader in his dive on the Me 262 but seconds later noticed another jet approaching the bombers from head-on. Turning away from Mast, Smith closed in on the jet as it banked to the left in front of the Marauders and then executed a steep right climbing turn

An Me 262 dives through an American formation.

that took it into the bomber formation. Smith levelled out at 30 degrees and fired a burst over the German aircraft's nose. For a moment, the German pilot continued his attack run and then must have become aware of the American fighter for he immediately embarked upon a series of violent, evasive turns and climbs. Despite this attempt to shake him off, Smith persisted in his chase and managed to fire several more bursts at the Me 262 which suddenly dived into the clouds. Smith at least had the satisfaction of watching his tracer strike home before being forced to return to his position and continue with the escort.

Meanwhile, Mast and Myers noticed that their Me 262 started to pull out from its dive at one point, but suddenly went into an even steeper dive, its pilot having probably become aware of the two P-47's pursuing him. The jet "...went into the ground and exploded" and Myers was forced to black himself out with a high "G" recovery in order to avoid hitting the ground himself.

Flying in the number 4 position of the third flight in the second box of the Marauder formation was B-26G coded K9-O of the 494th Squadron piloted by 2nd Lt. Doug R. Zimmerman. The aircraft's radio gunner was Sgt. Don E. Sinclair who was manning one of the waist guns and embarking on his fifteenth and final mission of the war: "We had just dropped our bombs and were headed back to base. We were all beginning to relax and take it easy for the return flight thinking there would not be any flak or fighters to contend with, when we were suddenly attacked by Me 262 jets that came up firing through our flight. I

Lt William H. Myers (left), 388th Fighter Squadron, 365th FG, was forced to black himself out during the high 'G' chase after Lützow's Me 262.

Captain Jerry G. Mast, 388th Fighter Squadron, 365th FG: he is jointly credited with shooting down Lützow's Me 262.

Left: The crew of B26G K9-O (below) of the 494th Squadron, 344th BG taken at Barksdale Field near Shreveport, Louisiana in December 1944 prior to departure for Europe. Four months later, the same crew would experience at first hand an attack by jet fighters of JV 44. Sgt. Don Sinclair (radio gunner) wrote: "It was quite an experience for me and the memory of it is still fresh in my mind." From left to right: 2nd Lt Doug Zimmerman (pilot), F/O Jack Dickert (co-pilot), F/O Bob Stoick (bombardier), Sgt. Glenn Tawney (engineer-gunner), Sgt. Don Sinclair (radio-gunner), Sgt. Norman Chapman (armourer-gunner).

heard their shells exploding near our left engine, but it was not damaged by their guns. Our top turret gunner, Sgt. Norman Chapman, fired at one jet as it passed by. The tail gunner, Sgt. Glenn L. Tawney saw one as it banked away and would have had a perfect shot as the jet had its belly and the underside of its wings exposed. In the instant that Glenn saw the jet, the two engine pods resembled the engines on a B-26 and he thought that it was one of our planes. When he realised it was an Me 262, it was gone and was too late to fire at it."

"One of the jets hung between my plane and the number 6 plane in our flight. As I aimed my gun at him, I could see the number six plane in my sights and I did not fire for fear of hitting the other B-26 in our flight. I could see the German pilot's face very clearly as he was that close. He was probably there for only a few seconds but at the time, it seemed a lot longer. In an instant, he was gone and the sky where had been was empty. In the distance, I saw a P-47 diving on the tail of a jet and in the next instant the sky in front of the P-47 was empty as the jet must have turned on his power and blasted out of sight. At least, for that one moment on that day in April 1945, we both looked each other over and each one went on our separate way. It was quite an experience for me and the memory of it is still fresh in my mind."

The German attack had faltered, though *Lt.* Klaus Neumann was able to fire his R4Ms at a *Pulk* of nine B-26s and thought that he saw two of the bombers go down before turning for home.

Shortly after their first attack, the four Me 262s endeavoured to re-group. *Hptm.* Walter Krupinski noticed that one of the Marauders was trailing black smoke from its port-side engine but still flying in formation and this may have been a machine damaged by Neumann's rockets. The German pilots were also aware of the numerically superior P-47 escort and had decided to return to München-Riem as quickly as possible. All four jets assembled in a loose formation and took a wide left turn on a homeward course, with Lützow's machine positioned furthest to the south of the attack formation. Radio contact had unknowingly been lost between Lützow and the other jets and he was observed by Krupinski to turn quite suddenly and inexplicably to towards

the south. Moments later, as Lützow flew away alone from the formation towards the mountains, Krupinski saw "...an explosion in the air" some 20 kilometres (12 miles) away.

"We broke away in a wide left turn on our homeward route – direction München", Krupinski recalled, "*Oberst* Lützow's change in course towards a southerly direction was completely incomprehensible to me and I therefore called him on the radio but did not get a reply. The explosion which I saw, or something very similar, occurred at a distance of at least 20 kilometres (12 miles). Everyone knows that at that distance, details can no longer be observed. In any case, my attempt at radio contact,

A contemplative moment for Lt. Klaus Neumann (left) and Major Erich Hohagen, München-Riem, April 1945. It is likely that Neumann accounted for at least one Marauder damaged on 24 April 1945.

prompted by *Oberst* Lützow's change in course, took place before I saw the explosion. Today, I no longer remember how many times I tried to call him. We couldn't fly after him as contact with the enemy Marauders had taken place quite late into the mission and we were compelled to fly home by the quickest route due to lack of fuel."

Research conducted by a British historian after the war confirms that on the afternoon of 24 April 1945, a fighter aircraft crashed into the small town of Donauwörth on an undeveloped tract of land between the Sternschanzenstrasse (Parkstadt) and a hill known as the Kalvarienberg. Donauwörth had been subjected to heavy American bombardment on 19 and 21 April when "three quarters" of the old, imperial town was destroyed and those inhabitants who remained and had not fled into the countryside, were largely women, children and the elderly. However, the crash was observed by staff from the nearby Messerschmitt works who reported it to an officer of the local *Landratsamt* but an official record of the crash appears not to have been kept by the authorities.

When the JV 44 pilots returned to München-Riem, they claimed three probable B-26 Marauders during what had been a ten minute engagement. However, official American records contradict the JV 44 claims. According to a Mission Summary of the Schrobenhausen and Landau raids prepared by the headquarters of the 9th Bombardment Division, "...no bombers were lost."

Gunther Lützow was reported missing and when Walter Krupinski later arrived at the Feldkirchen operations room, it was to discover that the "signal-marker" of the *Oberst's* aircraft on the IFF radar screen had blinked off at just about the same spot at where he had witnessed the explosion. His was the only Me 262 recorded as lost by the *Luftwaffe* that day.

"The Me 262 flew extraordinarily steadily when it was well trimmed," Walter Krupinski commented in 1986, "and I feel that *Oberst* Lützow was wounded during the attack on the Marauders and later became unconscious."

"What is my opinion about the explosion and the failure of Lützow's IFF system?" Johannes Steinhoff surmised in correspondence with the British historian, Nevil Basnett, in 1985, "I would not exclude that he was shot down. That he accepted a dog-fight whilst being alone is, nevertheless, quite unlikely. But Lützow was not very familiar with the Me 262. I happened to check him out and from the beginning I had the feeling that he was frightened. He had not been in combat for a long time – more than two years! Lützow was not exactly in love with the Me 262; did he make a mistake?"

"After all these years," Oliven Cowan wrote in 1982, "It seems very strange to learn that I was diving into a flight of jets led by Lützow who had 108 victories. We were really babes-in-battle compared with his record. We could have celebrated his death in 1945, but now it seems such a waste for him to have been killed so late in the war. Well, that's the way it was in the big war and all other wars for that matter."

The exact circumstances of Lützow's death still remain a mystery, though Captain Jerry G. Mast and Lt. William H. Myers are jointly credited with the destruction of an Me 262 that day.

AUTHOR'S NOTE: There is an anomaly here and I have taken the liberty of editing the text in the interests of keeping things understandable. However, something is not right. The author has a letter from Norman G. Farley stating he flew K-9D *Willie the Wolf* on the 24 April mission. The 494th Squadron post-mission loading list for this mission has Farley flying ship "no. 351" piloted by De Courcy. A post mission interrogation report lists De Courcy as flying K-9L. The author also has a letter from William P. Morton stating that *he* piloted K-9L on this mission, yet the post mission interrogation report lists Morton's aircraft as K9-C (If the group documentation is to be trusted then Morton could not have flown K-9L since De Courcy was flying that aircraft). In another letter in the author's possession, Don Sinclair states that he flew K-9O piloted by Doug Zimmerman. However, as the reader will observe from the photograph on page 134, the aircraft shown as K-9O is coded numbered "351". According to the 494th loading list, this is De Courcy's machine's number, ie K-9L! One explanation is that in the photograph, what appears to be a "O" maybe a "D", ie K-9D could have been Zimmerman's/Sinclair's aircraft on that mission - inferring that they flew *Willie The Wolf*. If any reader can unravel this, the author would be interested to hear.

Left: Hptm. Walter Krupinski was one of the last German pilots to see Lützow after the encounter with the Marauders and their Thunderbolt escort. He could not understand his fellow pilot's course of action, nor was he able to make radio contact. Abovet: Jet Killer: Cowan had already shot down an Me 262 in February 1945. Here he poses for the news camera in the cockpit of his P-47 while the squadron artist applies his skill to the fighter's fuselage.

FIFTEEN

FLYING TELEPHONE POLES?

The 323rd and 344th pay their compliments

Whilst Galland and his pilots recovered from the loss of one of the *Jagdwaffe's* most popular and accomplished officers, operating conditions at München-Riem were becoming more and more difficult with the airfield now crowded with the additional Me 262s "donated" from I./KG 51 and III./EJG 2. Yet of the 41 jet fighters registered as being on JV 44's strength on 24 April 1945, only 18 were serviceable and of the 92 fighter pilots available to Galland, 53 were trainees. In fact, such was the problem at München-Riem that OKL ordered that evening that no more aircraft were to be sent there and so as to ease the situation and to re-inforce Peltz's IX. *(J) Fliegerkorps*, 23 Me 262s were to be transferred to Prague, a clearly impossible order given the serviceability figures at Riem! Overcrowding meant a shortage of parts and maintenance of JV 44's jets frequently presented operational difficulties.

By 25 April, the Red Army had completed its encirclement of Berlin and even more symbolically, 100 kilometres (62 miles) south west of the capital, elements of General Hodges' US First Army linked up with those of the Soviet Fifth Guards Tank Army at Torgau on the Elbe. Germany was now cut into two. The northern flank of the Ninth Army had collapsed and Zhukov's tanks were driving relentlessly west towards Manteuffel's Third Panzer Army - virtually all that was left of Army Group Vistula. Hitler was now relying solely on a timely intervention by SS

Obergruppenführer Felix Steiner's ragged and depleted Eleventh Panzer Army to check the Russian advance. To the south, Göring was trapped in the labyrinthine tunnels that had been drilled into the limestone beneath in his villa-prison, as more than 350 Lancasters from RAF Bomber Command pounded Berchtesgaden into rubble.

A major reorganisation of the jet units had begun, with *Luftflottenkommando* 6 ordering the immediate disbandment of *Stab.* and III./KG(J) 54 and III./KG(J) 6 with their remaining available aircraft being placed at the disposal of the *Luftflotte*. Many of the personnel of these units were hastily "converted" into infantry.

JV 44 was active again on the afternoon of the 25th, though this time, its operations almost resulted in a fiasco when a formation of 13 jets including the volatile Me 262 A-1a/U4 experimental variant fitted with a nose-mounted MK 214 Mauser cannon and probably flown by *Major* Willi Herget, were readied to take off, the intention being to split the force into two elements; one to carry out "freelance patrols" against some of the hundreds of American fighters roaming over southern Germany that day, the other vectored to tackle more B-26s moving in to bomb the airfield at Erding and a nearby ordnance depot. However, of the Me 262s that took off to meet the bombers, five were forced to return to Riem shortly afterwards due to technical problems and two were recalled for unknown reasons. One of the aircraft probably recalled was Me 262 "White 11" flown by *Uffz.* "Jonny" Müller who took off at 17:11 returning sixteen minutes later.

Of the six machines that continued, three became engaged in combat with P-47 Thunderbolts in the Augsburg area without loss to either side and the remaining three including the Me 262 A-1a/U4 intercepted the B-26s of the 344th and 323rd BGs - the latter flying on what would be its last mission of the war - and A-26s of the 410th BG between Landshut and Erding.

The Me 262 A-1a/U4 was a standard aircraft but fitted with a colossal long range Mauser 50mm MK 214 cannon in the nose space normally reserved for the four smaller MK 108s. The development initiative for this highly dubious configuration can be said to rest with Hitler, who had lent his support for the idea in January 1945 after envisaging a weapon able to bring down bombers from outside their defensive fire-cone. Projecting some two metres (6.5 ft) from the nose, the MK 214 possessed a muzzle velocity of 920 metres (3,018 ft) per second. Herget took over tests in the prototype aircraft (W.Nr. 111899) from the Messerschmitt test pilot, Karl Bauer who had, by 26 March 1945, fired the weapon 128 times in a series of static and airborne test shots before all trials stopped as a result of malfunction and breakage. Once repaired, Herget was able to fire another six shots with the MK 214 against ground targets. Two further

flights were made on 16 April against American bomber formations, but on both occasions, the gun jammed yet again. Despite this, a second machine was equipped with the MK 214, but it is unlikely that it ever saw operational use. It is likely Herget then flew the first machine to München-Riem, since documentary, eye-witness and photographic evidence indicates its presence there later in the month.

In the early hours of the morning of 25th April, the teleprinter at the 344th BG's base at Florennes/Juzaine in Belgium chattered out the details of the day's forthcoming target as well as a short and worrying warning:

> *Target is portion of aerodrome at Erding. Recce a week ago showed 4 Me 262s and 20 other aircraft on the field; the next day there were 42 single-engine fighters. The aerodrome is serviceable and active. Your job is to post hole the area. One Group from each of the other wings will be hitting this aerodrome also.*
>
> *This is a deep penetration into the Redoubt area. Be alert at all times for fighter interception. Two groups in this wing had brushes with Me 262s yesterday.*

That day, Captain John O. Moench was flying in the group lead aircraft of a formation of 48 Marauders of the 323rd BG flying out of their base at Denain-Prouvy in France. Moench recalled in his own account of the mission: "As we briefed and loaded up for the mission to bomb Erding Airdrome, I am sure that no one

Below: Me 262A-1a/U-4 W.Nr. 111899 was deployed by JV 44 against B-26 Marauders of the 323rd BG on 25 April 1945 resulting in its 50 mm Mauser MK 214 cannon being described as resembling "...a giant telephone pole."

Inset: Lechfeld, March 1945: Karl Baur, the Messerschmitt test pilot, supervises the loading of the Mauser MK 214 cannon's vast 50mm shells as fitted to Me 262 A-1a W.Nr. 111899, the machine that Willi Herget would eventually take to JV 44.

thought that this would be the last mission of the 323rd BG. I was flying the command slot with Capt. E.C. Trostle in 131J - the Group lead aircraft. This was a combat check ride for Capt. Trostle... On schedule and with no fanfare, the two boxes of 24 Marauders each, formed into diamonds of four flights of six, passed over the airfield and headed out to target... The flight to the target was, if anything, akin to ATC boredom."

"We had been briefed that there were jets at the Erding Airdrome - whether they would attack was only a guess. Still, the aircrews had been hit by jets before and Marauder men had been lost. This was more than enough incentive to tighten up as we neared the bomb line. Visibility on this day of what would be the 323rd Group's last mission was very good and the air was smooth. Soon, the picturesque, snow-covered Alps mountains could be seen ahead and south of the flight path. Now tucked in close, speed was added as the target came into view. Then the bomb bay doors were opened."

According to the 9th Bombardment Division narrative covering the mission, a single Me 262 was sighted paralleling the height and heading of the Marauder formation away to the right and out of range shortly after the turn-off from the target. At 17.48, the jet circled around behind the third box of bombers and made one pass, approaching low at 6 o'clock, closing to within 400-500 yards and breaking away in a dive without opening fire at 9 o'clock

Moench: "Suddenly the intercom came to life with the call out of fighters taking off from the Erding Airdrome below. Almost instantly someone called out a fighter at one o'clock! I looked up and well out in front of us, swinging around for what looked like a frontal attack, was one of the *Luftwaffe's* Me 262s.

"Your job is to post hole the area... Be alert at all times for fighter interception." was how the 344th BG was briefed and warned for the mission on 25 April. In a classic photograph, Marauders of the 496th Squadron show here both the elegance and pugnaciousness of their design. Even German jet pilots had to take their chances and excercise considerable tenacity in dealing with Martin's creation at close quarters.

As the enemy pilot turned, the 50 mm cannon sticking out of the nose of the Me 262 had the appearance of a giant telephone pole. Seconds later, the Me 262 had passed well over the formation without firing a shot and well out of range of our .50's. Then we spotted him swinging around in a wide circle seemingly to get into position to make another frontal pass. Again, he remained out of firing range and disappeared."

"Almost instantly, there was a call from the tail gunner that an Me 262 was off the rear. Crossing from the right, the jet swung around and came back from the left. Nineteen of the gunners opened up on the Me 262 at maximum range and, apparently discouraged by the barrage of fire from the Marauders, the pilot broke off."

"The promptness with which the formation closed-up, presenting its massed fire-power," the Divisional narrative concludes, *"may have been an influencing factor in the decision of the hostile pilot to break off his attack without pressing home."*

It is likely that Herget was suffering from jamming problems with the Mauser cannon similar to those that he had experienced against American bombers in early April. Despite trying to use the gun operationally and performing test flights in the Me 262 A-1a/U4 at Lechfeld, Herget found his few attempts at combat flying

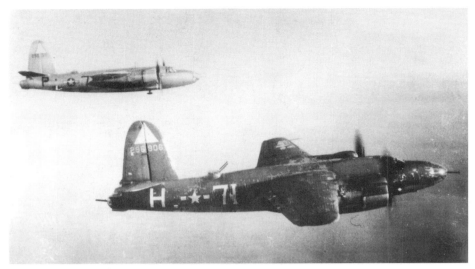

A pair of B-26s of the 497th Squadron, 344th BG photographed in formation over southern Germany in April 1945. The aircraft nearest the camera is S/N 42-95906 coded 7I-H. Behind is S/N 42-96311 coded 7I-P. This latter aircraft took part in both the 24 April mission to Schrobenhausen, piloted by Lt. J.N.Hellen, as well as the 25 April mission to Erding when it was flown by Lt. P .D. Gray's crew. Both missions were subjected to jet attacks.

claimed to have destroyed one) and one crashed due to engine flame out. No bombers were destroyed.

However, in a different encounter, two American aircraft did fall to the guns of *Uffz.* Franz Köster that day. Köster, who had very recently been transferred to JV 44 from JG 7, is credited with the destruction of one Mustang and one Lightning on 25 April.

Elsewhere, the 17th BG made a return visit to

the Me 262 unforgettable. He had been "amazed" at the speed of the jet fighter, but found that it was neccesary to raise the nose to slow the aircraft down because of vibration and the effect of manoeuvre. Furthermore, he found his reaction time had been affected due to the much shorter period he had to sight and fire.

One jet was damaged in the action over Erding (possibly by P-51s of the escorting 370th Fighter Group who erroneously

Schwabmünchen, where, escorted by 32 fighters, 14 of the group's B-26s dropped bombs on the ammunition dump.

Bombs explode and a pall of smoke drifts across Erding Airfield during the Ninth AF strike on 25 April 1945. This dramatic aerial photograph was taken from a B-26 Marauder at 8000 ft. The white circles, drawn by intelligence personnel, indicate the positions of German aircraft.

Mission #262 Erding Airfield April 25,1945 at 8,000Ft. 44,Aircraft. Circled German Aircraft

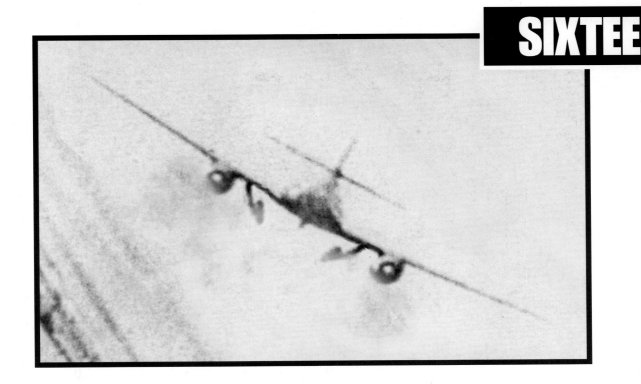

SIXTEEN

'DAMAGED AND PROBABLE' GALLAND DOWN

"Max Out - Trash and Burn..."

By late April 1945, the largest single piece of territory still controlled by the Third Reich stretched from the western half of Czechoslovakia, encompassed virtually all of Austria west of Vienna, most of northern Italy and Jugoslavia and extreme south-eastern Germany. Within this territory were to be found the most mountainous regions of central Europe. Throughout the second half of the month, SHAEF began to receive "substantiated" intelligence to the effect that thousands of German troops from the eastern Austrian front, from southern Germany and from Italy had regrouped within a tract of mountainous area spanning from Salzburg in the north and Klagenfurt in the south, west to Bolzano, Landeck and Bregenz. At the heart of this mountain fortress lay Innsbruck. This was the so-called "Alpine Redoubt", the anticipated citadel from where the Nazis would wage a last-ditch bitter guerrilla battle to the death. In the Allied camp, speculation was fuelled still further by a completely inaccurate report which stated that Himmler was now in München assigned to prepare the mountains for this dramatic last stand.

The reality, at least in military terms, was very different. *General Ritter* von Hengl was the man ordered to command the "redoubt garrison" but in a damning report to his superiors at OKW soon after his appointment, he voiced fears that the forces allocated to him were totally inadequate, for although a flood of ministry officials and civilian administrative agencies had already entered the area, not a single *Wehrmacht* division had been transferred. Ninety per cent of the 38,000 personnel in his billeting area were non-combatants and what army units that there were reaching the Alps, were doing so in fragmented groups. Von Hengl stressed that it was impossible to build adequate fortifications in the winter, transport would be difficult, thus making the establishment of industrial productivity impractical. There were few roads and railways in the mountains and thus the importation of food, machinery, clothing, bomb shelters, weapons and ammunition would also be impossible.

Nevertheless, the Allied belief in this "Alpine Redoubt" served to intensify American medium bomber activities against tactical targets in this area. The 26th April dawned with a mixed weather forecast for southern Germany; varying cloud at different altitudes with gaps, the ground only visible in about three tenths of the American tactical air forces' operational area. Notwithstanding the weather, a combined force of 1st TAF (Provisional) B-26s from the American 42nd Bomb Wing and the French *11e Brigade de Bombardement*, was assigned to bomb III./EJG 2's recently evacuated base at Lechfeld and ordnance targets in the Schrobenhausen area respectively.

The B-26-equipped French *11e Brigade de Bombardement*

Immaculate French B-26s of one of six Groupes de Bombardement operating Marauders fly through cloud and over mountainous scenery, the sun dazzling on their pristine bare metal finishes.

consisted of the *31e Escadre* (=group) - in turn comprising the *Gascogne 1/19, Maroc 1/22* and *Bretagne 2/20 Groupe* (=squadrons) and the *34e Escadre* comprised of the *Bourgogne 1/32, Franche-Comté 2/52* and *Sénégal 2/63 Groupe.*

Lechfeld had been selected as a target for the 42nd Bomb Wing because of what crews of the 17th BG had seen there during their return from the previous day's mission to the Schwabmünchen ammunition storage facility. Don Wilson was a twenty-two year old "throttle jockey" with the 95th Squadron, 17th BG. He recalls: "On April 25, the Group had flown a CAVU milkrun to the ammunition dump at Schwabmünchen some miles southeast of Lechfeld. After bombs away and Dijon bound, the K-12 cameras were busy at the waist gunner positions capturing images of anything in sight. Film processing that night revealed to photo-interpreters several Me 262s on the Lechfeld ramp that Group Operations considered to be sitting ducks for a mass attack next day. All squadrons were to max out with the first half of sixty-four B-26s loaded with fragmentation bombs and the second half with incendiaries. You know the drill: trash and burn."

For the Marauder crews, this mission was to be another important "maximum effort" raid. 2nd Lt. William W. Snead was a pilot with the 37th Squadron, 17th BG; he remembers: "Early on the morning of 26 April 1945, my crew boarded the truck for the drive from our tent area at the Chateau of the Count Desalverte to the airfield at Longvic near Dijon. We were given the standard briefing, weather en-route and possible expectation at the target. The bomb-load would be 15-250 lb. clusters of small fragmentation bombs. This was my only experience with this

type of bomb. It wasn't long however, before I was fully informed of these hazardous things. Due to their peculiarities, we would use a spread formation over the target to minimize the hazard to trailing aircraft. The normal vibration of the aircraft could cause the individual frag-bombs to fall from the clusters and they would become armed. There were recorded incidents when due to rough air or sudden movements of the aircraft they would explode on striking a bulkhead. Needless to say we sweated. However, in training, we had a crew who always bore the brunt of mishaps in our squadron. They crashlanded on two occasions without serious injury to any of the crew. For our part, we developed an attitude of invincibility - like if it happens, it will happen to "Langhoff" . We apparently carried this into our combat philosophy - *"it's going to happen to someone else.""*

"At the briefing, the intelligence officer advised us of the seriousness of this mission. The Germans had evacuated materials and supplies into this "Redoubt" area. Armament was apparently concentrated in and around Munich. We were told that aircraft were dispersed in every conceivable location. It was the belief at that time that the strength of this "Redoubt" situation must be destroyed before any reasonable settlement of the conflict could be effective."

German records state that *Jagdverband* 44 was reporting a total of 43 Me 262s on strength at sunrise on 26th. As the morning

2nd Lt William W. Snead of the 37th Squadron, 17th BG remembered seeing JV 44's Me 262s on 26 April 1945. At one point, they were so close to his aircraft he "... could have spit on them." Here the Snead crew line up for the camera in front of their B-26: 2nd Lt William W. Snead (pilot), 2nd Lt. Tom Owsley (co-pilot), F/O Sam Ciacio (bombardier), Sgt. Dean Friedendahl (turret gunner), Sgt. Bob Elmore (waist gunner), Sgt. Ed Donnellon (tail gunner).

progressed, warning of another incursion by enemy medium bombers into Bavaria reached the control room at Feldkirchen and JV 44 scrambled a force of 12 rocket-equipped Me 262s between 11:20-11:30 led by *Generalleutnant* Galland to intercept. One Me 262 was forced to turn back with engine problems.

The Marauders pushed on. William W. Snead remembers: "Our routine flight path was to climb out from Dijon, circle to join

Engines and tail ablaze, a B-26 purportedly of the 455th Squadron, 323rd BG, drops out of formation following a direct hit from Flak whilst on a mission to a Noball site at Dannes in France, 5 February 1944. Though this particular photo shows the results of Flak, similar results would have been caused by German fighters attacking from the rear of a Marauder formation.

up and climb on course just to the west of Colmar. Turning east to pass north of Selestat, we continued just to the south of Haslach. Since we were going east, we headed somewhat north and east, maybe towards Bobingen. Later, we turned south toward Munich. I recall at this time we could see our fighters attacking German aircraft even before they were airborne. I had never witnessed so much activity by our escort. On other occasions, I had heard their radio conversation and knew they were near and active, but we seldom saw them."

Thirty minutes after JV 44's jets had taken off from Riem, whilst over Neuburg an der Donau, they sighted the 60 bombers of the 42nd Bomb Wing flying in two tight box formations, the first of 36 aircraft and the second, flying slightly high and behind to the right, of 24 aircraft. Each box was further broken down into standard six aircraft flights. The B-26s, escorted by 63 P-47s drawn from four of the five fighter groups of the 64th Fighter Wing, had just aborted their bomb run some ten minutes before the target since increasingly adverse weather conditions (9/10ths cloud over the target) had forced them to turn back over Pappenheim.

Making their approach at 3,350 metres (11,000 ft) from 12 o'clock, the Me 262s passed over the bombers and then wheeled around in a dive for an attack from about 8 o'clock and below.

One day after his release from Unterföhring hospital and with his knee still weak from the injury received when baling out of his aircraft six days before over Kempten, *Uffz.* Eduard Schallmoser flying Me 262 "White 14" as Galland's wingman, fired his rockets into the enemy formation. As he swept up through the bomber *Pulk*, Schallmoser watched transfixed as a Marauder "...blew apart in the air."

In Me 262 "White 10", the former Siebel instructor, *Fw.* Otto Kammerdiener, selected a target and also fired his weapons.

Conversely, *Fhj.Ofw.* Leo Schuhmacher, formerly Heinz Bär's wingman recently arrived from III./EJG 2 and flying on what would be his only sortie with JV 44 against Marauders, lined one of the bombers up in his sights but found that his guns jammed. He was forced to fly through the formation without firing a shot.

Flying a little above Schallmoser, Adolf Galland armed his Me 262's four MK 108s and flicked off the safety to the R4Ms. Already, the Marauder tail gunners had opened fire at the approaching jets and as he closed in, Galland quickly selected as his target the outermost and rearmost B-26 of the first box. He depressed the rocket firing switch. To his astonishment, nothing happened – no rockets streaked ahead of him – and he realised that in the speed of the approach – a matter of seconds – he had forgotten to flick off the *second* rocket safety switch, probably as a result of the distraction of the return fire.

S./Sgt. Albert Linz was an Armourer Gunner with the 37th Squadron, 17th BG on board 1st Lt. Carl Johanson's B-26B (41-95771) *My Gal Sal* flying No. 6 position in its flight; he remembers: "As a crew, we joined the 17th BG late in the war. We flew our first mission during the winter of 1944-45 and the aborted mission of April 26th was, by far, the most memorable for us, despite the fact that no bombs were dropped on the target."

"Assuming that *Generalleutnant* Galland was leading the three jets which came in on us, the wing-man on his left selected us for a target and hit our left engine... Galland and his two buddies passed directly beneath us about three or four hundred feet, heading to the rear of our formation. This was my first sight of a jet plane and they sure looked strange with no propellers. As they continued to our rear, I kept reading their position to the rest of the crew, all the time hoping they had something important to do back that-a-way. About half a mile away, they started to make their turn and it became obvious that they were going to start their run."

"Since the Browning .50 calibre had its best pattern at about 250 yards, I was well aware that they were at a much greater distance. Despite the fact that this was our 29th mission, this was the first time any *Luftwaffe* fighters actually attacked us, so I had absolutely no experience at firing at a

Ofw. Leo Schuhmacher flew with JV 44 on the 26 April attack on the 17th BG. However, his guns jammed at the crucial moment and he was forced to fly through the bomber formation without firing a single round.

The crew of B-26B (41-95771) MY GAL SAL of the 37th Squadron, 17th BG pose by their ship, early 1945. Pilot Lt. Carl Johanson is to the far left and tail gunner S/Sgt. Albert Linz is to the far right.

moving plane, not even in gunnery school. But, having hunted lots of ducks back in Pennsylvania, I realised that a long lead was necessary. So, even at that distance, I commenced firing, assuming that eventually they'd have to run into those tracers... Galland was probably wondering what kind of jerk would be shooting a half-mile away. The more experienced gunners probably waited until they closed the gap. This was probably poor strategy on my part but it may have taken his mind off his work long enough to forget to release the safety switch on his rockets."

Though it was too late for the R4Ms, Galland still had his cannon. Racing through the bombers' defensive fire, Galland fired a burst of 30mm tracer at another Marauder which immediately exploded.

Lt Randle J. Dedeaux was aboard the lead ship of the 432nd Squadron, 17th BG: "I was flying co-pilot and we were all feeling relaxed, our parachutes were unbuckled and we were very comfortable. My thoughts: *Another milk run, the war will be over any day now.* Then I looked out the window off to my right and saw an Me 262 going up through our formation at a 45 degree

Taken during Combat Crew Training at Barksdale AFB, Shreveport, Louisiana in August 1944, this photo shows Lt John Sorrelle of the 432nd Squadron with the crew that would later accompany him to Europe. From left to right: Lt John Sorrelle (pilot), Lt Tyre (co-pilot), Lt Rodgers (bombardier-navigator), T./Sgt Cleo Wills (engineer-gunner), Cpl. Anderson (radio-gunner), Cpl. Walls (armourer-gunner). Cleo Wills was one of the 17th BG gunners accredited with damaging Adolf Galland's Me 262 on 26 April 1945.

angle. I was quite surprised and did not immediately identify it as a 262. This was the first one I had ever seen. My pilot decided I could fly the plane while he buckled his parachute on. I had my hands full for a minute or two as the formation made a left turn and I was trying to hold the squadron in position..."

Lt. Ed Brandt was the navigator-bombardier in the lead ship of the 432nd Squadron's low box. He remembers: "When still about 5-10 minutes from the target, we became aware of the jets' presence as our P-47 escorts dropped their gas tanks which then fell though the formation. Almost simultaneously with the falling tanks, I saw the box immediately in front of me erupt in disarray. It appeared that the No. 4 ship had been hit and, as it exploded, it veered right into the No. 2 and No. 5 ships. Shortly after this it became apparent that our box was also under attack. The intercom was alive with gunners reporting enemy fighters. The .50 Calibre machine gun available to me in the nose was of no use as it only fired directly forward. I then observed what looked like a yellow-nosed jet dive directly at us and pass in front of the formation."

"I was a 20 year-old flight leader flying in the No. 4 slot as deputy lead," recalls 1st Lt. John W. Sorrelle, a pilot with the 432nd Squadron, whose tail gunner was one those who registered strikes on Galland's aircraft. "Carrying a bombardier and a bomb sight, I was positioned to take over the flight should the regular leader be shot down. I recall being especially aware at the briefing that in the "Tail End Charlie" flight of the group formation, we would be extremely vulnerable to fighter attacks from the low rear, avoiding our top turret and waist fire."

"Flying at 12,000 feet (3,658 metres), tucked in tightly under the tail turret of the flight lead, we were weaving back and forth through broken cumulus clouds, some of which towered above us. Stratocu below covered most of the ground. I can remember thinking what a great day it was for enemy fighters lurking out of sight. My tail gunner, T./Sgt Cleo E. Wills, broke radio silence on the interphone: *"Bandits coming out of the clouds at 6 o'clock low,*

Right: Galland's nemesis - T./Sgt Henry Dietz of 34th Squadron, 17th BG at the waist gun position in a B-26 Marauder: "He was flying low, right into the sights of my machine gun. I shot a burst. Nothing happened. A little higher, a little lower, I just kept shooting."

Below: The crew of Major Luther Gurkin's Marauder (34th Squadron, 17th BG) - from left to right: S./Sgt Fred H. Loring, S./Sgt Earl L. Keith, S./Sgt Donald P. Edelen, T./Sgt Henry Dietz, 1st Lt Joseph S. Dziewicz and Capt. Luther W. Gurkin Jr. Edelen found himself momentarily looking at the pilot of an attacking Me 262.

climbing and closing fast. They look like 262s." I could feel my control column shuddering slightly as he began firing his twin .50-cal machine guns. The next events occurred in such rapid succession that I have no idea of the exact time sequence. *"I got him! I got him!"* Wills shouted over the intercom. Then the left wingman at my 10 o'clock position exploded and was gone."

A second or so later as Galland flew into the heart of the American formation, he fired at another bomber in the lead box, taking hits himself from the dense fire of the Marauder gunners among whom was T./Sgt. Henry Dietz, a waist gunner on board the 34th Squadron's lead ship piloted by Captain Luther Gurkin. Gurkin's Engineer-Gunner was S./Sgt. Donald P. Edelen. "As I recall, we had just arrived at the demarcation line and I was in the turret when something – a flash – caught my eye and I called Sgt Dietz on the intercom to look out at 9 o'clock level to see if he had seen anything out that way. He replied *"No."* Then, all at once, I looked out and saw an Me 262 taking a pass by us at 9 o'clock. The jet seemed almost to slow down momentarily and I found myself looking directly at the pilot who then pulled his plane up and turned back. As I was in the upper turret, I could not see what happened next, but I knew Sgt. Dietz was firing from his waist position and I heard him shout *"I got one!"* There were three Me 262s in their flight and they all attacked from the rear of our formation."

Nicknamed "Hermann the German" by members of his crew as a result of his last name, T./Sgt Henry Dietz had joined the Army Air Force in early 1944 having spent the previous two and a half years in the US Cavalry and the 10th Armored Division as a weapons instructor. Transferring to the 17th BG, he had flown more than fifty tactical missions over France, Italy and Germany since August. As he recalls: "Having been a weapons instructor in all of these branches, I naturally had a little experience with a .50 calibre machine gun prior to "meeting" *Generalleutnant* Galland. Probably the most important thing I remembered from gunnery school was to fire short bursts and forget about the tracer bullets – just use your sights."

"Our experience with the tail guns was that they repeatedly malfunctioned due to the under-powered motor feeding the ammunition belt. The waist guns were gravity fed and therefore you would empty a belt of ammunition without a problem."

"That day, we were flying as flight leader and we were about ten minutes from the target. I flew in the waist position from where I could see all mechanical parts of the aircraft. I had never seen a jet before. Galland slowed down to the speed of the B-26 to count the take... came back to observe and take score. I thought... *Dummy*. He was flying low, right into the sights of my machine gun. I shot a burst. Nothing happened. A little higher, a little lower, I just kept shooting."

His machine now damaged by the return fire and trailing smoke, Galland passed closely over his second victim and banked steeply to port to observe the results of his attack. "...I wanted to know definitely what was happening to the second bomber I had hit." Galland wrote in his memoirs, "I was not quite clear if it had crashed. So far I had not noticed any fighter escort."

JV 44's attacks against the Marauders of the Twelfth and Ninth Air Forces were usually made from below and behind the bomber formation.

It is still unclear which bomber was Galland's second victim, but one of JV 44's pilots had severely damaged *My Gal Sal* and smoke was pouring from her port-side engine. "As we fell out of formation," Albert Linz recalled, "the last thing I saw was our No. 5 plane completely enveloped in flames. However, I didn't see it explode."

For John Sorrelle and his crew, the speed of Galland's pass and the effect of his attack on the neighbouring plane meant trouble.

"My plane did a violent wingover to the left and dove straight for the ground," Sorrelle remembers, "Thinking I'd lost No. 1 engine, I idled both throttles to regain control. The aircraft was still rolling to the left. I advanced the throttles. Both engines were good. I started cranking in right rudder trim. It ordinarily takes 1 to 2 degrees to counter take-off torque and no more than 5 or 6 when losing an engine. I needed 11.5 degrees to straighten the plane out. The limit is 15. Airspeed redline for the B-26 is 353mph (568 kph). We were nearly past it. The ground was coming up fast. Fearing wing failure, I began gingerly using elevator trim tab. The airspeed bled off as the nose crept up. We were just above the treetops. The jets were gone and our squadron mates were barely visible in the distance. We used emergency power to rejoin the formation."

The crew of another Marauder of the 432nd Squadron – B-26G (44-68076) *Big Red* piloted by 1st Lt. Alf P. Shatto, fared less well than Sorrelle's aircraft. *Big Red* had just endured a screen of *Flak* around Neuburg before being attacked by Me 262s firing rockets. Fuel began to pour out of a damaged wing before the bomber "...nosed down and passed out of vision". The situation aboard *Big Red* as the jets swept over and above it was critical: "Approximately five minutes before reaching the target, our formation was attacked by German jet-propelled fighter planes," wrote 1st Lt. Charles E. Bryner, co-pilot. "All crew members were at their respective

stations including S./Sgt Robert J. Griffith who was in the rear bomb bays performing his duty as photographer gunner. When our plane was disabled by said German fighters to the extent that we did not have any control of the plane and were spinning out of control, the order was given to bail out. Evidently the rear section of the plane was shot up very badly."

Bryner's assessment was correct and is verified by the pilot of *Big Red*: "The damage to our ship occurred between the waist guns and the rear bomb bays," wrote Shatto, "Sergeant Griffith's position was in the rear bomb bays. It is my belief that Sergeant Griffith was killed when the shell exploded; however, I was unable to reach the rear of the ship and this evidence, as given, was related to me by my tail gunner, Staff Sergeant Louis N. Smith who baled out through the hole that was caused by the shell's explosion. Two other crew members were lost in this action, Sergeant Wilhelms (Radio-Gunner) and Sergeant Frank (Armourer-Gunner)."

"When the shell exploded, it disabled all the controls of our ship. I immediately ordered the crew to bale out as the ship was nosing upward very rapidly. I opened our bomb bays and released our bomb load with the salvo switch. The bombardier, co-pilot and I were thrown out of the ship at approximately five hundred feet (152 metres) above the ground. The ship at this time was in a severe spin. Before our aircraft started downward in this spin, we were pinned down, unable to move, due to the centrifugal force, caused by the ship falling over on its back and going into a dive toward the ground."

Smith's official account of the dying moments of *Big Red* was terse: "We were about four to six miles (6.5/10 kilometres) south-west of Ulm. Controls were knocked out by first hit. Radio gunner was killed. Turret gunner was seen to come out of the turret, but never baled out. Sergeant Griffith was never seen... Ship was

The carnage that the 30 mm MK 108 could cause: this is a B-26 of the 494th Sqdn, 323rd BG taken in late April 1945 following a cannon attack by a Me 262, probably from JV 44.

The crew of the 17th BG's B-26F-1 (42-96328) MARAUDER · 2nd Lt. Kenneth L. Bedor (pilot - standing far left) 2nd Lt Charles J. Howard (co-pilot), 2nd Lt Leranos F. Krasowetz (bombardier), S./Sgt Paul D. Geitgey (engineer-gunner), Sgt. Alfred E. Belt Jr (radio-gunner), Sgt. John J, Milkovich Jr. (armourer-gunner) - suffered at the hands of JV 44, when their bomb bay received direct hits. The "37th" sticker attached to the original photo indicates that the aircraft was assigned to the 37th Squadron.

"The aircraft I was to lead on began a slow descent. I followed him down possibly 500 – 1,000 feet. I knew we were to bomb at 10,000 feet and he had descended below that level. I was debating whether to break radio silence for verification of our action when suddenly he exploded. Almost immediately, my gunners informed me that the formation had turned to the left. Realising that I was in a very vulnerable position, I made a very steep quick turn to the left with all my engine controls to the firewall. As I looked back, there sat several Me 262s at our level, pointing right directly at us and oh, so close. I think I could have spit on them. I recall looking over those jets. I thought – *What are they waiting for?* I did not panic, but I saw no way of escape. Everything was in their favour. We were the proverbial sitting duck."

"I could not yet see the formation, so I continued my turning until I saw the squadron quite a distance away. I righted the aircraft to straight and level flight and headed for the squadron. I was now overtaking it at a very rapid pace. We had reached a speed of 225-240 mph. The formation was travelling at approximately 180 mph. All this time I expected to be intercepted by those German fighters, but none fired on us and none followed us. As time progressed, I realised I had beat them because the firepower of the formation was coming into play. We were back safe."

But fire from one Me 262 hit a B-26B-1 (No.42-43311) of 34th Squadron, *Spot Cash!* flown by 2nd Lt. Earle E. Reeves. A waist gunner in the last plane of the flight directly ahead of *Spot Cash!* saw a German jet make its first firing pass and then watched as the targeted bomber "...nosed upward then fell off to the left under partial control. I last saw it at 8,000 feet (2,438 metres) with smoke coming from both engines. No physical damage was observed. No 'chutes were observed."

reported by Germans to have blown up when it hit the ground."

Elsewhere, the JV 44 attack on the 17th BG had wreaked havoc amongst the American formation, particularly those aircraft of the 37th Squadron. Corporal Frank V. Towle witnessed the end of 2nd Lt. Kenneth L. Bedor's B-26F-1 (42-96328) *Marauder* which had been with the squadron since September 1944: "Ship No. 25 was flying No.5 in 5th flight. It was attacked by an Me 262 from 6 o'clock level. The tail gunner on No. 25 opened fire as soon as the jet began firing. Puffs of smoke from the cannon seemed to run between our wings and No. 25 must have received a direct cannon hit in the bomb bay or fuel tank as she made a loud puff and flames enveloped the ship from cockpit to rear bomb bay. Ship No.25 seemed to roll on one wing and nosed downward. One bomb bay door must have been blown off as I could still see bombs hanging in the bomb bay. I watched until they passed under our formation going downward to the 3 o'clock side."

Another pilot flying with the 37th Squadron that day, Lt William W. Snead, experienced a more fortunate but equally frightening encounter: "As we approached the IP, the clouds began to show. As I recall, this was not expected. There was a lower level of clouds partially obscuring the ground and a high cloud ceiling several thousand feet above us. No signal was given, so at the IP we picked up our target heading and began forming our target formation. I noticed some peculiar explosions which I thought were flak. The explosions were small and I could see red centres. I was soon informed that what I was seeing were 30 mm explosions from enemy fighters near us. I had not this point, observed any enemy aircraft since everything was immediately behind me."

Right: The crew of 34th Squadron, 17th BG's B-26B-1 (s/n 42-43311) SPOT CASH! taken earlier in the war. From left to right: Sgt. Richard K. Smith (armourer-gunner), S./Sgt. Francis Y. Siddoway (engineer-gunner), F/O Virgil B. Lightner (co-pilot), F/O Albert J. Collotta (bombardier, but replaced by Stockdale on 26 April mission), S./Sgt Andrew T. Poplos (radio-gunner) and 2nd Lt. Earl E. Reeves Jr. (pilot). Left: S./Sgt Allen H. Stockdale (bombardier, second from left).

The 34th Squadron, 17th BG's B-26B Spot Cash! *fell to the guns of JV 44's Me 262s on 26 April. The B-26 was hit in both engines and its tail was blown off. These photos illustrate the crude quality of the aircraft's nose art, which in the lower picture seems to have been recently enhanced.*

Crippled by the jet's attack, *Spot Cash!* went into a bad spin. At his waist gun position, engineer-gunner S./Sgt. Francis Y. Siddoway from Salt Lake City did not answer the co-pilot's enquiry of the crew's situation since his interphone had failed. Siddoway went to assist S./Sgt. Andrew T. Poplos, the radio gunner, who was wounded, just before the tail broke away. Siddoway struggled in vain to free the waist gun mount so that he could exit the aircraft through the waist hatch. In the end however, he was forced to push his feet through the window and he slid out over the top of the gun.

The bombardier on board *Spot Cash!* was S./Sgt Allan H. Stockdale from Seattle. He is remembered by former T./Sgt William D.Baird, a gunner from the 34th Squadron: "The enlisted bombardier that went down on that plane was my room mate and good friend, Al Stockdale. Al was a quiet guy, very self-contained. He went on combat to make money so his little sister could go to nursing school. His father was deceased.

"He and I had two rooms in a little house in Rouvres en Plaine. He slept in the back room while the rest of us played poker and drank cheap wine in the front room. He never complained about the noise. If they gave him a Purple Heart for that mission, it was his third.

"Al was Catholic. He grew up going to a parochial school; said he had to fight his way to school every day because the neighbourhood ruffians made fun of him for going to "church school". He probably would have made a priest had he lived. They lost a good one when they lost Al."

Flying as a flight leader with the neighbouring 432nd Squadron was the aircraft of Captain David Brackett. Brackett's armourer gunner was S./Sgt. Bernard J. Byrnes, who, on 26 April, was flying his 41st mission. He saw a 34th ship go down, probably *Spot Cash!*; as he recalls: "Our tail gunner, T./Sgt. Jack Hogan saw them first. They came up from below us and he fired the first shots that were fired by our flight. He held them off of our own tail until they came up to the level of my gun turret and then I turned and started firing at a jet at about 7 o'clock coming in high. All of a sudden, I saw a big flash and I turned the turret back to about 3 o'clock and I realised the other B-26 at the right side of us had gone. The Me 262 had blown it right out of the sky. He was still flying at our 3 o'clock position and he was going after another B-26 in front of the one he had shot down. In this way, he made a perfect set-up for me. I was able to fire a long burst into him. His canopy was badly damaged and as he flipped over and away, I thought I saw his canopy fly off, but I couldn't be sure. I know his aircraft was badly damaged. I don't know if he went down or not as I was too busy to watch as there were still fighters to watch out for and it kept me pretty busy turning one way or the other. In my notes that I wrote, Jack Hogan said he saw the one I shot up go down with smoke pouring out of his engines. The ship that I saw go down was from the 34th Squadron."

Lt Wayne J. Hutchinson, who had won the Distinguished Flying Cross in December 1944 for "extraordinary achievement" after holding a *Flak*-riddled Marauder steady over its bomb run and allowing his entire crew to exit the stricken aircraft safely, was piloting another 34th Squadron B-26 on 26 April 1945. Hutchinson was leading the third flight of six aircraft, maintaining a position to the left, below and behind the Group leader's flight and most likely also witnessed the destruction of *Spot Cash!*. "This position allowed us to slide into trail behind the second flight as we approached the target for the bomb run." Hutchinson recounts, "We would stack the flights down and each flight would make their own bomb run. I had most of my regular crew: Lt. Joe Dziewisz (co-pilot), Capt. Edgar Seefield (bombardier-navigator), Sgt. Fred Loring (top turret), Sgt. Freddie Fernandez (tail gunner) and a new waist gunner. About ten minutes from the target, the clouds appeared too dense for the formation to continue without getting into trouble. At the same time word came that we had six enemy fighters in the area."

"Now the problems started. Our Group leader appeared to have waited too long to make the decision to turn back and with the cloud build-up ahead, we had to make a steeper turn to the left than was manageable for my flight's position on the inside of the turn. As we made our turn, we were attacked from our left lower side with cannon fire observed not far in front of our windshield. My two left wingmen were hit; number 3 went down and I don't know what happened to the number 6 man. We were now within about 200 yards of the lead flight, still fighting for room in the turn, number 6 man in the lead flight *(possibly Spot Cash!/author)* looked like he was hit but apparently stalled out and rolled over onto his back and disappeared. About now my tail gunner hollered over the intercom to *"Pull up! Pull up! Pull up!"* which I did and a plane with the pilots blinded by Plexiglass dust in the cockpit from a stray bullet piercing the windshield, slid between my number 4 man and my plane, so close that the top of his rudder was bent over from having touched our belly as he slid under our plane. He then appeared on my left and slid directly across in front of us and disappeared to the right."

"We completed the turn and had some breathing room. Then, Lt Joe Dziewisz, my co-pilot, pointed out of his window. We now had three airplanes flying echelon on our right wing, nothing on my left wing, no planes under us and, of course, no one wanted to be on the lower left corner of the flight as that was where the next attack would have occured had there been one."

"The Me 262 attacks were deadly but that close collision call was equally as deadly. My crew and I had been shot down in December 1944 but that experience was

The mangled remains of a B-26 tail turret following an attack by a German fighter.

mild compared to this experience. The time involved seemed to have been several minutes but, in reality, everything happened in less than a minute. Galland has remarked about forgetting to release the second safety catch for his rockets and having to use only the four 3 cm cannon in his first attack. The possibility that we were the flight he had hit in the first attack seems a probability as we did not experience rocket fire, but just the cannon fire which hit my two left wingmen."

According to an official American account of the mission, JV 44 was seen to have made five simultaneous attacks against five different B-26 flights. The first attack, directed against the 5th flight came in high and from the left, dived under the bombers and swung up to approach from 6 o'clock low, closing to 100 yards (91.5 metres) before breaking off. In this attack the first of four B-26s was shot down. This was classified as "...the most damaging single attack". Seconds later a single Me 262 made a firing pass from 6 o'clock level at the 6th flight, breaking away in a wing-over manoeuvre. No damage was reported. The third attack, involving two jets, followed on the 9th flight from 6 o'clock low, opening fire with cannon from 800 yards (730 metres) and closing to 400 yards (365 metres) before breaking away in a vertical dive. The No. 3 position Marauder went down as a result of this attack. The penultimate assault was made on the 10th flight when three of JV 44's jets again approached from 6 o'clock level,

Up on the mission of 26 April 1945 with the 17th BG, was the crew of Capt. David Brackett of the 432nd Squadron. Here the crew is seen whilst still in training in the USA. From left to right: Capt David Brackett (pilot), 1st Lt. Paul White (co-pilot), 1st Lt Jack Rollow - replaced as bombardier for the 26 April mission by 1st Lt Francis Dougherty (not shown), T./Sgt Jack Hogan (engineer-gunner), S./Sgt Robert Macbride (radio-gunner) and S./Sgt Bernard J. Byrnes (armourer-gunner). Byrnes witnessed an Me 262 of JV 44 attack a neighbouring B-26 and "blow it right out of the sky."

Using unrelated photographs it is possible to reconstruct the angle of approach of a Me 262 against a Marauder formation. Above: A box of B-26s of the 17th BG. Inset: A Me 262A-1a of Erprobungskommando 262 sweeps past the camera.

with two breaking off in a diving turn to the left and the third swinging off high to the right. The B-26 in No.4 position was shot down. The last attack was mounted against the 8th flight by two Me 262s coming in from the favoured 6 o'clock level position and closing from 1,000 (915 metres) yards to 100 yards (91.5 metres), before both jets executed a split-S to 9 o'clock and down.

Of the four composite squadrons belonging to the 17th BG, only one escaped losing any aircraft to JV 44 on the Lechfeld mission – the 95th. However, as one of the squadron's pilots, Lt. Don Wilson recalls, the mission was not without its difficulties: "My aircraft was a "war-weary" that I'd had the misfortune to fly before. It would become airborne only after max everything including every inch of the PSP and retracting the gear just before skimming the canal at the runway end. But we made it once more."

"As the Group formed up and climbed out, I soon noticed that the windshield defroster was sick, or dead, so my left hand became the defroster of the left wing window while trying to hold in close to my flight leader in the right upper box. Usual procedure was to leave the *Flak* helmet on the floor beside the seat until crossing the bomb line or being attacked, whichever came first. So, the old hard hat rested there while I tried to keep it tight with an occasional quick glance at the clock and compass to estimate which part of the in-bound leg we were on and that all gauges were in the green. The cloud formations became more dense with some tops over 11,000 feet so the Group leader made a couple of turns and climbed higher to keep us all visual while my little world centred through the eight inch peephole I kept restoring in the wing window."

"Group lead started an unusually tight left turn which I guess was to avoid some higher cloud tops ahead. Then I felt the

old B-26 shudder a bit and concluded I'd stuck in a little too close and our left wing had encountered propwash. Another slight bump and our co-pilot, Chuck Darling from Boston, yelled *"Flak!"* as he picked up my helmet and dumped it onto my head all the way down to the bridge of my nose. I'm in a hairy turn, half blinded by the frosted plexiglass and now trying to see through a sixteen gauge steel helmet. I hastily pushed up the helmet, regained the peephole vision and heard lots of radio and intercom chatter that finally changed from *"Flak"* to *"fighters"*.

"These announcements didn't overly concern me because the operations briefing had promised fifty close-in P-47 escorts and 200 area escorts. That word "area" has never, even till today, been properly defined to my satisfaction. Was that "within sight"? "...On the ground?" "...Over all of Bavaria"... or exactly where? Hopefully this armada was close enough to help."

In fact, two of the four Thunderbolt escort groups flying with the bombers endeavoured to respond to the threat of the jets' presence. Just after midday, the 16 P-47s of the 27th Fighter Group flying 4,000 feet above the bombers, winged over and dived in pursuit of one of the small formations of German fighters, firing several bursts from their .50 Brownings and observing tracers hitting at least one Me 262 before they used their superior speed to outdistance the P-47s. The 27th FG later reported one Me 262 officially damaged.

"Jet Bandits!"

Also on the scene was 22 year-old 1st Lt. James J. Finnegan from San Francisco, whose squadron of sixteen P-47Ds of the 50th Fighter Group had been detailed to escort the French bombers to Schrobenhausen that day. Having taken off from its base at Giebelstadt at 10:19, the 10th Fighter Squadron – which was one of the three component squadrons of the 50th FG – was now flying above the *American* bombers at an altitude of just over 4,500 metres (14,765 ft). Finnegan clearly recalls his encounter with the commander of JV 44: "April 26, 1945: I remember it well because it was the first time I saw operational jets. We had been briefed on them because they had been expected and used since October 1944. Yet, like a lot of intelligence we received in those times, nothing ever materialised. The war had been winding down in April 1945. My tour overseas was completed (127 missions) but I was hanging around because I had fallen in love with a US Army nurse and was waiting for my C.O.'s approval to marry her."

"On the subject day, our mission was to escort a group of B-26 Marauders piloted by the French to a town known as Schrobenhausen. I was leading Green Flight, top cover. As such, I could oversee the entire scene below us; bombers, my own squadron, the ground and about 7/10 cloud cover. Suddenly, I watched two "darts" enter the bomber formation from the rear and saw two huge balls of flame emerge as the two "darts" went through the planes. One turned right and the other left. Somebody yelled *"Jet Bandits!"* over the intercom but there was no doubt in my mind what they were; I had never seen anything move that fast."

"I kept the "bandit" that turned left in my sight and watched the bombers from my 11 o'clock position. I told my flight I was going down after him, turned on my back in a "Split S" manoeuvre and caught him in my gun sight. Although the Me 262 was a great deal faster than the Thunderbolt, nothing could outdive it and I had the advantage of height. I pulled the big nose of the plane up so it obscured the jet – held the trigger for about a 1.5-2 second burst, dropped the nose and saw strikes on the right wing root. The ship pulled abruptly left and disappeared in the clouds. I claimed an Me 262 as "damaged and probable" and thought no more of it."

Lt. James J. Finnegan, 10th Fighter Squadron, 50th Fighter Group.

The Thunderbolts' timely intervention had been witnessed by Lt. Don Wilson in a 95th Squadron B-26, still struggling to see through a frozen windscreen: "Sometime during the attack, somebody identified the enemy as Me 262s firing cannon, which I soon verified by the sight of black puffs. Our Group leader remained in the tight left turn for a full 180 degrees while the air waves produced more exciting chatter. Through my small and only view I saw an Me 262 dive through the Group formation at about an 80 degree angle followed closely by two P-47s, one on each wing of the jet. I believe the Jug-jockies refer to this as having "boxed" him and the Juggies vowed they could keep pace with an Me 262 as long as he had his nose below the horizon. With that, my only view of the battle, I found some comfort that this Me 262 no longer had us in harm's way."

Henry Dietz observed: "I, nor any of my crew, remember seeing any P-47's in the area. If Lt. Finnegan fired at the Me 262, it must have been like shooting at a lame duck on its way home."

Galland: – "A hail of fire enveloped me... A sharp rap hit my right knee, the instrument panel with its indispensable instruments was shattered, the right engine was also hit – its metal covering worked loose in the wind and was partly carried away – and now the left engine was hit. I could hardly hold her in the air."

The jets reformed and made course for München-Riem having lost two aircraft during the attack with one pilot managing to bale out, though strangely only one jet was claimed as destroyed (by Captain Robert Clark). German claims were five bombers shot down, though the 1st TAF recorded only four Marauders lost and six damaged on 26 April. *Uffz.* Schallmoser accounted for one bomber destroyed and *Fw.* Kammerdiener another, though his Me 262 "White 10" received damage from

A well known but dramatic photo of an Me 262 caught by the gun camera of an Eighth AF P-47 Thunderbolt. According to US records, the Me 262, wheels down and preparing for a landing approach, was low on fuel. It did not make it as far as its home airfield and crashed in a field.

Ofw. Rudolf Nielinger (left) smiles down at the camera from the roof of a radio truck at München-Riem, April 1945. The other JV 44 pilot in the picture is thought to be Fw. Otto Kammerdiener who accounted for one Marauder destroyed on 26 April 1945, but whose own Me 262 received damage from B-26 defensive fire. Kammerdiener's right engine was set on fire and he was forced to make a shaky one engine landing.

the Marauder gunners and his right engine caught fire, forcing him to make a shaky one engine landing.

With the starboard side engine cowling flapping in the wind, for Galland, nursing his crippled Me 262 back to the relative sanctuary of Riem was a testing experience; one of Finnegan's .50 calibre bullets had hit the engine and passed through the cockpit obliquely from behind and it was the splinters from this bullet that had embedded themselves in his right knee and damaged the instrument panel. Another shell had hit the port-side Jumo engine and fragments from it had been sucked into the manifold, but, miraculously, the engine kept running. As Galland wrote: " I had only one wish: to get out of this "crate", which now apparently was only good for dying in. But then I was paralysed by the terror of being shot while parachuting down. Experience had taught us

that we jet-fighter pilots had to reckon on this. I soon discovered that after some adjustments my battered Me 262 could be steered again and, after a dive through the layer of cloud, I saw the *Autobahn* below me. Ahead lay München and to the left, Riem. In a few seconds I was over the airfield. Having regained my self-confidence, I gave the customary wing wobble and started banking to come in. It was remarkably quiet and dead below. One engine did not react at all to the throttle and as I could not reduce it I had to cut both engines just before the edge of the airfield. A long trail of smoke drifted behind me."

As Galland touched down with a flat nose wheel around 12:30, he was compelled to leap out of his aircraft and into the shelter of a bomb-crater because fighters of the American XIX TAC had chosen that moment to make a low-level attack on the airfield. But the commander of JV 44 was spared any further ignoble treatment when a mechanic drew up on a *Kettenkrad* and allowed the trembling *Generalleutnant* to hitch a ride to safety.

Though official USAAF records would credit Finnegan with a "damaged and probable" victory over Galland, the rear gunners of the 17th BG undoubtedly also inflicted severe damage prior to Finnegan's attack. John Sorelle remembers: "The Me 262s claimed 5 Marauders that day. They only got 4. I was fortunate enough to make it back. There is no way I can be sure whether T./Sgt Wills got a piece of General Galland's 262 before he was crippled by 1st Lt. Finnegan. Wills felt sure he did and reported such at the Intelligence debriefing. He was an outstanding gunner in the various stages of gunnery school and this was the only time he ever claimed to have scored on a *Luftwaffe* fighter."

"I didn't hang around the aircraft after we landed, just jumped on the truck for the debriefing and back to the billeting area for a much needed nap before chow. I found out the next day that my left wing man was damaged when the B-26 above and directly in front of him blew up. Wreckage striking his aircraft caused him to temporarily lose control and veer to his right, colliding with me. I suffered wing spar damage and serious misalignment of my vertical control surface. I was told later that the aircraft would never fly again."

Lt. Carl Johanson's B-26 *My Gal Sal* flew back to Allied lines on one engine and

"THE IRISH SHILLALAH": Lt. James J. Finnegan, 10th Fighter Squadron, 50th Fighter Group, seen here at Giebelstadt, the base from which the 50th mounted its escort operation on 26 April 1945. Finnegan is to the left on the P-47's cowling, while his crew chief sits to the right. After the war, Finnegan wrote that he considered himself "...very lucky " to have emerged unscathed from his encounter with "...the greatest German fighter ace of World War II."

crash-landed on an airstrip being used by P-47's at Luneville, France. Johanson and all his crew survived unharmed from the JV 44 attack. *My Gal Sal*, a Marauder which had joined the 17th BG at Villacidro, Sardinia in February 1944, was a write-off.

A revealing viewpoint on the mission from the American perspective, starting with the return from the target, is offered by Don Wilson: "Just after completing the 180 degree turn, the radio alarms of fighter activity quieted to be replaced by accountability of our losses which came through as garbled, scrambled, duplicated, denied and confused. The non-forecast high cloud tops and near solid undercast would not permit a clean bomb run and the old boast that "... AAF bombers always returned home with empty bomb bays" was certainly put to rest that day as we peeled off for individual landings with nothing expended but 130 octane gasoline, thousands of .50 calibre machine gun rounds, much perspiration and three B-26s. The debriefing was not a pretty picture."

For others, the memory of the jet attack would haunt them for a long time. William Snead remembers his own aircraft's close encounter with JV 44: "As a crew, we never discussed what happened on 26 April 1945. I know I had many sleepless periods for sometime afterwards. I never woke up screaming as I have heard of some. At a recent reunion, we discussed this and I believe for the most part, my feelings express somewhat at least all our feelings at that time. We now realise it was close. My crew and I thank God, even now, for His protection and deliverence in a dire situation we will never forget."

Another dimension to the JV 44 attack on the 17th BG, namely that of the confusion caused by the sheer speed of the jets, is described by Carl S. Schreiner Jr., a radio operator serving with the 34th Squadron, 17th BG on 26 April: "In the later stages of the mission, a P-47 was pursuing an Me 262 past the rear of our formation. Our tail gunners were firing at the jet but couldn't track it fast enough and we were later told that accidental damage may have been inflicted on the P-47. Also our tail gunner had his leg shot off and we were told that it was a .50 calibre bullet that did the trick..."

Henry Dietz wrote to Adolf Galland in 1991: "My own conclusion of our conflict is as follows: two B-26 gunners, Sgt. James A. Valimont and Sgt. Dick Dabling, were tail gunners in a flight above you, in the area at 12 o'clock high. They fired at about the same time I did and this is how you had so many .50 calibre hits and damage to your Me 262. You then quickly flew towards home... Jim Finnegan caught you in his sights while in a dive and hit your plane with more bursts. He was not foolish enough to fly into our fire while you were in your original position..."

When James J. Finnegan corresponded with Adolf Galland after the war, he wrote: "It is not my manner to boast about injuring another man, but if the Air Force's records are correct as to date and target, April 26, 1945, I consider it a high honour to be able to say I not only downed a German general, but I took out of the war the greatest German fighter ace of World War II

who is still alive. However, as you are most aware, I also consider the experience one of a very lucky circumstance and realise that if the roles were reversed, I might not be writing to you today."

In the course of some post-war correspondence Galland commented wryly: "Even today, I still have a little splinter in my

The crew of B-26B (S/N 41-95771) MY GAL SAL of the 37th Squadron, 17th BG pose once again for the camera, but this time as victims of JV 44's attack on 26 April 1945. Their bomber is seen here after having crash-landed at Luneville in France.

right knee which is the property of the United States government..."

For those stunned bomber crews who did make it back to base after their first encounter with the jets, life returned to normal routine remarkably quickly, for as the diarist of the 432nd Squadron recorded:

The resilience of the Marauder: despite being engulfed in flames and losing a bomb bay door, 2nd Lt. Kenneth L. Bedor's B-26F-1 (s/n 42-96328) MARAUDER *of the 17th BG crash-landed relatively intact after the 26th April mission.*

A light drizzle cancelled the league ball game in the evening. Supper was very good with hamburgers and pork chops constituting the main course.

By 18:00 on the 26th, JV 44 (including aircraft from *Stab*, I., II. and IV./KG 51) was reporting 31 Me 262s of which only nine were serviceable on strength and five Fw 190 D-9/11's. At midnight, OKL warned *Luftflottenkommando 6, Luftwaffenkommando West* and *Luftflottenkommando 4* of the very real possibility of an Allied thrust towards the Czech Protectorate from Passau. In such a case, OKW had decreed that German forces were to "split and spread south." JV 44 was to make itself available to offer close-support for the regrouping ground formations, a clear indication that it was to join the Bf 109s and Fw 190s of JG 53 and JG 300 who had been active that day bombing and strafing Allied columns in the Dillingen, Regensburg, Straubing and Regen-Cham-Passau areas.

For Galland, 26th April saw his last combat mission of the war. X-Rays taken at a hospital in München revealed that he still carried two of Finnegan's shell splinters in his knee. Recording the legacy in his diary, he wrote: "Since it was impossible to remove two of the steel fragments from my knee, it was put into plaster – otherwise, I would have been

Following events of 26 April 1945, from 27 April, field command of JV 44 effectively passed from Galland to Heinz Bär. The new commander is seen here with pilots from the unit at Riem late the same month: left to right - Major Brücker, Obstlt. Bär, unknown, Fhj.Ofw. Schuhmacher, Major Hohagen, Oblt. Stigler.

confined to a hospital bed. The plaster was therefore preferable. Although my own operative flying had come to an abrupt end, the history of my unit was to continue..."

This entry was perhaps a little optimistic, for though operations did continue during the last days of April, their measure and effect were on such a small scale as to be hardly felt by the Americans.

Uffz. Franz Köster, the JG 7 pilot who had recently joined JV 44, was in action again on the 27th, together with Heinz Bär and Willi Herget. The three pilots led by Bär, who was flying the six-cannon Me 262 A-1/U5 prototype machine, became engaged in a dogfight with American fighters as they made an attack on München-Riem. Bär and Köster each shot down two P-47 Thunderbolts and Herget claimed his final victory of the war when he made a single diving pass at one of the fighters and destroyed it, though whether this claim was made in the temperamental Me 262 A-1a/U4 with its 50 mm cannon which had proved so unreliable only two days earlier over Erding is unknown.

At this point, *operational* command of JV 44 passed from Galland to Bär, though despite his wounds, Galland remained in ultimate control of the unit. As far as Galland was concerned, Bär was the natural choice: "Bär was the most successful jet fighter pilot we had and he insisted on continuing to fight. Herget was now with me as my *Offizier z.b.V.*, Steinhoff was badly burnt and was in hospital, Barkhorn had been injured following his bad landing in an Me 262 and Krupinski did not have the experience that Bär had."

With Bär officially installed as *"Verbandsführer"* and Krupinski as his *"Adjutant"*, *Jagdverband* 44 was set to enter the final, cataclysmic few days of the war.

SEVENTEEN

ENDKAMPF

New Battle Orders addressed to all the jet aircraft units still operating on 28 April arrived at Riem late on the 27th. As an interim measure, JV 44 was to move urgently to Hörsching, an operational airfield designated as an emergency landing ground for Me 262s and located to the south of Linz in Austria. At the express orders of Hitler, this move would be followed by another transfer to Prague-Rusin where OKL was endeavouring to assemble other fragmented jet units. This decision to kove to Hörsching was tactically - if not technically - well justified; an American advance against the Passau-Linz area was threatening to disrupt lines of communication between the south and the Protectorate. From its new base, JV 44 was to be deployed in the threatened area as support for the army and as defence against the hordes of enemy fighter-bombers now active over the front. If neccesary - and depending on the fighting to the east - the *Verband* was also to be deployed against Soviet troop columns.

The staff of *Luftflottenkommando 6* further decreed that operations by JV 44 should be maintained "...as long as possible" but there was also warning that overcrowding on the rearward fields was to be expected and that operations could be restricted due to inadequate dispersal facilities. Furthermore, all surplus ground crew were to be transferred to the nearest Army units where they were to be hastily converted into infantry.

Adolf Galland however, was not prepared to accept these

orders. His argument was that the infrastructure at Hörsching was completely inadequate for the operation of jet fighters. In telephone conversations with both the staff of *Luftflottenkommando 6* and Hitler's Jet Aircraft Plenipotentiary, *SS-Obergruppenführer* Kammler, Galland reasoned that there were no fighter control facilities at Hörsching and that the ground support organisation there was virtually non-existent. Furthermore, weather conditions had deteriorated considerably; the forecast did not bode well, with 7-10/10 heavy cloud, heavy mist, rain and patchy fog predicted in southern Germany.

In reality though, Galland was endeavouring to keep his pilots and aircraft well away from Prague which was now seriously threatened by the Russians. Nevertheless, his argument was acknowledged by Kammler and an alternative suggestion was accepted; due to increasing "enemy pressure", JV 44 was to transfer to Innsbruck with all the Me 262s which had been undergoing "conversion and refurbishment" at the *Deutsche Lufthansa* hangars at Riem as soon as weather conditions had improved and local ground support there had been arranged. As a first stage, it would transfer to Salzburg and from there to temporary take-off and landing strips being made ready on the *Autobahn* between München and Salzburg, completion of which was expected in approximately two days once some overhead bridges had been demolished. In fact, the concept of converting straight stretches of *Autobahn* was not

A view of the hangars at München-Riem from a USAAF F-5 Lightning reconnaissance aircraft on 11 May 1945. Note the heap of Me 262s piled in front of the hangar and the Fw 190s further along the taxi-way.

new; work on at least four sites had been in progress close to the Sheppacher Forest near Augsburg and at Schleissheim during March and April.

Galland issued orders that any and all surplus jet fighters at München-Riem unable to take part in the first phase of transfer to Salzburg were to be moved to well camouflaged dispersal points just off the *Autobahn* in the Hofoldinger Forest due south of the city. Some Me 262s were flown the short distance to

Neubiberg airfield and from there towed by *Kettenkrad* tractors along one side of the road into the shelter of the trees or into the barns of nearby farms.

Wild rumours began to abound; *Fw.* Franz Steiner heard word that JV 44's Me 262s were being readied to be flown to Portugal and from there, shipped by sea to South America!

On the afternoon of 28 April however, as American advance units reached the western outskirts of München, the first Me 262s of JV 44 took off from Riem en route for Salzburg. As a result of his worsening knee wound, Adolf Galland reluctantly admitted himself to a military hospital in Bad Wiessee where he met up with Johannes Steinhoff who was still undergoing major treatment for his burns. He took with him *Hptm.* Hugo Kessler, from his personal staff and *Major* Willi Herget, his *Offizier z.b.V.* In the days ahead, Galland would need both of these men to carry out his final and perhaps most extraordinary venture of the war.

During his spell at Bad Wiessee, *Generalleutant* Adolf Galland, though probably still unaware of Adolf Hitler's suicide in Berlin on 30 April, had had time to reflect upon what course of action was needed to save the pilots and aircraft of the unit which he had personally established and commanded from falling into Russian hands or from being wastefully destroyed on the ground by Allied air attack. In view of the pace of the Soviet advance through Slovakia and Austria, Galland decided that the best option was to offer the pilots and aircraft of JV 44 together with their respective skill and technology to the Americans and for them to do with them what they wished. He knew that American forces were in control of München and reasoned that senior American officers would be in the city. What he needed were representatives from JV 44 to negotiate on his behalf.

"My intention was to avoid the destruction of the experience gained," he recalled, "The experience of the pilots, the experience of the technicians and mechanics; to keep the unit operational so that it could continue. I wanted to keep things going, not to destroy anything. It didn't make sense to do that. I hoped that they (the Americans) would take advantage of this and use it. I also thought that this would be more interesting than being a stupid prisoner of war."

Galland knew exactly what risks he was taking and for that reason kept his intentions absolutely secret. He was aware that should the nature of his plans be learnt by the SS, police or local Party authorities, there would be a strong possibility that he would be quickly and ruthlessly executed. "By that stage, life was dangerous because you only needed somebody to say - *"He was trying to surrender, he was doing something against the High Command"* - and it was enough to get shot."

Nevertheless, sometime on 30 April, he discharged himself from hospital and set up quarters at the villa of a local physician in the little town of Tegernsee on the shores of the Alpine lake of the same name. At this stage, he would still be able to maintain contact with Heinz Bär upon JV 44's arrival at Salzburg-Maxglan via telephone and had secured the services of a motorcycle and a single Fi 156 *Storch* liaison and reconnaissance aircraft which, with its negligible take-off and landing run, was able to operate from a small strip of open land close to the villa. In confidence, he asked *Maj.* Willi Herget and *Hptm.* Hugo Kessler to join him and to act as his personal emissaries in the forthcoming dialogue with the Americans. They agreed.

In the early hours of 1 May, Galland drafted a note in German which he intended his two aides to take to the Supreme Commander-in-Chief of Allied Forces, General Eisenhower.

Taking the note in a sealed envelope, Herget and Kessler took-off at daylight in the *Storch* and headed north for München. Their destination was the former *Luftwaffe* airfield at Schleissheim to the north of the city, now in American hands. Alone, in the vulnerable little observation aircraft, the two German officers flew towards München and circled low over the bomb shattered city. Somehow, miraculously, they landed at Schleissheim unharmed and were greeted by amazed and curious USAAF personnel who

listened to their request to meet with the most senior officer in the area. The events surrounding this extraordinary meeting and its outcome are detailed in the author's book *JV 44 - The Galland Circus* (Classic Publications, 1996)

JV 44's arrival at Salzburg-Maxglan on 28 April was somewhat dramatic, with the wary airfield *Flak* defences opening fire on the friendly jets as they made their approach. In a desperate attempt at recognition, one of the jet pilots landed and, scrambling from his cockpit, began to fire recognition flares across the field, before running, "screaming" towards the *Flak* positions. Remarkably no jets were damaged by friendly fire.

The remaining pilots due to make the transfer by air were delayed by weather and followed early the next morning, led by Bär. The Americans were working to encircle the northern half of the city but weather conditions had improved sufficiently to allow a loose interval formation to take off which included *Oblt.* Hans Grünberg in "White 1", *Uffz.* "Jonny" Müller in "White 23" and *Uffz.* Eduard Schallmoser in "White 14" - the third machine

Towards the end of April, Galland issued orders that all surplus Me 262s at München-Riem were to be moved away from the airport (where they were vulnerable to Allied bombing) to the relative safety of camouflaged, makeshift and temporary dispersals at the side of the autobahn running through the Hofoldinger Forest. This photograph and the one on page 175, taken by US Army personnel, show jets concealed in such a way, though in both cases their turbo units have been removed and the airframes damaged or sabotaged. Note also the crude parking ramp above built of sawn tree trunks bound together.

to land at Salzburg that morning, *Fw.* Otto Kammerdiener in "White 3" and *Fw.* Franz Steiner in "White 17". One by one, the Me 262s came into land on the 1,200 x 60 m runway, throttling back and taking care to avoid collision with the high tension cables immediately to the north of the airfield, though one jet, probably "White 22", came down just off the main runway and crashed into a pile of gravel.

The exact number of jets finally assembled at Salzburg has never been accurately established although is thought to have been between 20 and 26 machines. Those pilots known to have been at Salzburg include *Obstlt.* Heinz Bär, *Maj.* Erich Hohagen, *Hptm.* Walter Krupinski, *Oblt.* Hans Grünberg, *Lt.* Gottfried Fährmann, *Lt.* Klaus Neumann, *Lt.* Franz Stigler, *Fhj.Ofw.* Leo

Schuhmacher, *Uffz.* "Jonny" Müller, *Uffz.* Eduard Schallmoser, *Ofw.* Rudolf Nielinger, *Ofw.* Leopold Knier, *Fw.* Otto Kammerdiener and *Fw.* Franz Steiner. It is probable that they were also joined by the former instructor pilots from III./EJG 2.

Hptm. Werner Gutowski cleared the Feldkirchen operations room leaving it in the hands of a gang of Polish "guest" workers who had been employed to conduct repairs and maintenance to the airfield at Riem. He journeyed to Salzburg by road with the most qualified ground crews and technicians. He was also joined by *Maj.* Karl-Heinz Schnell and *Fhj.Ofw.* Herbert Kaiser. The remaining ground crews were sent to Bad Aibling to await further orders.

Facilities at Salzburg-Maxglan, though not damaged like Riem, were less geared up to accepting and operating a unit of Me 262 jet fighters; indeed it was only on 10 April that OKL had designated Salzburg-Maxglan as "...an alternative airfield from which (jet) aircraft can take-off again with tanks half full and/or with rocket assistance". Stocks of precious J2 fuel were rushed in.

The beautiful and ancient city of Salzburg, birthplace of Wolfgang Amadeus Mozart and dominated by its great Hohensalzburg fortress lay clustered around the banks of the river Salzach in western Austria. So far, as a result of little manufacturing output or war production, the war had been relatively kind to Salzburg. In total since October 1944, the city of Salzburg had been bombed on sixteen occasions and more than 500 of its inhabitants had been killed as a result of the raids. More

than 1,000 buildings had been destroyed or damaged and yet the city's airfield remained miraculously unscathed.

However, whilst living conditions for the pilots were considerably more comfortable than at Riem - with plenty of food and even more alcohol on hand - some conditions on the airfield presented operational problems. The Me 262s were parked in a line off a track under the shelter of some trees. Taking off from Maxglan had to be performed in a south to north direction towards the airfield buildings. The restriction in take-off run proved immensely difficult with the Me 262 and as far as is known, only one operational sortie was flown by JV 44 from Maxglan when, on 29 April, Heinz Bär flew the six-cannon Me 262 A-1/U5 and shot down a P-47 Thunderbolt over Bad Aibling.

The luckless *Uffz.* Eduard Schallmoser, plagued by recurring problems from his injured knee was admitted to hospital again.

By 1 May, the German forces of Foertsch's First Army facing the US Seventh Army's front were completely broken, unable to communicate with other commands and reduced to only 500 battle-worthy troops. The American drive on Salzburg began on the afternoon of 2 May with the Americans making

An Me 262A-1a (W.Nr. 170312) lies deliberately damaged and partially collapsed just off the autobahn near Frankfurt, Germany, 2 April 1945. Part of an engine cover, a bomb, a belt of cannon shells and the gun housing cover litter the ground around the aircraft.

Sgt Norman G. Farley, a B-26 armourer-gunner with the 494th Squadron, 344th BG, took these photos of an Me 262 in September 1945, abandoned whilst undergoing maintenance in a wooded clearing near Schleissheim. Farley was involved in occupation duty and based at Schleissheim prior to returning to the USA. Five months earlier, his unit had come under attack by Me 262s of JV 44.

quick work of dealing with the few pockets of light resistance that they encountered.

At Salzburg-Maxglan on 3 May, news of the speedy American advance had reached Heinz Bär but due to a breakdown in communications he was unable to contact Galland for further instructions. Gazing across the airfield he studied the 20 or so Me 262s now hidden in the trees near Kugelhof and contemplated the unit's next move. Galland's last orders were to remain in force; certainly there were now virtually no alternative airfields to which they could move other than Prague and those in the east, which would mean almost certain Russian captivity. The weather was deteriorating fast and fuel supply had now reached critical levels.

JV 44 was no longer bothering to report strength and serviceability figures or mission reports. Communication with most of Germany was now impossible. What remained of the OKL staff at Berchtesgaden was no longer in a position to control events. From Tegernsee, Galland sent a messenger to Salzburg with instructions for Bär to destroy all files, reports and documentation concerning the operations of JV 44

As dawn broke on the morning of 4 May, the pilots of JV 44, gathered in the draughty wooden barrack huts that served as their accommodation, could see American tanks massing on the far side of the Saalach, hear their engines. Even the *Autobahn* running north out of the city was clogged with American military traffic. The air was unseasonably cold and the ground was white with a fresh fall of snow.

After a brief artillery barrage on the city, intended as a show of strength, the Americans began to broadcast announcements to all German units in the area to surrender and to send a nominated representative into the city. Bär first ordered the ground crews to remove the Me 262 Jumo engine governors which would have the effect of immobilising the aircraft. These were to be given to *Maj.* Hans-Ekkehard Bob whom Bär assigned to lead a convoy of lorries into the mountains south of the city where the engine parts could be concealed and/or destroyed at some point in the future if neccesary. Next, he ordered *Maj.* "Bubi" Schnell and *Fhj.Ofw.* Herbert Kaiser to form the JV 44 delegation and gave them orders to investigate what was happening in the city. If possible they were to return to Maxglan with an American representative with whom surrender terms could be negotiated. Similarly, if they encountered any difficulties they were to return. The two *Ritterkreuzträger* left and the remaining pilots sat down to an early morning game of cards and to wait for whatever happened next, even ready to take off if neccesary, though to where nobody really knew.

Meanwhile *Hptm.* Walter Krupinski and a solitary mechanic sat warming themselves on the engine of a *Kettenkrad* tow-tractor at Kugelhof away on the eastern boundary of the airfield. They had with them a box of infantry hand grenades. Nearly two hours had passed when the tanks on the other side of the Saalach began to move. At around 07:15 and not having received any word or signal of an official surrender, Krupinski glanced at his watch and nodded to the mechanic.

"We had our aircraft in the woods and been waiting for something to happen." Krupinski recalled, "After about two hours, the tanks started to move towards Salzburg, over the Saalach. So I drove with a *Kettenkrad* and a mechanic and we drove from aircraft to aircraft putting hand grenades into the engines. I had already destroyed a lot of aircraft in Russia when we were on our way back, so I just decided to do it again, the way I knew how. We had enough to put one in each engine. We had to be careful because, three seconds later they exploded, so we had to drive very fast! I had to do it, due to the fact that the tanks were moving over the Saalach and as long as there was no official surrender... The problem was that the Americans had broadcast this radio message: *Do not destroy anything!* The tanks suddenly stopped and they must have wondered what was going on. They must have thought that the war had started again! They didn't shoot - maybe they had received a surrender notice by radio - but we hadn't."

One by one, the Me 262s exploded. Glumly, Eduard Schallmoser, now back at the airfield, watched his "White 14" "blow apart in the air." One young local resident heard the explosions and went to the window of his nearby second floor apartment from where he saw drifting clouds of black smoke rising into the sky from the airfield. Leo Schuhmacher recalled that it was a sight that made the JV 44 pilots "hearts bleed."

Having completed their task, Krupinski and the mechanic rode back to the barracks, leaving a line of smoking jet fighters. The final irony was yet to come, as Krupinski remembers: "About half an hour later, Schnell came back with an American Air Force intelligence officer and I thought to myself: *Why? Why? Why did you come back?*"

"White 22" was the only one of JV 44's jets known to have suffered damage on landing at Salzburg-Maxglan when it ran off the main runway on the morning of 29 April 1945.

EIGHTEEN

AFTER THE BATTLE
CAPITULATION AND OCCUPATION

On the morning of 4 May 1945, Major General John W. O'Daniel, commander of the US 3rd Division, accepted the surrender of the city of Salzburg under "...a sky still blanketed by post-seasonal snow, as a cold, damp wind whipped across the highways from the Tyrolean Alps."

Maj. Karl-Heinz Schnell and *Fhj.Ofw.* Herbert Kaiser drove into the centre of the city and made their way, as requested by the American broadcast, to the town hall to notify the liberators of the presence of JV 44 at nearby Maxglan. In the *Rathaus* they found scores of capitulating German military personnel from a host of different *Wehrmacht* units, but they were also mildly surprised at the fact that they were the only *Luftwaffe* people present at the surrender. A German army colonel introduced them to an American captain and they hesitantly began to explain about their unique unit.

Back at Maxglan, the Americans were almost on the airfield. "We were sitting in the barrack-hut of a former Labour Service Camp close to the airfield," recalled *Ofw.* Franz Steiner, "and we were playing *Doppelkopf* (a favourite card game among fighter pilots). In the distance we heard artillery fire and other similar noises. Things became a bit livelier in the camp. Then the door was opened, almost cautiously, and in the opening stood an American soldier with a machine-gun - completely typical, with his helmet crooked and chewing gum. We looked at one another briefly, then he said "OK" and shut the door from the outside. We

played on. One of us commented that we certainly hadn't heard him knock!"

Meanwhile the American intelligence captain took "Bubi" Schnell and Herbert Kaiser in a jeep back to Maxglan in order to see exactly for himself "who" and "what" was there. Schnell also carried a letter from the senior American commander in the area instructing JV 44 to stay where it was until arrangements were made to relocate it.

"That was very interesting," Krupinski recalled, "The American intelligence officer says: *"Stay here, I'll get some trucks and we will move you to a special place."* He disappeared. Ten minutes later, an American captain, an army captain, came up and said: *"Out! Go to the POW camp at Salzburg."* We tried to tell him that we had been ordered by one of his intelligence officers to stay put and wait for his return. But he had guns and so we got into our own vehicles and drove to the POW camp in the middle of the town. There was a large number of POW's there and the next day they took us in those big American trucks to Bad Aibling. We still tried to stay together, the pilots of JV 44 and we stayed in that camp on Bad Aibling airfield for two or three days."

Generalleutnant Adolf Galland surrendered himself to American forces at Tegernsee the next day, 5 May. Because of his knee wound, an American military ambulance took him to the nearby town of Bad Tolz where the US XXI Corps had set up its Command Post. The next day he met Colonel Dorr E.

Late April 1945: With Galland wounded, Steinhoff badly burned and Lützow missing, the exhaustion of combat and the strain of endless air raids shows on the faces of the three Ritterkreuzträger now in command of JV 44. From L-R: Major Erich Hohagen, Oberstleutnant Heinz Bär and Hptm. Walter Krupinski. Between them and by the war's end, these three officers had flown more than 2,600 combat missions and accumulated more than 470 confirmed aerial victories. Soon they would lead JV 44 into surrender and captivity.

Newton, Deputy Commander XII Tactical Air Command and the man to whom he had almost surrendered JV 44 five days earlier.

"I am of the opinion that Germany has lost the war but the future of all Europe lies in the hands of the Allies." Galland told Newton. He added *"...I have no place to go and no desire to go anywhere. I will be at your wishes at all times."*

USAAF Intelligence officers also agreed to Galland's request to launch an immediate search for his lost comrade *Oberst.* Günther Lützow and though this was carried out in co-operation with local German police around Donauwörth, it proved fruitless.

On the former airfield at Bad Aibling, where most of JV 44's ground crews had surrendered, Walter Krupinski and several other of the unit's pilots were getting used to captivity: "There were six to ten of us pilots," Krupinski remembers, "Some of the others had decided to go into the mountains when the Americans came - but that was before we had blown up the aircraft. Some of the pilots had signed the official *Soldbuch,* the serviceman's pay book which every soldier had in order to confirm, if necessary, that he had been released from service. These were the ones who wanted to go to the mountains - some of them went. But six to ten of us stayed. We went to Bad Aibling and from there, two or three days later, to Heilbronn, a very big POW camp with about sixty cages and in each cage, a thousand German soldiers. We had nothing to eat, no water. During the night there were thunderstorms - it was a terrible time. An American GI saw my *Flugbuch* and asked what it was. I told him, then he took it and I never saw it again. Four or five days later, an American soldier came with a megaphone into the cage and announced: *"I am looking for the pilots of General Galland!""*

"We were sitting together in a group - myself, Hohagen, Bär, Schnell, Gutowski and some others - and we looked at each other and wondered what to do. Prior to that, we had not registered

ourselves - nothing like that. No one knew who we were. Anyway, we all looked at each other and thought - *it's so bad here, anything is better than this* - and so we marched up to the gates and found this officer. He said: *"Gentlemen! Gentlemen!"* - In good German; he was one of those American Jews who spoke very good German - *"Now I have found you! I have been searching for over a week trying to find you!""*

"He had about nine men and three jeeps with him and we drove away from the POW camp and a little later they stopped the jeeps. The officer said: *"I know that you have had nothing to eat, it's been a very bad time for you, but now things will get better."* He opened some ration boxes and gave them to us and we ate them so quickly. Five minutes later, we were all sick!"

The officer who had plucked the JV 44 pilots from the Heilbronn camp had probably been either Major Max van Rossum-Daum or one of his staff. Van Rossum-Daum was the commander of the US 1st Tactical Air Force's Air Prisoner of War Interrogation Unit based at the time at Heidelberg some fifty kilometres (31 miles) north west of Heilbronn. Van Rossum-Daum was a concise and experienced interrogation officer and one of the first to interview Galland. Following an interrogation conducted on 14 May 1945 he observed:

"Galland was very enthusiastic about the capabilities of the Me 262, whose efficiency in combat he rated very highly. According to the statistics of his unit, the ratio was 5 to 1 of victories over aircraft shot down. He appeared to have uppermost in his mind the hope that his unit, with its experienced pilots and equipment, be used by US Air Forces "in the battle against Russia", which he was sure would come... In forming his unit, General Galland was determined to gather around him the very best that the GAF could offer. It was known in GAF circles that if you wanted to belong to Jagdverband 44, you had to have at least the Ritterkreuz..."

"...Galland blamed the top GAF officials for wilfully ignoring the facts and failing to plan ahead to counter the Allied air offensive by waiting until the last moment before protecting vital industries. He was very bitter about the fact that hard-working and hard-fighting air units were blamed for these mistakes and that the German public, realising that something was wrong, were told that the Luftwaffe was not doing its share to hold back the stream of Allied bombers. Galland admitted that some mistakes had been made by the units but the gravest and most telling were those committed by the leaders and the planners... Galland feels that Göring was fully cognisant of the conditions and the increasing threat of Allied air power. He accused Göring of deliberately choosing the easiest way out, by just ignoring the signs and following an ostrich policy."

Intrigued by what they heard of Galland's unit, the Americans began the search for its pilots; they wanted to learn more about the Me 262 from the men who had flown it in action. At Heilbronn they found some of them and relocated them to Heidelberg. Now they had Galland, Bär, Krupinski, Herget, Barkhorn and Hohagen.

Left: Soon after the cessation of hostilities and eager to acquire the benefits of German technology, American military intelligence personnel launched a concerted effort to discover more about the Me 262 both from the abandoned aircraft that lay on airfields and in forests across central and southern Germany as well as from pilots who had flown the aircraft in combat. Here a soldier from the US 12th Armored Division inspects an Me 262A-2a (W.Nr. 500079) "B3+DA" formerly belonging to the Geschwader Stab/KG(J) 54 at Giebelstadt, Germany in April 1945. Note the open gun canopy and the ejection chute and shell exit points for the MK 108 cannon. Another ejection chute lies on the ground behind the nosewheel and in front of the collapsed Jumo engine.

Right: Pilots belonging to a specialist USAAF evaluation unit under the command of Col. Harold E. Watson inspect the Me 262 A-1a/U4 coded V 083 and fitted with a 50 mm Mauser MK 214 cannon, which was a similar aircraft to that flown by Willi Herget of JV 44 against Marauders of the 323rd and 344th BGs over Erding on 25 April 1945. Watson's unit became known unofficially as the 'First US Jet Squadron' and 'Watson's Whizzers'. His men were distiguishable by the absence of propellers from their standard air force uniform insignia. They went on to find several Me 262s including fighter, reconnaissance and training machines. These aircraft, together with others, were then shipped to the USA aboard the Royal Navy aircraft carrier HMS Reaper and subsequently to Freeman Field, Indiana for further evaluation.

Left: A no doubt intrigued American officer examines abandoned Me 262s scattered around a forest clearing somewhere in south Germany in mid-1945. This was a scene which greeted thousands of US army and air force personnel as they pushed deeper into what remained of the Third Reich.

When Germany formally surrendered on 7 May 1945, US Army Air Force bomber and fighter groups, plus service units, were tasked with remaining in the country as the Allied Occupation Air Force. For some time there was the not insubstantial risk that die-hard groups of German troops would refuse to comply with the surrender terms and offer armed resistance. In that event airpower might still be needed. Consequently, fighter and bomber groups were stationed in Germany until this threat proved to be groundless.

Airmen also formed part of technical evaluation teams which had the enormous task of sorting and recording mountains of data on the German military effort, the effectiveness of Allied air attacks and overseeing the general disarmament of the German air, land and sea forces.

This was also a time for reflection and, of course, a little praise well earned; on 10 May, General Jacob L. Devers commanding the US 6th Army Group wrote to the commander of the First Tactical Air Force:

In the bitter struggle from which we have just emerged victorious, the infantryman learned quickly the importance of airpower and came to a grateful appreciation of the assistance rendered him from the air... The Seventh US Army, the First French Army, elements of the 6th Army Group have long been keenly aware that the capture of many objectives would have been delayed and many more casualties would have been suffered were it not for the brilliant and timely aid which the First Tactical Air Force (Provisional) furnished in all kinds of weather and against all degrees of resistance. I speak for all the troops in 6th Army Group when I express my sincere admiration and deep respect for the perfect teamwork and decisive action which your pilots always provided us.

Modern warfare demands split-second co-ordination and precise execution by all elements. Between your air force and the troops of my command, these requirements have always been met, and so it is with pride and gratitude that I heartily commend you, your officers and men for your magnificent achievements. May good fortune forever fly with you.

Around 14 May, Adolf Galland was flown to England and sent to the "Combined Services Detailed Interrogation Centre (CSDIC)" at "Camp 7" located in the wooded grounds of Wilton House, the country estate of Lord Chesham at Latimer in Buckinghamshire. Many other leading *Luftwaffe* personalities were here or about to arrive and all had been told by their British and American "hosts" that they were there to compile detailed

A lone US serviceman stands amidst a scene of carnage at the former Messerschmitt assembly plant at Obertraubling and jots down technical information pertaining to one of the Me-262s which surround him.

studies based on their respective experiences. Hidden microphones gave the British a considerable amount of additional fruitful material.

The group of JV 44 pilots assembled at Heidelberg rejoined their erstwhile commander at Latimer shortly afterwards, having been flown to England via Mannheim in a C-47 transport. Walter Krupinski remembers: "I can't remember where we landed but they took us to the camp by bus. There was Herget, Hohagen, Barkhorn and Bär. They took us into some barracks and everyone got a single room - very nice - but all the windows had iron bars on them. Before I even had a chance to look around the room, they had shut the door and there was no grip on the inside. I was absolutely on my own. The commander of the camp came by once to say hello and the food was fine."

"The next morning, I was reassembled with the other JV 44 pilots and some American officers came in, one after the other and tried to talk to us. We "talked" but gave away no military information; I gave just my name, just my rank. The whole time they asked: *"What did you think of the Me 262? Is it a good aircraft?"* But they didn't find out much because the others had acted in the same way, like ordinary POW's."

"After two or three days, they took us into the officers' mess and there was *Generalleutnant* Galland sitting there! That was the first time I had seen him since he had been wounded. They gave us a drink - the first time I had seen a whisky in a long time - but everyone was careful not to say too much. We whispered to Galland: *"They're wanting information."* Galland said: *"Okay, listen. For me, the war is over. They want to know something about the Me 262 - I have no objection for you to tell them what they're asking you."* From then on the doors were open. More officers came and they asked lots of questions. I even wrote a report!"

"After three or four weeks, they took us from that house to another one. They told us that it would only be for one night and that the next morning we were being returned home to Germany as one of the first groups to be released. Next morning, we travelled by train in a first-class compartment to Southampton with only one British soldier with us - myself, Barkhorn and Hohagen.

After a long, hard slog from Africa and across Europe and led by Major Ken Earl, the men of the 34th Squadron, 17th BG march through Dijon for their VE Day parade on 9 May 1945. According to the squadron diary entry for 16 April 1945: "Major Earl is hobbling around these days with a bad knee, the result of a spill while playing softball not so long ago!"

'Victory': H. Henry and R. Gibson of the 17th BG hold up 'The Stars and Stripes' Paris edition dated Tuesday, 8 May 1945 proclaiming the end of the war – at last.

Galland stayed behind for more interrogation. At Southampton, there were some of those so-called "Liberty Ships", a kind of transport ship built by the Americans and they were full of German POW's returning home from the United States after a long time in captivity there. We were taken on board one of these ships and we were put together in the same cabin. We then went to Cherbourg. I should point out that with the war over, we had taken all our medals and decorations off in those first camps, but in the UK everybody asked us why we didn't wear them! So we came off that ship at Cherbourg wearing all our decorations. There was a pair of very young looking French soldiers there who were leading us to some trucks and one of them tried to pull my *Ritterkreuz* from my neck, so I slammed my fist into his face. Barkhorn was behind me and he later told me when he visited me in hospital, that the other French soldier had used his rifle butt on my head! I was later moved to different hospitals in the south of Germany - to Wasserburg and so on. One day they moved me into the same room as Steinhoff. They told me I had blood on my brain but nobody dared to operate. They should have opened it up and taken some blood out but nobody was keen to risk it. They blew air into my head so that they could see whether the lump grew larger or not, but then, after two or three weeks, it grew smaller, so they decided not to operate - and the lump disappeared."

The specific responsibility of disassembling *Luftwaffe* equipment and facilities and preparing an inventory of the more important, i.e. most technically advanced, German aircraft that

The men of the 17th BG's 34th Squadron Engineering Section line up for an official VE Day photograph outside of the group's HQ at Chateau de Salverte, Rouvres en Plaine near Dijon, France, May 1945.

remained intact, was given to personnel of the 17th, 322nd and 323rd Bomb Groups and the 404th Fighter Group. Flyable examples of most first-line *Luftwaffe* aircraft but particularly the jet types, were to be prepared for shipment to the US for extensive evaluation, though not always.

Ronald Macklin was a Section Head with the 17th's 34th Squadron Engineering Section. He remembers his assignment in Austria: "My particular job was to survey 100 square miles for aircraft. If we found them, we wrote up a report on their condition and how many man hours it would take to them airworthy. We didn't know at the time what was going on. Some aircraft were new. We wrote up that it would take one man hour to make them airworthy, but orders came down to burn them. We found out later that no matter what we wrote, the order

The 17th BG was tasked with the destruction of many former Luftwaffe aircraft found in Austria. One of the hardest types to destroy was the Junkers Ju 52 transport aircraft. Here, a member of the 34th Squadron's Engineering Section takes an axe to the wing of such an aircraft.

always said *"burn them"*. We ran across some very interesting aircraft, but all of these were burned. Junkers Ju 52 transports proved difficult; they would not burn. We had a hell of a time getting them to light off. When we finished with one 100 square mile area, we went to work in another. It was interesting work..."

In addition, seven bomber and three fighter groups of the Eighth Air Force were originally assigned to occupation duty although plans changed rapidly in the first weeks of peace. In the event, the only Eighth AAF groups to be based in Germany for any length of time were the 55th, 355th and 357th Fighter Groups flying P-51s and the B-17-equipped 305th and 306th Bomb Groups.

After the headquarters (less personnel and equipment) of the Eighth Air Force was transferred to the Pacific island of Okinawa on 16 July 1945, most American groups designated for occupation duty were transferred, albeit temporarily, to the Ninth Air Force, if they were not already part of that organisation. In its last few months of existence the Ninth encompassed units flying a variety of aircraft types but in general, the occupation groups either retained the aircraft they had flown in combat or carried on with transition training on new types, as happened with some B-26 groups destined to receive Invaders.

Numerous examples of liaison aircraft and single and twin-engined fighters received the officially stipulated Allied Occupation Air Forces' recognition marking of two red and one yellow vertical stripe around the rear fuselage although the relevant order did not apparently extend to heavy bombers. As the most modern US tactical bomber for the foreseeable future,

"The order always said 'burn them'..." Setting fire to a Junkers Ju 52 on the ground was virtually impossible, but with persistence it could be done – eventually! The man behind the wing is throwing gasoline at the aircraft to keep it burning.

B-26G (s/n 43-34181) coded Y5-O LAK-A-NOOKIE of the 495th Squadron, 344th BG having landed with a blown tyre at Florennes/ Juzaine in May 1945. This aircraft usually flew with the crew of 2nd Lt. James L. Stalter and took part on the mission of 24 April 1945 to Schrobenhausen which was attacked by Me 262s led by Günther Lützow of JV 44.

the Douglas A-26 Invader was included in this relatively short-lived marking scheme.

On 16 August 1945, a further reorganisation of US air forces world-wide resulted in the establishment of a headquarters for a new command, United States Air Forces in Europe (USAFE). This was set up at Wiesbaden in September, at which point it was reinforced by XII Tactical Air Command, with two fighter wings, a reconnaissance group and a photographic group, plus air service, tactical control and other auxiliary units. To this force was added the European Air Transport Service, with one troop-carrier wing; the European Aviation Engineer Command, with an engineer aviation regiment; the AAF/European Theatre Reinforcement Depot; the Base Air Depot Area (which was located at Burtonwood in England) and the European Air Materiel Command.

Mulling over their redesignation as an 'air disarmament group' the men of the 323rd Bomb Group duly celebrated the end of the war, having moved to Gablingen, a grass aerodrome near Augsburg, on 8 May. C-47s flew the men in, and all had arrived by the 15th. Before tackling a new duty that was only vaguely defined, some of the pilots took the opportunity to obtain their instrument ratings while B-26s remained at Denain. As generally occurred in all the occupation groups, the 323rd gradually slimmed down as personnel were rotated home; some combat crews were re-assigned to the 397th BG, a sister B-26 outfit based at Venlo in Holland.

This was little more than a 'paper transfer' as these men

subsequently became part of the 387th Group before moving to Antwerp, their embarkation port. Officers bemoaned the fact that during the move, group records became lost and that many of the transferring aircrew were erroneously told that they would be sent, as Marauder units, to the CBI. In fact no such plan was ever implemented, as soon became all too obvious. Marauders were not to be flown anywhere, but were to be destroyed wholesale, in Germany.

Pilots of aircraft that had carried them through hundreds of hours of combat were ordered to fly to various airfields, the largest in these 'depot' terms being Landsberg (R-78), where the mass destruction of B-26s took place. There were more than a few heavy hearts as the pilots taxied into their allocated slots, climbed out and turned their backs on the lines of elegant medium bombers for the last time. An explosive charge was placed in the centre section of each one and detonated. The explosion tore each B-26 apart and turned hundreds of thousands of dollars' worth of perfectly good aircraft into scrap metal.

Elsewhere, there were accidents; 2nd Lt. James L. Stalter, of the 495th Squadron, 344th BG had piloted B-26G (No. 43-34181) coded Y5-O *Lak-a-Nookie* on the mission of 24 April to Schrobenhausen. As he recalls, he built up a respect for his faithful aircraft: "We flew a large percentage of our missions in Y5-O and it became my all time favourite B-26, though I was saddened when, on 12 May 1945, another pilot (Lt. Nogle) and crew returning from a practice mission in Y5-O blew a tire on

Major John O. Moench of the 454th Squadron, 323rd BG and the mysterious Luftwaffe Non-Commisioned Officer whose photograph Moench discovered at Augsburg.

landing, collapsed the gear resulting in considerable damage to the airplane. Although all the crew escaped without injury, Y5-O was dispatched to the scrap heap. Peace too, has its hazards. Our mount of the 25 April mission to Erding had been Y5-J and I presume its final fate was a tragic date with a cutting torch but I left the group in September 1945 to fly for the European Division of the Air Transport Command so I do not know Y5-J's final fate. I do remember that on 7 June (after a rather large party celebrating the first anniversary of D-Day), I and three or four other crews were called upon to transfer some airplanes; the trip was, sadly, one-way for Y5-D."

Emotions aside, the USAAF simply had too many aircraft in Europe. The fate of the Marauders was shared by the surviving A-20 Havocs, as both these older types had been earmarked for replacement by the A-26 Invader which had been designed to undertake both 'medium' and 'attack' roles.

Facilities at their new home were much appreciated by the Americans. Although Gablingen had been bombed, its sturdily-built barrack blocks had escaped virtually unscathed and once demolition charges (mostly consisting of German aerial bombs wired to explode) had been removed, the place was more than habitable. For the first time since leaving England, squadrons could house most of their personnel in one building. A German prisoner detail assigned to the 323rd was put to work to improve the wretched conditions of the inmates of a small and very squalid concentration camp-like compound situated on the edge of the airfield. *Luftwaffe* officers were summarily ejected from their off-base quarters and the American officers moved in. One officer of the 323rd BG, Major John O. Moench, experienced an unusual occurrence upon arrival at Augsburg.

As Moench recalls: "The war was over and my unit moved into Germany as an element of the disarmament and occupation forces. Our destination was Augsburg, Germany. And, to determine what we faced in the way of facilities and more, I took off from our base at Valenciennes, France, in a liaison aircraft

with another officer and with several five gallon cans of emergency fuel stowed aboard. We were terribly over-loaded but eventually we made it to Gablingen Airdrome which had been designated by headquarters as our next unit location."

"The *Luftwaffe* airfield was a mess. The main hangar had been destroyed by bombing; wrecked aircraft were everywhere; military equipment littered the area. The well-constructed German barracks had been looted and generally torn apart. Worse, the barracks and other buildings had been mined with aerial bombs wired together. But no one had set them off."

"We cut the detonation wires to the bombs, tried to figure out how to make liveable the barracks, tried to sort out relations with the remaining local government and more. Many of the men who shortly arrived by land, most of them already overseas for years, were angry at being kept on for the occupation duty and terribly unhappy with the German populace for a combination of things - among other events, the earlier savage happenings such as took place at Malmédy and now local observations keyed to such places as Dachau. I swear that many a man would have gladly stood at a roadside and shot every German in sight - and the hundreds of German military still in uniform and freely wandering about posed a serious problem - it was chaotic.

"I recall the German prisoner barracks at Gablingen - terrible lice-infested shacks with straw for bedding. We were allocated a number of German prisoners for work detail and they were "tossed" into the prisoner barracks that had previously been used for Poles and others. But we were poor prisoner guards - our job had been flying aircraft, not guarding prisoners. And, nightly, some of our prisoners escaped.

"At Augsburg, we quickly learned where the *Luftwaffe* family quarters were located and someone informed the local *Bürgermeister* that we were taking those quarters for our own use. I think the occupants were given some thirty minutes to vacate the premises. I recall that one stupid German sought to smuggle out a radio in a rolled rug - the guard did not shoot him - only fired a burst over his head. And that ended any smuggling.

"Subsequently, I and some others moved into an apartment in those *Luftwaffe* quarters. While in that apartment, I noticed some photos and one was obviously that of the *Luftwaffe* person who had been its occupant. I was stunned for I found myself looking at myself. A half century ago, I slipped that photo into my footlocker and have periodically returned to observe it. In this photo, I see not only myself but many of my family. He could have been me; I could have been him. The eyes, the ear structure and lobes, the eyebrows, the nose line, the lips, the chin, the bone structure, the neck, even the slight cleft of the chin - some would say that we were twins. But we were not twins; we were strangers and mortal enemies. Though, yes, I am of German ancestry. I have often wondered who he was. I am certain he fought for his country with the same vigour that I fought for mine. I still think about this *Luftwaffe* person whose apartment, kitchen, bath and bed I used. More important, I think that these two photos standing side by side reflect the incomprehensible nature of international conflict."

On 19 May a staff group from the 2nd Disarmament Wing arrived to brief the erstwhile medium bombardment group on its new duties. The upshot of this was that the sooner the demilitarisation task was completed, the quicker the men would be going home.

There was considerable discussion and no little doubt as to whether ordinary members of an AAF combat group could adequately undertake disarmament work, for which none of the men had been trained. While each combat group had its specialists, it ideally required the participation of experts in many fields. The official view was that airmen of one air force were basically able to evaluate the materiel and equipment of all kinds used by another. But the *Luftwaffe* of 1945 was in many important respects, quite unlike any other air arm in the world. Aside from the fact that as the men went to work vital records of revolutionary technical advances were lost, they were sometimes put into the situation of handling and destroying equipment of which they had little or no knowledge. There were inevitably, instances of injury suffered when an innocuous-looking piece of equipment was thrown onto a bonfire.

The men of the 323rd, in common with thousands of other Army Air Forces personnel saddled with similar tasks, were directed to take whatever they wanted. If an item was not required and it had some intrinsic military value, it was to be destroyed. Such actions were condoned under the rather naive desire to prevent Germany 'from ever again developing or building an air force' With the benefit of hindsight, it is obvious how short-sighted this policy was.

While the 323rd maintained a group headquarters at Gablingen along with the 453rd Squadron, the remaining members of the other three component squadrons were sent

Whilst serving on occupation duty in Austria, these former SS barracks at Urfahr served as HQ and accommodation to the men of the 17th BG. Note the sign placed outside the barracks which reads: 17th Bomb Group – "The Daddy of Them All".

elsewhere: the 454th moved to Innsbruck in Austria, the 455th took up residence at Leipheim aerodrome, about 35 miles west of Augsburg and the 456th moved into Kempten.

After rumours about being sent to Regensburg or Straubing, it was, from early June 1945, Linz in Austria which became "home" for the men of the 17th Bomb Group. From there, they would be tasked with similar duties to the men of the 323rd. The 34th Squadron's war diary describes the group's sentiments about its new location and work:

> *The 34th Bomb Squadron was a disappointed outfit as it moved from Dijon, France to a base farther inland at Linz, Austria. The war in Europe is over, and we had all counted on being sent home immediately. However, on second thought, it must be quite a task to plan for the return of so many thousands of men to the States, and we are just a few. Our mission in Austria is to comb the entire area for German Air Force material, and to disarm those portions of the German Air Force which we find in and around that part of Austria.*
>
> *Linz, Austria, has been an important hub of the war, and has also been a frequent target for the 15th Air Force from Italy. Most of the city is in ruins; however, a main residential section still stands unmolested, and the main bridge across the Danube between Linz and Urfahr is still standing.*
>
> *The Group took over a large SS barracks in Urfahr for our living quarters and office space. Each Squadron has been assigned a section of the building, with the 34th getting, what we think to be, the best section - naturally.*
>
> *We are surrounded by thousands of Displaced Persons who look and act very hungry. One of our hardest jobs is to keep the garbage in the garbage can where it belongs.*
>
> *Hörsching Airdrome, about ten miles from Linz to the West, is our base of operations. We have several aircraft there under the supervision of Captain Parkins, Group Engineering officer.*
>
> *The beautiful scenery of surrounding valleys and mountainside compensates, in a way, for the continued overseas duty. Every day different groups of men leave for*

vacations, rest camps, and just plain vacationing. Of course, on the side we're supposed to be doing disarmament work, but that takes us to the most scenic places.

On the violent side, two Concentration Camps are located very near here - at Gusen and Mauthausen. Thousands of graves can be seen, together with walking skeletons. Former SS men can be seen digging graves every day for the dying inmates who will never regain their health.

Much evidence of the German jet fighter programme had been left intact within the area assigned to the 17th and 323rd Bomb Groups and included in the long list of locations to be checked, were jet aircraft assembly plants at Leipheim, Gunzburg and Burgau. Allied Intelligence personnel were amazed when men from the 17th stumbled across a previously unknown underground Me 262 manufacturing plant at St. Georgen, east of Linz on the Gusen river.

The end of the fighting brought some grim discoveries for the men of the 34th Squadron, 17th BG, who visited several former concentration camps such as those at Mauthausen and Gusen. The sign in the photograph is self explanatory. Of Gusen, Ludwig G. Rosenkranz of the 34th Squadron S-2 Section wrote: "The atmosphere of death and suffering is not lessened by the hundreds of graves marked with crosses and Stars of David which fill the adjoining fields... It is with a feeling of relief that one leaves these horror camps with their electric fences. The unclean and morbid influence that pervades the place seems to stay with a person for some time afterward and the desire for bathing is foremost in everyone's mind." One former 17th BG veteran wrote to the author: "You cannot believe what a shock it was to see these people and what they had endured."

Sgt. George Stowell, a somewhat awestruck scribe from the 34th Squadron described the discovery:

Operating now as the 34th Disarmament Squadron, since this inactive theater no longer requires the services of the B-26 as a medium bomber, the Thunderbird ground men were assigned specific areas to police up for any technical intelligence and material left by the Germans and that might be used by the Japanese.

One of the most interesting of our targets turned out to be a huge factory for manufacturing complete fuselages for Göring's Me 262s. The factory itself isn't so amazing - it's the manner in which it is built and concealed entirely beneath the earth that compels one to admire the German engineering ability.

Nestled snugly in the hills of this sleepy little village on the muddy Gusen river, army experts call the factory "a modern miracle in engineering," which when finished would have been capable of turning out Messerschmitt 262s at the rate of 1,500 a month.

The plant today is just another job for us to comb for information and to neutralize, but a trip through the five miles of underground tunnels that house the works of this intricate machine is impressive, even to the most inexperienced layman.

Fourteen tunnels go to make up its five miles of workshops and assembly lines. The tunnels were dug into what was once a sand quarry and they reach a width of 30 ft at places. They are about as high as they are wide. Work on the tunnels went forward with typical German dispatch, a civilian guide told us. As the drillers knocked the sand down scaffolding was put in and cement reinforcement added. As each tunnel was finished, machinery was moved in and work on the jet propelled fighters begun. The factory has its own lighting and also an air conditioning system.

The plant is so hidden that it isn't obvious until one is directly upon it. The layout was started in March 1944, and 14 months later, when oncoming (Allied) troops stopped production, had turned out 1,041 twin-turbo aircraft, the type of which had already earned the healthy respect of our combat men who knew, from the last days of the war, what it was like to be jumped by 262s.

Finished fuselages still lay on the flat cars at the mouth of the assembly line tunnel when we visited the plant for the first time. The fuselages were to be transferred to another factory in Czechoslovakia where the turbos were to be installed. The factory operated right up until the time our troops took over.

The St Georgen factory never was bombed by American aircraft. the camouflaging of the exterior had been carried out to the "nth" degree but no anti-aircraft defense was employed, the Germans realizing, apparently, that the place was practically impervious to our bombs.

In Austria, a number of Me 262s were checked over and in individual instances, dismantled and readied for onward shipment to the United States. Discoveries were made in the most unlikely places. A synagogue yielded rocket propelled take off (RATO) bottles for the Me 262 and these were duly burned, much to the chagrin of the onlookers who were suddenly forced to run for cover as the heated bottles took flight! In a final

Above: American troops take a rest on a bare-metal Me 262 fuselage section outside the underground production facility at St. Georgen, east of Linz in Austria.
Above right: The entrance to one of fourteen tunnels which formed the St. Georgen underground aircraft production factory, near Linz. Note the railway track running into the tunnel and the Me 262 fuselage section to the left of the picture.

episode of irony, at Innsbruck-Hötting, a barely completed and primitively equipped airfield, 323rd personnel discovered a substantial number of Me 262s which had originally been deployed with JV 44. Their presence at this location reflects the desperate and wholly futile measures the Luftwaffe was adopting in the final days of hostilities.

One of the last officers to be officially transferred to JV 44 before the end of the war was twenty-eight year old *Major* Hans-Ekkehard Bob, a combat-seasoned *Ritterkreuzträger* with 59 victories who had flown throughout the war and who had been trained to fly the Me 262.

Bob had joined the *Luftwaffe* in December 1935. "I volunteered

for the *Luftwaffe*", he recalls, "because I already loved flying as a result of my involvement in glider flying and I therefore wanted to be a professional pilot. For me, the ability to fly was the most important thing. Everything else came second."

His first taste of aerial combat came in 1939 during the invasion of Poland but he later took part in the French campaign of May 1940 and fought over Dunkirk where some of his first victories were over RAF Gloster Gladiators. During the ensuing Battle of Britain, Bob led the distinctive "tiger-stripe" Bf 109 E's of 9./JG 54 on almost daily sorties against the British Isles, either on freelance fighter sweeps or as escort to bombers

As the Allied air offensive began to cripple German industry, drastic measures were adopted in an effort to maintain vital war production. Evidence of this is seen here at an open air assembly line for Me 262s hidden in woods near Obertraubling.

before experimenting in fighter-bomber operations in September of that year by using single 250kg bombs slung under the Bf 109's fuselage in several missions against the London docks.

He was awarded the *Ritterkreuz* in May 1941 on the occasion of his 19th victory and then moved with JG 54 to Russia, to cover the advance on Leningrad. In August 1944, he was given command of II./JG 3 whose Bf 109 Gs had been rushed to the Normandy invasion front from the Reich and with just enough fuel to operate, the *Gruppe* was one of those that fought a bitter battle of attrition against overwhelming Allied airpower. Just a month later however, in September 1944, Bob was transferred again, this time to the newly formed *Erprobungskommando* Lechfeld where, as result of fuel shortage, he received only two hours of very rudimentary training on the revolutionary Me 262 jet fighter.

By late April 1945, he received orders to transfer to München-Riem and report for duty with *Generalleutnant* Galland's

Major Hans-Ekkehard Bob

JV 44 now under the command of Heinz Bär. Getting there however, amidst the chaos of a virtually destroyed transport system, was a task in itself and when he finally reached Riem around 30 April, he found that Galland was hospitalised and that Bär had left for Salzburg. Having been in München for a only a few hours, Bob was instructed to proceed "immediately" to Innsbruck where he was to organise and supervise the necessary developments needed at the local airfield to enable operations by a number of JV 44's Me 262s expected to transfer there in the very near future.

"I was a pilot, trained for the Me 262," Bob recalls, "Even in possession of the advanced military pilot licence for multi-engined aircraft, my training having been received during peacetime - which included blind-flying - and yet nobody had thought of giving me an aeroplane. However, due to a lack of aircraft, I went to Innsbruck by car."

The decision to move some of JV 44's jets to Innsbruck had been taken on 28 April when Galland had proposed the idea to *SS-Obergruppenführer* Kammler as a compromise suggestion for a permanent operational base from which to continue operations as against relocation to Prague. Accordingly, a number of Me 262s which were undergoing repair and "conversion" at the Lufthansa sheds at Riem were readied for transfer.

When *Maj.* Bob arrived at Innsbruck, capital of the Tyrol, which had been thought of as the headquarters town of the "Alpine Redoubt", he discovered conditions there little better than primitive. The city was graced with two airfields, one being the old civilian aerodrome which had existed for some years before the war and which was located east of the city centre on the south bank of the River Inn. However, though this grass field was equipped with three small hangars fronted by a narrow tarmac apron and several six-gun defensive *Flak* positions, there were no organised dispersal facilities and climatic and geographical conditions in the area were known to be particularly unfavourable for flying as a result of regular ground fogs and the local *Föhn* (southerly wind) which frequently impeded flying activity. More importantly, maximum take-off and landing run of the field was far too little for Me 262s.

Below left: Abandoned Me 262s of JV 44 photographed at Innsbruck-Hötting by T./Sgt Lucien L. Couture, 454th Bombardment Squadron, 323rd BG.
Below right: T./Sgt Lucien L. Couture, 323rd BG endeavours to translate the message on the nose-wheel door of this Me 262 at Innsbruck on 9th June 1945, while Cpl Robert R. Gosselin admires the hydraulics. Translated into English - Achtung - Nicht am Bugrad Schleppen - means "Attention! Do not tow by nosewheel". Me 262s were mainly towed by Kettenkrad half-tracks from tow cables fixed to lugs on the mainwheels.

Me 262 W.Nr. 111857, designated by Messerschmitt Augsburg in March 1945 as an "improved series aircraft", before being assigned to JV 44 in April and subsequently flown to Innsbruck-Hötting. The reason for Messerschmitt's designation not known.

Four kilometres (2.5 miles) to the west, at Hötting, on the road to Telfs and just under one kilometre north of the Inn, another airfield had been in preparation for some time, though it was incomplete. No development work had been carried out for at least a year and the site was little more than rough open ground surrounded by mountainous terrain to the north and south.

As Hans-Ekkehard Bob remembers: "Upon my arrival at Innsbruck, I went to the airfield commander in order to make the usual arrangements for the arrival of a flying unit, in this case Me 262 jet fighters. At Innsbruck there were two landing grounds; the old civil aerodrome directly on the outskirts of the city with a grass runway of approximately 500 metres (546 yards) in length and west of it, a newly built airfield (at Hötting) also with a grass strip of approximately 800 metres (875 yards) in length. This grass strip was bordered by a small defile on the western edge which led to another grass field of about 400 metres (440 yards) in length. As usual - and ever since the beginning of the war - our aerodromes and airfields seldom had the reserves of equipment that flying units needed. There was neither adequate accommodation, nor splinter-proof standings, nor food, nor ammunition, nor the necessary J2 fuel needed for jet fighters. The landing strip was too short, as the Me 262 needed about 1,200 metres (1,312 yards) for take-off on grass."

"I reported all this to München-Riem and was ordered to arrange for an adequate extension of the landing strip to be made; although a simple operation, levelling the little defile to make way for an extension of the landing strip to a minimum of 1,200 metres (1,312 yards) could not be done quickly. The work was eventually done by using the services of a labour service unit acting under orders of the airfield commander."

"The Me 262s were transferred to Innsbruck early in May

although the landing strip had not yet been made ready for use. As far as I can remember, about twelve aircraft arrived, one of which landed inadvertently on the old aerodrome with the short landing strip. The machine came to a standstill just in front of the aerodrome buildings. To this day, I do not understand why those aircraft were sent to Innsbruck, the more so because nobody could possibly think that they could have taken off again. For that purpose, the take-off strip was far too short and the levelling of the defile would have taken at least 14 days despite working day and night shifts. Furthermore, there was no J2 fuel, nor anything with which to maintain the aircraft. The newly arrived pilots were accommodated in private quarters. Then we waited for things to happen - or not happen. Nothing happened!"

Bob did the best he could to speed up the extension work and established communications with the rest of JV 44 at Salzburg. "We received continuous reports about the enemy's position by telephone, made possible by the fact that the telephone lines between Mittenwald-Seefeld and Innsbruck were still working. As far as I can recall, it was rumoured that American troops were moving forward from Mittenwald to Seefeld across the Zirler Mountains to Innsbruck. Under no circumstances were the Me 262s at Innsbruck to be blown up, in order not alarm the local inhabitants. Consequently, we had orders to remove the regulators from each aircraft, which, of course, regulate the fuel/air mix to the correct ratio at all altitudes and are thus the "heart" of the mechanics."

The guts of the beast: Despite the removal of the Jumo 004 jet engine regulators by German ground crew as ordered by Hans-Ekkehard Bob just over a month earlier, there is still plenty to interest mechanics T./Sgt Guido J. Zanelli and Sgt James R. Hammerstone from the 454th Bombardment Squadron, 323rd BG on this Me 262 A-1a.

On the bitter, ice-cold morning of 3 May, instructions were received to move the regulators by truck to Salzburg for re-location. "We reported by telephone that enemy tanks had already passed Seefeld and that we were waiting to sight the first tanks with our vehicles ready to move off. When we saw them approaching at a distance of some five kilometres (3 miles) from the airfield, I gave the order for the ground personnel to proceed quickly to Salzburg. The aircraft were left intact on the airfield but without regulators which rendered them useless."

Bob and his small detachment of pilots and ground crew had probably seen advance units from the 409th Regiment of the 103rd Infantry Division of General Brooks' VI Corps who had just battled their way up from Scharnitz.

"On the evening of the same day, I arrived at Salzburg with my detachment and reported to *Oberstleutnant* Bär. Here too, I was told that the enemy was only a few kilometres from Salzburg. As I was equipped with lorries, I was firstly detailed to transport some consignments of food from the well supplied ration stocks at Salzburg. Our eyes nearly fell out at the sight of the delicacies in the ration stocks, the names of which we had almost forgotten! There were tins of meat, tins of fruit, chocolate, rice, filled biscuits and all sorts of sutlery items - rations filled with literally the most exquisite things! As we knew from previous occasions, the officials were not willing to let us have anything. This "obstacle" was easily dealt with and we were able to load our lorries with the most fantastic things."

On 4 May 1945, as the Americans neared Maxglan airfield, Heinz Bär gave Bob his final orders: "The Americans were close to Salzburg airfield which meant that we soldiers had to disappear. Firstly, the aircraft there were made useless, again by the removal of their regulators. I was ordered to go with the lorries and a detachment of sixteen men, well equipped with machine pistols and ammunition, and store the regulators safely somewhere in the mountains and then to be available for the defence of the so-called *Festung Alpen* together with a detachment that was there already. I took the lorries and drove with my men roughly in the direction of Bad Ischl and after four or five kilometres (2/3 miles) turned off into the mountains. I reached the village of Koppl where the road ended. There were no soldiers in the village. I gave my men sufficient food and ammunition and dispersed them around the farms. Together with two pilots - two NCOs from JV 44 - I established my "Headquarters" at a farm located at the highest point in the village. Again we waited for something to happen, but nothing did..."

Meanwhile, as darkness fell 150 kilometres (93 miles) away in Innsbruck and amidst a blinding snow storm, tank-mounted GI's of the American 103rd Infantry Division drove up Maria Theresienstrasse in the centre of the city to witness the bold splash of colour that was the Stars and Stripes fluttering in the fading light above the town hall.

As Bob remembers: "On the 8 May 1945, we heard the general declaration of surrender on the radio together with the instruction that all remaining German troops were to give themselves up to the nearest enemy unit."

"There was a small lake in the village and we firstly sank all the Me 262 regulators in the lake and left the lorries in the forest. My men received their preliminary discharge papers from me together with the "official stamps and signatures" and were given permission to walk off home under their own steam. We learnt from the radio that we were in a "foreign country" as Austria had once again been recently declared an independent state. After a few more days, American troops arrived in the village in a jeep and took all the men who had not gone into hiding and who were at the age where liable for military service away with them. My two pilots and I had hidden ourselves so well that we were not found. A few days later, we made an adventurous homeward trek on foot across Germany, partly with the aid of self-made passports. I reached my former home town of Celle after a 1,700 kilometre walk (1,056 mile) which took me six weeks. The story of events surrounding that walk from Koppl, near Salzburg to Celle, near Hannover and which led across many provincial boundaries and the enemy's demarcation lines is better than many Wild West films."

Hans-Ekkehard Bob and his two companions were some of the very few JV 44 pilots to evade capture. Other pilots, such as Leo Schuhmacher, were freed after nine weeks.

As personnel continued a task the magnitude of which had been significantly underestimated by Allied planners, there was widespread suspicion in the 323rd that campaign medals were being withheld. Under the AAF system, points were accumulated by each individual for length of service (one point for each month of home duty, two for each month overseas), battle stars (five points each) and dependent children (12 points maximum for up to three children) towards a total of 85 which earned him rotation. By May 1945, those 323rd men who were five or ten points short of the magic number eagerly anticipated the award of battle stars for the Ardennes, Rhineland and Central European campaigns, totalling 15 points. Had the awards been issued many men would have been on their way. But no battle stars materialised and the 'scuttlebutt' was quick to condemn what was seen as a rigged system designed to keep these men in Germany. The question was resolved, but it took longer than many individuals would have preferred and the last men did not leave Germany until December 1945. The 323rd was inactivated in the US on 12 December. Three days later the original B-26 Marauder group in the ETO, the 322nd, also officially ceased to exist.

Occupation duty for the US fighter groups tended to be similar to that experienced by the bomber men although there were of course, far fewer of them in terms of flight personnel. A trio of groups from the Eighth Air Force took up station on airfields in Bavaria: the 55th went to Kaufbeuren on 22 July and thence to Y-90 Giebelstadt. This latter base was to be home for some of the men who had flown P-38s and P-51s from Wormingford, England slightly longer for it was not until 20 August 1946 that the last members of the group left, the unit's residency having begun on 29 April 1945. The 55th is one group that appears to have lost most of its Mustangs in the run down of the AAF in Europe during the summer of 1945. The majority of its P-51Ds were stripped of useful parts and blown up.

The 355th Group shared Gablingen with the Marauder men, the fighter unit's residence officially beginning on 3 July 1945. Months passed before another move was made into the heartland of the former enemy, the 355th occupying Schweinfurt on 15 April the following year. This sojourn did not last and from August the group began its departure for the US to be stationed at Mitchell Field, New York. This 'phased move' was not apparently completed until November. Mitchell was the last base for the wartime 355th Fighter Group as it was inactivated there on 20 November.

When the 357th Fighter Group located at R-85 Neubiberg on 21 July 1945 it was to be more than a year before the last personnel bade farewell to Germany; occupation duty for this particular Mustang outfit was not completed until 20 August the following year. In that time the 357th became part of USAFE

Group aircraft were retained for necessary flying duties although few P-51s were destined to be shipped home; the USAAF had so many aircraft of all types on strength in 1945, both in the former combat theatres and at home, that mass transportation would have been uneconomical in both time and money. Fighter groups did not therefore escape the destruction meted out to the older medium and attack bombers and numerous examples of the Thunderbolt and Lightning joined the scrap piles. Relatively new, low-hours Mustangs were also axed, photographic evidence clearly indicating that substantial numbers of the

then-current P-51D/K models were destroyed along with earlier B/C model 'war wearies'. Despite this cull, the AAF still had more than 36,000 aircraft on hand world-wide on 1 May 1946.

An American presence in Germany was maintained even when evidence of German compliance with the surrender terms was irrefutable; in the aftermath of the most destructive war in history, Soviet Russia, which had done so much to speed the end of the war, became increasingly cool towards its former Allies. There was growing evidence, long before the term was officially adopted, that a 'cold war' war was developing between East and West. The nation still ruled by Josef Stalin became at best unpredictable, withdrawing as it was behind what Winston Churchill aptly termed the 'Iron Curtain'. A military presence in Germany was therefore a sound security measure, one that would soon prove its worth when Berlin was blockaded by the Russians in 1947.

In the meantime, US reorganisation of wartime air units continued. Neither of the P-47 groups that had crowned their operational existence by meeting JV 44's Me 262s in combat was part of the occupation air forces. The 50th only remained at Giebelstadt for two weeks after the war's end, as on 21 May it moved to Mannheim. On or about 22 June, group personnel prepared to ship out, a move that had been completed by August. The 50th was deactivated in the US on 7 November 1945.

Fritzlar continued to be home to the men of the 365th until a move to France was signalled in June 1945. By 29-30 July all three squadrons of the Hell Hawks had occupied Suippes, the group's final location in Europe before returning home for deactivation, on 22 September 1945.

The Ninth Air Force was itself deactivated in Germany on 2 December its sister tactical force, the Twelfth Air Force, having been similarly stood down in Italy on 31 August.

In a move that was finally to see the end of the P-47's service in Europe the six ex-Ninth (36th, 366th, 368th and 406th) and Twelfth (the 79th and 86th) Air Force occupation groups were gradually run down, with the 36th and 86th being deactivated in

Job done: scores of P-51 Mustangs predominantly of the Eighth Air Force's 55th Fighter Group gathered at Kaufbeuren in June-July 1946 awaiting basic dismantling and destruction. Some aircraft carry the red-yellow-red Allied occupation force rear fuselage bands together with standard squadron/group markings.

It's all over... To celebrate Allied victory in Europe, Lt. James J. Finnegan, 10th Fighter Squadron, 50th Fighter Group and the man accredited with shooting Adolf Galland down, shakes hands with his crew chief in front of a Do 24 flying boat on the Bodensee near Dornier's Friedrichshafen works in Germany.

Its three component squadrons were the wartime 525th, 526th and 527th Fighter Bomber Squadrons and these flew P-47Ds until 1950 when the unit received F-84E Thunderjets at Neubiberg.

Then, the formation of a new *Bundesluftwaffe* or West German Air Force lay less than a half-decade in the future. But the cadre of officers who planned the new force - which was officially raised in 1956 - and who would lead the first combat *Staffeln* included a number of experienced men who had last seen action at the controls of an Me 262 of JV 44. They included "Macki" Steinhoff who recovered from the burns he received in the terrible crash of 18 April 1945 to become one of the most enthusiastic and popular commanders of the new *Luftwaffe*. He, Walter Krupinski and others shouldered the awesome responsibility of 'holding the line' had the Russians ever attempted a conventional assault on the West before the Cold War came to an end.

February 1946. Not all of these original wartime group designations disappeared completely as in August 1946 the 366th, 368th and 406th were redesignated the 27th, 78th and 86th Groups respectively. Based at Nordholz, the 86th eventually absorbed all remaining personnel and aircraft from its sister units, and thus became, as a Composite Group and subsequently a Fighter Bomber Group, the only Thunderbolt unit in Germany.

A somewhat ignoble end for these B-26 Marauders at a nominated "graveyard" at Bad Wörishofen, Germany, autumn, 1945. Seen here are aircraft from the 322nd (coded SS, ER, DR, PN) and 397th (coded X2) BGs and the 1st Pathfinder Squadron (IH-X), awaiting their fate.

INFORMATION ON COLOUR ILLUSTRATIONS

1. **Republic P-47D-26-RA Thunderbolt, 42-28424/T5-L 'The Irish Shillalah', 10th Fighter Squadron, 50th Fighter Group, Ninth Air Force, Toul/Ochey, France.**

Although the pilot of this aircraft, Lt. James J Finnegan, was credited with 'damaging and probably destroying' the Me 262 he fired at and hit on 26 April 195, it was some time before he became aware that his opponent had been Adolf Galland. Once again the serial number of this P-47 is subject to confirmation although the one shown here is almost certainly correct. The red markings on the vertical and horizontal tail surfaces were applied in place of black P-47 'type recognition' stripes when the 50th Fighter Group became part of the US First Tactical Air Force (Provisional) in November 1944.

2. **Republic P-47D-28-RA Thunderbolt, 42-28439/C4-K 'Touch Me Not', 1st Lt. Oliven T Cowan, 388th Fighter Squadron, 365th Fighter Group, Ninth Air Force, Aachen, Germany.**

An aircraft of the famed 'Hell Hawks' group, the actual serial number of this particular Thunderbolt has thus far eluded research for this book. The individual code is based on conjecture, taken as it was from photographic evidence contained in the unit's recognised history. Rather than leave the serial number position blank, the authors and publishers have decided to employ that of the first production P-47D-28. Updates and corrections of these details would of course, be most welcome. Some 365th Group P-47s had an insignia blue panel below the cockpit on the port side to record pilot and ground crew names as well as victories and this machine had an Me 262 applied in such a fashion to record Cowan's February 1945 victory over an Me 262.

3. **Martin B-26G-25-MA Marauder, 44-68132/ WT-A, 456th Bomb Squadron, 323rd Bomb Group, Ninth Air Force.**

Based at Denain-Prouvy, this machine participated in the 323rd Bomb Group's heavy raid on Kempten on 20 April 1945. It was also included in a dramatic photograph taken by a USAAF crewman that proved to be one of the few, possibly only, exposures to show JV 44's Me 262s and their American targets in one frame. The 150 B-26G-25s were the 'last of the line', Martin completing the final Marauder on 18 April 1945 – about the same time as the Messerschmitt Me 262 was forcibly demonstrating that the era of the piston-engined bomber was passing into history.

4. **Martin B-26F-1-MA Marauder, 42-96256/RJ-J, 455th Bomb Squadron, 323rd Bomb Group, Ninth Air Force.**

An aircraft borrowed for the maximum effort mission of 20 April 1945, 'Ugly Duckling' was, notwithstanding its impressive mission record, something of a lame duck on that day. Defective in a number of ways, it was far from pilot James Vining's first choice for the mission. However, Vining duly flew the aircraft from Denain-Prouvy into the teeth of JV 44's attack against the 323rd Bomb Group's raid on Kempten. Ill luck decreed that 'Ugly Duckling' would not make it back to base after a further attack by Me 262s of KG (J) 54. Despite the heroic efforts of Vining and James Mulvihill, the co-pilot who took over the controls when Vining was wounded, the aircraft crashed and was totally destroyed when it hit anti-tank obstacles at Uberherrn.

5. **B-26 Marauders of the 344th BG taxi out at the start of a mission to Cologne in February 1945**

6. **Martin B-26G-25-MA Marauder, 44-48115/K9-L, 494th Bomb Squadron, 344th Bomb Group based at Florennes, Belgium.**

This aircraft had a 'nose art' design consisting of a shark and two masks depicting the traditional 'tragi-comedy' faces of the theatrical world. It should be said that the reference from which this painting was created was not of the highest quality and the actual design and colours could be slightly different to what is depicted.

7. **Martin B-26B-40-MA Marauder, 42-43311/09, 34th Bomb Squadron, 17th Bomb Group, Twelfth Air Force.**

Based along with the rest of the 17th Bomb Group at Dijon, France, 'Spot Cash' was flown by 2nd Lt. Earle E Reeves on the mission of 26 April 1945. It received fatal cannon-fire damage during an attack by JV 44's Me 262s and was seen by eye-witnesses to be hit in both engines before going into a spin, shortly before its tail broke away. In common with the majority of Twelfth Air Force Marauders originally based in North Africa, this aircraft had its lower pair of forward-firing 'package' machine guns removed. The overall olive drab upper surfaces had the typical 'tan brown' weathering of this shade when subjected to the desert sun for any period of time. Numerous faded shades show up in contemporary wartime photographs. The artwork colours shown here are speculative and the number of sorties that might have been recorded on a port side scoreboard (the most common location) is not known.

8. **Martin B-26C-45-MO Marauder, 42-107729/17, 34th Bomb Squadron, 17th Bomb Group, Twelfth Air Force.**

Piloted by 1st Lt. Fred J Harms, this aircraft was one of the first victims of JV 44's Me 262 rocket attack on 24 April 1945. Attached at that time to the First Tactical Air Force (Provisional), 'Stud Duck' lead aircraft of a Window Flight supporting raids on a variety of tactical targets. It was destroyed by R4M rockets with the loss of all its crew, apart from one gunner. The aircraft, which eye witnesses confirmed had taken fatal hits in the vertical tail, crashed near the town of Babenhausen.

9. **Me 262A-1a W.Nr. 111745, 'White 5', Jagdverband 44**

Photographic evidence suggests that JV 44 started life with a batch of aircraft finished in a single dark colour (which we have interpreted as RLM (German Air Ministry Colour) green 83) on their upper surfaces, extending in a solid application right down the fuselage sides and with their undersides probably in RLM 76. Aircraft in this upper surface scheme exhibit varying degrees of patchiness in their finish, with a lighter colour showing through on some of them. Whether this second colour was camouflage paint proper or just primer still visible through a cursory spray finish remains open to question. Also apparent on many examples is the filler paste (often a yellowish-green in colour) used to smooth over the joins in the aircraft's skin.

Tactical numbers on this initial batch of machines were in white, ahead of the rear fuselage cross although on later replacement aircraft, as evidenced by aircraft abandoned at Innsbruck-Hötting, these numbers were omitted. This feature can be seen on a number of Me 262s and does not appear to have been the monopoly of any unit. The highest number known from documentary evidence to have been displayed on a JV 44 Me 262 is RLM 'White 21'.

In addition, anecdotal and documentary evidence shows that JV 44, officially or otherwise, acquired aircraft from numerous other Me 262 Gruppen and there is no good reason to suppose that the conditions of the last two weeks of the war were conducive to much repainting to achieve conformity with their new unit's colours.

'White 5' had the usual set of crosses and carried its Werk Nummer (Works Number) in black with the individual digits quite widely spaced. There is a possibility that this Messerschmitt had previously been coded '3' since this appears to be the number on the nosewheel door and there is a patch of seemingly fresh paint on the fuselage, over which the 'white 5' has been applied. The dark green paint on the fuselage is unusual in having been carried round the 'corners' of the triangular cross-section to impinge on the undersides. On the nacelles there is again quite a hard edged division between the green and the undersurface pale blue-grey.

10. **Me 262B-1a (W.Nr. not known), 'White S', Jagdverband 44, (probably formerly EJG 2)**

One of the few Me 262s of any sub-type to be graced with the solid white (H3a) Hakenkreuz (Swastika) but otherwise a standard machine as regards both its RLM 81/82/76 camouflage and national markings. The white 'S', outlined thinly in black and placed quite high in respect to the fuselage Balkenkreuz (Balkan Cross), would in all likelihood have been repeated on the nosewheel door. The fuselage and nacelle sides and fin and rudder are very 'clean' on this aircraft, with very little mottling. The demarcation between upper and lower surface camouflage colours on the fuselage is quite high up.

11. Me 262A-1a/U4 W.Nr. 111899, Jagdverband 44

A normally camouflaged Me 262 from the tail to the forward wing-roots, this aircraft featured a modified nose section (and nosewheel) to accommodate the enormous MK 214 5cm cannon. Mottling was densely applied and carried right down the fuselage sides. The new nose section was unpainted metal, cross-hatched with the by now familiar filler paste. An especially prominent line of paste had been used to fill the joint between the modified nose and the fuselage proper. Essentially a prototype, the machine was without tactical markings. The Hakenkreuz was a black/white H2a and remaining Balkenkreuze were B5 on the fuselage with B2 and B6 on the lower wings respectively. Interestingly, this machine was flown operationally by Willy Herget.

12. Me 262A-1a (W.Nr. not known) 'White 22', Jagdverband 44

'White 22' again lacks a Werk Nummer and its crosses are all 'normal.' It is distinguished by a pale rudder with a somewhat darker trim tab: these items may well have been left as natural metal, their contrasting appearance the result of their different angles with respect to the sunlight in the photograph. The upper paint finish is insufficient to mask the darkening effect of the filler paste where the fuselage panels join and there is, between the starboard wing root and nacelle, what looks like the diagonal dividing line of a segmented camouflage pattern (although none is evident on the fuselage). It is therefore possible that 'white 22' had a wing (or set of wings) fitted which carried the standard Me 262 splinter pattern in Braunviolett RLM 81 and RLM Hellgrün 82.

13. Me 262A-1a (W.Nr. – possibly 170063, previously 'White 11' of Ekdo. 262), 'White 4', Jagdverband 44

'White 4' lacked a (visible) Werk Nummer, perhaps because of the overpainting and the oversized H2a Hakenkreuz which monopolised space on the fin. Other crosses were 'standard issue.' The camouflage demarcation on the nacelles was fairly hard edged and in this case the forward part of each cowling was painted in the camouflage colours.

14. Martin B-26C-15-MO Marauder, 41-34929/30, 34th Bomb Squadron, 17th Bomb Group, Twelfth Air Force.

Piloted by 2nd Lt. Kenneth L Bedor, 'Marauder' was shot down by Me 262s of JV 44 on 26 April 1945. As only the starboard side of the aircraft is shown in available photographs, it is not certain how many missions this or any previously assigned crew might have recorded on a port side scoreboard – the most common position for such markings.

15 and 16. Martin B-26G-1-MA Marauder, 43-34181/Y5-O, 495th Bomb Squadron, 344th Bomb Group, Ninth Air Force.

Named 'Lak-a-Nookie' when the group was based at Cormeilles-en-Vexin, the aircraft was flown by Jack Lyons' crew before passing to 2nd Lt. James L. Stalter for the mission of 24 April 1945. The 'two tone' tactical camouflage depicted was widely adopted for operational B-26s despite camouflage paint being officially dropped from most US aircraft following a directive of 13 February 1944. Field commanders, worried that their 'silver' aircraft would be highly visible on forward airfields within range of German aircraft invariably welcomed this passive method of protection and numerous Marauders were partially painted to be less visible from above. By the time that this particular 344th aircraft met JV 44 in combat during April 1945, the horizontal bomb mission symbols may have risen to considerably more than the total only partially visible here. It had apparently completed 88 missions by February 1945 when the aircraft was repaired after being damaged in a crash.

17. Martin B-26B-45-MA Marauder, 42-95771/37, 37th Bomb Squadron, 17th Bomb Group, Twelfth Air Force.

'My Gal Sal' was flown by Lt. Carl Johanson. This Marauder's numerical squadron markings contrast with the British-derived letter codes generally used by Ninth Air Force groups. By April 1945 the two US air forces, originally based many hundreds of miles apart in England and North Africa, were almost flying missions together, attacking targets in the relatively small area of Germany that was still holding out. The colour of the number and the rear fuselage band on this aircraft denoted the 17th Group within the markings system adopted for US medium bomber groups in the Mediterranean Theatre of Operations in July 1943. An impressive mission scoreboard, typical of hundreds of wartime B-26s, is shown in yellow bomb symbols with the fiftieth sortie depicted in red.

During the unequal combat with Me 262s in the spring of 1945, 'My Gal Sal' was one of the lucky ones; hit by Galland's jets on 26 April, it lost an engine but was able to crash land at Luneville without any crew injuries. It was return fire from B-26 gunners of the 17th Group that contributed to Galland's own forced landing that day.

18. Me 262A-1a (W.Nr. not known) 'White 1 and S', Jagdverband 44

This machine bears the hallmark tail camouflage of Kommando Nowotny, making it perhaps one of the oldest surviving operational Me 262s when the war ended. When it served with the Commando this aircraft was painted in the standard RLM 81/82/76 finish, the camouflage paint being heavily mottled, obscuring any 'formal' segmentation on the fuselage at least, and carried right down the sides. The upper surface colours were also taken back along the fuselage sides beneath the tailplane as far as the leading edge of the rudder. As frequently seen in the Kommando, the forward nacelle sections were in natural metal. The hard-edged blotches of the fin and rudder camouflage were in RLM 82 over a base of RLM 76 (or perhaps an even paler shade of blue-grey). The visible Balkenkreuze were all normal with an H2 black/white Hakenkreuz. The white 1 appeared on each side of the nose just aft of the gun access panels and was repeated on the nosewheel door; aft of the cockpit was the narrow yellow fuselage band characteristic of Me 262 operational training units; beneath the tailplane, on the fuselage sides, was a small white 'S.' The Werk Nummer appears to have been overpainted on the fin.

At Innsbruck in Summer 1945 these markings remained much the same, although the 'S' appears to have been repainted, altering its form slightly. As for camouflage, the fuselage between the gun hatches and the yellow band had been crudely resprayed in Hellgrün 82, unevenness in the colour showing how quickly the spray had been moved back and forth. Both forward engine cowlings were now camouflaged, although the port engine appears to have been changed since the paint on the adjoining sections does not match up.

19 and 20. Me 262A-2a W.Nr. 111685, '9K+FH', Jagdverband 44

9K+FH sports a complete set of codes for 1./KG 51 although dark patches of paint behind these characters suggest that they may have been repainted or changed at some stage. On the starboard side the 'H' is not completely upright but tilted back somewhat toward the 'F', perhaps because the painter's stencil was not properly aligned. There is a white fin/rudder tip but the nose cone has not been painted in the Staffel colour. The white 'F' is not repeated on the nosewheel door. On this occasion the Hakenkreuz is the all-black H3 variety. None of the photos allows us to be sure whether bomb racks were still fitted but it would appear not. KG 51's initial complement of Me 262s was finished in RLM 81/82/76 but not in the familiar segmented pattern; instead the RLM 81 was sprayed in meandering lines over the 82 base colour of the upper surfaces. This aircraft seems to exhibit a variation of that scheme with the base shade showing as blotches through an irregular 'lattice' of oversprayed RLM 81. The starboard rudder area displays something more like the normal 'scribble'. By the time the dumped aircraft was photographed after the war, filler paste was also showing through the paintwork.

21. Me 262A-2a W.Nr. 111712, Jagdverband 44

Unlike its pristine predecessor off the assembly line – the well known W.Nr. 111711, delivered to the Allies by Hans Fay and later evaluated in the USA – W.Nr. 111712 had at least received the beginnings of a camouflage scheme. Camouflage paint (RLM Braunviolett 81) had been applied to the rudder, rear of the nacelles and front removable cowling panels. There is grey primer (RLM grey 02) on the tail assembly but the remainder of the fuselage is in natural metal interspersed with yellowish-green filler paste. Markings consist of an H3 solid black Hakenkreuz, B4 Balkenkreuz on the fuselage and B6a on the upper wings which were normal for an unpainted Me 262 and necessary to stand out from their light coloured background. Beneath the wings are the normal B2 crosses. Individual markings are confined to the last three digits of the Werk Nummer on the fin in black and repeated below the fin/fuselage junction. An additional number '56' in black was painted, probably denoting a part number, on the tailplane root fairing. The white patch on the edge of the swastika could be a bullet hole repair. This machine had not only bomb racks but steel plated head armour for the pilot.

SOURCE NOTES

SELECT BIBILOGRAPHY

I wish to express my acknowledgement to the many authoritive military writers whose books – unfortunately too numerous to mention here – provided me with the fundamental platform for my research. Following is a list of some the primary published references from which I have drawn:

Austin, Lambert D. (Ed.). 344th Bomb Group (M) "Silver Streaks" – History & Remembrances World War II (Southern Heritage Press, St.Petersburg, FL, 1996)

Boehme, Manfred. JG 7 – The World's First Jet Fighter Unit, 1944/1945 (Schiffer, Atglen, PA, 1992)

Craven, Wesley Frank & Cate, James Lea. The Army Air Forces in World War II Vol.III Europe: Argument to VE Day (University of Chicago Press, Chicago, 1951)

Earl, O.K.. The Thunderbird Goes to War – A Diary of the 34th Bombardment Squadron in World War II (Braun-Brumfield Inc., Ann Arbor, MI, 1991)

Forsyth, Robert. JV 44 – The Galland Circus (Classic Publications, Burgess Hill, 1996)

Frayn Turner, John. & Jackson, Robert. Destination Berchtesgaden – The Story of the US 7th Army in World War II (Ian Allan, London, 1975)

Freeman, Roger A. The Mighty Eighth – A History of the US 8th Army Air Force (Macdonald, London, 1970)

Freeman, Roger A. Mighty Eighth War Diary (Janes, London, 1981)

Galland, Adolf. The First and The Last (Methuen, London, 1955)

Gilbert, Martin. Second World War (Weidenfeld and Nicolson 1989)

Girbig, Werner. Six Months to Oblivion – The Eclipse of the Luftwaffe Fighter Force (Ian Allan, London, 1975)

Havener, J.K.. The Martin B-26 Marauder (TAB/Aero Books, Blue Ridge Summit, PA, 1988)

Irving, David. Hitler's War (Hodder & Stoughton, London, 1977)

Irving, David. The Rise and Fall of the Luftwaffe – The Life of Erhard Milch (Purnell, London, 1973) Moench, Major-General John O. Marauder Men – An Account of the Martin B-26 Marauder (Malia Enterprises Inc, Longwood, 1989)

Murray, Williamson. Luftwaffe (George Allen & Unwin, London 1985)

Nielsen, Andreas. The German Air Force General Staff (Arno Press, New York, June 1959)

Obermaier, Ernst. Die Ritterkreuzträger der Luftwaffe 1939-1945 Band I – Jagdflieger (Verlag Dieter Hoffmann, Mainz, 1966)

Obermaier, Ernst. Die Ritterkreuzträger der Luftwaffe 1939-1945 Band II – Stuka- und Schlachtflieger (Verlag Dieter Hoffmann, Mainz, 1976)

Price, Alfred. Battle over the Reich (Ian Allan, London, 1973)

Radinger, Willy & Schick, Walter. Me 262 – Entwicklung, Erprobung und Fertigung des ersten einsatzfähigen Düsenjägers der Welt (Aviatic Verlag, Planegg, 1992)

Radtke, Siegfried. Kampfgeschwader 54 von der Ju52 zur Me262 – Eine Chronik nach Kriegstagbüchern, Dokumenten und Berichten 1935-1945 (Schild Verlag, München, 1990)

Rust, Kenn C. The 9th Air Force in World War II (Aero Publishers Inc, California, 1967)

Scutts, Jerry. B-26 Marauder Units of the Eighth and Ninth Air Forces (Osprey, London, 1997)

Shores, Christopher. Luftwaffe Fighter Units, Europe 1942-45 (Osprey, London, 1979)

Smith, J. Richard, Kay. Antony L., & Creek, Eddie J. German Aircraft of the Second World War (Putnam, London, 1979)

Smith, J. Richard & Creek, Eddie J.. Jet Planes of the Third Reich (Monogram, Massachusetts, 1982)

Smith, J. Richard & Creek, Eddie J.. Me 262 A-1 – Monogram Close-Up 17 (Monogram, Massachusetts, 1983)

Steinhoff, Johannes. The Last Chance – The Pilots' Plot Against Göring (Hutchinson, London, 1977)

Suchenwirth, Richard. Command and Leadership in the German Air Force (Arno Press, New York, 1969)

Toliver, Raymond F. & Constable, Trevor J. Fighter Aces of the Luftwaffe (Aero Publishers, Fallbrook, 1977)

Toliver, Raymond F. & Constable, Trevor J. Fighter General – The Life of Adolf Galland (AmPress, Nevada, 1990)

DOCUMENTARY AND UNPUBLISHED SOURCES

The documentary and unpublished material used in the writing of the manuscript has been collated from many different sources, both public and private, in Germany, the USA and the UK. For a more extensive and detailed listing of such references in respect to the formation and operations of *Jagdverband* 44, readers are advised to refer to the source notes listed on pages 339-344 of my earlier book, *JV 44 – The Galland Circus*.

In précis, the primary material used for the German perspective was drawn from:

CSDIC Interrogation Reports at the Public Record Office (PRO), London

ADI(K) Report No.373/1945 "The Birth, Life and Death of the German Day Fighter Arm" (via Pegg)

Miscelleaneous documents in the AIR 20 Class at the PRO, London

The DEFE3 series of Ultra signal decrypts at the PRO, London (microfilm).

AHB 6 Microfilm, Imperial War Museum London

Nachlaß Galland – General der Jagdflieger – Aufgabenbereich und Tätigkeit: Privates Tagebuch des GenLt a.D. Adolf Galland – Bd.2: III.Teil: Die Auflösung E. 1944-1945 (Bundesarchiv-Militärarchiv, Freiburg, N 211/2)

Misc. Documentation from *Luftflottenkommando 6* – microfilm printounts from NASM, Washington

Gollob, Gordon: *Kritische Anmerkungen und Ergänzungen zum Buch von J.Steinhoff: "In letzter Stunde" – Verschwörung der Jagdflieger* (*Jägerblatt* via Schliephake)

Various OKL Luftwaffe Org.Stab documents from the BA-MA, Freiburg and private collections.

The research papers of Mr Nevill Basnett (Eduard Schallmoser and Günther Lützow – refer Source Notes in Forsyth, *JV 44 – The Galland Circus*)

Various pilots *Flugbuch* – private collections

Private correspondence and interviews with Adolf Galland, Walter Krupinski, Wolfgang Späte, Erich Hohagen, Klaus Neumann, Hans Ekkehard Bob, Herbert Kaiser, Bodo Dirschauer, Franz Stigler, Werner Roell, Werner Gutowski.

The primary material used for the American perspective was drawn from:

Various Missing Air Crew Reports (MACRs), HQ, 1st TAF (Prov), (via NA&RA, Record Grp. 92 & misc. US sources)

Operational Summaries, 323rd, 394th Bomb Groups, 27th Fighter Group, 64th Fighter Wing, 42nd Bomb Wing, 1st TAF (Prov.), SINTREP, 1st TAF (Prov.) via USAFHRA, Maxwell AFB, USA

War Diary, 34th Bomb Sqdn, April 1945

War Diary, 37th Bomb Sqdn, April 1945

War Diary, 95th Bomb Sqdn, April 1945

War Diary, 432nd Bomb Sqdn, April 1945

34th, 37th, 95th and 432nd Sqdns., 17th BG Aircraft identification sheets (B-26 Marauders – WWII Combat Ops) (via 17th BG).

Unit History, 17th BG (M), April 1945

Operational Organzation of the First TAF (PRO/AIR 40/1097)

Battle Narratives, 344th Bomb Group and 9th Bomb Division

Milk Run – Offical Newsletter, 344th BG Association

Sortie – Official Newsletter, 17th BG Reunion Association

The Marauder Thunder

Les Marauders Francais – 11e Brigade de Bombardment par Georges Bernage (via E.Larger)

Correspondence between Mr Nevill Basnett and Adolf Galland and James J. Finnegan

Private Correspondence with James L.Vining, Robert M. Radlein, John O. Moench, William Allan, Robert L. Harwell, Don Sinclair, Norman G. Farley, W.P. Morton, James L. Stalter, Robert A. Hobbs, Henry Pryce, Warren E. Young, William H. Myers, Oliven T. Cowan, Ronnie Macklin, James J. Finnegan, William W. Snead, Don Wilson, Wayne J. Hutchinson, Bernard J. Byrnes, Henry Dietz, Lillian and Donna Maria Couture, Ed Brandt, Edward M. Cole, Randle J. Dedeaux, Orrin Cloud, Don Edelen, William Baird, Carl S. Schreiner Jr., Donald Mushrush, John W. Sorrelle Jr. and Jack Havener

INDEX